DATE DUE

Compromised Campus

Compromised Campus

THE COLLABORATION OF UNIVERSITIES WITH THE INTELLIGENCE COMMUNITY, 1945–1955

Sigmund Diamond

New York · Oxford · OXFORD UNIVERISTY PRESS · 1992

Oxford University Press

Oxford   New York   Toronto
Delhi   Bombay   Calcutta   Madras   Karachi
Kuala Lumpur   Singapore   Hong Kong   Tokyo
Nairobi   Dar es Salaam   Cape Town
Melbourne   Auckland

and associated companies in
Berlin   Ibadan

Published by Oxford University Press, Inc.,
200 Madison Avenue, New York, New York 10016

Oxford is a registered trademark of Oxford University Press

Library of Congress Cataloging-in-Publication Data
Diamond, Sigmund.
Compromised campus: The collaboration of universities
with the intelligence community, 1945–1955 / Sigmund Diamond.
p. cm.   ISBN 0-19-505382-6
1. Political crimes and offenses—United States—Investigation—History—20th century.
2. United States. Federal Bureau of Investigation.
3. Higher education and state—United States—History—20th century.
4. Academic freedom—United States—History—20th century.   I. Title.
HV6285.D53   1992
364.1'31—dc20   91-15668

9 8 7 6 5 4 3 2 1

Printed in the United States of America
on acid-free paper

To My Grandchildren
Susannah and Rebecca and Sarah

Let me tell you why I had to write this history:

THOSE WHO UNDERTAKE to write histories . . . take that trouble . . . for many reasons . . . ; some of them . . . to show their great skill in composition . . . : but others there are, who of necessity . . . are driven to write history, because they were concerned in the facts, and so cannot excuse themselves from committing them to writing, for the advantage of posterity; nay, there are not a few who are induced to draw their historical facts out of darkness into light, and to produce them for the benefit of the public, on account of the great importance of the facts themselves with which they have been concerned. Now of these several reasons for writing history, I must profess the last two were my own reasons.

FLAVIUS JOSEPHUS,
Antiquities of the Jews

Acknowledgments

ONCE WHEN I was a graduate student the room in which I took my final examination in a course on Westward Expansion was also being used for the final in another course. The instructor for the other course had been, years before, a college classmate of mine. We had not seen each other for many years; while we were talking he spotted the teacher of my Westward Expansion course and introduced me to him. Harvard courses were very large, and there was no guarantee that students and teachers knew each other at all. On being introduced to me, my teacher, Frederick Merk, who was the kindest of men, said, "Of course I know Mr. Diamond. He and I collaborate in giving the course." My part of the collaboration consisted, on the invitation of Mr. Merk who knew that I needed the money and was taking the course anyway, in showing slides, drawing the blinds, and opening the windows to reduce 8:30 a.m. sleepiness. When, in later years, I came to know Mr. Merk better I realized that he was not being kind; that was the way he looked at the world and at work—all who helped were collaborators.

I have another memory. On the mosaic floor of an ancient synagogue in Jericho there is a Hebrew inscription that, in translation, runs roughly as follows: "It is not necessary to record here the names of those who built this place. God knows who they are." Perhaps God does, but I should like my readers to know who my collaborators have been.

Three young attorneys gave me legal advice from the very start and did the work, at no cost to me, that was necessary to bring a suit against the FBI in the Federal Court of the Southern District of New York. I am forever grateful to Thomas Daugherty, Helen Hershkoff, and Stephen M. Diamond, my son, for the advice and encouragement they gave and for the work they did. In the years that followed Steve gave more than legal advice; he listened to my argument and provided perspective and information that saved me from errors and taught me things I had not known. The legal work on my case was taken over by the distinguished firm of White and Case, who accepted me as a client pro bono; I am grateful to the firm, to Ms. Dorothea Regal, and, above all, to Halliburton Fales II, who gave the help I needed.

The research was not inexpensive; there were the costs of reproducing the documents, court costs, postage, and the like. I greatly benefited from grants given by the following organizations and persons: the Columbia Council for Research in the Social Sciences; the Office of the Vice-President for the Arts and Sciences, Columbia University; the Fund for Investigative Journalism; William H. Ferry and Carole Bernstein Ferry. Mr. and Mrs. Ferry were also generous in the moral support they gave; I want them to know how much it was appreciated.

A number of libraries gave permission to use documents in their custody, and so did the heirs of persons who left their papers to these libraries. I wish to thank the staffs of the following: the Harvard Law School Library and the Nathan M. Pusey Archives; Special Collections and Central Files, Columbia University; the Oral History Collection, Columbia University; the Yale University Archives and Library; Dartmouth College Library; the Carnegie Corporation; the University of Texas Library; the Waterford, Connecticut, public library. I am grateful also to the heirs of the late Grenville Clark and Merle Fainsod.

Some of the material in this book originally appeared in different form in journals and other publications, and I record my indebtedness to them: *The American Quarterly, The History of Political Thought, Labor History, The Midwestern Archivist, The Nation, The New York Review of Books, Our Right to Know* (Fund for Open Information and Accountability), the Historical Society of Israel and the Zalman Shazar Center for Jewish History, and Temple University Press.

A great many persons talked, listened, typed, tracked down clues, interceded for me, and helped in countless ways:

Dora Arenas, Yehoshua Arieli, Joellyn Ausanka, the late Robert R. Brookhart, Jonathan Cole, India Cooper, Esther Davis, the late Herbert A. Deane, Dr. Betty Diamond, Barbara Goodwin, Harold Goodwin, Shirley Hazzard, Haggai Hurvitz, the late Herbert H. Hyman, Marion Jemmott, David S. Landes, Sonia Landes, Dr. Edgar Leifer, John Lohmann, Sheldon Meyer, the late Edith Nagel, the late Ernest Nagel, Victor Navasky, Charles O'Connell, the late Hubert O'Gorman, Servando Ortoll, Marshall Perlin, David Sacks, Eleanor Sacks, Dr. Leon Salzman, Clara Shapiro, Robert Silvers, Peter Temin, Athan Theoharis, Adam

Ulam, Dr. Bruce Volpe, Mary Wamby, Marlene Warshawsky, Zvi Yavetz, and Viviana Zelizer. And, of course, my students at Columbia and Tel-Aviv Universities; they listened, and I think some heard.

My greatest debt is to Shirley. It began long before the ten years of labor on this book; it started forty-eight years ago in Detroit. If what this book has dealt with comes out of my life, it comes out of hers as well.

> Think when man's glory most begins and ends,
> And say my glory was I had such friends.

Contents

Compromised Campus

Introduction

THIS BOOK HAS been more than ten years in the making, and many of the twists and turns in the roads that were traveled have been forgotten—many, but not all, and certainly not the start of the journey. I had been a graduate student in American history at Harvard, received a Ph.D. degree in 1953, and during the following year, on the invitation of McGeorge Bundy, dean of the Faculty of Arts and Sciences, held an administrative position there. In the spring of 1954, again through Dean Bundy, I was offered another administrative position, but this time with teaching duties. That offer was withdrawn when, after telling me that he had reason to believe that I had once had an association with the Communist Party, Bundy asked what my position would be if I should be asked about the matter by "civic authority"—meaning the FBI or a congressional investigating committee—and I answered that I would speak about myself but not about others.

The question Dean Bundy put to me was not at all uncommon in universities and elsewhere in the 1950s, though exactly how common it was, even at Harvard, we shall probably never know. The Cold War was well under way and, not coincidentally, so was the hot war against dissent at home. The link between the wars, hot and cold, was the identification of disagreement with foreign-directed subversion. Alternatives to existing policies, whether those alternatives were in fact Communist inspired or not, were stigmatized as subversive. Opposition could be treated as treason. It was a remarkably effective strategy, so effective that it would be a serious error to assume that only McCarthyites joined in. So did others, university presidents and deans among them, sometimes out of agreement, sometimes hopeful that a display of bloodlust would buy immunity for them.

In April 1977 I wrote an article in the *New York Review of Books* about one section of a recently published book by Seymour Martin Lipset and David Riesman, *Education and Politics at Harvard,* the section written by Lipset on how Harvard handled the political purge of the 1950s. The publication of the book provided an opportunity for a second look at the domestic side of the events of a quarter-century earlier. What had been revealed, what had been forgotten, what had been learned?

I concluded that though Lipset knew about my encounter with Bundy, both from me and from others, he had made it appear that Harvard, which acted in a fashion that made it complicit in the behavior of the Federal Bureau of Investigation and the congressional investigating committees, was standing firm for university autonomy and academic freedom. Lipset's account was complacent, not penetrating; it provided support for what many wanted to believe.

I decided to request my FBI dossier under the Freedom of Information Act (FOIA). Perhaps there I would find what the FBI felt it knew about me, whether it informed Harvard of what it knew, and whether Harvard on its own account gave information to the FBI. I did find at least partial answers to some of my questions—the FBI did give information to the university and was kept informed about Harvard policy regarding appointments; and Harvard did give some materials—including a photograph of me—to the FBI. But it soon occurred to me that far more important matters could be explored here than what had happened to me. That was biographical, of interest to me and perhaps a few others; but the relation of the FBI to major institutions in our society was far more important. Could not the Freedom of Information Act be used as a tool of research into more general problems, for example, how much autonomy really was still retained by major "private" institutions in the United States? Detailed knowledge of who did what to whom— what one might expect from the FBI records, at least as I saw them in my own dossier—might lead one to question how much separation still existed between "public"—that is, governmental—and "private"—that is, autonomous.

I dropped my own case in order to concentrate on these larger problems. I decided to begin my research by requesting the FBI documents on the two organizations that I knew best—Harvard University, where I had been for six years, and the United Automobile Workers of America–CIO (UAW–CIO), for which I had worked in Detroit, mainly in research and education, for a number of years in the 1940s. Universities and labor unions are institutions of critical importance to democratic society; I thought that by beginning with those I knew best, I could test the FBI records against my own remembered experience and, at the same time, find a point of entry into the study of the larger problems in which I was interested. Accordingly, I filed FOIA requests for FBI documents relating to both organizations.

There are a number of illusions about the Freedom of Information Act. Like all pieces of legislation, it needs to be interpreted, administered, and enforced; it is not self-executing. Perhaps the most widespread misimpression is that all a petitioner has to do to obtain documents is to request them. If only it were so. The act permits an agency to withhold documents partially or in their entirety, or to release them in censored and expurgated form—the deletions ranging from a few words to the entire document—if they fall under one or another specified exemption. Objections to these deletions may be made in requesting an administrative appeal. Only rarely does the administrative appeal result in a reversal of the agency's decision; in a few cases, it may result in the release of some documents in a less censored form. If the petitioner still has objections, he or she may file suit in the federal district court—the start of a long and costly process—and follow as far as the judicial appeal process allows.

In my own research, deletions were most often justified by citation of the following exemptions:

- (b)(1)(A) and (B), which allow properly classified documents, under criteria established by an Executive Order, to be kept secret in the interest of national defense or foreign policy
- (b)(2), which relates solely to the internal personnel rules and practices of an agency
- (b)(7)(C), concerning records or information compiled for law enforcement purposes that could reasonably be expected to constitute an unwarranted invasion of personal privacy
- (b)(7)(D), concerning information that could reasonably be expected to disclose the identity of a confidential source, including a state, local, or foreign agency or authority or any private institution which furnished information on a confidential basis

Exemption (b)(1)—the "national defense" and "foreign policy" exemption—has been used to withhold and censor documents dealing with undergraduate student organizations in the 1920s and 1930s. Exemption (b)(2) has been used to deny access to materials having to do with the policies and administration of the FBI itself. Exemption (b)(7)(C) allows the FBI to refuse to disclose its full record of surveillance and harassment by "protecting" the privacy of those who invaded the privacy of others. Exemption (b)(7)(D) allows the FBI to delete the names or any distinguishing characteristics, including jobs, of its informants and keeps us from knowing the level at which it worked out its "arrangements" with cooperating private organizations, such as universities and labor unions.

But even before these decisions are made, there are other decisions that affect what will be released and how much. What is the attitude of those who administer the law—to do so in a way that allows its purposes to be achieved, or to confine it so that it can be sabotaged into destruction without the necessity of repealing it? Users of the Freedom of Information Act conclude that the Department of Justice under Attorney General Edwin Meese was particularly restrictive in its administration of the law. Perhaps that policy was related to the fact that, as we now know, President Ronald Reagan himself was what the FBI calls a "Confidential Informant," providing information on a regular basis to the FBI on the Screen Actors Guild and other organizations of actors and artists. He seems to have begun his informing at least as early as 1941 and was still at it as late as 1947.[1]

An executive order signed by Reagan on April 2, 1982, gutted an earlier order by President Jimmy Carter providing that documents be declassified within a specified period, that those already declassified and released could not later be reclassified, and that all doubts involving the classification of documents be resolved in favor of a broader, less restrictive interpretation of the law. In October 1986 authority was given to withhold documents whose release, in the administration's view, might compromise certain investigations, including the right to refuse to admit whether certain documents exist at all. When scholars have no right to enter the agency's archives, they have no way of knowing whether certain materials exist except by asking. To be sure, they could have been lied to before, and no doubt often were; now, they do not need to be answered at all.

In my own case, the FBI provided an especially interesting variation on the general theme of nonresponsiveness. When I became aware that it had carried on a massive and continuing investigation of what it called "Communist Infiltration of Education"—along with similar investigations of "Communist Infiltration" into labor, the press, foreign films, religious organizations; the list is endless—I requested the documents. And when I learned that the file captions appeared in several forms— "Communist Infiltration" of education, higher education, schools, for example—and that documents might be filed under any of these captions or under the name of a particular university, in which case it might not be sent to me since I had not specifically requested it, I wrote to the FBI requesting a list of file captions under the general title "Communist Infiltration." On February 22, 1980, the FBI replied that it did not have to answer my request for a list of the file captions because to do so would produce a new record and under the law it was obligated to provide only already existing records.

Still another, not inconsequential, restriction on the use of the Freedom of Information Act is the cost of photographic reproduction of the documents. The FBI charges ten cents per page; the charge is not assessed when the document is withheld entirely, but it is when it is sent in censored form, even when the deletions are so numerous as to include virtually the entire document. It need not be so. The FOIA itself contains a provision for a waiver of fees where the request is in the public interest. The legislative history of the act makes clear that Congress intended the fee waiver provision to be broadly construed; requests for documents in connection with historical research, presentations to professional organizations and in scholarly journals, non-profit-making purposes, and the discussion of important public issues were explicitly mentioned as conditions qualifying for a waiver of fees. Some petitioners have received such waivers. My requests were rejected.

My first FOIA request to the FBI—for my own dossier—was made on May 16, 1977. I received the documents, heavily censored, on October 14, 1977. My first request for documents relating to Harvard was made on January 30, 1978; my first request to the FBI for information relating to the strike of UAW-CIO Local 248 against the Allis-Chalmers Company was made on March 7, 1979. According to my calendar of correspondence, from October 14, 1977, until April 19, 1991, the FBI and I had exchanged 1,718 letters relating to my requests, complaints about delays, administrative appeals, and the like. The letter of January 19, 1988, is especially instructive. The FBI says that it is sending documents I had requested concerning what the FBI called its "Responsibility Program" and "Dissemination Policy," subjects of importance to this book. The FBI claims that for this collection of documents 882 pages were reviewed, of which 759 were being released. Fully 14 percent of the documents were being totally withheld, with no indication of their content; of the 86 percent that the FBI calls released, many were so heavily expurgated that nothing remains except an occasional date or file symbol written in the margin by an FBI clerk in Washington. But the details of how to sabotage an act of Congress are better revealed in the record of the delays in releasing the documents.

That letter states: "This release concludes the processing of your requests regrading the Responsibility Program (FOIA #218,531) and Responsibility of the FBI in the Security Field (FOIA #218,540)." It seems so straightforward and easy that one might be tempted not to enquire further. If one did, however, one would find that from first to last, the FBI and I had exchanged forty-four letters and seven and one-half years had passed—and I had had to pay more than $1,000 for documents for which no fee at all could have been charged. All this for only one file category—the "Responsibility of the FBI in the Security Field."[2]

Such delays in the enforcement of the law help only partly to explain why it has taken so long to finish this book. Part of the reason lies in the kinds of documents the FBI released and the form in which it released them. As to the kinds of documents: very rarely did the FBI release documents that permitted an entire story to be told about even some limited episode at a particular time and place, a particular university, for example. As to the form of the documents: so many were so heavily censored as to make it difficult to construct a complete narrative. The situation was entirely different from what I had become accustomed to in earlier research. Then, I had been in control—I defined the problem, decided what the appropriate sources would be, tracked them down, designed the research to help produce an answer to the problem I had set, and decided what constituted proof. But here I was not in control—the FBI decided what I would be allowed to see, and its decision as to what evidence to disclose or even admit it had often meant that I could work not on the problems I had defined but only on some compromise. And the all-too-frequent withholdings meant that even with regard to the problems I was forced to work on, rather than those I wished to work on, my own standards for completeness and the adequacy of the evidence could not always be met. To work on "The Relations of the FBI and the Universities and the Labor Unions" as a historian would wish to do it was impossible; the documentation provided—whatever existed in the files of the FBI—simply did not permit generalizations to be made at the level I would have liked. It took a long time before I arrived at an alternative solution; it seemed all the longer in retrospect because the solution was so simple. Since I could not write the book I wanted to, I would write the one I could, given the limitations of the evidence I was permitted to see. Accepting those limitations, I would write the narrative—a biography, as it were—of a research project: how it began, where it began, where it led. The goals of completeness and breadth of generalization would be sacrificed—they could not be achieved in any case—for detailed examination at the places where I was able to insert a probe. I could not write about "the American university" with the concreteness I wanted, but I could insert my probe into some universities—Harvard and Yale, for instance, where the documentation was especially rich—and into some FBI practices, like selective leaking from its files, that affected all universities. Case studies would be the product; illustration would be the technique.

  The fact that this book is now, in effect, the biography of a research project helps to explain why, contrary to my original thought, it makes use of a good deal of material that does not come from the archives of the FBI. Still, the FBI documents provided the point of departure for the research. In many of the topics I have dealt with—Harvard University, William F. Buckley, Jr., Yale University, for example—the story begins with the FBI documents, but then moves on to other types of documentation. Some of the accounts that follow are, indeed, based as much on these other types of documents as they are on the FOIA materials. These chapters may, therefore, deal with matters other than relations with the FBI, but these other matters help put the actors and the FBI relationship in a broader political context.

In the shift from what was desirable to what was possible, much was lost. My deepest regret is that, though I have collected thousands of pages of documents on the subject, I was unable to write about the role the FBI played in the internal affairs of labor unions. I remain convinced that the operations of the FBI in labor unions had incalculable effects, which will persist for years to come, not only on unions but on society as a whole, and not only in connection with what many would consider parochial trade union issues but issues of the greatest national and international importance—the civil rights movement and the Vietnam War, for example. Two kinds of organizations, universities and labor unions, crucial to the functioning of democratic society because they provided both the sources for alternative versions of society and the muscle to achieve them, were brought to heel. Who would now cry Havoc?

Necessity has made for certain regrettable losses, but it has also made possible at least one gain. Had the FBI documents been made available in their most usable form, I think I would have been content to use only them; their richness would have seemed so overwhelming as possibly to suppress serious thought that more was possible. But the FBI documents left gaps. If, however, they were seen as providing clues as well as answers, then they pointed in the direction of additional sources, sometimes supplementary, sometimes even more important. That led to searches in the libraries of a number of universities, to the extent that the universities allowed, and in the papers of foundations, like the Carnegie Corporation, and persons who had no objection to examination of their papers. The FBI documents were the point where I began; they were not where I finished. By the time I had finished, the book was the product of research in both public—that is, the FBI—and private archives, and the network of relationships revealed by research in the two sets of archives is more complex and more troublesome than would have appeared if reliance had been placed on the FBI documents alone.

Having said that I am particularly interested in the details of these relationships—who did what to whom, at what cost, to whose benefit?—I must nevertheless confess that I have attempted to relate these particulars to some general issues. But which, since there were so many to choose among?

These specific details might be related, most obviously, to the history of police forces, especially the secret police and the intelligence activities of the police.[3]

There are other persistent problems to which our details may be connected, among them the autonomy of organizations and professions and academic freedom. Do threats to autonomy arise mainly from the intrusion of outside agencies, especially government, or, to a large degree, from changes within the organizations and professions themselves? Autonomy and academic freedom have been sacrificed to obtain grants, federally financed programs, and government-supported benefits that are felt to be professionally advantageous, and to ward off the threat of loss of funds, public and private, because of the behavior of some teachers and students who are less concerned with "professional" advancement than with enquiry into themselves, the institutions they are part of, and the world they live in. The increasing violation of autonomy and the narrowing of the range of views that will be protected by academic freedom to those that the profession defines as "significant" are costs of professionalization. Professionalism is a mode of achieving internal discipline, and whether or not the profession comes to the aid of those accused of breaking that discipline or abandons them—by saying that they have been "unprofessional" in their work or behavior—helps to define the social and intellectual boundaries of enquiry.[4]

If the question of what belongs to the state and what to the citizen is one of the general questions to which the particularities of the 1950s may be related, another is how secrecy affects the power of government to get the answers that it prefers. Who helps to keep the secrets, and what ensures their silence?

What were the secrets all about? Clearly, about universities and government, about power. McGeorge Bundy was well aware of the connection between the specific and the general when he spoke on "The Battlefields of Power and the Searchlights of the University" at the School of Advanced International Studies of the Johns Hopkins University. He seemed to be talking of the here and now when he spoke of area studies as providing "a powerful connection between the higher learning and government":

> It is a curious fact of academic history that the first great center of area studies in the United States was not located in any university, but in Washington, during the Second World War, in the Office of Strategic Services. . . . It is still true today, and I hope it always will be, that there is a high measure of interpenetration between universities with area programs and the information-gathering agencies of the government of the United States . . . so that this kind of assessment can be part of the regular business of contemporary life.

Bundy really valued a vision of a world in which people moved easily between the battlefields of power and the campuses of the university, a vision nourished by "the kind of history which is possible only when there is a deep engagement of sympathy to the battlefield of politics and to the way the men on that battlefield conceive of their war. . . . I think it is wrong to suppose that the university is usefully disconnected from this society. I think rather that there is gain for both the political world and the academy from an intensified process of engagement and of choosing sides and of engaging in the battle."[5]

Bundy approached the relationship of the academy to political power with a certain defensiveness, which he hoped would be offset by reference to Thucydides and classical historiography. The subject needs no such legitimizing today; it is what the professions take for granted. The report, approved by the Governing Board of the National Research Council, of the conference convened in 1981 by the Institute of Medicine of the National Academy of Sciences and the United States Secret Service, entitled *Behavioral Science and the Secret Service,* shows the connection between the problem the conference was called to address—how to prevent assassinations—and broader political interests. The issue is not whether the academy should be concerned with assassinations, but rather whether its involvement with government intelligence agencies may make it an accomplice in activities that have as much to do with political objectives as scientific. Prior to the conference, meetings were held with the Secret Service to make sure which questions it wanted to raise.

Before they had concluded their work, the conferees roamed pretty widely.

Concerning what information the Secret Service should obtain about "dangerous" persons:

> . . . history of unemployment or employment difficulties. . . ; "wanderlust" (no permanent home or participation in stable social relationships); exaggerated concern with the world situation; idiosyncratic gripes about the government, and especially feelings of having been cheated or taken advantage of by the government. . . .

Concerning groups other than the "mentally disturbed" and the maladjusted and marginal:

> More attention . . . should be devoted to anticipating new and different potential sources of danger: women and minorities, terrorists, violent radical extremists, and political dissidents or persons and groups with legitimate policy concerns or grievances against the government . . . to name a few. . . . Some conferees speculated that whatever the present level of female threat activity, with the general liberation of women in the United States, threats from women are likely to increase in the future. As with women the Secret Service caseload of blacks, Hispanics, and other minorities is increasing. Because minority groups have become politically visible and vocal in recent years, conferees thought the Secret Service should anticipate a higher level of threat activity from such groups in the future.

The goal of greater cooperation between the Secret Service and the "mental health community" should be "cooperation without cooptation." Both formal and informal relations should be developed, on the model of the "informal consulting relationship that has recently been developed between the Boston field office of the Secret Service and the McLean-Bridgewater Program of Belmont, Massachusetts," under which Secret Service personnel learn about "dangerousness" and "observe clinicians interviewing violent patients (with the informed consent of such patients)." There was considerable support for the view that, as one member of the planning committee put it, "the decision to protect the community and reveal confidences is clearly and obviously ethical." Finally, the conference recommended the creation of an advisory panel to "stimulate research by behavioral scientists in the academic and private sectors on issues of concern to the Secret Service."

It would be difficult to conceive of a closer relationship between the Secret Service and the mental health community than one in which the professional problems of the two were defined as so similar that work done on problems set outside the academy—in the government—was given professional sanction. In fact, the suggestion was that the relationship be made even more intimate; intelligence problems and research problems were the same, and intelligence organizations and professional organizations had become the same. Robert Michels, professor of psychiatry at Cornell University Medical College and psychiatrist-in-chief at New York Hospital, told his colleagues that "perhaps the most important thing that mental health consultants can do for the Secret Service is . . . to facilitate its becoming a specialized part of the mental health system, linked (with appropriate controls) to the rest of the system."[6] The world according to Bundy, in which a shuttle service operates between government and university, had become, within a few years, a world in which the boundary between the two had disappeared; both were assimilated into a more comprehensive category—the profession. Perhaps this is the ultimate in academic *Gleichschaltung*.

Accepting the view of government that social science can be helpful means accepting its criteria of "realism" and "practicality."

In the academy, administrators and professors have tended to pursue the interests of those who could support them, as in the Wars of the Roses the bravos supported those who could provide livery and maintenance. Not all approve; some have said that every acceptance of a project grant is a political as well as a scientific choice, and would agree that "every behavioral investigation or attitude survey potentially affects the interests of its subjects; and . . . no people, except on their own terms, ought to be made an object of the kind of study that could lead to the further rationalization of social controls over them."

The writer of those words did not know that, at the time he wrote them, the basic techniques of only U.S. Army surveillance of citizens—not including FBI, Central Intelligence Agency, or Secret Service surveillance—depended upon conceptual, methodological, and technological developments in which social scientists, many of them doubtless unaware of the ultimate consumer of their research, were intimately involved. The army intelligence archives for which they were consulting architects ran from many volumes of records on "Individuals Active in Civil Disturbances" to eight million case records plus files on suspected subversive groups and persons and reports on incidents of domestic political activity thought to represent a threat to civil authority, including files of the Directorate for Civil Disturbance Planning and Operations in the Pentagon, established in 1968 when the army expected political protest to explode into urban guerrilla warfare.[7]

The last of the general problems involved in the specific details we shall examine is the one that interests me the most: the importance of history in suggesting how to assess our present situation and, therefore, choose the course of action to lead us to the future we want. In the Argentine movie *The Official Story*, a little girl sings wistfully of the connection between memory and direction:

> In the land of "remember-not"
> I take three small steps and get lost.
> A small step toward there, I can't remember if I took it,
> A small step over there, oh, how frightened I am.
> In the land of "remember-not"
> I take three small steps and get lost.
> A small step backward, and I take no more steps
> Because already I forgot
> Where I put my other foot.

Remembering and forgetting are not for lullabies alone. In *The Fixer*, Bernard Malamud writes:

> Once you leave you're out in the open; it rains and snows. It snows history, which means what happens to somebody starts in a web of events outside the personal. It starts of course before he gets there. We're all in history, that's sure; but some are more than others. . . . In or out, it was history that counted—the world's bad memory. It remembered the wrong things.

Why does society forget, or remember the wrong things? The great French historian Marc Bloch suggested two reasons: "the negligence which loses documents; and, even more dangerous, [the] passion for secrecy . . . which hides or destroys them." Bloch had his sardonic side, which he showed when he chided his fellow historians for their propensity to accept the documents of "official authority" as truthful because they are official. On April 21, 1834, prior to the prosecution of the secret societies, Prime Minister Louis Adolphe Thiers wrote to the prefect of the Lower Rhine: "I advise you to take the greatest care to furnish your share of documents for the great forthcoming investigations. The correspondence of all anarchists, the intimate connections between events in Paris, Lyons, Strasbourg, and, in a word, existence of a vast conspiracy embracing the whole of France—all this must be made entirely clear." Was the "official" character of the documents provided at Thier's instructions reason for belief or skepticism, proof of their reliability or evidence of the creation of an "official" story? Bloch was a professional historian, and his critique was directed against those who produce the histories we accept. Perhaps it took someone even more sardonic, and a nonprofessional, to raise questions about the complicity of others in the production of official stories:

> I would gladly be wise.
> The old books tell us what wisdom is:
> Avoid the strife of the world, live out your little time
> Fearing no one,
> Using no violence,
> Returning good for evil—
> Not fulfillment of desire but forgetfulness
> Passes for wisdom.
> I can do none of this:
> Indeed I live in the dark ages![8]

In the pages that follow we shall find much to support both Bloch's criticism of the producers of the official stories and Brecht's criticism of the consumers of those stories, the lotus eaters for whom "not fulfillment of desire but forgetfulness passes for wisdom."

My greatest regret, as I have said, concerns the absence from this account of the FBI's involvement in the labor movement.

The similarity in behavior between many corporations and universities in relation to the FBI deserves closer attention. In 1953, when the United Electrical Workers (UE) and the International Union of Electrical Workers (IUE), which had been chartered by the CIO after the expulsion of the UE, were locked in an election struggle at the Lynn, Massachusetts, plant of General Electric to determine which would have the right to represent the workers there, GE announced a new policy, GE Policy No. 20.4. Rank-and-file leaders of UE locals were then being called before the McCarthy committee. Ralph Cordiner, GE president, announced the new policy: GE employees who refused to testify under oath "when questioned in public hearings conducted by competent public officials"—in other words, "refused to cooperate fully"—would be suspended. It was the first official blacklist of union militants since the early 1930s, and it was a harbinger of what, as we shall see, the universities would do. It is likely that GE policy would have been what it was without government consultation, but in this case, as in the case of the universities, cooperation led to coordination of policy, secretly, of course.

GE Policy No. 20.4 was worked out at a secret meeting at the Mohawk Club in Schenectady, New York, by GE representatives and Roy Cohn and George Anastos of the McCarthy committee. Universities, too, had their private conferences with FBI and congressional committee representatives.[9]

Official stories bloomed, made possible by the careful cultivation of seedling secrets.

It is in connection with its investigation of Communist infiltration of the press—especially of the *New York Times*—that the similarity with the secret arrangement worked out between the FBI and high university officials is so marked. On October 2, 1953, Assistant FBI Director Louis Nichols wrote Clyde Tolson, J. Edgar Hoover's closest associate, that he had been visited that day by General Julius Ochs Adler, general manager of the *Times*, to discuss matters of mutual interest. Adler had left a letter, dated October 1, 1953, for Hoover. Nichols wrote:

> Adler further stated he is very glad to cooperate with the Bureau in any respect in this matter, and while he appreciates the confidential character of the Bureau's work, he wondered if the Bureau could possibly assist him. Adler further advised, of course, he doesn't want any Communist on the New York Times.

In the margin of Nichols's memorandum, Tolson wrote, concerning Adler's request for material in the FBI files: "Let us see what we have—then we can decide."

The meeting of Adler with FBI officials on October 2, 1953, was not his first. On March 5, 1953, D. M. Ladd notified Hoover that Adler and General Edward Greenbaum (of the law firm of Greenbaum, Ernst, and Wolff) had been in to discuss "allegations made by Harvey Marshall Matusow and Louis F. Budenz [FBI informants] relative to Communist infiltration of the New York Times." The New York office of the FBI turned up the names of forty-six persons "who are presently or were formerly employed by the New York Times who have Communist sympathies."

Nor was Adler the only person connected with the *Times* who provided information to the FBI. The names of the others have been deleted from the FBI documents. One of them, according to a teletype from SAC (Special Agent in Charge) New York to the director, November 8, 1954, notified the FBI that Vice-President Richard M. Nixon had interested himself in the matter of Communist infiltration of the *Times* and intended to discuss it with President Dwight D. Eisenhower and Hoover. According to a memorandum from FBI official Alan Belmont to Ladd, June 15, 1953, Assistant SAC Whelan of New York had called that very evening: "[Name deleted] of the New York Times had informally discussed with him a campaign being waged by the Rosenbergs and the Communist Party for clemency or a stay of execution." The informant "wondered whether it was not possible for the Government to hit back through the medium of newspapers to counteract this propaganda." He realized that the government might not be in a position "to carry the ball," but "perhaps he could be of assistance through the New York Times. . . . if the New York Times was going to attempt to counteract the propaganda, it would have to be on their own." He wondered whether "there was any slant we would want to give the New York Times for this purpose."[10]

In this episode, and in others—those we have examined and those we have not yet been able to—we have some answers to the questions raised by Marc Bloch and Bertolt Brecht: How are "official stories" created? Why does forgetfulness pass for wisdom?[11]

1. Square One: Veritas or Hallucination

SQUARE ONE—THE point of departure for the entire investigation—consisted of my article on Seymour Martin Lipset and David Riesman, *Education and Politics at Harvard* (New York, 1976), one of more than a hundred reports and volumes produced under the direction of the Carnegie Commission on Higher Education; McGeorge Bundy's reply to that article and my rejoinder; a lengthy letter from Professor Robert Bellah setting forth his experience at Harvard during the Bundy regime, together with comments by Bundy and me; and letters from Clark Kerr, director of the Carnegie study and president of the University of California, Lipset, and some of Bundy's Harvard associates.[1]

I wanted to know, among other things, what Lipset said about firings at Harvard for political reasons. I myself was one, but I didn't know how many others there were. Perhaps Lipset had found out, and perhaps he would reveal, how Harvard got information about political "suspects" and what it did with that information. Lipset's discussion of the Harvard situation was shallow rather than searching; it was an account that helped perpetuate what Harvard wanted others to believe of it—that it had been a fortress of resistance to the political purges of the period. What made his account all the more curious is that several of the Harvard faculty members whose assistance he acknowledged knew about my situation, and so did his collaborator, Professor Riesman, who had talked to me about it at the time it happened. In my article I discussed the work I was doing at Harvard, on invitation of Dean Bundy, during the academic year 1953–54, and the offer I received from him in the spring of that year, in a letter I possessed, of a five-year appointment to an administrative post with some teaching duties. I described a visit at my office on April 21, 1954, from two FBI agents who had with them a recording machine they wanted to use in their discussion with me about political associates years before in Baltimore, my refusal to talk with them, and my interview by Bundy almost immediately thereafter when I was asked if there was anything in my past that might embarrass Harvard if the appointment that had been offered were to be made. I told him that I had earlier been a member of the Communist Party but no longer was. He then came to the point that on this occasion and again in a second interview was of most concern to him—what my position would be if I should be asked about my political beliefs and activity by "civic authority." I answered that I would talk about myself but not about others. Bundy told me that this was not good enough, but that he would present my appointment to the Harvard Corporation if I would talk about others as well. He urged me to talk about the matter with Harvard faculty members whom I knew, and he scheduled another appointment with me. Both the first and second conversations were recorded on a disk, which revolved on a machine in plain sight. None of the faculty members with whom, at Bundy's suggestion, I discussed the situation supported Bundy's position that I "cooperate by giving the names to the authorities." When I saw Bundy at the second and final meeting, in early May 1954, I called his attention to some *New York Times* articles from April 1938, which showed that Harvard had not always required informing as the price of continued association with the university. Thomas W. Lamont and George Whitney testified in the trial of Richard Whitney of the New York Stock Exchange that they knew he had violated the law but had seen no need to inform the authorities. Harvard had not insisted that they be removed from their positions on the highest governing boards of the university to demonstrate the "complete candor" that was now a requirement for association with the university. I also wrote in my review that a number of faculty members went to see Bundy, and that I had agreed, after discussion especially with law professor Mark Howe, to speak to the FBI about myself but not about others. Under those circumstances, they felt that President Nathan M. Pusey could be prevailed upon at least to meet with me and possibly to proceed with the appointment. He did meet with me; that meeting, too, was recorded. Pusey said virtually nothing, though he promised to be in touch with me in a few days; I never saw him again for twenty years—and then by accident.

I ended my article by asking, first, how Harvard obtained "derogatory information" about me and others—voluntarily from the FBI or at the request of Harvard; second, whether Harvard passed on the information to other universities; third, how many faculty members were actually fired by Harvard or forced to resign; fourth, whether Harvard had one policy—a "public" policy—for those called before congressional committees, and another policy—a "private" policy—for those not called; fifth, how many people were refused appointments or fellowships at Harvard because, when asked about their political activities, they refused to "cooperate fully"—that is, to inform on others.

Bundy's reply emphasized two matters. One, the position I had been offered was administrative, not academic, and therefore was not covered by the privileges and immunities of academic freedom. Two, his discussions with me had not been recorded: neither he nor President Pusey, "either at Harvard or anywhere else, has ever recorded any conversation with anyone, either face-to-face or over the phone." My memory was "wholly wrong," the result of my having been "in a state of great stress." He concluded by quoting from his letter to President Pusey, May 6, 1954, stating that I had made a "serious error" in not having admitted my previous membership in the Communist party after he had offered the position to me.

In my rejoinder to Bundy I quoted a part of his letter to Pusey that he had not cited. He was withdrawing his recommendation of my appointment and suggesting that it be rescinded by the corporation if it had already been approved. In short, he had made an offer of appointment, had withdrawn that offer after learning of my past political affiliation, and was prepared to reconsider the offer if—as his letter to the *New York Review of Books* stated—I agreed to name my former political associates. I also took up the matter of the recording of our discussions and said that I had been authorized by Professor David S. Landes to say that he, too, had been recorded when he spoke to Bundy about my situation. As to his distinction between "administrative" and "academic" appointments, I pointed out, first, that in his letter to me offering the appointment he wrote that there would be some teaching duties, which he hoped would increase in the future; and second, that his view was that administrative employees had none of the immunities of academic freedom. Concerning the possibility that there might have been two Harvard policies—a "public" one and a "private" one—I quoted another section of Bundy's letter to Pusey that he had not referred to. In it he recommended that my two then-current appointments—as adviser to faculty fellows, and research fellow in entrepreneurial history—should be allowed to run their course because if I "were removed now, we should not be able to avoid extensive public discussion of his situation." If my appointments were allowed to expire, however, "we may well be able to end his connection with the University without publicity," which would be "unpleasant" to Harvard and "damaging" to me. Publicly, Harvard was asserting its defiance of Senator Joseph McCarthy. Was its willingness to do otherwise privately an indication that the course Harvard actually followed—in how many cases?—was based more on political expediency than on notions of justice or academic freedom, or any moral principle?

When Professor Robert N. Bellah of the Sociology Department of the University of California at Berkeley described his experiences with Bundy while he was a student at Harvard, the controversy was renewed. He was writing, he said, to confirm that Bundy's letter was proof that "Harvard's capitulation to McCarthyism is still being defended as a form of resistance to McCarthyism." He reported the threats he had received as an undergraduate and graduate student that he would not be able to get an academic job if he persisted in behavior that was embarrassing to Harvard but that the university could not publicly penalize because it wished to cultivate the reputation of defending academic freedom. Bundy told him that he had an obligation of "complete candor" to inform the FBI or any other "authorized" body about his former associates as well as about himself; otherwise, his fellowship would be revoked and his academic future "clouded." Subsequently he was interviewed by FBI agents, to whom he maintained the position he had taken with Bundy—to talk about himself but not others. Bundy continued to press for "complete candor" and requested that Bellah visit an official at the Harvard Health Service. What followed was what Bellah called the strangest episode of a strange story—the attempt of the doctor to determine whether he had ever committed sexual acts for which he could be blackmailed. Bluntly, was he a homosexual? He concluded that Harvard, possibly as early as 1949, "cooperated with a massive effort to suppress political dissent." Privately, all its efforts were directed at cooperation with the political purge then under way, not resistance.

Bundy's rebuttal did not deny pressing for "complete candor"—as he put it, "the Corporation did publicly attach a negative weight to incomplete candor on the part of ex-Communists, even for teaching appointments; that weight lasted until about 1956"—but insisted he was less fierce and single-minded than Bellah suggested. As to the episode with the psychiatrist and the threat of blacklisting, they simply did not happen as Bellah described. His account, after twenty years of silence, "reflects the mixture of animus and self-pity, and also the assumption of conspiracy, that can recapture many ex-Communists still." Bellah had nothing to fear from Harvard, only from the government.

I pointed out that the distinction Bundy had made so much of earlier between teaching and administrative appointments was clearly fictitious. Here was an appointment that was in no way administrative and yet took account of the political beliefs of the appointee. That, according to Bundy, simply did not happen at Harvard. I pointed out, too, that Bundy's suggestion that Bellah see a psychiatrist and his characterization of Bellah as prone to "leaps of fancy . . . animus and self-pity" showed that those who do not accept the official portrait of Bundy—and Harvard—risk being dismissed as unstable. Psychiatry was in the service of politics, as the Harvard administration was in the service of the government, insisting upon full confession, not "complete candor," threatening loss of employment if appointees did not inform on others, and requiring cooperation with the FBI and congressional investigating committees. And I asked if it were really true, as Bundy implied, that it was the corporation's policy, not his, to require "full disclosure"?[2]

Square One looks different now that I have been through so many other squares. I wonder why Bundy was so vehement in his denial that he recorded our discussions of 1954, especially when the issue of recording was insignificant as compared to the issue of Harvard policy. Why should Bundy have been so obsessed with the issue after twenty-three years? Perhaps he was worried that it raised questions concerning what he and President Pusey did with the recordings.

A few other aspects of this earliest exchange are noteworthy in the light of later discoveries. One is the distinction Bundy made between administrative and teaching positions and the different way in which the principle of academic freedom applied to them. It was a distinction that was affirmed when convenient, discarded when not convenient. Bundy himself disregarded the distinction when, as Harvard's representative to the "Listening Post," an informal committee of leading academic administrators, he supported limitations on the academic and political freedom of teachers and students. "There was no 'working in tandem' between Harvard and the FBI," Bundy wrote. The minutes of the meeting of the Listening Post of December 8, 1954, at which Bundy, acting for Harvard University, met with staff members of the Joint Committee on Internal Revenue Taxation, reveal that each university representative reported that "any derogatory information received by the university [was] a basis for an investigation of some sort" and that, since none of the universities had a regular investigating staff, "they obtain such information as they can from Government investigating agencies." The minutes also show that the universities were irked that the Department of Justice and the FBI "are not today following up and prosecuting cases which the universities have already handed over to them under existing law." (See chapter 2.)

Commenting on Professor Bellah's letter, Bundy wrote, as we have already noted: "The Corporation did publicly attach a negative weight to incomplete candor on the part of ex-Communists, even for teaching appointments; that weight lasted until about 1956." The corporation's "negative weight to incomplete candor" is Bundy's elegantly abstract way of referring to reprisals for refusing to confess and inform to government agencies. I did not know in Square One what I learned about Bundy's language by the time I reached Square *N*. Consider, for example, his statement about what he knew of the CIA's special squad, called "Executive Action," to assassinate foreign leaders. Executive Action was apparently an outgrowth of the CIA's "Health Alteration Committee," whose mandate was to "incapacitate" foreign officials. Richard

Bissell of the CIA told the Church committee of the U.S. Senate that he had authorized Executive Action in 1961 and had informed Bundy, national security adviser to the president, about it. Bundy did not remember the episode as well as Bissell did. He admitted he knew that Executive Action involved killing individuals, but he thought that the policy, as discussed with him by Bissell, was merely an "untargeted capability." He neither approved nor disapproved the CIA plan since it did not call for the assassination of a specific individual. Executive Action was "purely preparatory." If a specific individual had been named as a target, would Bundy have approved? Would he have so testified to the Church committee?[3] But we are left with nothing to wonder about concerning Bundy's candor; it was less than "complete," the requirement imposed on others. Reporting to the Listening Post, Bundy did not make the distinction he made later between administrative and academic appointments and why the former were not affected by academic freedom. Did he really believe the distinction was valid? Testifying to the Church committee, he showed himself quite capable of making refined distinctions: assassination of unnamed targets was simply an "untargeted capability," which did not need his approval, as, presumably, their naming would have. Did he believe that distinction was valid?

What was the actual behavior of the universities? How did verbal distinctions aid in the creation of official stories?

Bundy himself was responsible for the fact that so many squares followed Square One; indeed, he provided the impetus for the research that followed.

On April 15, 1977, before I had a chance to see my article in printed form, I received a telephone call from Bundy's secretary at the Ford Foundation, of which he was then the president. When Bundy got on the line he told me that he had read the article. He was especially concerned about what I had written about a recording he had made of our discussions in 1954. As soon as the call was over, I made notes, but even if I had not I am sure I would remember what he said. My notes read as follows:

> BUNDY: You are hallucinating. It didn't happen. I never made any recordings, with you or anyone. Never.
>
> DIAMOND: That's your memory, not mine.
>
> BUNDY: No, its the fact.
>
> DIAMOND: That's your story.
>
> BUNDY: No, you're hallucinating. It's the fact.
>
> DIAMOND: Mac, that's not the truth.
>
> BUNDY: Well, I guess that breaks communication between us.

DIAMOND:	There hasn't been any.
BUNDY:	There are some other errors. I suppose I'll just have to correct them.
DIAMOND:	You will do what you must do, and I'll do what I have to do.
BUNDY:	I'm sorry.
DIAMOND:	Mac, I've been sorry for twenty-three years.
BUNDY:	Good-bye.

On April 19 I received another call from Bundy. He asked me to come to his office the following day so that he could show me a copy of the only document relating to the episode that he was sure was in the Harvard files—a letter he had sent to President Pusey on May 6, 1954. He invited me also to look at the reply he was preparing: "Let's not have bloodshed over this thing," my notes record him as saying. When I saw Bundy the next day, I refused to look at the letter he was sending to the *New York Review of Books*. Once again he brought up the issue of the recording; nervous and angry, he said again that I was hallucinating, that he had never recorded conversations in Cambridge or Washington. In an interview in the *Harvard Crimson*, April 17, 1977, Bundy repeated that I was hallucinating: "I have no doubt that he [Diamond] believes it, but he must have had a hallucination. I never recorded any of my conversations; I strongly disbelieve in doing it." Pusey also denied recording the discussion I had had with him; indeed, he could not remember the episode at all, though Bundy had written him about it on May 6, 1954. Just before our conversation in his office ended, Bundy asked me why, since I had obviously felt deeply about the matter, I had never called him. I answered that in my second meeting with him in early May 1954 and in my meeting with President Pusey at about the same time, each said I would be hearing from him within a few days. I never did hear from Pusey; I heard from Bundy twenty-three years later.

Bundy's insistence that I was hallucinating rankled. I knew, of course, that I was not hallucinating, but I did not know what Harvard knew about my past, or thought it knew, and how it was informed.

What really needed to be inquired into—the alleged state of mind of the participants, or the facts of what happened?

Let us begin with Harvard.

2. Harvard and the FBI: "A Most Cooperative and Understanding Association"

THIS CHAPTER PRESENTS the Harvard–FBI relation essentially as the FBI saw it—what activities at Harvard most concerned it; what parts of the university most attracted its attention; how it obtained information about the university, and from whom. How the FBI looked at Harvard and what it claimed to see there are important, but they are only part of the story. What was Harvard's view of the relationship: who acted for Harvard; was the relationship a matter of policy or something into which the university drifted; who even knew about the relationship; was it the result of well-considered views of the kind of organization the FBI was, or was it derived from more general considerations of Cold War politics? The answers to these questions require access to a different set of documents—not in the FBI archives but in the records of the universities, their professors, and the other private organizations, like foundations, that were involved in the relationship with the FBI. Harvard's fifty-year secrecy rule on official corporation records has walled off critical documents, but the records of the Russian Research Center have been made available, as have the records of the Carnegie Corporation—so deeply involved in the affairs of the Russian Research Center—and of specific individuals whose papers, at the Harvard Law School Library and at Dartmouth College, are not bound by the fifty-year rule. These documents provide the basis for three later chapters.

═══

In retrospect the decade of the 1950s assumes the character of a prolonged and raucous—and often violent—binge. Unlike most binges, however, this was less spasmodic than systematic, less the product of those who could not be contained than of policy that aimed at achieving calculated goals in part by making use of the uncontrolled tempers of others, exploiting fears, and holding out promises of reward to those who became political vigilantes. Central to the policy was the FBI, although—thanks in part to its carefully constructed image of being non-political—it was not generally seen to be as controlling as it in fact was. For the FBI and for other organizations and individuals as well, "non-political" had a very special—and intensely political—meaning. What under other circumstances would be considered "political" views, under the special circumstances of the Cold War were not "political" at all. They were beyond the pale of politics; activities that would follow logically from opposition political views could be treated as if treason itself. Opposition was not seen as proof of democracy and a safeguard against the coerced order that can end in totalitarianism. It was seen as subversive—of nation, of family, of social order itself; it was to be hunted and uprooted.

At the center of this massive purge, which affected all aspects of American life and culture, was the FBI. Its connections with other administrative agencies of the federal government, with state and local police departments and investigating agencies, with private organizations, including universities, labor unions, corporations, churches, and veterans' organizations, were intricate and most often secret. Indeed, it was generally the strategy of the FBI to deny its true role, to allow its partners to be boastful where it was reticent.

Whether Communists, former Communists, or suspected Communists were or should be permitted to be members of college faculties was the focus of public attention on the problem of subversive infiltration of the colleges in the 1950s, but FBI concern was not so limited. Students as well as faculty members attracted the attention of the FBI, and at Harvard the interest of the FBI began well before the 1950s, was directed toward an unusually wide range of student activities, curricular and extracurricular, including even the surveillance of student organizations, and depended in large part on the secret cooperation of university administrators.

On January 14, 1954, some agency of the U.S. government, whose name has been deleted but must have been Washington FBI headquarters, wrote to SAC Boston about the pending congressional investigation of Communist activities at Harvard University. The subject of the memorandum was "CP, USA, Dist. #1, Harvard University branch, Internal Security—C": "In the event it becomes necessary to do any research along these lines in the event of requests from the Bureau attendant upon investigation by Congressional investigating committees, it is suggested the following central files be consulted." Many of the file captions and numbers have been deleted, but enough remain to show how wide-ranging the FBI interest was:

100-28110	House Committee on Un-American Activities
100-28260	Cominfil into Education
100-20916	Defected Communists
100-22702	Cominfil of American Colleges
100-16094	Harvard Liberal Union
100-28245	Jenner Committee
100-20951	National Council for American Education—Red-ucators at Harvard
100-23675	Red Influence at Harvard
100-23744	Faculty, Harvard University Law School
100-18912	CP, USA—Education
100-28341	Harvard Student Union
100-9504	John Reed Club of Harvard
100-1263	American Youth for Democracy
100-23986	Labor Youth League
100-1661	National Lawyers Guild

The names and file numbers of at least twenty-six other organizations have been deleted. For some organizations the records began to be kept in the early 1930s, and even at that relatively early date the FBI depended on cooperation from the university administration.

An internal FBI memorandum of June 23, 1941, from R. P. Kramer to P. E. Foxworth reports a telephone call from SAC Boston in response to a headquarters request for information as to whether the Boston office was conducting an investigation of the Harvard Student Union or any other Harvard undergraduate organization. SAC Boston "advised that no outright investigation of the Harvard Student Union had been or was being conducted, but that in connection with a general investigation which the Bureau had requested of the American Student Union, some inquiry had been made and reports had been submitted by the Boston Office concerning the Harvard Student Union, which is a branch of the American Student Union [ASU]."

SAC Boston also reported that in connection with an FBI investigation of a Harvard undergraduate "who was reported to the Bureau as being an active Communist . . . Agents had contacted [2 lines deleted] Harvard and [name deleted] has furnished considerable information concerning various undergraduate organizations at Harvard."

The report by SAC Boston was in response to a request for information of June 23, 1941, from Acting Attorney General Francis Biddle to J. Edgar Hoover. Congressman Thomas Eliot of Massachusetts had asked Biddle whether the FBI was investigating the "Harvard Liberal Union, the Harvard Student's Union, or other undergraduate organizations at that University," and Biddle asked Hoover to let him know "whether any investigation of the members has been made, to what extent, and under what circumstances." At 10:00 the next morning, Foxworth notified Hoover's office that he had been in touch with SAC Boston and had asked whether the Harvard Student Union, Liberal Union, or any other student organization was under FBI investigation. He was told "that the Boston Office is not conducting an active investigation; however, they have an informant at the University who has been sending in information on these organizations." Foxworth told SAC Boston to make sure "the Bureau had been furnished all of the information obtained by the Boston Office regarding these organizations" and to call if any additional information became available. When Hoover answered Biddle's memorandum with one of his own on June 24, 1941, he was characteristically evasive: "I should like to advise you that no specific investigation of any undergraduate organization at this University is being made. However, this Bureau has for a number of months been accumulating information concerning the American Student Union, reportedly a Communist front organization, together with a number of other alleged front organizations for the Communist Party." It was in connection with "the gathering of information" concerning the ASU that "some data have been accumulated with regard to the Harvard Student Union."

Was the Harvard Student Union being investigated or was it not? Hoover was less than clear: "No active investigation of the Harvard Student Union has been conducted, but information has been obtained from available sources. . . . Considerable data with regard to the Harvard Student Union and its connection with the American Student Union, the American Youth Congress and the Young Communists [*sic*] League were obtained . . . and this information has been incorporated in the Bureau's file." Hoover told Biddle that in August 1940 the FBI had been asked by the attorney general for information about a number of organizations "operating to interfere with the passage of the Burke-Wadsworth Selective Service Act," among them the ASU. He told Biddle that the FBI memorandum showed that the ASU opposed "military preparations" in the United States and would "fight against any legislation designed to outlaw the Communist Party." His memorandum ended with a characteristic insinuation:

> You may be interested in the fact that Mr. Joseph Lash, the National Secretary of the American Student Union, in testifying before the House Committee on Un-American Activities on December 1, 1939, stated that the Harvard Chapter of the American Student Union had cooperation "with Tom Elliott [*sic*] in his campaign for Congress in order to get practical experience in politics, because Mr. Elliott [*sic*] represented ideals in which the A.S.U. believes."

For the FBI the atmosphere of a university, a labor union, a newspaper, a church was susceptible to pollution and required constant monitoring. Organizations were especially to be watched, but so were student activities not under the direction—at least not known to be under the direction—of any organization. Perhaps sufficient investigation would show that the activities were not so innocent after all, but were evidence of a conspiracy wider and more insidious than hitherto suspected.

Why else should the FBI have been so twitchy about the annual Ames Competition at the Harvard Law School in 1948?

On April 20, 1948, SAC Boston wrote the director that the final competition for the Ames award had been held. He enclosed three documents—the record on appeal in the U.S. Circuit Court of Appeals for the "Ames Circuit," the brief for the appellant, and the brief for the defendants. The documents presented the arguments made in the mock case, which, as SAC Boston wrote, "involves action against Richard A. Hood and other special agents of the Federal Bureau of Investigation in connection with alleged violations under the Fourth and Fifth amendments to the Constitution in which money damages are sought for unreasonable searches and seizures and deprivation of liberty without due process." The Gardner Law Club, arguing for the appellants, had been declared the winner by the judges, Deans Young B. Smith of Columbia, Erwin Griswold of Harvard, and Wesley A. Sturgis of Yale. The issue, as stated by SAC Boston, was whether the protection afforded by the Fourth and Fifth Amendments against deprivation of liberty without due process included the right to recover in federal court for money damages for violation of the rights guaranteed. The case had arisen "as a result of arrest by FBI agents of members of an organization known as 'Mankind United' after indictment for violation of the wartime sedition laws." On January 23, M. A. Jones sent Assistant FBI Director Nichols a twenty-six-page analysis of the case.

Hoover was outraged. At the end of Jones's memorandum he wrote:

> It seems to me that this is certainly a vicious smear of the FBI. While it is a moot court case and facts are therefore suppositions, yet in drafting facts they could have adhered at least to more realistic facts as to how FBI acts and not portray it as a Gestapo—breaking [doors?], taking doors off hinges, using firearms improperly, etc. and other typically Communist portrayals of the FBI.—H.

Within a few days, SAC Los Angeles had called the attention of the director to the Ames Competition and suggested that the Boston office obtain copies of the documents. SAC Cincinnati sent along a full set of the documents that somehow had been "made available by Dean Griswold to Special Agent [name deleted] of the Cincinnati Office."[1] We may have a clue as to how SAC Cincinnati obtained the documents from Dean Griswold. On February 8, 1949, the agent wrote to the director describing a recent meeting of the Harvard Club of Cincinnati at which Harvard College Dean Wilbur J. Bender had spoken. Bender did not know of any Communist Party members at Harvard College, but he did know of one organization "which is 'close to it,' consisting of nineteen members who may be either Party members or fellow travelers." Bender said that both students and faculty at Harvard were considerably to the right of the American people. In the recent presidential election, the faculty favored Dewey four to one; as to the student members of the Communist-front organization, they were "unattractive, repulsive, and neurotic persons," who would be martyred by taking action against them. The SAC was making this information available to the director "inasmuch as the remarks of Dean Bender are one of the few public expressions concerning Communism at Harvard." He himself was given "the information by S.A. [name deleted], a member of the Harvard Club of Cincinnati, who attended the afore-mentioned meeting." It is not at all unlikely that the special agent had written to Dean Griswold requesting the briefs and that Griswold sent them to the Harvard alumnus.[2]

Of all Harvard student organizations it was perhaps the John Reed Club that most attracted the attention of the FBI—and of military intelligence. The reason may have been purely historical. As early as 1932, Washington FBI headquarters was being sent reports of John Reed Club meetings and copies of pamphlets from cities throughout the country— New York (Jack Conroy, Meridel LeSeuer, Allan Calmer, Joe Jones, Nelson Algren, Philip Rahv, and Alfred Hayes had spoken for the American League against War and Fascism), Boston, Baltimore, San Pedro, Milwaukee, Buffalo, Chicago (Nelson Algren had written an article for *Left Front* on "the Southern Illinois situation").[3]

On May 14, 1943, the Office of the Director of the Intelligence Division, First Service Command, War Department, prepared a report on "The John Reed Society of Harvard University (Marxist organization)." It was described as a "professedly Marxist student organization, conducted as a study and action group." It was not a membership group— indeed, it was reported as having only three members—but it provided an opportunity to "study Marxist social science both in theory and practice." It published the *Harvard Vanguard* from Leverett House and sponsored a weekly discussion group. In addition, six special meetings had been held, one of which, addressed by Jack Green, secretary of the New England District Communist Party, was attended by "thirty-three college students (including two Negroes)." The FBI also noted that a petition with 546 signatures had been sent to President Franklin D. Roosevelt, "asking that an inter-racial unit be established in the United States Army." Later reports by military intelligence, which attempted to bring the record up to date, were based on confidential reports from informants who had access to information in the office of the dean of Harvard College:

According to a confidential report, the John Reed Society "was synonymous with intellectual Marxism, and probably indicated membership in the Communist Party. It was a registered organization in the University (Harvard) whereas the Young Communist League was never a recognized group in college circles, and thus it met, if at all, secretly. . . ." Subject society is still a registered organization at Harvard University. Its current sponsors are Professor Kirtley F. Mather (connected with many CP front organizations) and Professor F. O. Matthiessen, a leader in PCA [Progressive Citizens of America] activities.[4]

By May 24, 1943, the FBI had begun what was to become a lengthy dossier on the John Reed Society of Harvard. Most of the information it contained was from a regular confidential informant of the FBI, almost certainly a member of the Harvard administration. It concludes: "Will, at intervals, recontact [name and title deleted] for any further information, which he may be able to give regarding the John Reed Society, its organization and members." Later reports, based on documents given to the FBI by officials of Widener Library, show that the society protested the university's refusal to allow Communist leader Earl Browder to speak in a university building and organized a John Reed memorial meeting, sponsored by Professors Gordon Allport, Harry Levin, Perry Miller, Ralph Barton Perry, Theodore Spencer, and Dirk J. Struik of MIT, at which a portrait of John Reed was dedicated at Adams House.[5]

Meetings of the society were regularly attended by agents or informants of the FBI. On March 10, 1947, the FBI decided to reopen its investigative file on the society upon learning that it had been "reactivated at Harvard University and is presently sponsoring a series of public lectures on 'Marxism and Modern Thought.' " The first of the lectures, by Howard Selsam, director of the Thomas Jefferson School in New York, was attended by an audience "composed principally of persons who by their appearance and demeanor were students at Harvard." Later meetings, all reported by the FBI, were addressed by Dr. Joseph B. Furst ("The Marxist Theory of Neurosis"), who made "frequent favorable reference . . . to lectures by Professor Gordon N. Allport"; Paul M. Sweezy, who "pledged a constant continuation of capitalism as an economic theory" [sic]; John Gates, legislative director of the Communist Party; Professor Bernhard J. Stern of Columbia University; and F. O. Matthiessen, who was "the subject of an Internal Security investigation by the Boston Division." Harvard College regulations required that undergraduate organizations register with the college and record the names of their officers and members. All reports by the FBI on the John Reed Society give the names of the officers and members, the speakers at the organization's meetings, and the topics of discussion groups. On July 16, 1948, SAC Boston wrote to the director requesting bureau authority "to continue established contact with [two-thirds of line deleted] and such other contacts as may be desirable on the campus at Harvard University . . . in connection with" the John Reed Society, "which is a student Marxist group operating with strong Communist Party influence." Within days, authority to continue the established contacts was granted.[6]

All Harvard undergraduate organizations concerned with politics were subject to investigation involving surveillance and reports by "unofficial" informants and regular confidential informants in the employ of the university. As late as November 29, 1960, a Boston FBI agent, "while contacting" a confidential source (name and title deleted), was told about an article in that day's *Harvard Crimson* dealing with a movie, *Operation Abolition,* showing "the violence developed during the hearings" of the Un-American Activities Committee in San Francisco in May 1960. The film had been shown by the Naval ROTC unit at Harvard; the *Crimson* article was considered "inflammatory" by the FBI informant, who inquired whether the FBI agent would "mind talking with [half line deleted]." The informant was a Harvard officer who

> had made arrangements with the Department of Naval Science to have the film shown . . . at a subsequent date so that they could more accurately report on it to President Pusey of Harvard, as well as to the Board of Overseers if necessary.

On December 2 the informant called the FBI agent at his home to report that he had received a number of telephone calls from faculty members who supported the showing of the film. A week later he "called in members of the Harvard-Radcliffe Liberal Union" and demanded an explanation of "the circularizing of a one page sheet," which had been passed out on Harvard property, protesting the propagandistic character of the movie.

The episode was enough to cause an FBI investigation of the author of the leaflet, who was identified as chairman of the Emergency Public Integration Committee (EPIC), "an anti-discrimination group interested in the problem of lunch counter integration as well as discrimination on college campuses and in housing." And, of course, the Harvard-Radcliffe Liberal Union was investigated. The FBI was told that the organization had fifty members; it found no derogatory information in its files concerning the three officers of the Liberal Union or its two advisers, Professors Arthur M. Schlesinger, Jr., and Samuel H. Beer. Nevertheless, Boston "completed arrangements with [name deleted] to pay the closest attention to the organization in the future, particularly for any evidences of CP infiltration."[7]

On January 21, 1947, an FBI agent sent a report to SAC Boston concerning an antilynching rally he had attended at Jordan Hall, sponsored by the Intercollegiate Committee to End Lynching. His report was placed in the files of all the undergraduate clubs sponsoring the event, including the Harvard Liberal Union, but it was captioned "Foreign

Inspired Agitation among American Negroes in Boston Field Division—Internal Security—C." The report listed the sponsoring organizations: twelve undergraduate clubs at Boston University; the Calvin Coolidge College American Veterans Committee; three undergraduate clubs at Harvard, two at Wellesley and Tufts, and one each at Northeastern, Radcliffe, Wheaton, Portia Law School, and the Samuel Adams School for Social Sciences. The FBI report of the meeting is as notable for the evidence it does not present on "foreign-inspired agitation among Negroes" as for what it does report.

Reflecting the scope of FBI interest in undergraduate organizations was the forty-eight-page report by SAC Boston on May 20, 1949, on the activities of the Young Progressives of Massachusetts (YPM). The activities are those of an undergraduate organization forty years ago, but long sections of the report are now blacked out on the grounds that their disclosure would compromise the present national defense or foreign policy of the United States government. What remains is revealing of FBI interests:

- the names of the officers of college chapters of the Young Progressives throughout Massachusetts
- the names of speakers who supported the campaign of Henry Wallace for the presidency
- the names of members of YPM committees (organization, program, resolutions, nationalities, teenage, community, religion, and the like)
- the names of the officers, members, and faculty advisers at Harvard—obtained from university informants—of Students for Wallace, together with many excerpts from *Harvard Crimson* articles dealing with opposition to the draft and the Smith Act prosecutions ("Allen F. Westin, first-year student at Harvard Law School [protested] this attempt to legislate a minority political party out of existence. . . . We do not intend to sit idly by and watch the Bill of Rights and academic freedom violated by camouflage Red spy tales.")
- the record of participation by YPM in "inter-racial activities," such as Negro History Week (with a talk by the baritone Kenneth Spencer), a Lincoln–Frederick Douglass rally (with an appearance by Zero Mostel and a hootenanny with members of the Weavers), a report on the activities of the Committee to End Job Discrimination in the Roxbury–South End Area (entirely blacked out), and the picketing of the Timothy Smith Department Store for discrimination (also largely blacked out)

Concern with undergraduate organizations and cooperation with Harvard authorities—and not only on the part of the FBI—was continuous. On March 10 and 16, 1953, First Army Headquarters on Governors Island, New York, sent on to the FBI and a number of other intelligence agencies reports on the Harvard Student Union and the *Harvard Progressive*, based on "the records of the Archives, Widener Library, Harvard University . . . examined in the presence of Mr. Kimball Elkins, series assistant."[8]

But the affairs of Harvard University were of greater interest and concern to the FBI than the affairs of Harvard College, and to place them under adequate scrutiny required more subtle procedures. Those, in turn, required negotiations with university authorities at a higher level.

On June 9, 1949, the *New York Times* reported the recommendation of the National Education Association's (NEA) educational policies commission that Communists "should be excluded from employment as teachers." The exclusion of Communists, the commission had concluded, far from being an "abridgement of academic freedom, would serve a contrary purpose":

> Such [Communist] membership involves adherence to doctrines and disciplines completely inconsistent with the principles of freedom on which American education depends. Such membership, and the accompanying surrender of intellectual integrity render an individual unfit to discharge the duties of a teacher in this country.

The report warned that teachers should not be called Communists "carelessly and unjustly." Such charges, "with their usual accompaniment of investigations, book burning, and efforts at intimidation," could seriously impair the efficiency of the school system if they became "too violent, frequent, and widespread":

> The whole spirit of free American education will be subverted unless teachers are free to think for themselves. It is because members of the Communist party are required to surrender this right, as a consequence of becoming part of a movement characterized by conspiracy and calculated deceit, that they should be excluded as teachers.

The undergraduate editors of the *Harvard Crimson* dissented. How could Communists be barred from teaching without encouraging "too violent, frequent, and widespread" charges and thereby impairing the efficiency of higher education? And how could Communists be barred as teachers without investigating faculties? There was no "just and fair method" of investigating faculties for Communists, the *Crimson* concluded: "Competence alone should be the standard."[9]

On campuses throughout the country the investigation of faculty members—by congressional committees or otherwise—had become a divisive issue. At some public universities the issue was not merely being debated; investigations had already begun. Nor were private universities immune. At Harvard, Frank B. Ober, an alumnus of the Law School who as a state legislator had sponsored the Maryland Subversive Activities Act of 1949, was urging alumni to stop contributing financially until the university ceased being a refuge for "reds" and "pinks." The distinguished attorney and Harvard Corporation member Grenville Clark responded to Ober's call by affirming that no threat of financial sanctions would deter the university from its traditional defense of academic freedom.

Clark's response seemed to suggest that Harvard had adopted a policy of rejecting any review of its faculty's political activities. But had it? On June 22, 1949, in a talk before the Harvard Fund for Advanced Study and Research, Harvard President James B. Conant sought to reassure both his faculty, who in an opinion poll had supported the NEA position, and his students, who had rejected it. He reaffirmed the position he had taken as a member of the NEA commission, that Communists should not be permitted to teach, but then added that "as long as I am president of the University I can assure you there will be no policy of inquiring into the political views of members of the staff and no watching over their activities as citizens."[10] How did Conant propose to detect Communist teachers without investigating the political activities of faculty members?

FBI documents confirm that the FBI's Boston field office—and other federal investigative agencies (for example, military intelligence)—closely followed the activities of the Harvard faculty and, in the process, developed sources of information on the Harvard faculty and staff. Whatever the basis for this cooperation—to curry favor, to forestall an investigation of oneself, to do one's patriotic duty—FBI officials were concerned that it be discreet. Section 87, paragraph 5A, of the *FBI Manual for the Conduct of Investigations* specified the restrictions governing interviews "with individuals connected with institutions of learning." Before "initiat[ing] a security investigation of a faculty member," FBI agents had to obtain authorization from FBI headquarters. Prior authorization was not normally required in the case of students or nonacademic employees "providing no unusual circumstances exist which would require advice from the Bureau prior to initiating the investigation":

When requesting Bureau authority to conduct a security investigation of an individual connected with an institution of learning, the letter should set forth the identity of the subject, his position, and the reason for which the investigation is desired. Information concerning the individual's identity should be obtained from the Registrar's office unless some specific reason exists which would make it undesirable to contact the Registrar's office.

Once bureau authority had been granted to conduct a "security" investigation, the FBI agent could "contact all established reliable sources including those connected with the institution of learning." A principal source was the university registrar:

> If the Registrar is reliable and can be depended upon not to divulge the Bureau's identity, Bureau authority is not needed in these cases to contact the Registrar's office to obtain background data useful for identification purposes, to develop other proper investigative leads or to verify connection with the institution of learning.

If it became necessary to "interview a student, faculty member, or other employee of an institution of learning who is not an established reliable source," prior bureau authorization was needed. In that event, "a positive statement concerning [the person's] discretion and reliability" had to be provided.[11]

On March 12, 1953, in a memorandum to the FBI director captioned "Harvard College Observatory/Information Concerning" SAC Boston reported a telephone call from a Harvard official, whose name and title have been deleted, requesting that an FBI agent visit him at his office so that he could provide "information of interest to the Bureau." "SA [name deleted], *who acts as liaison agent at Harvard* [my emphasis], was designated to interview [name deleted]." At that interview, the informant gave the FBI agent a copy of a letter to Harvard Provost Paul Herman Buck from Professor Donald H. Menzel, acting director of the observatory. Menzel's letter was attached to the agent's report; it stated:

> Someone in the Observatory is distributing or attempting to distribute sizable quantities of Communist literature, real red propaganda an investigating committee would love to pick up. For the moment we have decided to keep quiet, holding the documents as they come in, although my first reaction was to destroy them and send a note around to the Observatory personnel that nothing was to be placed in the box but pure science. I should appreciate having your advice.

The Harvard official who provided the FBI with a copy of Menzel's letter said that Menzel had

> stated such activities, if made known to an investigating committee, would add to the woes of Harvard University officials especially in the light of the projected HCUA [House Committee on Un-American Activities] investigation among members of the Harvard University faculty. He added he "well realized Harvard was on the spot" and re-

quested SA [name deleted] to discuss the matter with Dr. Menzel, the
original complainant, who was greatly concerned about the matter.

The FBI agent did interview Menzel, who told him "he had been advised by [name deleted] that he, Menzel, would be visited by a representative of the FBI." Menzel was urged to provide "anything which he
thought would be of interest to this Bureau."

That Menzel provided information to Provost Buck and to the FBI
about "Communist infiltration" into the library of the Harvard Observatory raises questions about the complex reasons for informing. Is it
done for patriotic reasons, for money, to curry favor, to remove suspicion
from oneself? In Menzel's case, as in so many others, the record allows
us to be more definitive in our judgment of the FBI than in our judgment of the informant.

By 1953, when the FBI investigated the incident at the observatory,
Menzel had already been under FBI scrutiny for a number of years—as
he must have known—and he was to remain so for some time to come.
In 1948 he was investigated by the FBI for the Atomic Energy Commission in connection with an application to be a consultant at Los Alamos.

The FBI report on Menzel, attached to the Personnel Security Questionnaire he was required to fill out as a prospective consultant with the
Atomic Energy Commission, dated August 25, 1949, was especially concerned with the fact that he was an associate of Harlow Shapley and
Walter Orr Roberts at the Harvard Observatory. Some of those interviewed by the FBI spoke highly of Menzel. Others were suspicious. One
found Shapley and Roberts not "particular[ly] stable in their political
views. . . . Shapley has been very interested in the past few years in
doing what he can to avoid any future war with Russia, but it was [name
deleted] opinion that Dr. Shapley is possibly wrong in his approach to
the situation, and has become affiliated with organizations . . . of a
questionable nature, inasmuch as these organizations have been considered to be rather closely affiliated with the Communist Party." Another felt that "Dr. Menzel possibly shares the views of both Roberts
and Shapley, and for this reason is a poor security risk." The FBI was
also interested in the fact that Menzel's personnel questionnaire showed
that he had visited Russia with a scientific group in 1936 to observe a
total eclipse of the sun and, for "several months" in 1937, had been a
member of an organization Menzel remembered as the "American
Committee of Democracy." The New York office of the FBI turned up
the fact that in November 1942 he had spoken at a conference called by
the Congress of American-Soviet Friendship to celebrate the twenty-
fifth anniversary of the USSR. He spoke about the trip he had made in
1936, wartime damage to Russian observatories, and his hope that the
meeting would contribute to "the free intercourse of scientific men."
The FBI noted that the American Council on Soviet Relations, which

had organized the Congress of American-Soviet Friendship, was on the attorney general's list of proscribed organizations under Executive Order 9835.

The Boston FBI report of September 1, 1949, stated that the American Committee for Democratic and Intellectual Freedom, in which Menzel had admitted membership, had been cited by the House Committee on Un-American Activities as "subversive and un-American." The FBI was also informed that Menzel had been invited to attend "a small private luncheon for the British Nobel Prize winner P. M. S. Blackett, whose book, *Fear, War, and the Bomb,* was called by the *New York Times* 'the best defense and explanation of the Russian viewpoint on the control of atomic energy.' " On March 22, 1950, SAC Albuquerque notified Hoover that the AEC Security Office at Los Alamos was no longer considering Menzel as a consultant. But that did not end the matter. In May 1950 the Air Force Loyalty Hearing Board requested all the information collected by the FBI so that it could make its own investigation. On May 10, 1951, Hoover notified SAC Chicago that Menzel "was denied clearance in connection with his contemplated employment by the University of California at Los Alamos" but was "again being considered for employment and . . . an inquiry had been made by the Director of Security, AEC, Chicago. . . . You are requested to maintain contact with the local AEC Security office and advise the Bureau in the event this individual is granted clearance." Back came the answer: the matter had been checked; Menzel was not an applicant for a position.[12]

———

Talcott Parsons, of Harvard's Social Relations Department, and his wife, Helen, administrative assistant at the Russian Research Center, were problems for the FBI. Though Parsons gave every assurance of his loyalty, the FBI was uncertain that his wife could be made an informant. On February 16, 1949, FBI agent Thomas McLaughlin, Jr., in a memo to SAC Boston, reported that "[name deleted] believes that Mrs. Parsons holds liberal views with respect to political and social matters and would possibly not be a desirable contact in connection with any information desired relating to the Russian Research Center. Informant has no information relating to the loyalty or responsibility of Mrs. Parsons but provided this information as indicative of the attitude Mrs. Parsons might take in the event direct contact were made through her for information relating to the Russian Research Center and its program." Who the FBI informant was we do not know; the name and other identifying material have been deleted to maintain the confidentiality of the source and the information the source was "regularly" providing to the FBI. Professor Parsons was another matter.

In 1953 and 1954, he was the subject of an intensive loyalty investigation by the FBI in connection with his employment as a consultant by UNESCO. The investigation produced enough "damaging" evidence—

going back to FBI inquiries dating from 1923 when he was reported to be a member of the League for Industrial Democracy, and extending to 1953 when, in the words of a Harvard informant, he was "perhaps the 'hidden leader' of a group of Professors . . . who are devoted to furthering Communist Party projects"—to warrant a hearing. On May 17, 1954, while on leave at Cambridge University, England, Parsons submitted a lengthy notarized affidavit in response to a series of questions by the International Organization Employees Loyalty Board. His answers suggest that he had second thoughts about some of his earlier activities and was in thorough agreement with the current political orthodoxy—that to be a Communist was cause for dismissal from a teaching position.

The board was especially interested in the "nature of [his] association" with Harlow Shapley or "any other Communist or Communist Party member." Had Parsons "organized, aided or sympathized with Mr. Shapley or any other individual in the performance of Communist activities"? Parsons's response was that, aside from seeing Shapley at some faculty meetings, the only association he had with him was to discuss including the social sciences in the proposed National Science Foundation and in the program for the 1948 centennial celebration of the American Association for the Advancement of Science. With one exception, he had only tenuous connections with a few other persons who were later identified as Communists; the exception had been "quite openly Chairman of the Harvard Trotzkyist (*not* the official Communist) student group at Harvard," whose "renunciation, a good many years ago, of Communist-type views and activities was sincere and complete. Moreover, I have reason to believe that his Harvard education, including my influence on him, had a good deal to do with his change." His having been a faculty sponsor of the John Reed Club was entirely pro forma and did not imply agreement with its views. Besides, "knowing what I do now of the abuses which Communist-front organizations have consistently made of the privileges of free speech I would not today accept sponsorship of such an organization."

Parsons responded to "Explain where your sympathies lie in the ideological conflict between the United States and the Soviet government" as follows:

> I am strongly opposed to Soviet Communism and its influence in the United States and elsewhere for four main reasons. First, the Communist Party advocates and works for revolution by violence and refuses to accept the legal procedures of Constitutional Democracy. . . .
> Second, it works by conspiratorial methods which are incompatible with the requirement of a democracy that differences of political opinion, which we treat as legitimate within a considerable range, should be

openly threshed out before the forum of public opinion and decided by constitutional processes. Third, the Communist Party in the United States is known to be not an independent movement of free Americans. The fourth reason is that I do not like the Communist ideal and where they have gained ascendancy, their practice, of what a society should be. . . .

I subscribe to these views, which I understand to be taken for granted by all loyal American citizens, without reservation.

At his hearing before the examiner and a board member of the International Organization Employees Loyalty Board in New York on November 9, 1954, he admitted to having been opposed to the California loyalty oath, but said he had "no objection to taking loyalty oaths to the government of the United States." He did oppose singling out the teaching profession for such oaths. He felt that a Communist had no moral right to be a teacher.[13]

The FBI dossier on Alexander Gerschenkron, professor of economics and head of Harvard research in Soviet economics, has been gutted by deletions, but enough remains to show that, because he was a consultant for the Rand Corporation, he was the subject of searching investigations by the FBI and the Office of Special Investigations of the air force even before he was appointed at Harvard. He had taught at the University of California at Berkeley and, while employed at the Federal Reserve Board in Washington, at George Washington University. His FBI report from Boston, August 16, 1950, states that in both San Francisco and Washington, D.C., the FBI "will through Confidential Informant and established reliable sources determine whether the subject was engaged in any activities at" either university "considered inimical to the welfare of the United States." In San Francisco, no derogatory information was produced; to the contrary, one informant at Berkeley, who claimed to have had "adequate opportunity to become familiar with the subject's associates, organizational affiliations and teaching during the years they worked together," felt that he was "thoroughly loyal . . . , never a member of any organization which was subversive in nature and . . . never willingly associated with persons who were members of such organizations." The reason: "At one time the subject's father owned a factory in Kiev, Russia, but was forced by the Soviets to give up his business and leave Russia because he was a Capitalist. . . . In view of the treatment of his family and himself by the Soviets, the subject not only hates Communism for its ideas but also for what it has done to him." But in Washington, D.C., where he had been investigated earlier in connection with his government employment, he had been placed under physical surveillance in 1946, and letters to him written in Russian and German were opened by the FBI and translated.[14]

The FBI sought to obtain information concerning the Harvard faculty in unobtrusive ways from individuals employed by or associated with the university. A few examples will suffice.

On January 7, 1954, the Boston field office notified FBI headquarters:

> [Name deleted], Corporation office, Harvard University, advised her records indicate [name deleted by S.D.] currently residing at [deleted by S. D.]. . . . These same records indicate that on September 15, 1953, [name deleted by S.D.] received a Corporation appointment. . . . On July 1, 1953 . . . [name deleted by S.D.] had been appointed Research Fellow. . . . According to information in her files [name deleted] stated [name deleted by S.D.] was interviewed by McGeorge Bundy, Dean of Harvard College, prior to his appointment.

Was the FBI relationship with its informants purely personal, or was it a covert institutional arrangement?

A number of memoranda between SAC Boston and FBI headquarters, beginning in June 1950, shed light on this question and further suggest that some understanding between the FBI and Harvard antedated even the first of these reports.

1. The FBI has refused to release the first document of this series, but we know that it is a two-page memorandum, dated June 16, 1950, captioned "Harvard University/Cambridge, Massachusetts/Confidential National Defense Informant [CNDI]."

2. The second document of the series, dated June 29, 1950, and marked "Personal and Confidential," is also a memorandum from the Boston field office to the FBI director. It is captioned "Bernard A. DeVoto/Information Concerning." On January 7, 1982, in response to a court order (U.S.D.C., S.D.N.Y., Ca 79-Civ-3770), the FBI released a second version of this document, which does not delete, as the first version did, the caption of the document and the whole of paragraph four. Some deletions still remain, but the document deserves being quoted at length because of what it reveals both by content and tone:

> [Three lines deleted] asserted that while the Harvard University authorities were desirous of cooperating with the Bureau, and while the Bureau's interests and those of the university were identical, there was a constant fear that some independent agency of the government might assert itself in connection with the Bureau's records and thus cause embarrassment to the University in its cooperation with the Bureau.
>
> It is noted that as a result of [half line deleted] on this date, arrangements have been completed for a most cooperative and understanding association between the Bureau and Harvard University.
>
> [Name deleted] stated that it was his judgment that many of the conditions existing today, referring to internal security problems, were

most distasteful and obviously some action was necessary in order to correct them, but he felt that in most instances the methods utilized in order to effect the correction were not in good taste, and tended in some instances to destroy the real effectiveness of the work done. He asserted that information came to his attention some time ago with respect to a condition involving immorality and homosexuality among State Department employees and he felt that some action should have been taken by the State Department some time ago. . . . He asserted, however, that he did not believe that a Senate Investigating Committee was the proper method to be used. . . . He did not offer any suggestion as to what methods might be utilized in this respect.

[One and one-half lines deleted] article by Bernard DeVoto, appearing in the October 1949 issue of Harper's Magazine under the general caption "Easy Chair" [few words deleted] gave the definite impression that he felt if DeVoto had some complaint with respect to the Bureau, and its activities, that the method he used, namely an open statement in a national magazine, was obviously not the fair and judicious method of bringing such matter to the attention of proper authorities. [Few words deleted] did not specifically condemn DeVoto, but gave the agent . . . the definite impression that he was displeased with the method which DeVoto utilized in that connection and was using that as a further illustration of the fear which may exist in the minds of some university authorities who desire to cooperate with the Bureau in its work but are conscious of the possibility that a Congressional inquiry or directive might usurp the confidential character of the Bureau's files.

As indicated previously [name deleted] has been most cooperative in his contacts with the Boston Office and this information is provided the Bureau for information purposes with the request that no dissemination be made under any circumstances.

Even allowing for the possibility that SAC Boston overstated the relationship with Harvard, several things seem clear: there were those at Harvard who had more confidence in the FBI than in congressional committees; some kind of "arrangement" existed between the university and the FBI for sharing information; the FBI was pleased by this cooperation; the topics discussed included political belief and activity; Harvard officials would be embarrassed if some "blundering independent agency of the government"—a congressional committee, perhaps—would reveal the university's cooperation with the bureau.

The references to the well-known journalist Bernard DeVoto are intriguing. DeVoto was the subject of an extensive FBI file that began at least in the 1940s and extended until his death in 1955.[15] His offending article, "Due Notice to the FBI," published in the October 1949 issue of *Harper's* magazine, had urged refusal to answer questions asked by FBI agents. Hoover was enraged; DeVoto's article became the subject of a blistering series of letters between Hoover and other FBI officials and the editors of *Harper's*, between Hoover's friends outside the agency and

Harper's, between officers of the Office of Naval Intelligence and the FBI. "Let me get what ONI has on DeVoto," Hoover wrote at the bottom of one of the memos he received.[16] David Jacobson, a journalist who claimed that he had been commissioned to write an article on Hoover by *Harper's,* called Louis Nichols, assistant FBI director, to say that *Harper's* editor, Frederick Lewis Allen, deplored the DeVoto attack and now followed what Nichols called "the Roger Baldwin line"—namely, that what was improper "was the use made of some of its work, which was not the Bureau's fault but the fault of others."[17]

But what was there, if anything, about DeVoto and Harvard to lead the FBI to link them? The interview between the Boston FBI agent and the unidentified Harvard official with whom he had discussed DeVoto took place in June 1950, a full eight months after publication of the article Hoover found so offensive. The FBI agent might have been sensitive to the issue because he was aware of Hoover's concern. Like a dog worrying a bone, Hoover could not let go of it, nor could he bury it. Indeed, the amount of energy the FBI devoted to the matter was astonishing. On November 10, 1949, Assistant Director Ladd told Hoover that he had been in touch with SAC Soucy of the Boston office to request an investigation of DeVoto's statement that he could get affidavits from Harvard professors attesting that they had been asked whether applicants for government jobs read the *New Republic:* "I instructed him to review all of the loyalty cases in the Boston Office promptly. . . . Mr. Soucy called back on the morning of November 10 and stated that he had assigned forty Agents to reviewing all loyalty files in the Boston office and that they had found no incidents where Harvard professors or DeVoto had been asked any such question." No such question had ever been asked in applicant or loyalty cases.

More intriguing is the very strong possibility—indeed, the likelihood—that the DeVoto matter was brought into the conversation not by the FBI agent but by the Harvard informant. Why should he have done so? And what does that suggest about who the informant might have been?

On September 20, 1949, FBI official M. A. Jones wrote to Louis Nichols that the impetus for still another anti-FBI article by DeVoto had come from two articles in the June 4, 1949, issue of the *Harvard Crimson,* in which the accusation had been made that the FBI, with the cooperation of the authorities at Yale, was deeply involved in the screening of faculty members there. (See chapter 8.) We know now that this cooperation was a fact, but at the time it was vehemently denied by both the FBI and the Yale authorities. Yale President Charles Seymour had made a statement that many took as defiance of the widening political purge: "There will be no witch hunts at Yale because there will be no witches." The student editors of the *Crimson* were skeptical about Seymour's statement in exactly the same way—and for exactly the same reason—that they were skeptical about the meaning of Harvard President Conant's statement that there would be no investigation of the faculty but that to be a Communist made a teacher unfit to be a faculty member. How could Communists be banned as teachers without investigating faculties, the *Crimson* wanted to know.

And so did DeVoto.

In his "Easy Chair" column in *Harper's* in September 1949, DeVoto congratulated the universities for showing some opposition to the order of the House Un-American Activities Committee that they submit copies of course reading lists. But, he added, the colleges "have already lost the battle of the outposts, and have lost it by voluntarily retreating from a position of great strength." Even Harvard, which had published a brilliant reassertion of the principles of academic freedom in the form of the reply of corporation member Grenville Clark to alumnus Frank Ober, backed off from its own position when Conant called Communists " 'out of bounds as members of the teaching profession.' . . . Presumably Harvard will not have them on its faculty, although Mr. Conant binds it not to inquire into the political views of its teachers and not to tolerate investigation of their loyalty or review of their private activities." He concluded:

> Already one leading university whose president has denounced the witch-hunt has been publicly accused of having consulted the FBI before making certain faculty appointments, and Mr. J. Edgar Hoover's denial fell short of convincing at least me. Is there any other way out? If a college is to protect the freedom by which alone it exists in the tradition of democratic education, it has got to run the risk. The full risk.
> . . . The colleges . . . have got to say: on this campus all books, all expression, all inquiry, all opinions are free. They have got to maintain that position against the government and everyone else. If they don't, they will presently have left nothing that is worth having.[18]

The Harvard official who spoke to the FBI agent in June 1950 was "desirous of cooperating with the Bureau" and gave every assurance that "the Bureau's interests and those of the university were identical," but he was afraid that embarrassment to the university would come from a rampaging congressional committee's access to the bureau's records, which would reveal the facts of the university's "cooperation" with the bureau. For that reason he was "displeased" with DeVoto's "Easy Chair" column. The informant had "been most cooperative in his contacts with the Boston Office" of the FBI. His opinions were those of a friend, not an antagonist.

But who was the Harvard official? We may never know, because of the passion for secrecy on the part of both the FBI and Harvard. But it must have been a high-ranking officer who could speak so knowledge-

ably and freely about Harvard's relations with the FBI. At the time of
the DeVoto incident, the second highest official at Harvard, "Mr. Inside" to President Conant's "Mr. Outside," was Provost Paul H. Buck.
He was certainly in a position to know what Harvard–FBI relations were,
indeed, to have been instrumental in establishing them.

From October 12, 1978, to August 29, 1980, I wrote three FOIA
requests to the FBI for documents relating to Buck and submitted evidence of his death, thereby eliminating the argument of invasion of privacy as the grounds for refusal to provide the documents. On October 3,
1980, I was notified by the FBI that I would be charged for documents
relating to Buck, but on January 23, 1981, I was informed that nothing
would be sent to me because of specific exemptions of the Freedom of
Information Act having to do with national security, the character of FBI
investigation procedures, the privacy of third parties, and the disclosure
of information that might identify informants. I appealed this decision
on February 2, 1981; on March 9, 1981, my appeal was rejected, but I
was told that the Justice Department Review Committee was recon-
sidering the question of whether the documents should continue to be
classified.[19] On November 21, 1983—five years after my original request—I was notified that all the documents had been declassified by
the Department Review Committee but would still be withheld on the
grounds that their release would tend to identify an informant. To this
date I have not received a single word from any FBI document about
Buck. And yet the very reason stated as the basis for the denial of the
documents reveals information of considerable importance—they would
disclose the identity of confidential sources. The reason given for denying access to the Buck documents suggests that Buck was one of the
FBI's "confidential sources" at Harvard and possibly the Harvard official who expressed his disapproval of the DeVoto article to the FBI agent.

3. That FBI Director Hoover understood Harvard's need for discretion is shown in a memorandum he wrote to SAC Boston on July 31,
1950:

It is noted from your letter of June 16, 1950, [withheld in its entirety]
that arrangements have been perfected whereby information of interest
will be made available to the Bureau on a confidential basis [several
words deleted]. This arrangement will be effective in connection with
Harvard College and the Graduate School of Arts and Sciences.
　　[Three paragraphs deleted.]
　　[One line deleted] should, of course, not be contacted at any time
without specific Bureau authorization.
　　In contacting [name and title deleted] who is approved for contacts
by the Bureau, prior Bureau instructions must be followed regarding
investigations on campuses of colleges and universities.

4. At this point in the file, a two-page letter from the Boston field office to FBI headquarters, dated August 28, 1950, has been withheld in its entirety. The series resumes with another letter, also dated August 28, 1950, captioned "Harvard University/Cambridge, Massachusetts/ Potential CNDI's." Heavily expurgated, this letter reports:

> The [July 31, 1950] letter in authorizing continued contact [one line deleted] should not be contacted without specific Bureau authority.
> [Paragraph deleted.]
> [Five lines deleted] it would appear that contact with him on applicant and other matters will be of frequent occurrence. The Bureau is requested to advise whether in each specific instance, authorization must be obtained. [Two lines deleted.]
> [Paragraph deleted.]
> [Entire page withheld.]

5. Hoover replied on October 5, 1950, in a letter also captioned "Harvard University/Cambridge, Massachusetts/Potential CNDI's":

> Provided the files of your office show no reason to the contrary, there is no objection to your office contacting [one line deleted] with Harvard University in accordance with arrangements [five lines deleted].
> With respect to [name and title deleted] the Bureau feels that this person should be contacted only if there is no other manner or means of obtaining the desired information. You are, therefore, requested to advise whether there is a more prudential method of procuring information [several words deleted] rather than contact [name and title deleted].
> [Paragraph deleted.]

6. Exactly what Hoover meant by "a more prudential method of procuring information" is not clear. Some light is shed by SAC Boston's response of October 26, 1950:

> With respect to the authorization contained in the [October 5, 1950] Bureau letter relating to the contact [one line deleted]. Harvard University in accordance with arrangements [twelve lines deleted].
> [Three lines deleted] would assure that no embarrassment would come to the Bureau by contact [name deleted] inasmuch as [two lines deleted].
> The Bureau is assured that every precaution will be exercised in connection with this matter and [half line deleted] under the authority granted in Bureau letter of August 5, 1950, will be exercised only after careful consideration. [Name and title deleted] was assured that any contact for the purpose of obtaining such confidential information from

Harvard University files, would be on a selective basis and this policy has been closely adhered to.

7. The FBI director was pleased that the arrangement precluded the possibility of embarrassment, especially to the FBI. He replied on November 20, 1950:

> Reurlet dated October 26, 1950, which states that you feel the arrangement completed [name and title deleted] assure that no embarrassment would come to the Bureau by contact with [name deleted] inasmuch as [two lines deleted]. You assure that every precaution will be exercised in connection with this matter and contact with [name and title deleted] will only be had after careful consideration.

CNDIs—"Confidential National Defense Informants"—were not people whom the FBI interviewed during routine applicant investigations. They were individuals of importance. Can we obtain information about their mission as confidential national defense informants and their importance in the Harvard hierarchy? At Yale cooperation between the FBI and the university existed at a level at least as high as that of provost and secretary of the university, and there was an official administrative position—liaison officer—whose occupant, H. B. Fisher, boasted of supervising relations with the "one hundred and twenty six different investigative bodies who have and are using Yale records and files and faculty for background and information concerning Yale men." [20]

We cannot fully resolve the question of the level of importance of the FBI informants at Harvard until all FBI documents have been released (and the extensive deletions filled in) and Harvard releases its documents. We do have, though, some information about these informants.

The FBI has submitted affidavits further detailing its reasons for deletions and for withholding certain documents entirely. Most of the deletions are said to be needed to protect informants. The FBI had several levels of informants, ranging from those who furnished information "during a single interview" to those "from whom information was regularly received under an expressed assurance of confidentiality." The latter sources were informants "within the common meaning of that term and not merely conscientious or cooperative citizens." To protect their identity, FBI documents cited them by source numbers and not by name, and information was obtained from them "only at locations and under conditions which guarantee the contact will not be noticed." [21]

In justifying its refusal to release certain documents in their entirety, the FBI claimed that these involved confidential sources "reporting information to the FBI on a regular basis, the release of which would lead to the sources' identification." Most of the deletions were made to "protect the name, symbol number, position and place of employment pertaining to a confidential source reporting to the FBI on a regular basis." Can these informants be identified more precisely?

I had requested from the FBI all documents pertaining to Harvard University. In explaining why one document was withheld entirely, the FBI claimed that it "was outside the scope of the plaintiff's request because it pertains to an invitation from Harvard graduates to the Director" while my FOIA request sought correspondence only from Harvard employees.

In fact, I had not requested FBI documents relating only to Harvard employees, but *all* documents bearing upon the relationship between Harvard and the FBI. The FBI's response in this instance confirms that the documents the bureau released involved only Harvard employees. We now know, therefore, that the informants whose names were deleted from this series of released documents were reporting to the bureau on a regular basis and were employees of Harvard University—faculty or staff—not students or alumni.

Can we ascertain the level at which the Harvard–FBI "arrangements" were made?

Pursuant to the order of the federal district court, the FBI released a second version of a memorandum from which it had originally deleted the name of a Harvard official—President Conant. That memorandum, dated February 9, 1949, from SAC Boston to the FBI director, concerns the Russian Research Center. The center's work, the memo reports, had "greatly expanded" over the years:

> It is believed that the results of the work of the international program and the Russian Research Center can be made available to the Bureau officially through contact with President James B. Conant of Harvard University, who has on occasion indicated his respect for the Bureau's work and his understanding for its many and varied interests in connection with internal security matters. It appears that a presentation of the Bureau's desire to be informed on such matters to President Conant personally would make available the current programs and results of research work of the Center on such basis that the interests of the Bureau would not be revealed to the personnel of the particular program and in that way no possible embarrassment could possibly come as the result of any inquiries being directed in an attempt to obtain . . . items of interest in connection with this matter.

By the 1950s at least, cooperation with the FBI as a defense against accusations by congressional committees seems to have become the policy of Harvard and a number of other universities.

As we have already noted, on December 8, 1954, representatives of seven universities, together with two attorneys, who together made up the Listening Post, met with members of the staff of the Joint Committee on Internal Revenue Taxation. Arts and Sciences Dean McGeorge Bundy represented Harvard. The university spokesmen described how they handled or were prepared to handle loyalty questions concerning present and prospective faculty members:

(1) No present member of the Communist Party or anyone subject to Communist discipline would knowingly be retained as a faculty member or given scholarships and fellowships. (2) While not in itself a cause for dismissal, use of the Fifth Amendment would precipitate a thorough investigation and review of the user's fitness to teach. (3) These reviews were conducted by faculty members or others having a responsibility to the university. (4) "Any derogatory information received by the university [was] a basis for an investigation of some sort." (5) None of the universities had a regular investigating staff; they "obtain such information as they can from Governmental investigating agencies but find this of limited usefulness because of the refusal of such agencies to disclose sources." (6) A faculty member under Communist discipline or one who refused to be "completely frank" with the university investigating board would not be protected by academic tenure. (7) As a result of their investigations, some universities had refused to renew contracts of nontenured faculty members, some had dropped faculty members with tenure, and some were in the process of making investigations.

Had "present-day investigative procedures . . . been in effect" earlier, some of the current difficult cases would not have occurred. These new procedures had to be continued to guard against subversion and to retain public confidence "in the integrity of the universities and of the teaching process." Responding to a taxation committee staff member's suggestion that the universities might be helped if there were a statutory oath requiring the affiant to swear he was not a member of the Communist Party or under its discipline—which "would bring the FBI and the Department of Justice into operations which the universities now have to undertake"—the university representatives pointed out that the Department of Justice and the FBI "are not today following up and prosecuting cases which the universities have already handed over to them under existing law."[22]

The FBI may or may not have forwarded all its investigative findings to university officials, but it did intensively investigate political activities in scores of universities.

Research into the FBI documents has so far produced some findings and many suggestions that cannot always be pursued because some institutions are even more reluctant than the FBI to make available the documents needed to confirm or refute statements made in the bureau reports.[23] Harvard's official documents are withheld, but we do have the papers of the Russian Research Center, of many Harvard professors and one distinguished member of the corporation, of the Carnegie Corporation, and of Yale and Columbia, which have not restricted access to their documents, all of which shed light on the Harvard view of these matters. What happens when the two views are brought into focus? We begin with the Russian Research Center. What was its origin and prehistory; what was its connection to the intelligence agencies, CIA and State Department as well as FBI; who knew about its connections; how did the FBI operate there; what does the history—not the "official" story—of the research center tell us about intelligence agency–university relations? The FBI felt it had "a most cooperative and understanding association with Harvard." So did other intelligence agencies. Did Harvard agree?

3. The Russian Research Center, 1: Informing and Surveillance

FOR OBVIOUS REASONS, the interests of the intelligence agencies—the CIA and the State Department, in addition to the FBI—and those of Harvard were most likely to intersect at the Russian Research Center—and they did. Each side of the relationship provided opportunities for the other, and also risks. For the agencies, there was the chance to obtain information and trained personnel and, if the matter were handled with discretion, to influence the direction of scholarly research. But there was also the danger that the center would attract security risks and other unsavory characters. For Harvard, there was the opportunity to establish connections with agencies that could hire its students, suggest projects, help to finance them—though at arm's length—and solve some of the problems of conducting research abroad at a time when that was both politically and financially difficult. But there was the fear that association with the center might cause trouble with an agency like the FBI, whose ability to discriminate among different ways of opposing communism was cruder than that of the more academic agencies. J. Edgar Hoover was no George Kennan. To take advantage of opportunities and to minimize the risks, all parties were agreed on the need for secrecy. Not that the relationship between the agencies and the research center was denied; it was rather that the real relationship was concealed behind a camouflage of official stories. We have no contracts to do classified research, was one such official story; as if the absence of a written contract meant the absence of an unofficial understanding. All our research is generated out of our own scholarly interests, was another; as if government agencies are scornful of or uninterested in scholarly matters, or may not, indeed, under certain circumstances, suggest that the academy undertake particular scholarly investigations.

The Russian Research Center was the locus of fruitful collaboration between the intelligence agencies and Harvard, fruitful but not entirely free of tension. The agencies had their own agendas; Harvard had its— and the agendas were not always identical. For those who had responsibility for the Harvard agenda, certain political convictions were necessary, but so was subtlety. Some activities, like cooperation in bringing to the United States persons who had a record of collaboration with the Nazis, were at the time in violation of the law, or close to it. How far should Harvard go in bringing such persons to the United States—offering them jobs on the staff; hiring them for particular research projects? With whom, in the university and in the government, should such matters be cleared? Not to talk about them at faculty meetings was politically understandable, if morally objectionable; many faculty members, after all, would find those activities impermissible, some on political grounds, some on moral, others on the grounds that they were a violation of the principle of academic autonomy. But not to talk about these matters to, say, J. Edgar Hoover was entirely different. What guarantees were there that he would not leak the story to some Red-hunting congressional committee or newspaper columnist eager to find a sensation? No one could seriously entertain the possibility that Hoover might be told, so that Harvard would be in the clear, yet kept in check. No one—not the president, not the attorney general, not the courts—rode herd on Hoover.

We have seen what the FBI thought of Harvard. To discover what Harvard thought of the FBI and other intelligence agencies requires a look at documents other than those in the FBI's own archives, especially those in Harvard's official archives and in the papers of persons and other organizations involved in the intelligence agency–Harvard complex.

The effort to obtain the Harvard documents led to lengthy correspondence with President Derek Bok over the "fifty-year" rule. What is that rule? How did it affect the creation of Harvard's "official" stories about its relations with the intelligence agencies and the effort to disclose its "little secrets"?

On December 9, 1977, the *Harvard Gazette* announced, after a number of requests from scholars for permission to do research in the Harvard archives on the McCarthy period, that the policy of sealing official university archives for fifty years would be continued.

My correspondence with President Bok lasted for a number of years. Bok was adamant in refusing to modify the fifty-year rule in any way. He conceded that the Harvard files might contain records of the political activities of various persons, but despite that, and despite the letters he was sent showing that SAC Boston had written Hoover about the "most

cooperative and understanding association between the Bureau and
Harvard University," he could not be budged. Moreover, no selections
from his letters to me could be quoted.[1]

—————

Our task now is to supplement what we have learned about the FBI–
Harvard association directly from the FBI documents with what might
be learned from documents, at Harvard and elsewhere, not withheld
from scholars by official secrecy regulations. Specifically, what light do
these documents shed on the origin and purposes of the Russian Research Center and how it attracted the interest of the FBI; what light do
they shed on Russian Research Center personnel and activities that might
have had the same effect, and on how the FBI attempted to satisfy its
curiosity?

The first question has to do with context and is easily answered. The
wartime Office of Strategic Services (OSS) and the early postwar CIA
were staffed overwhelmingly by university personnel, and considerable
thought was devoted to how the intelligence-university connection could
be both strengthened and perpetuated. A recent student of the subject,
Yale historian Robin Winks, who has shuttled between the intelligence
establishment and the academy, discusses the intimate relations between Yale's Institute for International Studies and Institute of Human
Relations and government intelligence agencies. In the first case, relations were made closer by the old-boy network that bound Yale and
government, particularly the State Department, so tightly together. As
to the Institute of Human Relations, after its director, Mark A. May,
announced that it would accept contract work from any government
agency, it shifted its focus to areas of greatest interest to the government.

When James Phinney Baxter, president of Williams College, became
head of the Office of Research for the Coordinator of Information, predecessor of the OSS, he acted also as chairman of a board of analysts
responsible for the mobilization of American scholarship for intelligence
purposes. Military personnel on the committee were outnumbered by
professors of history, political science, economics, geography, and law
from Harvard, Yale, Michigan, Duke, and other universities. In the fall
of 1942, the Research and Analysis Branch of the OSS began to contract
out research projects to specialized institutes at various universities, first
at Stanford and Berkeley, then at Denver, Columbia, Princeton, Yale,
and others. William L. Langer, the Harvard historian who had succeeded Baxter, appointed the Committee on Relations between Government Intelligence and Research Work and the American Universities.
One report submitted by a member of the committee struck the note, in
tone as well as content, that was to become characteristic of the govern-
ment-university symbiosis. Anthropologists, geographers, art historians,
archeologists, and others would quickly turn their professional knowl-

edge into intelligence. Since such scholars would be "under more or less constant surveillance" if they ventured abroad, they could not do truly clandestine work, but their work could be subsidized by American intelligence, "and a project might be redirected to include intelligence reporting."

When in 1948 the National Security Council (NSC) authorized a study on intelligence coordination, Norman Holmes Pearson, a Yale professor with considerable OSS experience, recommended that each university have on its staff informal talent spotters who would forward the names of likely agents to the CIA. Each university should designate a faculty member to act as adviser to students considering careers in intelligence, and the CIA should maintain up-to-date lists of students with unusual talents or skills that might someday be useful to the agency. Nor was it contemplated that the role of universities would be restricted to research and analysis. By 1947, with the Cold War well under way and with a critical election in the offing in Italy, Langer, "whose reputation stood high because of the wartime successes of R & A, strongly argued for covert measures."[2]

When former national security adviser McGeorge Bundy said that all university area studies programs "were manned, directed, or stimulated by graduates of the OSS," he was writing more than history; he was giving a prognosis of the future and making policy. There always had been and always would be "a high measure of interpenetration between universities with area programs and the information-gathering agencies of the government of the United States." There were more than faint echoes of Clausewitz: "I think rather that there is gain for both the political world and the academy from an intensified process of engagement and of choosing sides and of engaging in the battle."[3]

As to the origin and purposes of the Russian Research Center and other area programs, the belief is that, as Professor Stephen Cohen, a leading Soviet specialist, has said, "American Sovietology was created as a large academic profession during the worst years of the Cold War. . . . Throughout the 1950s and early 1960s, the field's leaders generally denied any cold-war influences on Soviet studies. . . . A different opinion formed in the late 1960s and 1970s, reflecting the general mood of academic self-criticism provoked by Vietnam and Watergate." Policy considerations threw their weight on the scale along with historical precedent:

> From the beginning, the partnership that created Soviet studies and caused their extraordinary expansion in the 1940s and 1950s—a planned collaboration initially of government agencies, the Rockefeller and Carnegie foundations, and university scholars—candidly emphasized the "urgency of their studies and . . . their relevance to questions of national policy."

All of this was intensified by the anti-Communist political purge and the feverish atmosphere surrounding the emergence of the loyalty-security issue in domestic politics.[4]

Operation Dropshot, presented by the National Security Council on November 23, 1948, set forth the philosophical and political underpinnings of the cold war: "(1) . . . Peaceful coexistence . . . is an illusion and an impossibility. . . . (3) . . . There can be, in the long run, no advancement of the interests of the communist and the noncommunist world by mutual collaboration. . . . (5) . . . Spontaneous collaboration between individuals in the [two worlds] is evil and cannot contribute to human progress." The Joint Chiefs of Staff on August 18, 1948, proclaimed that the "gravest threat to the security of the United States [stems] from the hostile designs and formidable power of the USSR, and *from the nature of the Soviet system*" [my emphasis]. The "formidable power of the USSR" was an appropriate target of the application of military force; the "nature of the Soviet system," of political and psychological warfare.

The relation of military to political warfare had already occupied the attention of the State Department. Addressing itself to the problem of how to govern Russia after its forthcoming defeat—total occupation of the country being out of the question—the State Department concluded that there must be a political settlement with a non-Communist regime: "Who would constitute such a government? . . . At the present time there are a number of interesting and powerful Russian political groupings among the Russian exiles . . . any of which would probably be preferable to the Soviet Government from our standpoint as the rulers of Russia."

A Joint Chiefs of Staff directive to Lt. Gen. J. E. Hall concluded that atomic bomb air strikes against the USSR would not produce the desired result, because of insupportable losses to U.S. planes and air crews and logistical difficulties—a conclusion that had the effect of emphasizing the importance of political warfare. It was a logical conclusion, since the Soviet system as well as Soviet power already had been declared the enemy.[5]

How might these general considerations have affected the establishment of the Russian Research Center?

Professor Winks writes that by 1947 the experts, including academic experts like Langer, were convinced that "something covert was called for since few wished to take on the Soviet Army." But who would run the covert operations, and what were they to be? "The secretary of state, George C. Marshall, refused, since he believed most such operations ultimately became known and would compromise foreign policy. Still, he thought covert operations, if housed elsewhere, to be necessary." Perhaps the government could do something. On December 19, 1947, Roscoe Hillenkoetter, director of the newly created CIA, was ordered to do what he could, including covert operations, to influence the impending elections in Italy. James J. Angleton helped set up a Soviet Division in the CIA, which reached out to the universities, providing money for language study and specialized area training. Professor Cohen tells us that "university Sovietologists established many open and reasonable relationships with government agencies, but also some that were covert and later troublesome."[6]

Writing within a few years of the events he was describing and indeed participated in, George Fischer, who played a key role in laying the groundwork in Germany for the Russian Research Center's main fieldwork operation, made clear the connection between the political context of the period and the center's most important activity, the interviewing of Soviet émigrés as part of its study of the Soviet social system. He was disturbed because the hopes and plans of the center—and of other institutions as well—to bring some of the émigrés to the United States might run afoul of recent legislation barring immigration of those who had been accomplices of the Nazi regime. Fischer found the anti-Soviet potential of such émigrés more important than their Nazi past: "It is part of the tragedy surrounding Soviet opposition that in such circumstances there was simply no place for what has been the proud Western principle of political asylum." Echoing the main conclusion of the NSC on the relationship between political instability and warfare in the Soviet Union, he wrote in the conclusion of his study of the Vlasov movement in World War II that now (1952), as "in 1941, the Stalin regime is apt to disintegrate only if so hard a blow is struck that its hold over the country is relaxed for a significant period. . . . Such a decisive blow would perforce be a World War III."[7]

With the enemy so clearly defined, both patriotism and scholarship pushed the research center in the same direction.

⸺

The FBI had its version of the history of the Russian Research Center, and its documents make clear how it intruded in the affairs of the center.

First, as to the history of the center: one of the very earliest documents in the FBI file, a memorandum from SAC Boston to the director dated December 12, 1947—even before the center officially opened for business—reports that the center would be funded by grants from the Carnegie Corporation of New York

> to provide the United States, including the State Department and other governmental agencies, with systematized information about contemporary Russia. . . . The project was approved at a recent meeting of the corporation's Board of Trustees, which was attended by Secretary of State Marshall, a board member. . . . *It was understood that findings and conclusions made during the study will be made available to the*

State Department and other federal agencies, including the central intelligence groups, through informal channels long before publication by the university [emphasis in original]. The close contacts made between Harvard professors and government officials during the war were emphasized as a link binding the research group to the State Department.

The memorandum concludes with information in the files of the Boston office about each of the four faculty members appointed by Provost Paul H. Buck to direct the center:

Clyde Kluckhohn is reported to have been the subject of an FBI investigation by the El Paso office for an incident on the Navajo reservation.

Talcott Parsons is identified as having been an adviser to the undergraduate John Reed Society, "a Marxist organization devoted to the establishment of a program of lectures and discussion groups tending towards creating a better understanding of the fundamentals of Marxism."

Donald C. McKay is reported to have been the subject of a full employee investigation in 1942 when he was hired by the Office of Coordinator of Information and, later, to have been contacted by a suspected subversive who knew J. Robert Oppenheimer.

Edward S. Mason is identified as dean of the Graduate School of Public Administration and professor of economics. Aside from that, all information—two full paragraphs—has been deleted.

Given the distinguished patronage of the center, the nature of its research interests, and the extraordinary sensitivities of the FBI to subversion and to the possibility of co-opting others in the hunt for subversion, it was inevitable that the center should remain a focus of its attention. The increasing closeness of the relation between them is attested to by a constant stream of memoranda between FBI headquarters and the Boston office; exchanges of reports between the State Department and military intelligence agencies, on the other hand, and the FBI, on the other; repeated efforts by the FBI to recruit confidential informants among the research center staff; and considerable evidence of information being provided to the FBI by center personnel.

Contacts were sought at every level, from President Conant down. The FBI documents as they have been released do not permit us to know without a doubt whether Conant was approached to provide the information the FBI wanted and was sure he would give. Knowing him as we now do, it was almost certain he would have responded favorably had he been asked. The fact is, though, that he did not need to be asked; others were also available to do the task.

On December 31, 1948, SAC Boston wrote:

It is believed desirable that contact be established with a responsible person or persons within the [Russian] Research Center in order to have an indication of the programs being developed and perhaps have available for review purposes, results of these programs. . . . Accordingly, the Bureau is requested to advise what information they [*sic*] might have in its possession relating to the background of the above-named individual [name deleted] and authorization is requested to establish contact with him which contact can be commenced on a pretext basis, developed and expanded providing the circumstances warrant and justify such expansion in the light of his interest and availability of information relating to this project.

The FBI arranged to deliver a "packet" to him, and he "stated he would be pleased to be of assistance or cooperation with the Bureau whenever his services might be desired." SAC Boston later requested approval to recruit this potential informant in the Russian Research Center.

On February 25, 1949, SAC Boston forwarded the "confidential informant's" report that the "two members" of the Russian Research Center "faculty who disturb[ed] him more than all the rest" were

Isaiah Berlin and Harold J. Berman. The latter person has been the subject of separate correspondence between the Bureau and Boston. Berlin arrived in the United States in January, 1949 from England. He is a native of the latter country. [Berlin is a native of Riga, Latvia.] He is giving a course entitled "The Development of Revolutionary Ideas in Russia."

We may know the identity of this "confidential informant," thanks to a slip by the FBI censor. On May 5, 1949, SAC Boston reported on the Russian Research Center and cited the February 25, 1949, report "wherein the Boston Field [Office] stated that it would check its indices against the 'list of staff members' provided by confidential informant [name deleted] and the names of the project workers in that program, entitled 'Programs and Census of Current Projects—January 1949' *also provided by confidential informant Charles Baroch* [emphasis mine]." Baroch was a graduate student on the staff of the research center, working on "The Russian Peasantry and Its Political and Social Institutions."[8]

It is not always possible to know whether the impulse to cooperate came from conviction—ideological or patriotic—or was the product of anxiety lest activities engaged in for professional reasons might be misunderstood by government authorities. In the FBI files there is an internal State Department memorandum, dated December 20, 1955, from Walter J. Stoessel, Jr., to Warren M. Chase, about Assistant Professor Richard Pipes of Harvard University, who "recently had a series of contacts with Soviet historians at the International Conference of Historians at Rome. He has since entered into correspondence with them. Recently on a visit to Harvard I discussed this matter with him and told him that the Department encouraged contacts between loyal American scholars and their Soviet counterparts." Pipes was not wholly reassured: "Security developments of the last years have made him nervous about contacts with Soviet citizens and he has asked that his contacts be made a matter of record in the Department." Attached to Stoessel's memorandum is a letter, dated December 6, 1955, from Pipes to Marshall Shulman of the Russian Research Center, setting forth the reasons for his concern. At the September 1955 meeting of the International Congress of Historical Sciences in Rome, his paper on nineteenth-century Russian conservatism had been criticized by Professor A. L. Sidorov of the Soviet Academy of Sciences, and he had criticized Sidorov's paper. Later they had a two-hour private breakfast and promised to send books and other materials to each other. On his return to Cambridge, Pipes wrote Sidorov reminding him of their meeting and of Sidorov's promise to send "data concerning the original manuscript of Karamzin's work, written in 1811, which I am presently editing." Sidorov had replied that he was sending the microfilm of a manuscript and asked for "two books published by the U.S. Senate in the early 1920s dealing with the finances of World War I. . . . I shall try to locate these books for him, and I promise myself considerable scholarly advantage from this exchange." Pipes promised to keep Shulman posted on future developments. Pipes was able to demonstrate that he was a "loyal American scholar," and his later career seems not to have been affected by the episode.

Other scholars at the Russian Research Center came under FBI scrutiny, and many of them felt, as Pipes did, the need to demonstrate their loyalty. There was a readily available means to do so. In all probability, judging from the documents now available, the FBI opened a file on everyone associated with the research center, but some obviously were subjected to more searching scrutiny than others.

Both Clyde Kluckhohn, director of the center, and Robert Lee Wolff were subject to especially rigorous investigations. Kluckhohn, who had been hand-picked to be the director, had top-secret clearance from the Research and Development Board of the Department of Defense. By the time he obtained his clearance, he had assured the FBI that he had been "very apprehensive of Soviet interference in the operation of the Russian Research Center, though he has had no indication that such interference has been attempted. It is his opinion that it would be much in the interests of the Soviet Union to ascertain the sources from which statistics are being compiled in order that the U.S.S.R. could eliminate this source from availability and thereby better maintain their Iron Curtain. To this extent he believed a security problem is involved which would indirectly affect the United States."

On August 17, 1951, SAC Boston submitted an extensive report on the Russian Research Center, based largely on interviews with informants. The first half of the first sentence of page 2, paragraph 3 of that report has been deleted; the rest of the paragraph reads:

> While the intention of the Carnegie Foundation was to set up a strictly private research institute, they also wanted a more personal contact with United States government agencies. One of the jobs of [Clyde] Kluckhohn is to obtain pertinent information requested by government departments and, within limits, shape the research program of the Center to the needs of the United States. He cited as an instance of this application [*sic*] the State Department would communicate with him to suggest they were short in a certain aspect of Soviet activity. Kluckhohn would then suggest to a graduate student at the School that he might do a thesis on this particular problem, making no mention to him of the fact that the State Department was also interested. Subsequently the results of the individual research could be brought to the attention of the State Department.

That Kluckhohn may have felt pressure to cooperate with the FBI is suggested by an October 27, 1952, FBI memorandum "Re: Russian Research Center, Harvard University" marked "Secret," which contains FBI reports on all the directors of the center. In that memo the FBI claimed to have information that, if leaked, could have subjected Kluckhohn to humiliation.[9]

In all probability, Wolff gave the FBI even less concern as to his loyalty. The opinions he provided to the FBI were appropriately orthodox. In his dossier is a quotation from a letter he wrote to the *Harvard Crimson* on November 17, 1951: "I believe that members of the Communist Party should not (repeat NOT) be employed as teachers in American universities."

On May 1, 1951, SAC Richmond (Virginia) reported on Robert Lee Wolff's recent public appearance in Richmond. Formerly director of the Balkan Section of the Research and Analysis Branch of the Office of Strategic Services, Wolff at the time was an associate professor of history at Harvard and a director of the Russian Research Center:

> Graduates of this Russian study school either go into Russian Research Center or are individually placed by Wolff . . . in government positions in Washington, D.C. . . . Wolff states that Harvard University feels that this is a contribution to good government. . . .
>
> As an example of the type work which the Russian Research Center is doing, they are presently conducting a mass interview project of Russian escapees and defectors coming from Eastern Germany into Western Germany in an effort to do a mass sampling proposition for the benefit of the government on a variety of problems. . . . The results of the sampling, he stated, are being sent to the "necessary" agencies of the government. . . .

Dr. Wolff appeared to me to be a very stable and unusual individual who, I feel, would be of immeasurable value to the Bureau as at least a SAC contact for the Boston Office. He was very friendly to me and highly complimentary to the Bureau. . . .

It is suggested for the benefit of the Bureau, if it has not already been done, that Dr. Wolff and Professor Kluckhoehn [sic] be contacted by the Boston Office in order that those studies and published results be made available to us; and further, that the New York Office similarly ascertain the situation at Columbia University.

Whether the FBI succeeded in making Wolff a regular informant we do not yet know. We do know that on occasion he provided information to the FBI. On May 24, 1951, SAC Boston notified Washington headquarters that as early as April 16, 1947, Wolff had "turned over to the FBI" a letter he had received from a government employee requesting sources of information bearing on the question "of the guilt or innocence of Mihailovitch"—the leader of the Chetnick resistance to the German occupation of Yugoslavia and a fierce opponent of Marshal Tito's guerrilla movement—on which Wolff had just published an article in the *Atlantic Monthly*. Wolff thought the matter would be of interest to the FBI.

On June 20, 1952, Hoover sent SAC Boston a memorandum that throws light on two paragraphs of an earlier memorandum the FBI deleted for "security" reasons:

Reurlet May 29, 1952. The Bureau has no objection to a contact with Robert Lee Wolff. For your information, the LGE [Loyalty of Government Employee] investigation concerning Wolff failed to develop any information which would preclude his use in a confidential capacity. The Bureau agrees with your suggestion concerning the method of contacting Dr. Wolff in order to determine his attitude toward cooperation.

On April 12, 1949, FBI agent Brenton S. Gordon reported on an April 1 telephone conversation with a Harvard informant. The informant "felt this Bureau would be interested in a man whom he had seen touring the Harvard Research Center on that day. He identified this individual as Owen Lattimore," a leading Far Eastern scholar who had been accused of being a "master" Soviet spy. On April 4, 1949, the informant reported Lattimore's earlier appearance at Harvard as the guest of Professor John K. Fairbank. He gave a full record of Lattimore's lecture on that occasion and "further reported that Fairbank, while not explicitly endorsing everything Lattimore had said, gave every indication to the audience that he supported Lattimore in spirit."

As a result of a court order, the FBI made available a second copy of this memorandum, disclosing three words that had been deleted in the first released copy. Those three words, the very last in the memorandum, are "cc Michael Karpovich."

The reference to Karpovich, the distinguished professor of Russian history at Harvard and member of the Executive Committee of the Research Center, is tantalizing. It could mean that Karpovich had been sent a copy of Gordon's memorandum. But why should an internal FBI memorandum have been sent to Karpovich? Or could it mean that a copy of Gordon's memorandum had been placed in Karpovich's file? But why should the FBI have maintained a file on Karpovich?

One possible answer is suggested by another Gordon memorandum to SAC Boston, also dated April 12, 1949. After two long paragraphs that have been totally deleted to protect the identity of "an informant reporting on a regular basis," Gordon reports that his informant had at an earlier date provided information that Karpovich was not in the good graces of the authorities at the Russian Research Center; he was too much a supporter of "the fallen Kerensky regime." The mutual dislike between the authorities of the Russian Research Center and Karpovich, the informant advised Gordon, created an opportunity for the FBI. "In the opinion of Karpovich the men operating this institution were exceedingly pro-Communist and he was, therefore, exceedingly unwelcome. . . . [Name deleted] stated he feels certain if the Bureau desires to interview Mr. Karpovich it will probably be able to obtain additional facts upon which the former [the informant] predicates his opinions and conclusions." [10]

The FBI had begun its file well before the informant suggested the possible usefulness of Karpovich to the FBI; it contained correspondence and memoranda covering his speeches and political views extending back to the early 1930s. In November 1944, for example, the secretary of the Friends of Russian Culture in New York City informed the FBI that Karpovich had lectured at meetings of the society from 1930 to 1939; "Military Intelligence, New York City, advised the New York office that the Society of Friends of Russian Culture was organized to create a love for Imperial Russia and was anti-Soviet." In more recent years, the FBI file notes, he had denounced Anna Louise Strong's *I Saw Poland* as "pro-Russian and non-factual," joined Professor Arthur M. Schlesinger, Jr., in attacking Henry Wallace, was one of five Harvard professors to oppose the Cultural and Scientific Conference for World Peace in New York as supporting "the Communist Party line," opposed the University of California loyalty oath, and signed a petition sponsored by the Harvard Young Progressives against the imminent execution of a black prisoner, Willie McGee. [11] Also noted was an invitation to Hoover from Ben M. Cherrington, director of the Social Science Foundation at the University of Denver, to "assign some of your investigators" to attend a month-long Institute on Russian Affairs, at which Karpovich would be one of four speakers from the research center. During the previous year, when a similar institute had been conducted by four members of the Columbia University Russian Institute, "a few representatives of the Army and Air Force Intelligence Services attended and expressed satisfaction with what the Institute had given them." [12]

Karpovich's political views were less clear-cut than Hoover would have liked. When an official of the Cambridge, Massachusetts, Department of Education wrote Hoover that the department had received a request from "the Society of Russian Immigrants, Inc., and the Russian Clubs of Boston," for permission to use a high-school auditorium for a lecture by Karpovich, he wanted to know whether "the persons involved have any connection with Russia or it's [sic] communistic government?" The investigation conducted by the FBI was less than wholly reassuring. Hoover replied that the bureau did not "make valuations" concerning individuals or organizations, but on the bottom of the office copy of that letter, which was sent to the Boston office of the FBI, the conclusion of an FBI inquiry appears:

> Your attention is directed to your file 100-23668 entitled "The Russian Dramatic Club, aka., Russian American Club, The Russian Club, The Hub Club, The Hub Dramatic Club, The Russian Education Club, Internal Security—C." It is not known whether the organization listed in correspondent's letter is identical with the above-captioned organization. The Russian Dramatic Club was the subject of investigation by the Boston Office in 1950 and 1951. . . . This investigation indicated that the Club had been in existence for twenty years or more and that at some of its meetings in the past it had speakers who espoused the Communist line.

Someone in Hoover's office wrote at the bottom of the file copy: "No action. Karpovich—anti-Soviet." [13]

Another member of the staff of the Russian Research Center who was of continuing interest—as a suspect, a possible informant, or both—to the FBI, the CIA, military intelligence, and the House Committee on Un-American Activities was Raymond A. Bauer. Bauer, a lecturer in the Department of Social Relations and research associate at the center, who also had a connection with the Center for International Studies at MIT—"writing an essay on a classified Soviet project" for Director Max Milliken—headed the group of analysts that the research center sent to Germany in 1950 to interview a large number of displaced persons from the Soviet Union in connection with one of the center's major research projects, the Project on the Soviet Social System. His "travel to Munich was by an AGO card which is a Military Travel Permit issued to military personnel or personnel of military contractors. The employees of the Russian Research Center would fall in this category." The project itself was financed by a grant from the Human Resources Research Institute of the U.S. Air Force, Maxwell Air Force Base, Alabama. The essays he wrote for the classified MIT project were based on "materials" developed by Bauer during the interviews conducted in Germany on the air force contract.

By at least 1954, Bauer was employed by the Human Resources Research Organization (HumRRO) of George Washington University, which functioned as a kind of holding company for several government intelligence and military agencies and engaged in its own research in a number of locations throughout the country and in coordinating the research that it subcontracted to universities, including Harvard, Columbia, Stanford, Michigan, Chicago, and others. He was a consultant for whom it sought to obtain security clearance for classified research. The connection with the research center project and the application to obtain security clearance would have been enough to launch an FBI investigation. But there had already been an investigation of Bauer.

From 1944 to 1946, he had been in the U.S. Navy as a junior officer studying Russian in New York City and in Boulder, Colorado. In both places, and later on a few occasions in Washington, he had had dinner and gone horseback riding with a fellow student, William W. Remington, who was later convicted of perjury in denying that he had ever given confidential information to Elizabeth Bentley (whose testimony before various congressional committees provided the basis for some of the most lurid spy scares of the Cold War) or that he had known of a Young Communist League group at Dartmouth College while he was a student there. He told the FBI of his connections with Remington in 1950 and spoke of his membership in the American Student Union at Northwestern University in the 1940s, but he denied that he had been a Communist and insisted that he had opposed the national leadership of the ASU: "I was aware before joining of the fact that a communist clique was either in control or threatened to gain control. I worked . . . in opposition to the foreign policy program which the national group proposed." He also admitted membership in another organization in which the FBI was interested, the American Veterans Committee.

On May 16, 1950, he testified in executive session before the House Committee on Un-American Activities about his knowledge of Remington and the ASU. His appearance before the committee was the result of a subpoena; he was "disturbed that . . . his testifying before such a committee might affect his appointment at Harvard University." An FBI informant in the navy, to whom Bauer had spoken about Remington, reported that Bauer had told him that it was "only because his appointment at Harvard was in the mill" that he was worried about testifying. The committee had "nothing on him as he is not and never has been a Communist. The only thing the Committee may have on him . . . was his connection with the American Student Union." He was dismissed without actually being called as a witness. The 1954 investi-

gation of Bauer came to an end when HumRRO withdrew its request
that he receive a security clearance, but the FBI maintained a sporadic
interest in him. In 1966 Bauer, by then a professor at the Harvard Business School, was the subject of still another FBI report because in a
book he edited, *Social Indicators,* an essay skeptical of the FBI Crime
Index statistics appeared.

It is clear that the FBI's interest in Bauer arose from his connections
with the Russian Research Center, HumRRO, and William Remington.
What is not clear, because of the censorship of the documents, is the
degree to which Bauer cooperated with the FBI and other investigative
agencies and, if he did so, whether it was because, as he told the FBI,
"his testifying before such a committee [as the House Un-American Activities Committee] might affect his appointment at Harvard University."
He might have thought that cooperation in the present would offset the
historical record. Perhaps we could answer that question if we knew why
several of the FBI reports on Bauer bear on their first page the following
notation: "2xc [2 copies]—W[hite] H[ouse] (Erlichman). By Liaison, 11-
10-69. JFM; pjg." There is no hint as to why one of President Nixon's
two main assistants was interested in Bauer.[14]

4. The Russian Research Center, 2: Scholarship and Intelligence

THE "OFFICIAL STORY" is that Harvard established the Russian Research Center with the help of a preliminary grant of $100,000 from the Carnegie Corporation of New York to provide information to the State Department and other government agencies about contemporary Russia. An article in the Boston *Traveler* of December 5, 1947, the basis for an FBI memo of December 12, reported that the results of the Harvard research would be "made available to the State Department and other federal agencies, including the central intelligence group, through informed channels long before publication by the university," though the university declined to do any classified (secret) research.[1] The State Department, though convinced of the importance of covert activities, was reluctant to engage in them itself. So were many professors, who were also eager to establish a permanent university-government relationship. We are led to wonder, therefore, whether the "official story" is the full story. What, if anything, do the Carnegie Corporation records add to our knowledge?[2]

By mid-1947 John Gardner of the Carnegie Corporation was in touch with a number of universities for information about the state of Russian studies. He asked for recommendations concerning how interest might be increased, especially among psychologists, sociologists, and anthropologists. On July 11, 1947, he reported for the file on his recent trip to Washington to determine the extent of government research in Russian studies "and to estimate the attitude of various government people toward further development of such research in the colleges." There was no

difficulty about that. Government agencies were so harried by day-to-
day work that there was no possibility of serious, long-term research.
They "would welcome any help from any source" and would make materials available for research: "The men from C.I.G. [Central Intelligence Group] pointed out that there were, for example, bales and bales
of captured German documents pertaining to Russia which haven't even
been opened up because no one had time to do anything with them."
The major shortcoming of Russian research was the "complete lack of
any adequate research of a social psychological nature." Cooperation
with private researchers was required and would be encouraged, but
since the circumstances of government-private cooperation were pretty
well defined, there would be difficulties. On July 14, 1947, someone,
probably Gardner, prepared for the Carnegie Corporation a six-page
memorandum—"Russian Studies"—describing the kind of research center
Carnegie had in mind and where it should be located. What was wanted
was a "research and training program centering on the application of
social psychology, cultural anthropology, and sociology to Russian studies." It was to be a center where, in addition to the collection, analysis,
and interpretation of current information—involving "a radio analysis
section, press analysis section, a section which devoted itself to interviewing men just back from Russia, a section which sent men into Russia or into neighboring countries to interview and gather information"—
there would be concern with a "variety of problems which require a
more intensive approach or a historical approach." The day-to-day approach, suggested by psychologist Alexander Leighton, was useful for
studying "Russian attitudes toward war . . . the factors involved in these
attitudes and to record the ups and downs in Russian willingness or
determination to keep the peace." The alternative approach, favored by
the author of the memorandum, was more conducive to the study of
especially significant problems:

1. "Attitudes of Russians toward their homeland in relation to the rest
   of the world"—the sources of Russian patriotism, including religious, cultural, social, and political attitudes.
2. "Attitudes toward Authority, Hierarchy, Suppression of Individual
   Freedom"—"without this understanding" we will never "be able to
   assess the internal stability of the communist regime."
3. "The Attitudes and Guiding Beliefs of the Communist Bureaucrat"—"no social psychologist will be satisfied with a diagnosis . . .
   based simply upon the official prescription"
4. "Communist Ideology and Its Impact"—"what parts of that ideology
   are readily assimilated because they simply provide new verbal symbols for old value-systems. . . . what parts are unassimilable and
   remain mere words."

There were three possibilities for the location of the center:

Harvard: By far the best bet at the moment. . . . A first-rate nucleus of social scientists, several of whom would be extremely useful in a program of the sort contemplated. . . . Harvard is having a tough time getting a foothold in the Russian field. It will take ten years to catch up with Columbia, if it tries to compete with Columbia on the latter's ground; whereas it might forge into an important position overnight if it chooses to develop an extremely important aspect of the field which Columbia has altogether neglected.

Columbia: The best Russian Studies program in the country—by far. Good sociology, mediocre anthropology, weak psychology. The worst disadvantage here is that the head of the Russian Institute is not at all likely to view such a program with either sympathy or understanding.

Stanford: An inadequate program of Russian Studies, which might be bolstered. Good psychology, one good anthropologist, weak sociology. . . . The Hoover Institute would be an ideally flexible setting for such a program. But Stanford would be handicapped by distance from the other academic centers and from Washington.

For Gardner, Harvard was "first choice for the headquarters or central coordinating point of the project." To direct the center, he favored an executive committee and a chairman. "I am going to assume that Harvard will be the headquarters," he wrote, and "will only name such individuals as seem likely to be available for the duties indicated." These were Clyde Kluckhohn, Talcott Parsons, and Alex Inkeles, from Harvard; Alexander Leighton from Cornell; and Leonard Doob and Carl Hovland from Yale. He concluded with a "Plan of Action": to explore the possibility of Harvard as the site for the center; to select an "Exploratory Committee to examine the whole program"; and to "consider the setting up of at least two projects at Harvard"—"Leighton's project, with Raymond Bowers as project director," and a "Planning Seminar devoted to continuing exploration of the field, formulating problems, suggesting methods, etc. . . . the seed-bed for men who will later undertake direction of research projects."[3]

During the late summer and fall of 1947, Gardner and Charles Dollard of Carnegie exchanged letters and had additional conferences with Harvard and government officials refining their program. All parties would benefit. As Gardner told Kluckhohn, "The need for such research has been strongly endorsed by everyone I have talked to—experts on Russia, State Department personnel, and the people in Central Intelligence, as well as the various psychologists and anthropologists interviewed." He continued to press for the two-track approach set forth in his initial Carnegie memorandum. He made it clear that Harvard was the preferred location.

Dollard noted that General Frederick Osborn, director of the army's Information and Education Division, supported the program and had told him "that if any question arose at Harvard as to the interest of the State Department or the U.S. Delegation to the United Nations in having more systematic information about Russia, we were free to use his name without reservations. He volunteered also to address Conant personally on the subject if this were advisable, Conant being one of his consultants."

Gardner reported that Kluckhohn, Parsons, and Frederick Mosteller strongly favored the continuing analysis of developments in Russia—"of the sort carried on during the war in connection with Japan"—while Donald McKay of the History Department was "immensely attracted by the idea of a research seminar." By October Provost Paul H. Buck and Francis Keppel of the School of Education had been drawn into the discussions, and Buck had presented a budget for an exploratory eight-month period and, if that were accepted, for an additional five years. Dollard and Gardner had the "firm impression that Buck had a reasonably good understanding" of the program and "was prepared to give it firm support"; the clearest indication of that was his "strong support of Clyde Kluckhohn as director of the program."

Further conferences were held with Harvard authorities and government officials—including J. M. Maury of the CIA and Alexander Gerschenkron. Gardner was ready to propose to the Carnegie Corporation on October 15 that $110,000 be given to Harvard with the likelihood that a five-year grant would be made later; "it would seem to be unwise to support the experimental phase unless the Corporation were fully prepared to back the five-year program." The argument for the research contemplated at the center "is admirably set forth in the recent article on Sources of Soviet Conduct by X in Foreign Affairs"; the precedent for it was the analysis of Japanese civilian morale by army intelligence based on prisoner interrogation and systematic scrutiny of other sources.[4]

The Carnegie Corporation kept careful records of its activities in connection with the research center. Its inventory of "Follow Up Correspondence and Conferences Relative to the Russian Research Center of Harvard University" shows seventy-three items from October 20, 1947, to June 2, 1948. Most have to do with evaluations of personnel and budget, but some deal with matters closer to our interest, the relations between Harvard and the intelligence agencies.

Gardner met with a CIA representative, among others, in Washington on October 16, 1949. Earlier, on January 5, 1948, Walter Ellis of the CIA had "stopped in at Carnegie headquarters in New York at the suggestion of Knight McMahon of CIA to ask about the Russian program at Harvard." He was introduced to Gardner. The memorandum mentioning his visit to Carnegie headquarters is not listed in the Carnegie inventory, though it does appear in the Carnegie file on the Russian Research Center.[5] Item 40, described as a letter from Kluckhohn to Gardner, February 10, 1948, appears in the inventory but not in the files. It was written less than three weeks after the official establishment of the center on February 1 and is inventoried as follows: "Inquired as to the advisability of telling the New York FBI that Irene Hay (bibliographer) would probably visit Communist bookstores and people the FBI may be watching."

Though that letter is not in the Carnegie files, a copy of it is in the Russian Research Center files. Kluckhohn wrote Gardner that research center staff member Irene Hay was fearful that her visits to Communist bookstores in New York and with "such people as Mrs. Ruth Fischer whose activities the FBI may be watching" might bring her to the attention of the FBI. Kluckhohn felt that she was exaggerating but did have a point. "Rather than having her go directly to the New York FBI," he wrote, "I thought it preferable to have her explore the matter with you to see if by any chance you or some other officer of the Corporation wishes to initiate this contact."

Gardner wrote a memorandum for the file on February 18, 1948, on his meeting with Hay, who was not only a bibliographer but a researcher on the center's staff. He noted that Hay, after having made surveys of Russian materials in Boston and Washington, was now working in New York, where useful current materials "are most readily obtainable through Communist bookshops and similar channels." But Hay, though an American citizen, was Russian-born and therefore "reluctant to explore these sources without some sort of prior understanding with the FBI." Gardner answered:

> The Russian Research Center would have to establish contact with the FBI in any case, and . . . the contact should be made with the FBI's Boston office. Miss Hay had thought that CC might wish to get in touch with the New York office of the FBI, but JG suggested that all such relationships be carried on through Harvard University.

Why did Gardner feel that the center would have to establish contact with the FBI "in any case"? What did he mean when he "suggested that all such relationships be carried on through Harvard University"? Was he implying that there was a liaison relationship between Harvard and the FBI and that matters concerning the center would be handled accordingly? Was he suggesting that such a relationship should be established and that Harvard, not Carnegie, was the organization through which it should be done?

Nothing in the Carnegie files clarifies the matter, but the advice that Harvard establish contact with the FBI was repeated. On February 24, 1948, only six days after he had spoken to Irene Hay, Gardner met with H. Stuart Hughes, assistant director of the center. Hughes "touched briefly on the problem of establishing relations with the FBI and JG reiterated the judgment previously expressed that such relationships should be accomplished through Harvard with the Boston office of the FBI."

The nagging questions remain. What did Hughes mean when he spoke of establishing relations with the FBI? Twice Gardner writes that relationships with the FBI should be carried on through Harvard University, not through the research center. Was Gardner simply distinguishing between Carnegie and Harvard, through which he wanted the FBI contact maintained? Or was he distinguishing between the research center and Harvard in general? In that case, was he implying that matters concerning the research center could be handled through already existing channels or channels that should be established? Most important, what were the matters that Harvard and the FBI should be discussing—the possible appearance of center personnel in suspicious quarters, of course; but were there other center activities or projects about which it would be useful to inform the FBI and obtain information from the FBI? Aside from Gardner's views and those of the center authorities on this matter, might it not be useful to the FBI to obtain information about center programs and policies?[6]

Two other items on the Carnegie–research center agenda for the academic year 1948–49 are of special interest.

The first has to do with European fieldwork and interviewing for which the center was preparing itself. Plans were made to send Professor Merle Fainsod as temporary cultural attaché in Moscow for a month prior to the Salzburg summer seminar, Professor Talcott Parsons to Stockholm and Prague, and two graduate fellows, one of whom was Raymond A. Bauer, to Helsinki and Vienna. Bauer was to become a student at the University of Vienna, where "he will establish contact with Austrians who have had first-hand experience with Russians in the occupying forces and will attempt to make an evaluation of this type of source." The final proposal for field work had to do with interviewing Soviet displaced persons (DPs) in Germany. An interim report, "prepared by Stuart Hughes in collaboration with" Kluckhohn, recommended the project and referred to a report sent to the center by "a psychologist of Baltic origin, Dr. Bakis, who is now teaching at an improvised DP university in Schleswig-Holstein," who had already been interviewing DPs.[7]

The second item of special interest to the parties concerned efforts, at Harvard and elsewhere, to increase the visibility and prestige of the center and enhance its usefulness to the two worlds of government and scholarship. On March 30, 1948, Gardner noted that

> Kluckhohn makes the sensible point that until the program is solidly entrenched at Harvard and until it has established good relations with other institutions in the Russian studies field, there is little point in moving on to establishing relations with the government, the military,

and other circles. He believes, however, that by midsummer the Center will be fully prepared to develop its contacts with the State Department, etc.

What Kluckhohn and Gardner called "the public relations problems facing the Center" could be handled, first, by enlisting the cooperation of important members of the Harvard faculty and recruiting able people from the outside, like Harold Berman of the Stanford Law School and Alexander Gerschenkron from Berkeley and the Federal Reserve Board; second, by a joint strategy in which it was Harvard's responsibility to serve as the "primary source of information" while Carnegie would confine itself to a curt "No comment." Finally, the "public relations" problem would be helped by a series of small dinners at which President Conant and officials of the center would solicit the advice and "moral teaching of the best men of the country." Charles Dollard suggested to Kluckhohn that Conant host the following guests in New York: Arthur Ballantine, Allen Dulles, Brooks Emeny, Walter Gifford, Devereux C. Josephs, Nicholas Kelley, Roy Larson, Walter Mallory, Charles Merz, Arthur Page, Geoffrey Parsons, Robert Patterson, Geroid Robinson, and Gordon Wasson. Kluckhohn began to make the necessary arrangements with Conant. He also suggested to Dollard that documents describing the work of the center be sent to "Allen Dulles and the other people whom you suggested" be invited by Conant. Things were working out well. Gardner noted that Kluckhohn had informed him that requests for assistance on the part of government agencies were increasing:

> Last week [Gardner's memorandum is dated June 1, 1949] there were 17 official visitors from various government agencies. They had received a variety of requests to undertake contract research for government agencies. And the demands upon his staff to serve as consultants in this or that capacity is a growing drain on their energies.[8]

Carnegie was so pleased with the performance of the research center that it voted to appropriate $150,000 annually for five years beginning with 1952–53. The grant was to enable the university to do the planning required to maintain the research center team that led Carnegie to extend the original grant even before the first five-year period had expired. For the same reason, General Osborn requested that the center staff not be drawn into military service:

> Their staff is largely made up of reserve officers in the three Services and, in addition, they are now sending a team to Europe under contract with and under the administrative jurisdiction of the Air Forces. If I am right in believing that the Center comprises an appreciable fraction of our country's intelligence potential on Russia, it is important that its personnel should be kept on its specialized work and not drawn into the Services.[9]

There were, however, indications of stormy weather ahead; the Cox committee of the House of Representatives was about to investigate the foundations. Charles Dollard informed Conant that the investigation "was bound to put the spotlight on the Russian Research Center." He himself was sure that the investigators would find no substantial ground for criticism, but he suggested that it would be well for Conant to bring himself up to date on the center's activities. In preparing its own defense against the expected attack by the Cox committee, "D.D.T." of the Carnegie staff drafted a memorandum for the corporation counsel that provides additional information about the origins of the center. It confirms that conversations with the Harvard authorities and government officials began in midsummer 1947 and adds the comment "most revealing . . . is the ease with which the Corporation moves around Washington." Various items in the files, the memorandum emphasizes, "indicate rather close cooperation with administrative offices of the government in the *planning and development of the Center*" [my emphasis]. Moreover, the memorandum refers to certain documents, apparently not now in the files, which deal with possible appointments to the staff: Edward Shils of the University of Chicago; Hans Speier of Rand; Gardner Murphy of CCNY; Ruth Fischer; "Stewart [*sic*]" Hughes, "Kluckhohn's first choice to be executive secretary"; Joseph Freeman, who was now "strongly anti-Communist."

With an eye for the names of people who might be "pertinent" to the Cox committee, "D.D.T." mentioned that William Remington had been suggested for a position. This is not the only indication that the memorandum was written with a weather-eye out for the kinds of questions the Cox committee might be interested in. Concerning a member of the faculty of Champlain College who was being considered for a research center appointment, the memorandum states: "He is not one of the Champlain teachers under FBI suspicion." About a lengthy report commissioned for General Osborn by the center from Adam Ulam, a member of the staff and of the Harvard Government Department, the memorandum states that it contains "certain small things which people might criticize—for instance, a sentence such as this . . . . : 'It is naive to expect a change of regimes in Russia as the result of a popular uprising or dissatisfaction among the masses. . . .' This may be perfectly correct, but there are those who are espousing just such a popular uprising, or are awaiting it." And finally, the memorandum for the counsel conceded that there was "some indication . . . of Corporation intent not to reveal its role to the public." For example, it deleted references to Carnegie from an article prepared by Harvard for *Reader's Digest*.[10]

By 1955 there had been major changes in the direction of the research center, but not in the relation with government agencies and with intelligence. A memorandum, "Notes on Russian Research Center

Achievement," based on a telephone conversation on May 19, 1955, between Marshall Shulman of the center and William Marvel of the Carnegie staff, reports that six of the fifty-five persons who had worked at the center had gone into government service (including the CIA); 40 percent of the graduates of the Regional Studies Program had gone into government, and 40 percent continued graduate work. The Regional Studies Program had "two people a year from CIA for [the] last several years, has trained 8 Foreign Service Officers during the last 5 years and had six German Foreign Service Officers during 1950–51." In addition, the center had recently performed several special services for the government: a two-day conference with representatives from Harvard, MIT, and the American Committee for Liberation from Bolshevism; instructing six German army officers in the United States under government auspices in research techniques; discussing with air force officers the effect of Soviet atomic capability on foreign policy; consultations by the center's director and associate director in Washington with the State Department and CIA, and in Cambridge with representatives of the Office of Intelligence Research of the State Department.[11]

Twenty years or more after these events, a number of officials of the Carnegie Corporation and of Harvard University, interviewed by the staff of the Oral History Research Office of Columbia University, revealed details of the Carnegie–Russian Research Center connection—and, indeed, Carnegie relations with government agencies in general—that go considerably beyond the statements in the documents.

The interview with Harvard Provost Paul H. Buck presents an alternative to the "official" story of the origins of the center. The idea of the center was not generated within the university as an autonomous activity of the academic profession; it was brought to Harvard by Charles Dollard and John Gardner and was based, Buck thought, on a suggestion first made by Carnegie trustee General Frederick Osborn to study Russian behavior. "It was their initiative and it was their wise observations that an anthropologist should direct this study." The model for both the Russian Research Center and the Harvard Social Relations Department was, according to Buck, the OSS. In 1947 Buck sent his assistant Francis Keppel, whose father had been president of Carnegie, to see Dollard to discuss Harvard people who had OSS experience and wanted new programs and "a new organizational setup in which they could pool their activities in a common study of these new international problems which have become so vitally important." Keppel had a lengthy meeting with Dollard, Gardner, Donald C. McKay, Talcott Parsons, Clyde Kluckhohn, and Frederick Mosteller on October 6, 1947. A day later he wrote a memorandum paying tribute to the support given by General Osborn and reporting that Dollard and Gardner had already settled on Harvard as the site for the Russian Research Center.

The corporation never imposed any limitations on the freedom to do research, Buck said: "We've never engaged in any secret research. There may have been certain aspects that were done under the grant of the Air Force that approached it." But the research center staff itself "voluntarily accepted . . . that they would not participate freely in politics that would bring them into controversial positions in regard to present government policy towards Russia." In all this "there had to be a certain direction." For example, the center told the FBI about its purchase of Communist literature, and it procured Russian books at the suggestion of the Library of Congress because this was less likely to arouse congressional opposition than purchasing them on its own motion. There was, however, "one exception to all I've said, and this is the part I hesitate to have on the record yet because it does involve some very important people. Maybe you've heard about the Stuart Hughes affair in 1948."

Hughes had been active in the Henry Wallace presidential campaign in 1948. Gardner and Dollard came to Buck, "and they were very embarrassed." Kluckhohn was also at the meeting. "And another friend of mine, a man I respect greatly, said that this was causing embarrassment for the Carnegie Corporation and could we possibly remove Hughes from the assistant directorship. . . . Well, I didn't like it. It violated some of my principles, and yet, on the other hand, I had authority to remove him" because his was an administrative appointment. Buck told Hughes he was making a mistake by "sticking his neck out on issues too soon in his life. . . . Stick to [your] knitting as an historian for a while and then develop into [the] same position" later. "He followed that advice. He later told me it was the most important advice he ever got in his life. And, of course, what I said has become true. He is now very influential." And how was the matter handled with the Carnegie Corporation, which did, after all, pay Hughes's salary? "Now, I did tell the Carnegie people, and they willingly agreed, that they'd have to take over his—make a gift to Harvard—remaining four of his five-year professorship. They did that willingly. I don't know how that appeared as a gift, but at any rate they paid his salary for the remaining assistant professorship years." Buck's interviewer was not sure she understood the situation. Buck clarified it:

Let's look at some of the implications here. Here was a grandson of a Chief Justice of the United States involved in a corporation which had just added General [George C.] Marshall to its board of trustees . . . and the first action was the dismissal of Hughes. Now, I'm sure General Marshall didn't know a damned thing about it; he'd never been to a meeting up to that time. But I didn't see that the scandal on this would be of benefit to anybody and certainly not of any benefit to the well being of the nation, so we handled it very quietly. And I don't think that Hughes suffered; quite the reverse.

When Buck's interviewer remarked that Hughes was in a position to "make an embarrassing fuss," Buck replied: "And that was my role, largely to tell him how ill advised he would have been to do that. . . . He took the advice." The interviewer pressed on with more questions about the origins of the center: "I understand that preliminary talks were held in Washington to make sure that it was understood at the State Department by some key government figures that this was not going to be a subversive or a trouble-making outfit, but rather a helpful one and one that was needed by this country. Are you aware of these movements?" Buck certainly was: "I know there were discussions." He also knew that, as his interviewer put it, it was "required that arrangements be made with government people" to interview the defectors who were the main source of information for the center.

No one interviewed for the Carnegie Corporation project denied what was most important in Buck's account—namely, that Carnegie officials had had prior consultations with government agencies and had broached the idea of a Russian research center to Harvard. Some were less solicitous of Hughes than Buck and more ready to approve of foundation and university connections with intelligence agencies.

General Osborn took credit for having first raised the idea of a Russian research center at Harvard with Carnegie officials. He "determined, from the State Department, that they would be interested in having such work done for them but that they were not prepared to do it themselves. They didn't have the allocations for it and there might be some political problems arising from doing it, but they felt it would be great if Carnegie Corporation would do it. . . . They were very enthusiastic and sent John Gardner around the country to see where the strong points were and where the Corporation could start building." As to the hiring of politically controversial people, Osborn was "pragmatic"; a foundation should not jeopardize its projects by hiring them: "I think that, at the time of the McCarthy investigations, it was essential that any foundation or institution find out who it was hiring. It wouldn't be sensible for it to injure its own usefulness very greatly in the attempt to protect the rights or liberty of the single individual. . . . The chances are that a man who is agin his government and is a Communist is something of an oddball and that this would interfere with solid work on his part."

Professor Talcott Parsons was able to supplement Buck's account from the Harvard perspective. Gardner approached him to set up a meeting with Buck to discuss the establishment of a Russian center. Parsons was certain it had already been agreed that Kluckhohn, "who had been consulted along the way," was to be the director, and that it had already been decided that Harvard would be the site of the center. On the dismissal of Hughes, he had been consulted by the Carnegie "twins"—Dollard and Gardner—and Buck, and he was sure Buck would not approve any infringement of Hughes's right to teach as "a contravention of academic freedom. But when he was in an administrative capacity in a very sensitive area, it was better that he not stay in it. That was the way it was resolved." Wasn't the Russian Research Center in a vulnerable position? "Yes, of course it was. . . . I think this was one of Clyde's greatest contributions, that he managed such a very delicate thing with really an absolute minimum of political trouble. . . . Generally speaking, I think there was an avoidance of getting what you might call political fireballs [sic] onto the staff, either pro- or anti-Soviet. I remember, for one year, as a visitor, they had Isaac Deutscher here, but, of course, he is an old Trotskyite and therefore was very anti-Stalin." Interviewer: "So that was respectable?" Parsons: "So it was neutralized, as it were."

Perhaps what is most impressive about the interviews with the Carnegie executives is the straightforwardness with which they discuss government-foundation relations.

Carnegie President Devereux Josephs made clear why the issue was so sensitive and who wanted the research to be done. Soon after World War II the USSR was going to be "our great competitor" and we would have to learn more about it. To his interviewer's point that it would be good to learn more about the USSR and whether it was a friend or enemy, he answered: "That's right. But we [the corporation] had tended to be more interested in things closer to home. . . . I can remember that, at that time, the State Department was very anxious to see us do this." But to show interest in Russia was enough to arouse suspicion; it was necessary, therefore, in planning the Russian Research Center, "to discuss this with our trustees, both at a board meeting and individually, to explain what we were after." And what were they after? "We wanted to be very clear that we were not trying to embrace the Russians. . . . That was one reason why we were very anxious to get the endorsement of the State Department; that spread a little holy water on it. . . . So we had ourselves fully endorsed."

Nor did Josephs dissent from the decision to drop Hughes from the Russian Research Center. He was reluctant to reveal Hughes's name— "He's still up there in Cambridge"—but it was surely necessary and proper to have him removed: "How do you do such a thing as politely as possible, so that nobody's feelings were hurt?" He would do the same today: "After all, what you're trying to do is start an institute. . . . You're not battling for an individual; you're not battling . . . academic freedom or anything else like that. Why do you work with something that is not wholly satisfactory? You want the thing to flow easily."

The testimony of President Dollard would, in any case, be of considerable significance. Since Gardner's oral history memoir is still under restrictions, Dollard's takes on added interest and importance.

Large as the corporation's interest in the research center was—our "most substantial investment," Dollard called it—it was not as large as the government would have liked. According to Dollard, the government wanted Carnegie to oversee all the research the center did for the air force, with the money funneled through the center, but the corporation rejected the idea. Was it because the contemplated relationship presented some kind of "philosophical or ethical problem" to the corporation, or "was it purely a practical matter"? "It's a practical matter, I think. . . . I don't think it was a matter of ethics so much as a matter of style." In any case, the ultimate relationship among government, foundation, and university was brought about by the foundation: "It was an unusual program, in the sense that we went to Harvard; they didn't come to us. . . . Paul Buck was then the provost. We started with him."

Was it necessary for Dollard and Devereux Josephs to do much spadework with the corporation trustees and with government officials to get agreement that this was "a well-intentioned and legitimate program"? The trustees were a bit anxious, but there was no anxiety in the government; Russian experts, such as those produced at Philip Moseley's Russian Institute at Columbia, were snapped up as quickly as possible. As to relations between the government and the foundation (and the center, its satellite), Dollard wavered between finding them to be institutional in character or simply personal. Sometimes he regarded them as the product of an understanding between the organizations involved; sometimes, as the product of the wartime experience of particular individuals "who were being asked to work with federal agencies. . . . It was personal involvement and not the Corporation program." But if the relationships were based exclusively on personal considerations, why was the corporation so anxious to demonstrate its willingness to cooperate with the FBI, for example, and with congressional investigating committees like the Cox and Reece committees? "Our position with the FBI was always that we would tell them anything we knew," Dollard said. "But as for giving them documents, I think that if they had asked, we would have made them subpoena them. . . . we did a great deal of work for the Cox Committee . . . and had a very good relationship." It was a disagreeable experience only "because it took so much of our time. . . . It did us no harm and probably did us some good." But, he was asked, did not the staff wonder if they should be concerned about the politics of grantees? Not more than usual.

Dollard's comment about the degree of interest the corporation took in the political views of its beneficiaries was at least ambiguous, perhaps cagey. Some trustees were more blunt. W. Randolph Burgess said he probably would have opposed naming Gunnar Myrdal as director of the famous study on race relations because of his political views. "Do you think that foundations should know who its . . ." His interviewer did not even have time to finish the question when Burgess interrupted: "Yes, what their leaning is, because you want to get an objective job done." Was there any such discussion in connection with the Russian Research Center? "Didn't this center a little around the personality of Stuart Hughes?" Burgess asked. Stuart's father, Charles Hughes, was his intimate friend: "I think Stuart was very disappointing," but the corporation had been quite right in not interfering with Harvard. The university had been "a sucker" on some of its appointments, which were "very reprehensible," but Carnegie could not be faulted for its grants to Harvard: "If Carnegie had been running the program, Hughes would not have been hired, but since Harvard ran it, Carnegie should not have interfered." Burgess's response leaves it unclear whether he even knew of the role Carnegie played in the elimination of Hughes.

Trustee and Brown University President Henry Wriston certainly knew: Hughes had been removed because of his political views, and it was done "without any noise because of his grandfather." The research center was getting its "money from the Navy [in this, Wriston was wrong] and I think he wouldn't get clearance." But was it not Harvard policy not to do classified research? "That's not the issue. The point is that the Russian Institute, whether you like it or not, had access to classified material. Now, the results may not be classified, but it's access, and a person without clearance can't get access."

For the distinguished biologist Caryl Haskins, relations of foundations and universities with government raised no ethical questions, only policy issues. What about the CIA and universities? "I'm not one of those who blames the CIA for having done it, because it seems to me that what the CIA did was to step into a breach that they were asked to step into from the highest authority." Does not the Russian Research Center transmit information to Washington "which cannot be disclosed?" "This is certainly true. It is a web, it's a very complex web, and of course it is terribly important that this kind of transmission occur, too. A Russian Research Center will necessarily have to make its own judgments of what kinds or sorts of information it must keep secret, what it must transmit to Washington, and what parts simply become scholarship. . . . There is a continuum between the things . . . on which national policy must depend, and which have to be so guarded, and the other kinds which simply raise our cultural level." Scholars who work for a "national cause by working for a government agency of any kind— the CIA, State, or anything else—can be patriots, very great patriots" and are not "untrue to their scholarship." Scholars who work in "that peculiarly difficult business of non-public information" are doing a "much harder job for [the] country than other people."

Where Carnegie trustees were ignorant, or partially ignorant, of particular cases or, like Haskins, saw them in a broad context of policy issues, the corporation staff, especially those of the middle level, saw them more matter-of-factly. William Marvel was asked whether there was some connection between the development of area studies programs and congressional investigations. He was sure that there was; there had to be "a certain amount of informal clearance of some of these schemes." When the Harvard Russian Research Center

> was started, this was just when the cold war was building up really good, there was a lot—there is no doubt about it. . . . I think it would vary a good deal according to the sensitivity and the sort of critical nature of our foreign relations problem at that time with the countries that were being studied—how much consultation there was with Washington.

The most difficult aspect of academic-community–intelligence-agency relationships is that "the standards, the mode, the conscience, the attitude toward his own colleagues and everything else of the individual scholar" are called into question. "This is much more important than anything you can easily legislate about or easily control by administrative action." The paradox was that nothing much could be done from the outside about academic-community–intelligence-agency connections. But had the problem arisen specifically in connection with the Carnegie Corporation? "Did the question of government (CIA or any other government agency) approaching foundations in respect of programs arise at Carnegie?" Marvel's answer was direct: "In terms of government-foundation relations [it] is an everlasting theme, you might say." [12]

Carnegie Corporation archives dealing with the Cox committee in 1952 and the Reece committee in 1954 throw light on the strategy adopted by Carnegie to answer the charges made against it. They help explain relations with the government as the foundations and the universities saw them, though they reveal less about the specific relations of Carnegie to the Russian Research Center. In part, the reason is that some documents may simply have disappeared from the files. A memorandum written sometime after 1966, entitled "Briefs Prepared for Congressional Investigations," reveals that the Carnegie staff had "prepared detailed information about all the organizations to which grants had been made that might conceivably appear to be 'left-wing' or Communist-infiltrated." The briefs were about to be thrown out in 1977, but it was felt that "many . . . contain[ed] material gathered from numerous sources that might be useful to researchers of the future." Accordingly, the individual briefs were kept and filed under the names of the organizations and individuals to which they pertained. Listed among the ninety-five organizations and individuals on whom such briefs were prepared, ranging from "Adamic, Louis" to "Yale University, Seminars on National Policy," appears "Harvard University, Russian Research Center, 7/8/52." The date is that on which the brief was prepared.

That document is almost certainly the one entitled "Memorandum for Counsel, Harvard Russian Research Center, July 8, 1952," initialed "D.D.T." It consists primarily of a calendar of the correspondence and conferences with the center, and it points out certain phrases—as in Adam Ulam's report to General Osborn—that the Cox committee might be expected to snap at. Appended to a twelve-page list of microfilm reels is a note explaining that the sixteen reels were "microfilmed at the beginning of the Cox investigation on advice of counsel [because he] thought there was a possibility of our files being subpoenaed by the Committee, in which case we would have nothing to work with in answering questions." In 1978, however, the reels could not be found, "and it was assumed they were destroyed"—except for two reels on the Gunnar Myrdal study on American blacks—"having served their purpose."

The strategy adopted by the Carnegie Corporation to defend itself from the Cox and Reece committees was similar to that devised by the universities for their defense. Carnegie cooperated closely with the Rockefeller Foundation in working out a common policy, just as the universities worked out a common strategy. The "Working Papers, Cox Committee" file in the Carnegie Archives contains many exchanges of letters and briefs between Carnegie and Rockefeller counsel on the matter. Both foundations not only conceded the right of the congressional committees to proceed as they were, but acknowledged the existence of Communist subversion and of a serious loyalty-security problem. The strategy of both the foundations and the universities was to demonstrate that they were aware of subversion and therefore could be relied upon to police themselves. Such a strategy required Carnegie and Rockefeller to defend traditional principles of freedom of inquiry while at the same time conceding the right of the state to impose limits on that freedom. Like the universities, the foundations found themselves on the defensive. Carnegie policy in "handling problems of disloyalty" involved four major considerations:

> The first is that our funds shall not go to support communism or communist causes. But we cannot rest with any such narrow construction of those who should be excluded from our grants. Therefore our second consideration is that we shall not support any person or institution where the evidence of disloyalty is of such a nature as to leave in doubt the scholarly or professional objectivity of the potential recipient. This certainly includes those committed to a system of beliefs that deny the assumption of free enterprise in the world of the mind and spirit. The third consideration is that we will not use our funds to control the thoughts and opinions of those who receive our grants. We are sensitive to the basic importance of academic and intellectual freedom. . . . Our concern for loyalty and . . . for academic freedom leads us to a fourth consideration which is that each case will have to be treated independently. We must use our best judgment to make sure that the freedom

we protect covers only those who wish to extend that freedom to everyone.

Sounding remarkably like the report of the universities' Listening
Post, a May 15, 1952, memorandum for counsel laid down seven "Basic
Principles to be employed in CC presentations and defense of operations." These included its agreement not to "finance the work of a proven
communist or organization successfully infiltrated by communists"; the
assumption of "primary responsibility for taking appropriate action with
respect to a recipient institution where communist infiltration has been
established"; agreement to "entertain proposals representing many beliefs and shades of opinion except those of proven communists and successfully infiltrated organizations." At the same time, it argued that it
was in no position to conduct its own investigations to determine Communist affiliation.

The Rockefeller Foundation had the same policy. Counsel Lindsley
Kimball stated: "Now our enemy is insidious. . . . He invades not only
our shores, but our society as well. . . . The Rockefeller Foundation
cannot live in isolation." Senate and FBI investigations of the Institute
of Pacific Relations and the charges of the Cox committee "indicate the
belief in at least a few minds that the Rockefeller Foundation is either
unwittingly giving support to the enemies of our country or is itself fuzzy-
minded, unrealistic, and even pinkishly inclined." He recommended eight
steps for coping with the situation, two of which are particularly important: (1) "The RF should not be committed to that extreme conception
of academic freedom which converts it into academic license. . . . In
our society we go a long way in preserving the right of an individual to
think and talk as he pleases. There is no concomitant obligation to endow the soap-box. . . . At any given time in history there can be only
that degree of academic freedom which is compatible with the dominant
sentiments, purposes, and needs of the particular society in which it exists." (2) "We must remember that the RF position is not impregnable.
Tax exemption is a privilege tendered by the people rather than a right
which we can assert. We must therefore recognize public opinion as a
fact." [13]

How deep was the involvement of the intelligence agencies—the FBI,
military intelligence, civilian agencies—in the research center? What were
the activities that attracted their interest, and how might this interest
affect the work of the center? How did the center respond to these agencies and in what forms—as idiosyncratic responses to pressure or blan-
dishment or as policy? If the latter, was the policy made known to the
academic world or even to the staff of the center?

The best-known activity of the center was the Harvard Project on the
Soviet Social System. It conformed closely to the desiderata expressed

by the Carnegie Corporation. It was multidisciplinary, applying the methods and findings of social psychology, cultural anthropology, and sociology to Russian area studies; it combined short-term monitoring of current conditions with investigations of long-term historical factors and trends; and it attempted to analyze a "total" society through consistent application of a particular theory. In their acknowledgment in the final report of the project, the authors, Raymond A. Bauer, Alex Inkeles, and Clyde Kluckhohn, give some clues to the answers to the questions that concern us:

> Our obligations are manifold, both to United States Air Force Person-
> nel and to academic colleagues. Within the Air Force our thanks should
> first be expressed to Dr. Raymond V. Bowers, formerly Director of the
> Human Resources Research Institute (HRRI). The initiative and much
> of the original conception were his, and he continued to give excellent
> support and assistance. . . . It is also necessary to call attention to the
> collaboration of the Munich Institute for the Study of History and Cul-
> ture of the USSR. Its Scientific Council made up of leading represen-
> tatives of the *émigré* community, particularly its Director, Mr. Boris Ya-
> kovlev, were of great help in our relations with the refugee community.
> We wish also to acknowledge the technical collaboration provided our
> field team by the group from the Bureau of Applied Social Research at
> Columbia University, particularly its senior staff members, Mr. Lee
> Wiggins and Mr. Dean Manheimer.

Among those at the center immediately connected with the project, the following were singled out: Professor Merle Fainsod and Paul Friedrich, who "conducted the pilot phase of" the investigation, and Dr. George Fischer, who "performed invaluable services in establishing friendly relations with the *émigré* groups in Europe and in generally launching the Project under favorable circumstances. . . . beginning with the first informal explorations of the Center in the German-Austrian area which he carried out in 1948." Professor Talcott Parsons "advised and aided the Project in countless ways."

The book itself is described as a series of observations and conclu-sions based mainly on data from questionnaires administered to Soviet DPs and from "experience in working directly with the refugees through many hours of intimate personal contact." Such surveys had been used sporadically by a few individuals and organizations, but their objectives were limited or their findings were restricted by security classifications.

In the spring of 1950 Harvard accepted support from the air force "for a more systematic exploration of this source of information," a de-cision made on the basis of pilot studies by senior members of the Har-vard faculty in 1949. The air force provided "funds and logistic sup-port"; "As basic research, the work was under the sole technical direction of the Russian Research Center at all times."[14]

Following the 1962 convention of the American Sociological Association, a volume of invited papers was published; Raymond V. Bowers wrote the chapter "The Military Establishment." It provides indispensable material for understanding the relation between the military establishment and academic sociology in general, and the importance of that relation in the development of the Harvard project.

In the National Security Act of 1947, Congress set up a research and development board to review and stimulate research and development programs in the armed forces. The behavioral sciences were specifically included within the mandate of the board; and a committee on human resources, with special responsibilities in psychophysiology, training, manpower, and human relations and morale, was organized to oversee the possible uses of the behavioral sciences. The air force was particularly responsive to the promise of the social sciences and established three in-service research centers by 1949, including the Human Resources Research Institute at Air University, Maxwell Field, where most of the programs in human relations and morale were assigned. The Human Resources Research Office (HumRRO) at George Washington University, on the basis of its own research contracts and subcontracts it let to other universities and organizations, did most of the work for the army.

As to intelligence-university connections: "The rise of cold-war tensions and limited warfare" focused attention on deficiencies in our knowledge of "those countries most likely to be aligned against us" and led to the conclusion that steps had to be taken as quickly as possible to assess the social, psychological, political, and economic weaknesses and strengths of the "major closed foreign social systems. Later this interest was extended to other countries as well." The story begins in 1948, when it was recognized that, while the intelligence agencies were doing a creditable job in handling day-to-day questions, what was needed was "basic improvement" in the information required for the larger questions. This need was communicated to the Committee on Human Resources of the Research and Development Board, and by it to the panels of advisers to recommend the general types of research to be pursued.

Knowledge of the Soviet social system was "established as the number-one priority of that time," and a program was begun in 1950 through a contract between the air force's Human Resources Research Institute and the Harvard Russian Research Center, "specifying Clyde Kluckhohn as principal investigator." Harvard had its own reasons for supporting such a study. Bowers leaves no doubt as to the government's:

Its objectives were to develop a method for (a) understanding how a relatively inaccessible foreign social system "looks from within" and (b) predicting how it would react to various strains and stresses placed on the pattern of interrelationships existing among its social institutions, administrative and political controls, and social and socioeconomic groups.

The unique source for the study was the day-to-day experience of Soviet citizens derived from approximately seven hundred intensive interviews and twelve thousand lengthy questionnaires obtained in Europe during 1950–51 from Soviet refugees, escapees, and émigrés. Bowers admits that the study produced no mathematical model of a social system. Still, individual reports provided military planning offices with data and predictions unavailable before; members of the research center staff were often used as consultants on "classified strategic and psychological warfare planning studies"; "sets of the interview protocols were made available to the intelligence community in Washington"; a special "restricted" *Guide for Interviewing Soviet Escapees*, written by Alice H. Bauer, was prepared "for the use of the military intelligence operator"; and finally, the products of the study found their way into the reports of the MIT Center for International Studies "and other research groups serving the military establishment."

Among the innumerable examples of military-university cooperation in sociology, Bowers cites one that is of particular interest, in its own right and in connection, as we shall see, with the Harvard study. In 1951 the air force's Human Resources Research Institute (HRRI) contracted with the Bureau of Applied Social Research (BASR) at Columbia University, with Professor Kingsley Davis as principal investigator, to develop files of basic information about each of the major cities of the world. On the academic side, "these data would enable analysts to make comparative studies of urban and regional complexes. . . ."; on the military side, the data would permit the development of "more dependable methods of the selection of air targets." When Professor Davis left Columbia University he took the project with him to his Institute for International Urban and Population Research at the University of California at Berkeley.[15]

Additional information of interest about the research center can be obtained by following up some of the clues provided by Raymond Augustus Bauer and Raymond V. Bowers.

We have already seen that Raymond A. Bauer was of considerable interest to the FBI both because of his connection with the research center and his employment as a consultant by HumRRO, which did contract work for the army. The FBI took careful note of his attempt to obtain a passport for travel to France, Switzerland, and Austria "for the purpose of carrying on studies in connection with the Russian Research Center, Harvard University."[16]

By 1952 HumRRO itself had become the subject of a massive investigation by the FBI and army intelligence because they suspected that it had been designated as a prime target for Communist infiltration. The investigation throws light on the relations between the military services and the universities and, more specifically, on particular projects at Harvard and Columbia.

On December 16, 1952, FBI official M. A. Jones notified Louis Nichols that the day before an employee of HumRRO had come to FBI headquarters to discuss "new techniques in psychological warfare." He wanted to learn what techniques had been developed by the FBI to obtain "additional information from persons who for one reason or another came from behind the Iron Curtain into the territory held by the Western nations."

He was told that a request by him for more information would be entertained, but within the next few months, the FBI and military intelligence—prodded perhaps by "the indications that the McCarthy Committee will conduct hearings regarding HumRRO in the near future"—launched an investigation of several hundred HumRRO employees because of suspicion by army intelligence that "HumRRO constitutes a prime target for Communist infiltration. . . . Should this matter become known to the press considerable publicity might result." Because of that danger, the investigations must be completed quickly and quietly: "Under no circumstances should you contact President Marvin of George Washington University and other university officials *except those individuals who are listed as confidential sources in your office*" [my emphasis].[17]

Among the documents sent to the FBI by army intelligence was its own security survey of HumRRO, prepared in January 1954. The information in that survey concerning research projects and subcontracting agencies shows that among its more important research projects were (1) "research on methods of interviewing foreign informants" and (2) "a study of the reactions of Soviet military personnel to U.S. propaganda as reported in interviews with Soviet defectors."

Most of the projects listed were undertaken by HumRRO staff members, but a number were subcontracted to other organizations—the Human Relations Area Files of Yale, the Hoover Institution at Stanford, American University, New York University, the University of Minnesota, the National Opinion Research Center at the University of Chicago—in all, a total of seventeen subcontractors, nearly all of them academic institutions. That list, however, does not begin to exhaust HumRRO's connections to the academic community. Appended to the report is a list of all consultants, most of whom were from universities, with a statement of the degree of security clearance they had been granted. There is also a list, dated April 27, 1953, of the organizations from which "HumRRO Library is currently receiving reports." Included are "Harvard University—Project on the Soviet Social System" and "Columbia University—Project AFIRM."[18]

Bowers writes that the HRRI's contract with the BASR at Columbia involved the development of a "World Urban Resources Index" of basic information on the major cities of the world. He is silent about Project AFIRM and, indeed, about any other aspect of the HRRI–BASR contract. The archives of the bureau give a glimpse of a broader relationship.

By the time BASR Project B 0390 left the bureau, twenty-five volumes of reports had been written, not all of which dealt with urbanization in the usual sociological sense. The first seven volumes of reports, several of which were written by Fred Iklé, who later became a high official in the Department of Defense, dealt with the effects of the bombing of large cities in West Germany and Eastern Europe.

While the studies were based on historical episodes of World War II, they were quite concerned with a contemporary problem. As Iklé wrote in his report "The Long-Range Effect of Destruction upon Urban Population Distribution Compared with the Short-Range Effect: Hamburg as an Illustrative Case": "The population displacement in Hamburg, both short and long-range, gives an approximation of the demographic effects of an atomic bomb (of the size exploded in Japan) in a large city." In general the conclusions of the reports were rather reassuring. Not long after the bombings, the social and demographic patterns of the cities reverted to their prewar tendencies.

Bowers's description of the World Urban Resources Index as enabling "analysts to make comparative studies of urban and regional complexes and develop more dependable methods for the selection of air targets" is expanded by Kingsley Davis, in his progress report on the project, March 1, 1952:

> The idea of the Index is this: To gather and transcribe into a systematically arranged file the quantitative data for the cities of the world with over 100,000 inhabitants. By a logical and readily accessible arrangement of the file, quick reference can be had to any particular city or to any particular aspect of all cities or a limited class of cities. . . . The selection of data to be included in the files has been made from two points of view: (1) information important for military intelligence, and (2) information important for economic, political, sociological, and social psychological purposes. In most cases, these two points of view result in the selection of identical types of data, but we will necessarily be aided by detailed instructions from the Human Resources Research Institute and the operational agencies in the determination of military relevance.[19]

We know that the Harvard Project on the Soviet Social System was largely dependent on the interviewing of Soviet DPs. We know, too, from the FBI documents on HumRRO, that Columbia was involved in a project called AFIRM, about which Bowers is silent. What was AFIRM, and what connection, if any, did it have with the Harvard project?

The description of Columbia Project B 0390 reads: "Urban Analysis Project (Air Force). This research on urban analysis methods is a distinct part of the overall Columbia–Air Force Project which includes a section on interview methodology (B 0391)."

AFIRM, which was also directed by Kingsley Davis, yielded five volumes of reports. Volume 1 is concerned largely with instructions to interviewers in Germany about how to handle their sources, for the most part German soldiers who had returned after spending some time in Soviet prisoner-of-war camps. To help train the interviewers, written reports evaluating their performance were required. These were called the [Project] WRINGER Report Evaluation Forms and were to be filled out by the Directorate of Intelligence Personnel Headquarters, USAF. Another form, to be filled out by the questioners immediately after the interview, dealt with interviewing techniques:

> Check whether you used this technique with the source?
> 11) a) Shared common experiences with Source
>   b) Had to "squeeze" Source to get information . . .
>   f) Impressed on Source common interest in aiding struggle against Russia
> Why did the source agree to cooperate?
>   Wants favors from U.S.
>   Tell of experience
>   Revenge
>   Feel important
>   Curiosity
>   Payment
>   Response to orders or fear of U.S.
>   Help the West

Volume 2 consisted of reports and memoranda on a variety of subjects, including technical advice to the Harvard Russian Research Center, written to Professor Davis by Dean Manheimer and Lee Wiggins of the BASR staff. Of special interest is their progress report of December 14, 1950, on methodological research:

> The work being done for the Air Force . . . is to provide the research groundwork for possible improvements in the techniques used in intelligence, target selection, and psychological warfare, insofar as these have social and social-psychological aspects. . . . On the side of interview methodology, our first task was to work with the Harvard Russian Research Center in connection with its project for interviewing Soviet personnel in Germany.

The mutuality of interests was emphasized in the hope for "close liaison with intelligence officers of the Air Force, both for the purpose of getting indispensable suggestions from them as to what they view their main problems to be and for the purpose of aiding them in understanding and putting to use any results that we may obtain."

The BASR also produced a number of reports for the United States Information Agency on the content and audience of Voice of America and other foreign broadcasts in Poland, Czechoslovakia, Hungary, Russia, and Bulgaria, based on interviews with people from those countries made by Foreign News Service, Inc. Grateful acknowledgement was offered to Alex Inkeles, David Gleicher, and Raymond A. Bauer, senior research staff members of the Harvard Russian Research Center, who were deeply involved in their own interviewing program.[20]

There was considerable collaboration between the Harvard Russian Research Center and the BASR in trading information and training personnel in both sophisticated methodological refinements and in the nuts and bolts of interviewing. In these matters the intelligence agencies had a deep and obvious interest. The universities also had their interests; they were not always identical, but, in Kingsley Davis's words, "these two points of view result in the selection of identical types of data."

One of the problems that had to be met was the selection of persons to be interviewed. This had a political, as well as intellectual and methodological, side. How were the United States authorities, and those of the other governments in the Western zone, to be convinced of the importance of the research task? How were the Soviet DPs, divided into many antagonistic political groups, to be convinced to suspend their animosities at least to the point of cooperating with their questioners? There was a new party to the enterprise—the organizations of émigrés. What was in it for them? Harvard needed their cooperation, but what could it offer to obtain it?

How important—and sensitive—the interviewing of DPs was for the research center may be seen from the assignment given to Professor Talcott Parsons, whose role in the gestation and early years of the center was as important as that of Clyde Kluckhohn.

Parsons, of the Social Relations Department, was without doubt the preeminent American sociologist of his time. Others excelled him in the application of quantitative methods to social analysis, but none rivaled him in influence as a theorist, either in the scope of his theory or in the systematic attempt to apply it to the description and analysis of all parts of a social system, from small, "simple," face-to-face relationships to massive, complex systems like the United States and the Soviet Union. His writings were the official canon of Parsonian structural-functional analysis, and they influenced the research and writing of an extraordinarily large number of glossators. The agenda he set was not confined to the highest levels of abstraction; considerable attention was paid both by Parsons and his followers to the analysis of social problems that seemed to follow logically from his theoretical formulations. Parsonian theory, in short, did not stand alone; it implied a set of social problems and suggestions for their solution.

Parsons was one of the original members of the Executive Committee of the Russian Research Center. The "official story" of the center's Harvard interview project, and Parsons's role in it, is as follows:

> Unfortunately, various attempts to do scholarly research within the USSR were blocked by the Soviet government. It has been possible to support field study in adjacent or related areas such as Finland, Czechoslovakia, Poland, and Yugoslavia. . . . During the summer of 1948 Professor Parsons made an initial exploration of the possibilities of an interview program in Europe with Soviet escapees. The following summer Professor Fainsod and a student assistant undertook a highly successful pilot study with Munich as headquarters. This led to discussions with Dr. Raymond Bowers, Director of the Human Resources Research Institute of the United States Air Force, on a substantial field project. The Human Resources Research Institute agreed to support an intensive program which was to be basic research rather than intelligence research. . . .
>
> While reports are submitted to the Human Relations Research Institute, these are all non-classified because Harvard University does not accept, in peacetime, Government contracts involving the classification of research materials or findings.

In short, the flow of influence ran from the research center to the Human Resources Research Institute, and the raison d'être of the research center was basic research, not intelligence research. We have already seen that this is, at best, a partial description. Perhaps we can learn more if we inquire further into the work done in the summer of 1948 by Professor Parsons, who made an "initial exploration" of the interview program. What did he do? Whom did he see? What did he discuss? Fortunately, it is possible to give reasonably full answers to these questions because Parsons wrote at least ten letters during that time to Clyde Kluckhohn. They were handwritten; Kluckhohn then had them typed and forwarded to Merle Fainsod, who was himself sent to Germany as a scout for the research center.[21] The first of the letters is dated London, June 19, 1948; the tenth, Salzburg, August 22, 1948.

Between the first and tenth letters, Parsons wrote to Kluckhohn from Frankfurt, Berlin, and Stockholm; his letters covered meetings he had in those cities, and in Garmisch and Heidelberg as well, with officials of the Office of Military Government of the United States for Germany (OMGUS), the State Department, and the intelligence agencies; with officials of the intelligence agencies of other governments; and with a number of émigrés themselves.

He was, in his own words, doing a "press agent job" for the research center with the American officials, who were needed to run interference among the émigrés. Those officials were in a position to provide such cooperation if they desired, because they had been using the DPs for intelligence purposes for some time and had amassed reams of information—some false, some true, much of it rumor—about the background of potential informants for both Harvard and the government. Whether it was Parsons's persuasiveness that did the trick or the demands of the situation, the needed cooperation was provided.

The letters stress a number of points. One of them, raised in the very first of the letters (London, June 19, 1948) is the connection with the émigrés themselves. Parsons and the research center had knowledge of some of the émigrés even before Parsons's discussions in Europe. On June 27, 1948, writing from Frankfurt, Parsons told Kluckhohn that he had phoned one of the Soviet émigrés, Dudin, and had spent the night with him at his home in Immenstadt, from which he and his host had been picked up the next morning by a car provided by U.S. Army Intelligence. His host was working with American intelligence officers in "political orientation" matters but had been in correspondence with Parsons before Parsons's arrival in Germany. He had been a language professor at the University of Kiev and had helped edit Ukrainian- and Russian-language newspapers during the German occupation. In 1943 in Berlin, he wrote radio scripts for the Nazi Propaganda Ministry.

Parsons also met at least two other émigrés who had been relatively high-ranking Soviet officials, one in the army, Colonel Vladimir Pozdnakoff, who had been captured by the Germans and then joined the Vlasov movement. The other Parsons thought it best not to identify in a letter: "Let's call him Mr. N." All were now "working up materials" for Lt. Col. Theodore F. Hoffman, whom Parsons met, who was in command of "a special intelligence school for Russian experts. . . ; some of the men there have had a year at Columbia." Hoffman was "a very congenial young fellow who seemed anxious to play ball with us." He was not under Theatre Command but reported directly to military intelligence in Washington. Hoffman and other military colleagues felt that "Dudin and a few of his confreres would be more useful to the U.S. if brought over." They would "clearly have to be given jobs at Harvard— but naturally I was very cautious on that score. Nevertheless, we might consider something of the sort." If that could not be arranged, he had two other suggestions: (1) that someone on the research center staff fluent in Russian be sent to Germany for several months to interview a large number of émigrés, a suggestion that, though "feasible," would require "a good deal of clearing with intelligence etc."; (2) that some of the émigrés be commissioned to write reports on special subjects.

In Heidelberg Parsons saw Colonel Schow, deputy director of intelligence in the European Command. Schow was "cordial." He had been in touch with John Paton Davies, Jr., of the State Department, "who was here a few weeks ago. He thinks there should be a coordinated program for bringing these Russians to the U.S. Naturally I didn't mention the difficulties we had run into. He said that if any of us knew whom they wanted they could in most cases be brought in under the new D.P. law. They would of course have to be screened by MIS [military intelligence] in this theatre. In cases like Mr. N. who are on forged papers there might be serious difficulties." Parsons felt the urgency of the situation: "In general this seems to be something damned important that we ought to follow up—I should think also pretty fast. I wonder whether you ought not to do some work on the Washington end—find out just where Davies' plans stand. . . . If I knew the result I might be able to do more at this end. Also do you want to even think of the possibility of bringing any of these people to Harvard?"[22]

Through Harvard professor Carl J. Friedrich, who was in Berlin at the time, Parsons met some "useful" Germans who promised to put him in touch with a new group of Russians in Stuttgart who "claim to have a functioning information service from there [Russia] now. I am to stop there on the way to Salzburg and meet some of them."

Possibly the most interesting of Parsons's contacts with émigrés was Nicholas Poppe. Through Friedrich, Parsons met Lawrence de Neufville, deputy director for OMGUS, who told him that the British had snapped up most of the Nazis' German experts on Russia and installed them in a hotel in Herford, near Hannover. They were reluctant to talk about the matter to U.S. intelligence. But, as Parsons wrote Kluckhohn, de Neufville finally "came up with the name of our friend Poppe. He told me that Poppe was under the protection of the British Intelligence people but they want to get him to the United States. He is very hot for them because he is explicitly wanted by the Russians." An intelligence officer named Rhodes had confirmed de Neufville's story:

> The dossier he had on his desk on P. [Poppe] was by the way marked Top Secret. He told me that when General Walsh [chief of intelligence in Europe] was in Washington this spring he tried to get the State Dept. to admit P. but failed and felt he was lucky that they wanted to keep the case open.

Rhodes told Parsons that if "he [Poppe] can get into the US the British will take care of letting him out of Germany. . . . Rhodes was most emphatic on the importance of keeping it entirely confidential. I should think Kennan was almost the only channel that could help. Maybe [Edward S.] Mason—Kennan."

Who was Poppe, and why the interest in him? How did Parsons know about him? At the end of December 1946, he was being hunted by the U.S. authorities for extradition to Russia; he had worked for the Germans since 1942. By the spring of 1949, he was working for U.S.

Army Intelligence. His Counter-Intelligence Corps file card contained the notation "Nothing Derogatory." He had been in touch with the Far Eastern Institute at the University of Washington in search of a job and had been promised one contingent upon obtaining an immigration visa and admission to the United States. Having done so, he spent the rest of his academic career in Seattle.

Born in 1897 in China, the son of an imperial Russian consular official, he studied in St. Petersburg and by 1925 was professor of Mongolian at Petrograd University. By 1932 he had conducted research in Mongolia and became a member of the Soviet Academy of Sciences. At the time of the German invasion of Russia, he moved with his family to the Caucasus. With the German advance there, he became an interpreter. As the Russian counterattack began, he left with the Nazis. He joined the Germans because he wanted to emigrate to Great Britain or the United States, he said, though he "did not have the faintest idea if and how this could be accomplished." While in the Caucasus he accepted an offer from the SS to go with his family to Kislovodsk and Nal'chik, which had many "Mountain Jews," whom he calls Jews by religion but Iranian by ethnicity. The SS wanted to kill all Jews, but the Mountain Jews were saved, according to Poppe, because of a memorandum he wrote establishing the fact that the czars had never considered them to be Jews.

He was in Lwow in the spring of 1943, when it was decided that he should go to Berlin, where "specialists on Soviet nationalities were badly needed." He was assigned to the Wannsee Institute, whose function was "to study various aspects of the Soviet economy, politics and science and make reports to the German government. . . . The institute was an intelligence organization," part of the apparatus of SS chief Ernst Kaltenbrunner. One of his tasks was to compile a large work on Siberian history, ethnography, culture, and natural resources. He also taught at the University of Berlin. He then worked with the East Asian Institute of Dahlem and Marienbad, but in May 1945, fearful of the advancing Russians, he went to West Germany, to the "large Böckel estate" he claimed belonged to a remote relative. Böckel is close to Herford, where the British closeted their Russian experts.

After the war he solicited help from an old acquaintance, Dr. Karl Heinrich Menges of Columbia University, who was sure there were job possibilities for Poppe in the United States. He made efforts through British intelligence to get to England, to which he could not get a visa, and, through Menges and his connections with American intelligence, to get to the United States. His Harvard connection was through Professor Serge Eliseev, whom he had known since his days in St. Petersburg. He claims to have been promised a job at Harvard, "half my salary coming from the Far Eastern Department and the other half from the Center for Russian Studies." He was informed a short time later by

Kluckhohn that "for various reasons, which [Kluckhohn] did not specify, I could not get the appointment." Before going to the University of Washington, where he was appointed, he spent the spring and summer of 1949 in Washington, D.C., under an assumed name, writing research papers for the State Department and meeting with intelligence officers and with a former official of the Nazi foreign office, Gustav Hilger.[23]

The second important theme of the Parsons letters is his discussion with U.S. military, intelligence, and political officers in Germany and Austria, and ultimately in Washington, D.C., attempting to enlist the support of the appropriate agencies to make possible the work of the research center. Parsons spoke with innumerable military intelligence officials; the officer in charge of DP affairs for OMGUS; those in charge of documents from the German Foreign Office and Chancellery archives in Berlin; the political officer of the Berlin Military Government; the secretary general of the Control Commission, U.S. Group, and the editor of the official U.S. newspaper for Germany—both of them, fortunately, from Harvard; and the chief of the Civil Administration Division of the military government, who proposed a formal connection between the Russian Research Center and his division through an appointment in military government to one of the Harvard people, provided Harvard would pay the salary: "This would certainly open all kinds of doors and should I think be taken very seriously." What Parsons learned at these meetings he passed on to Kluckhohn for further action in Cambridge and Washington.

When he was informed, for example, that plans were ready to announce the organization of a Western-sponsored university in Berlin as soon as the crisis over the Berlin blockade "quiets down"—an announcement in which "the American part . . . is not to be emphasized"—he suggested that Kluckhohn speak to Provost Buck about a Harvard connection with the new university. Parsons wrote Kluckhohn that he had been assured there would be no difficulty about "getting access to intelligence material at least as far as this side [American intelligence in Germany] is concerned." Those intelligence reports were sent on to Washington, and it might be possible to obtain them through the good offices of George Kennan.

The Information Control Division of the army, which maintained a running analysis of Russian propaganda as part of its counterpropaganda campaign, would be pleased to have the research center do a long-term study of Soviet propaganda and would make its material available. He met with uniformly favorable responses from U.S. officials in Germany and Austria: "I have the definite feeling that they very much welcome what we are doing and think it may help them. There was none of the standoffishness and suspicion I gather you have encountered in Washington. One might say these people are too close to the firing line to be snooty." Parsons also established connections with nongovernmental organizations and persons—with the German Social Democratic Party, which had excellent "political intelligence" on the Soviet Zone ("I think we can arrange to get some of their mimeographed reports and of course our man here could go to their center and interview the people"); with a German sociologist who had studied Russian forced laborers during the war; with German writers and with *New York Times* correspondents.

He wrote from Salzburg after a particularly important meeting with Carmel Offie, a high-ranking official in the Office of Policy Coordination, which, though located in the State Department, was funded by the CIA to collect intelligence data and run covert operations. Offie spoke to him about "a whole group of . . . Russian informants and German experts on Russia" working for him "in some segregated place." Parsons wrote Kluckhohn what the three most important tasks of the research center were: (1) "One is the DP thing (bring to the U.S.) through Davies and all that. My own feeling is that we ought not to try to do too much on our own but definitely ought to be in on what is done." Davies "had got both a promise of money and official approval for his project of a Russian experts' center. . . . I think you probably ought to get in touch with him right away." (2) "Second is the matter of representation here." He suggested Merle Fainsod. (3) "The third thing is at a high level to try to [gain?] access to some of the documentary materials available in Washington. I think it can and should be done." He also recommended, after meeting with General Balmer, deputy high commissioner in Austria, that someone on the research center staff be sent to Austria. Kluckhohn and he should use the September meeting of the American Association for the Advancement of Science in Washington to discuss "the clearance problem" with the proper authorities. "I am more convinced than ever that the D.P. operation ought to be handled in a relatively large framework," he wrote in the final letter of the series.

On his return to the United States he reported to the Carnegie Corporation. President Dollard described the discussion Parsons had with him and John W. Gardner:

> Parsons made a very encouraging report on a series of conversations which he had with our military and political people in Berlin during the past summer. He said that by and large they were very anxious to cooperate with enterprises like the Russian Research Institute [*sic*] and promised every facilitation to any Harvard personnel that might come over. They also gave Parsons the names of key people in Washington whose sympathetic cooperation would be important to the Center.[24]

Germany was very much on Parsons's mind. On July 1, 1948, he had written Kluckhohn that "Berlin is the major center of all the political pulling and hauling that is going on between the Soviet influenced and the Western influenced Germans." He returned to the theme when he was visited by William W. Marvel of the Carnegie staff in late September 1952:

> Talcott Parsons has a present concern which he told WM that he had been meaning to communicate to JG [John Gardner] for some time but he never quite had the opportunity. This is the idea that the foundations and universities interested in area studies should be getting themselves concerned a little bit about German affairs. Parsons apparently thinks that ten or fifteen years hence Germany is not going to seem the pygmy alongside the Russian monster she seems today. . . . Presumably, he would suggest an attack on the problem something like that represented by the Russian Center.[25]

Parsons approved attaching universities to the intelligence apparatus of government—covertly; bringing persons accused of collaboration with the Nazis to the United States—covertly; using Harvard connections to influence government officials to ease their entry to the United States—covertly; breaking down the distinction between research and intelligence. As late as 1974 he was serving as consultant to the CIA on the effects of the student rebellions of the 1960s and on the personality of potential CIA recruits.[26]

The record of Talcott Parsons may puzzle many people who know that he had "security" problems with some agencies of government. Parsons may have been bewildered. How could he, loyal soldier as he was, be suspected of disloyalty? All that was needed to dispel the doubts was to tell of the many services he had performed. He could have done it; Harvard could have done it; the intelligence agencies with which he worked could have done it. But as far as the documents now available reveal, none did. Why not? Parsons would not only have been taken off the hook, but would have been honored by those who thought that scholars should live in Camelot, not in ivory towers. But to have revealed these matters would show the existence of an intelligence-university complex that would have embarrassed the parties and jeopardized the relationship. Parsons chose to fight communism and Russia in a particular way—favored by some, disapproved by others. The very qualities that commended him to the former were proof to the latter of his untrustworthiness.

———

The Munich Institute for the Study of the USSR was vital to the work of the Harvard Russian Research Center. It paved the way for the research center among Soviet émigrés, established contacts that enabled the center to obtain informants, and provided a number of special reports on selected Soviet problems for the center. From early 1951 until 1971, when its CIA connection was revealed by Senator Clifford Case, it received financial assistance from the CIA, but before that it operated under the intellectual imprimatur, and with the financial assistance, of the Harvard Russian Research Center.[27]

Some ambiguity shrouds the early history and even the description of the Munich Institute. In 1959 Alex Inkeles and Raymond Bauer of the research center described it as an institute "composed of Soviet scholars of the wartime and postwar emigration . . . [including] persons of the widest range of political and nationality affiliations that it appeared possible to assimilate and hold together in a single group." In 1960 it was described in its own journal as having been organized ten years before by eight Soviet scholars, under the direction of Boris Alexandrovich Yakovlev, to establish a library, organize conferences, and distribute publications having to do with "the theory and practice of various aspects of the state and social order of the USSR." In 1983 it was said that both the Munich Institute and Radio Liberty were funded by the American Committee for the Liberation of the Peoples of Russia, Inc., established in New York on February 8, 1951, later called the Radio Liberty Committee. Ostensibly financed by "endowment" funds but actually, as Senator Case revealed, by the CIA, the committee had a New York office and also a European office at the same address as the Munich Institute. In addition, it has been agreed that the covert operations branch of the CIA, the Office of Policy Coordination, provided "guidance" and "aid" in setting up the Munich Institute.

In the spring of 1950, George Fischer, a Harvard junior fellow and son of journalist Louis Fischer and Markoosha Fischer, who had recommended the use of Yakovlev's library to the Russian Research Center, and Frederick Wyle, a Harvard student, were sent to Europe on behalf of the Harvard Refugee Interview Project to solidify Harvard's relationship with the émigré community in Germany. Fischer met in England with British experts in the field and with U.S. State Department officers; in Germany, his way having been paved by Clyde Kluckhohn, he met with the Director of U.S. Air Force Intelligence. He was also advised by Inkeles and Bauer on the use of Yakovlev and other émigré contacts and on relations with State Department officers Francis B. Stevens and Frederick Barghoorn, who were setting up their own interview project. But Fischer's most important assignment was to help establish an émigré organization that would legitimate the Harvard interview project to Soviet DPs and establish a system by which Harvard could obtain respondents and informants.

The official reports and correspondence of Wyle and Fischer and the replies they received, particularly those of Kluckhohn, show that their task was above all a political one—to organize, so far as it was possible, a coalition of anti-Soviet dissident factions. The problems were formidable; they included well-nigh unbridgeable breaches among the refugees themselves and fear on their part that Harvard, suspected of being

under leftist influence, would jeopardize their security by providing information about their wartime activities to both Soviet and U.S. officials.
The rumors that the research center would inform on DPs to either Soviet or U.S. intelligence authorities were being overcome by the "construction of a rather complex contact system built upon strict anonymity,
and the sponsorship of various respected personalities in the place of
refugee consultation," Wyle reported to Bauer on November 15, 1950.

The "bigger problem," with which Fischer and he would continue
to wrestle, was "the great amount of political dissension within the refugee community." Too close a reliance upon the Munich Institute would
court the danger of alienating some political groups not represented on
the institute's council; every effort was made, therefore, to supplement
the informants and respondents provided by the council with those obtained from other political groups or directly from the camps through
"local contact men."[28]

Supplementing the list of informants provided by the Munich Institute meant going to sources like U.S. military intelligence. In a memorandum on his conversations with Russian members of the faculty at the
military intelligence school at Regensburg, Professor Merle Fainsod reported that, thanks to the cooperation of commanding officer Lt. Col.
T. E. Hoffman, he had on earlier occasions spoken to Dr. Mylk, who
had escaped from the Soviet zone as recently as 1946, and with Dr. N.
[Nyman]. Most recently he had spoken with members of Hoffman's staff—
Krypton, Krylov, Osipov, Vasiliev. Krypton, an émigré, was especially
impressive: "I would strongly suggest that Mr. Shimkin [Dimitri Shimkin,
a senior official of the research center in Cambridge] get in touch with
him. There is a distinct possibility that Mr. Krypton may come to America, and I have urged him to contact the Institute [*sic*] if he does." Through
the good offices of Frederick Barghoorn of Yale, Fainsod was put in
touch with another member of the Regensburg faculty, Joseph Baritz,
an economist and planner. Military intelligence was willing to have him
prepare materials for the research center, and he had made a favorable
impression on both Barghoorn and Fainsod, who recommended him to
Alex Dallin of the research center. So, too, had "Kunta (Avtorkhanov)
. . . and Shteppa," both of them anxious to get to the United States.[29]

The cooperation of Lt. Col. Hoffman and the work of George Fischer
in obtaining that cooperation were of critical importance in getting the
Refugee Interview Project off the ground. Cooperation involved more
than sympathetic understanding on the part of military intelligence; it
involved the contribution of informed personnel. And gratitude on the
part of Harvard involved more than an expression of politeness; it involved notifying the military of the plans of the project. Kluckhohn wrote
Hoffman of Fischer's acknowledgement of "the generous assistance" of
Detachment R, which assured the cooperation of several members of
Hoffman's staff—Grigorich, Mylk, Kunta, Redlich, Aldan, Osipov, and

Artemiav. "You may be interested in some of our present plans," Kluck-hohn wrote as a kind of quid pro quo, and he proceeded to tell Hoffman the tentative interviewing schedule, the purpose of the study, and the role of the Russian Library in Munich. Hoffman was kept informed of personnel and administrative changes in the Refugee Interview Project and of the changed relationship of their research center to the Munich Institute. That Hoffman had a special connection with the Munich Institute was made clear by Kluckhohn: "I will be very grateful to you if you could transmit a translation of the text of this letter to every member of the Council of the Institute."

If Kluckhohn left any loose ends in his letters to Col. Hoffman, Alex Inkeles knotted them up. He described the objectives, personnel, and scheduling of the "Defector Interview Project" in considerably greater detail than Kluckhohn had. He hoped that the information he had provided "can be of use to you in discussing the Defector Interview Project with others interested, and in extending your always welcome advice and assistance to the Russian Research Center in Germany and to the Russian Library of Munich."

Col. Hoffman was important for the Harvard refugee interview program and for Harvard's possible use of refugees in other ways as well. Talcott Parsons, after testing the political and intelligence waters in the summer of 1948, told Hoffman that he and Kluckhohn had had a long talk with Evron Kirkpatrick of the State Department about plans for establishing a general research center utilizing "a considerable number of DPs. We hope this plan works out." If so, the DPs would be accessible to the Russian Research Center. One of the DPs Harvard was interested in was Ivar Nyman. On July 7, 1948, Kluckhohn wrote Parsons in Germany to be sure to interview Nyman in Oberammergau. Parsons probably did, for Col. Hoffman later wrote to Harvard's President Conant recommending Nyman for a position at the Russian Research Center or elsewhere.[30]

The solution to the problems of the political organization of the DPs required major changes in the structure of the Munich Institute. In this, George Fischer was a major architect. At stake was not only the success of the Refugee Interview Project but "the future relationship of the Center with the Soviet refugees in Germany" aside from that project, as Fischer explained to Fainsod. The Academic Council of the Russian Library had not proved to be a success for both personal reasons—some members had thrown their weight around, and other significant people had not been invited to join—and structural reasons—the council had no real control over the operations of the library, which remained under the direction of Yakovlev, who was well known as the leader of one political faction. Under pressure from Fischer, Yakovlev agreed to create a new organization with standing under German law, which would make it possible for the Russian Research Center to "engage in extensive collaboration, including financial," without constant fear of the council's disintegration. The act of incorporation required obtaining seven signatories; Fischer succeeded in convincing Yakovlev that "while Harvard and I personally had no intention of effecting individual selections, it was most important for our project to maintain a balance as regards political affiliation." Fischer drew up the list "of the men who finally became the founders—and therefore members of its Council—of the new organization," now called the Institute for Research on the History and Institutions of the USSR.

The very first meeting of the council was with Boris I. Nicolavesky, who was touring West Germany after attending the Berlin Congress of Cultural Freedom with Yakovlev; Nicolavesky had been instrumental in getting some of the members of the council to sign up.[31]

Given the shadowy pasts of the eight persons (including Yakovlev) in the directorate of the Munich Institute and the deceptiveness of the records, it is difficult to obtain full information regarding them. A reasonably complete account is possible of four; skimpier accounts, of the others. Briefly, the record shows:

All eight, including Yakovlev, the director, assumed new identities and shed old the way a snake sheds its skin; Yakovlev alone used thirty-three aliases. All eight had collaborated with the Nazis. Several had participated in the Vlasov movement, and some were brought to the United States after service with military intelligence in Germany and with the CIA. A number received financial assistance from the East European Fund of the Ford Foundation.

Yakovlev and another director, Kunta, sent Inkeles the minutes of the meeting at which the council accepted the research center's plan for the conduct of its interviews.[32]

By 1950 the Munich Institute had been granted official recognition as an academic corporation. Some political problems remained; for instance, the rivalry between prewar and postwar Soviet émigrés was still so great that the right-wing was likely to call any group that worked with the postwar DPs "Soviet *agents*."[33] But the financial problem was the major one to be solved. In the short run it was handled by Harvard, which paid for services incurred in the interview project and for special research essays.[34]

The financial arrangement between Harvard and the institute was not put in "writing [in] any kind of contract, or any detail in any formal document." The Harvard financial office and the center preferred to "regard it as an informal arrangement, to be made in part orally and in part through informal correspondence. In particular" it was not desired "to involve the University or the Contract Office in the signing of any papers or making of any agreements." R. M. Hinchman, the university contracts officer, wanted the center to provide a justification for the monthly fee to the institute in case there should be objections from the air force accountants. He felt that the justification would "considerably fascillitate [*sic*] the extent to which we would be able to perform operations of a similar nature, that is, operations which are outside the usual chain of operations in government contracts. Therefore we would benefit all around." He provided detailed advice on how the payments to the institute would be handled and how the billing, particularly for advances, would be done.

William F. Diefenbach, who handled financial matters for the research center in Munich, kept detailed records of the fiscal arrangements between the center and the institute.[35] The money paid to the institute for its services was obtained by Harvard from its air force contract that financed the entire Soviet Social System project. The financial arrangement with Harvard did not last very long. In the fall of 1950, Raymond Bauer informed the center that the institute was in negotiations with Spencer Williams of the CIA–sponsored American Committee for the Liberation of the Peoples of Europe, who was exploring the possibility of uniting the political groups among the Soviet émigrés. When Harvard finished the field phase of the interview project in March 1951, it ceased to pay the institute for research papers.

But not all relationships between the two organizations came to an end. Fischer was a consultant to the State Department's Office of Intelligence Research, under the direction of Evron Kirkpatrick. In that capacity he urged, "both for research and long-range morale and political reasons," continued U.S. support for Soviet émigrés in Germany, the basis for such support being Harvard's "initial exploitation of the defectors." On August 18, 1950, Fischer wrote Kluckhohn that Kirkpatrick thought that funds for the institute could probably be arranged from both the State Department and the CIA, and that "such government-financed research by Soviet refugee experts might well be channeled through the Russian Research Center. This may be desirable both for purposes of cover and in view of the possible difficulties of a government contract with any non-U.S. establishment like the Munich Institute." Whatever the difficulties, they were surmounted, and Fischer was able to tell the State Department that Kluckhohn was delighted that the State Department would now be the sponsor of the Munich Institute and that Harvard had been of service in the affair: "Its own research project was to a considerable extent a 'holding operation' for just such government undertakings."

A "holding operation for just such government undertakings"—both by nature and nurture the research center was the child of the intelligence agencies and the universities. There were times when it responded to its social science parent, as when Fischer wrote Kluckhohn, Inkeles, and Bauer that it would be necessary to place more limits on the military than the military wanted to place on itself. The refugees had been promised confidentiality; that promise would be broken if military personnel, "in civvies or otherwise," were on the center staff as some of the military wished. Nor did Fischer have total confidence in the ability of military counterintelligence to do an effective job of screening institute and center employees to weed out Soviet agents and sympathizers; as a test of the Counter-Intelligence Corps (CIC), he had had Yakovlev himself checked, and he was "far from sure that he himself may not be a Soviet agent." And there were occasions when the center staff and military intelligence officers themselves were reminded that social science research and intelligence research, while certainly not antagonistic, were different. Writing to Brigadier General M. Lewis, director of intelligence, U.S. Air Forces in Europe, Inkeles set forth the difference between the two and expressed his conviction that conflict was unnecessary:

> I trust that you will be completely frank with us in indicating whether or not any particular request we might make is either unreasonable or cannot be met without undue strain for your staff. At the same time, we will naturally be considerably dependent upon assistance from you and your staff if we are to successfully fulfill our mission under our contract with the Air Forces. . . . Although our operation is defined as being primarily a fundamental social science investigation, having as its final purpose the construction of a working model of the functioning of Soviet society, we naturally expect to uncover a considerable amount of material which may be of immediate and direct relevance to Air Force Intelligence operations. This being the case, I should like to indicate that we naturally stand fully prepared to make every effort to make such information available to you and your staff in the shortest possible time and in the most useable form. In addition, as you may see from some of our working memoranda, we have already begun to include in our questionnaires a variety of questions which have specific relevance to the interests of Air Force Intelligence as we understand its requirements. Naturally, the detailed working out of such direct collaboration . . . should be left until such time as I can meet with your staff to discuss these matters directly.[36]

His concern for the widest possible collaboration was effusively seconded by Kluckhohn. The research center's problem, how to accommodate the somewhat contradictory claims of both parents, proved rather easy to solve, in part perhaps because the political views and the scholarly interests of important staff personnel were quite compatible. When, for example, Serge Belosselsky of the Russian American Union for Protection and Aid to Russians Outside of Russia, Inc., wrote an open letter to President Conant, complaining that his compatriots were fearful that their confidences would not be respected, Ivan D. London, in charge of the research center's program of interviewing Russians in the United States, attempted to mollify him by his assurance that "our common enemy is communism. It is truly a pity that ill-considered action [the open letter to Conant] should be allowed to hinder what should be a joint fight." On the same issue, the interviewing of Russian DPs in the United States, Dallin wrote to Inkeles: "A final point: did you plan to pay the DPs here something too for the interviews, or shall we try to get them 'for the sake of the cause'?"[37]

For some, subscribing to the "cause" was no doubt a political commitment; for others, the price that had to be paid to get money from the air force to pursue the research center's "scholarly" interests. In any case, it led to the collection of intelligence information by the center that was hardly of decisive importance in a study of how the Soviet social system works.

At a planning session of research center staff members on July 18, 1950, a report was made on a recent meeting of Inkeles and Bauer with officials at Maxwell Field, at which Inkeles and Bauer were under two types of pressure: "one type from the military dimension, by which Alex means Air Force Intelligence and the people actually in Europe whose guests we will be, one type based on a misconception of what social science is in very general terms. . . . This can be straightened out over time." The air force assumed that "we can produce things that are useful to Air Force Intelligence. This doesn't mean hardware, but it does mean the sort of thing that Air Force people are interested in. They don't have the kind of data they want and they'd like as much of it as they can get. The only possible answer to that is that *naturally* [my emphasis] insofar as we can get such data which will not interfere with our prime mission that's fine." Inkeles let the staff know the situation "so that (1) anybody who wants to quit can quit, (2) anybody who is not used to the way of the world will be prepared for a certain number of day-to-day problems and difficulties of just this kind." The research center staff were reminded that "we promised Clyde that a memo would be gotten out indicating to each staff member our desire that they keep in mind the relevance of their material to the Air Force and . . . U.S. policy in general." This was to be worked into the regular staff reports and analysis; in addition, they were to keep " 'poop' sheets of anything from a few lines to several pages which could be forwarded directly to the Air Force when they thought of or came across relevant materials."

On November 15, 1951, Brigadier General W. M. Garland, assistant for production, Directorate of Intelligence, U.S. Air Force, reported to Raymond V. Bowers concerning a recent meeting between Kluckhohn and officers of the Directorate of Intelligence that was so "fruitful and productive" that "I hope this excellent method" of facilitating "direct contact between outside research personnel and operating personnel who will use the research product . . . will be repeated and extended." Many of the research center's "proposed interim studies as listed on page six of the 21 August 1951 Analysis Plan" were so interesting that it was difficult to express "our priority of interest." Some air force concerns were rather remote from a social science investigation of the functioning of the Soviet social system: for example, determining Soviet concepts of the employment of air power, secret Soviet doctrine as distinguished from doctrines proclaimed by Lenin and Stalin, and the recruiting methods, indoctrination, discipline, training, security measures, and morale of the air force and the naval air force.

The Air Targets Division had its special requirements "for social science information." These included information on the bombing of those targets that "would maximize positive psychological reactions toward the attacking force," estimates of the positive and negative effects of warning potential target areas and the degree of panic reactions to "various weights of air attack," and recommendations of specific military operations that would intensify cleavages between the Soviet government and the Soviet people.

The relation between psychological attitudes and sociological contexts was of special importance to the research center, given its interdisciplinary character. It is a relationship that can be studied in a wide variety of situations, but the center was not interested in the full range of these situations. As Inkeles wrote to Wyle:

> Another matter! We are interested in getting at an interesting psychological dimension in certain social situations; namely, how do Russians behave when forced to live for extended periods of time in small groups in very close contact with each other? For example, isolated weather stations, long trips in small boats, submarines, and small remote communities of one type or another, etc. for special purposes, etc. If you can get a list of people who can serve a sources of information in this area, we should be happy to have one.[38]

Interviewing Soviet DPs—at the core of the Russian Research Center's major enterprise—and facilitating their entry drew it into direct connection with military intelligence and the appropriate intelligence bureaus of the State Department. Two of the most important State Department personnel in that enterprise were John Paton Davies, Jr., and Evron Kirkpatrick, under the direction of George Kennan. The complementarity, not to say identity, of interests led to the collaboration of Davies with Kluckhohn and Parsons, in which the role of chief matchmaker was almost certainly played by John Gardner of Carnegie.

At the time Gardner was canvassing universities to find the one best suited to house an interdisciplinary center in Russian affairs, the State Department was already well along with plans to bring to the United States a significant number of DPs to act as informants. On March 4, 1948, Davies, of Kennan's Policy Planning Staff, produced a "Secret" report entitled "Utilization of Refugees from the Soviet Union in U.S. National Interest." It was approved by Undersecretary of State Robert A. Lovett and passed along to the State–Army–Navy–Air Force Coordinating Committee (SANACC), the Office of Intelligence Research, the National Security Council, and the CIA "for implementation." The plan was to "increase defections among the elite of the Soviet World and to utilize refugees from the Soviet World in the national interests of the U.S."

The effect of such "desertions" was clearly spelled out; it "would create wide repercussions in the ruling classes of the Soviet World. All-pervasive distrust and suspicion would be aggravated, denunciations would be compounded and repressive measures multiplied. Such a chain of events would have a stifling effect on the creative capabilities of the Soviet World, damage its overall productive efficiency and generally tend to exert a demoralizing influence." What was damning up the hoped-for flood of refugees was the "absence of assurances of asylum for political refugees," symbolized in the agreement under which "the U.S. authorities are obligated to return deserters to the Soviet authorities." Moreover, if a refugee, despite the "inflexibility of our present immigration legislation," did manage to get to the U.S., "there is no organization charged with responsibility for assisting him to find a secure place in American society."

To increase the flow of the disaffected and at the same time add to our knowledge of the Soviet system, the State Department made a number of recommendations to "encourage the desertion of the elite of the Soviet World" and to utilize "refugee resources . . . to fill the gaps in our current official intelligence, in public information, and in our politico-psychological operations." These recommendations included prompt removal of present deterrents to DP immigration and a screening program—under the direction of the State Department, the army, the navy, the air forces, and the CIA—to select refugees and obtain documentary material "with a view to obtaining intelligence regarding the USSR and its satellites. The screening process should result in the selection of not more than 50 qualified social science scholars . . . to be brought to the U.S." The selection was to be made by "a representative of the Social Science Research Council or some other qualified body of American scholars. . . . Not more than 50 qualified specialists . . . for use as broadcasters, script writers, translators, etc., by the Voice of America and other propaganda activities" were also to be admitted. No limitation at all was placed on the number of physicists, chemists, and other specialists in the physical sciences and technology.

Two additional recommendations of the Policy Planning Staff deserve attention. As a result of the first, SANACC, including a representative of the Department of Justice, was given the responsibility of studying the "security and legal problems involved in bringing these three categories of selected refugees to the U.S. and with recommending measures necessary to facilitate their movement to and residence in the U.S." The second recommendation was that the government should encourage efforts by America scholars and educational institutions to establish in Washington a "social science institute composed of refugee and American scholars for the purpose of doing basic research studies on the Soviet World." To that end, the "Department of State . . . [was] charged with maintaining contact with the academic world." As to how "the mass of refugees . . . can be effectively utilized . . . CIA should be requested to prepare a report and recommendations on this subject."

The Harvard authorities knew quite well what Davies and his associates were doing.

But official Washington was deeply involved in bringing German and DP specialists on Russia to the United States well before 1948, the year of the Davies memorandum, indeed, before the Cold War had officially—or unofficially—begun. The policy began even before Kennan, Davies, and Kirkpatrick took over its close supervision. In 1944 a committee of the National Academy of Sciences, working under the auspices of the Office of Scientific Research and Development and the National Advisory Committee for Aeronautics, prepared a paper on "Treatment of German Scientific Research and Engineering from the Standpoint of National Security." It was a blue-ribbon committee of corporate executives and government, corporation, and university scientists, including I. I. Rabi, Nobel laureate from Columbia. The committee proposed that German scientists not be brought to the United States, but remain at home to reconstruct German science and industry. But its reasoning provided the basis for potential change in the policy and, in addition, helps explain why the American academic community had no great reluctance to enlist in government-sponsored military projects.

The concern of German scientists during the war, the committee concluded, was not with politics or victory, but "with their future professional status." The majority were "as little influenced by Nazi teaching and doctrine as any group in the population." Indeed, the professors were "an island of nonconformity in the Nazified body politic." They withdrew during the war into "the traditional ivory tower which offered the only possibility of security." They could be expected in peacetime gladly to reenter the international scientific community and "publish as freely, even as eagerly, as had been their practice in the past." Moreover, because of their objective, realistic, and scientific attitudes about politics, they would provide for greater political stability at home; "any wholesale emigration would interfere with the rehabilitation of their nation."

There seemed to be a contradiction in the National Academy's conclusion: if the German scientists were not concerned with politics or victory, but with "professional status," from whom did they get the rewards that bestowed such status? And, as a sheer matter of fact, were the German universities into which the scientists had withdrawn really "ivory towers . . . of security" for any but collaborationists? Prominent German scientists had propounded theories of Aryan genetic superiority; party members had been given laboratories and research institutes; grants had been discriminatingly administered; professional licensing bodies refused to allow anti-Nazis to practice; Jewish and other scientists and scholars had been dismissed; elaborate screening procedures had been established; important scholars were given honorary Nazi and SS memberships. But the National Academy's conclusion that German professors were impeccably professional made it logical, once the international political situation heated up, to admit German and other specialists to the United States.

And that, in fact, was what was done.

Between May 1945 and December 1952, some 642 German scientists were brought to the United States under Project Paperclip. By 1949 they were placed at Cornell, Penn State, North Carolina State, RCA, Bausch and Lomb, AVCO, Dow Chemical, and elsewhere. During the decade of the 1950s they were placed on the faculties of Yale, Michigan State, Wisconsin, Oregon State, Minnesota, MIT, Louisville, Kansas, Washington, Chicago, and Ohio State and on the staffs of Boeing, Raytheon, Lockheed, General Electric, Rand, Northrop, RCA, Westinghouse, and other corporations. It was agreed that a "suitable statement" would be issued only after the program was in effect. On September 24, 1946, on Dean Acheson's recommendation, President Truman approved the importation of a thousand German and Austrian scientists, who were promised citizenship, financial support for their families, and other concessions.

All that really remained was to extend the number and range of admitted scholars to include social scientists and non-German specialists, especially on Eastern Europe, and to establish appropriate contacts with American universities that could use their services and those of the government intelligence apparatus for which they worked.

That was the work of Kennan, Davies, and Kirkpatrick. Kennan, head of the State Department's Policy Planning Staff, dominated policy from covert action to political warfare. The importation of German and DP specialists was to be handled in such a way that "any U.S. government responsibility . . . is not evident to unauthorized persons and that if uncovered the U.S. government can plausibly disclaim responsibility." As it happened, the Kennan operation, including the covert relations with the Carnegie Corporation and the Harvard Russian Research Center, did not have to use the technique of plausible deniability, though many facts about the operation were known to the press. Brigadier General Robert A. McClure, commander of U.S. Army psychological warfare activities in World War II and during much of the Cold War, referred to Carl D. Jackson of Time-Life and William Paley of CBS as "my right and lefthands [*sic*]. . . . [They] know more of the policy and operational side of psychological warfare than any two individuals I know of." [39]

As early as January 15, 1948, Donald McKay wrote to Donald Young, director of the Social Science Research Council (SSRC), informing him that Davies, a friend of John K. Fairbank, distinguished professor of Chinese history at Harvard and an associate of the research center, had written to Fairbank about the interest of Kennan's "small group" in the State Department in the kind of work the research center was about to undertake. Kennan's group was "independently interested" in such a project and "moderately interested" in setting it up at Harvard. Such a group in Washington would pull scarce personnel away from Harvard and Columbia, with adverse effects on serious university research. McKay told Young that Davies had just written Fairbank about his attempt to get in touch with the SSRC representative in Washington "with a view to that body's taking over the responsibility for blue-printing the form which the institute should take. The implication is that if the SSRC recommends Harvard, the State Department will go along with that." He ended by appealing to Young to meet with Fairbank, Kluckhohn, and himself to learn why "it is in the national interest" to avoid establishing another research center on Russia in Washington.

Davies was an important connection for Harvard. At the end of 1947, when relations between Harvard and Carnegie were still in flux, John Gardner wrote Kluckhohn that he had set up a meeting with Davies in New York on January 6: "I suggested that Davies bring Kennan along if Kennan has the time." By midsummer Kluckhohn, Davies, and others were in consultation about plans to bring Soviet émigrés to the United States. As Kluckhohn wrote to Davies on July 21, 1948: "If your plans for bringing Russian D.P.s and others over for your projected Experts Center have crystallized, in any way, I should be grateful if you could inform me. I hope very much that some mutually satisfactory arrangement can be worked out whereby the Russian Research Center could also have a fraction of the time of some of the people you bring over."

Davies turned the matter over to Evron Kirkpatrick. By that time, Kluckhohn had already been in touch with Kirkpatrick. One of Kluckhohn's "senior colleagues is in Germany at the moment and it would be enormously helpful to us if we could know as soon as possible how this matter stands." "This matter" was, of course, the importation of DPs in general and of Nicholas Poppe in particular.

No policy had yet been developed concerning "foreign personnel," but Kirkpatrick was sure that once the policy had been established "it will be possible to develop arrangements whereby the personnel could be made available to" the center. He anticipated a close association with universities: "We plan to have a Board of university people interested in the Russian field to help with planning and implementing the program of the Institute. This should lead to joint projects, exchange of personnel, and other procedures that would be beneficial to all concerned."

As to Nicholas Poppe, Kluckhohn had been in touch with both Kirkpatrick and Davies since early May about bringing him to Harvard as a research associate of the center and lecturer in Far Eastern languages, his interest in Poppe having first been aroused by Davies. Provost Buck had assured Kluckhohn that he could proceed with an offer to Poppe if he could "obtain from the State Department or the Army a statement in writing to the effect that the U.S. Government would consider Mr. Poppe's presence in this country in the national interest." Davies had told Kluckhohn informally that this was indeed how the State Department viewed the matter and that a university offer to Poppe would probably result in his being flown here at government expense.[40]

Research center relations with the CIA seem more closely guarded than those with the State Department, but they were no less cordial and are especially important for showing that the CIA was present at the creation and enjoyed a concealed relationship with Harvard at the highest university level. "When I talked with the Central Intelligence Agency people last Thursday," McKay advised Kluckhohn in November 1947, "Captain S. B. Frankel, USN, the head of their Russian work, expressed a desire to have a talk with you at some length about your mutual problems." McKay reminded Kluckhohn that CIA director Admiral Hillenkoeter was "very gracious and distinctly helpful in his wish to establish continuous relationship between their organization and ours." Colonel Theodore Babbitt, a former Yale professor, was the CIA's assistant director, head of its Office of Reports and Estimates, and Frankel's superior: "Since our personnel relations will all clear with him—it might be useful to shake his hand when you are in the office as well."

On March 8, 1948, McKay sent Kluckhohn an intriguing note enclosing a letter from Harrison G. Reynolds, "the representative of the CIA." Unfortunately, McKay could not remember all that had been said during their "long conversation . . . a couple of weeks ago." Exactly "what Dr. Shockley's expertise is" he had forgotten, "but it lies in your field and I remember his saying it was important. Perhaps you will speak to him about it when you talk to him next." The letter he enclosed from Reynolds, typed on stationery without letterhead and having as its return address only "P.O. Box 2292, Boston 7, Mass.," does not identify Reynolds but does identify Shockley. He was Dr. William B. Shockley, described by Dr. Edward C. Bowles of MIT as "the scientist of scientists." "I have read his report," Reynolds wrote McKay, "and I feel that his contribution to Dr. Kluckhohn's work will be most valuable." Reynolds was sure that Shockley "would be glad to assist the Russian Research

Center in any way that he could." Since he identified Shockley at the time as head of the Bell Telephone Laboratories, it is possible that what he had in mind was some aspect of communications research. In the light of what we now know to be Shockley's interest in genetics and the alleged mental consequences of racial differences, however, it is possible that Shockley's "report" was more closely related to social science.

Conversations between CIA representative Reynolds and the research center must have been, as McKay's letter suggests, fairly regular. A few months after the Shockley discussion, Dimitri Shimkin of the research center staff wrote to Kluckhohn about a problem on which he needed a decision from Kluckhohn before taking action:

> Our friend, Mr. Reynolds, visited here yesterday and desires information on the current operations and plans of the Center. I gave him a general oral survey but await your instructions before providing any written material. He is interested in receiving essentially the report of the Center's operations during the summer and the list of our staff members who would be capable of presenting materials and acting as consultants in fields of research in the USSR of significance to Reynolds' organization.

Whether Kluckhohn provided written documents we do not know, though it is likely that he did. In any case, Reynolds could have obtained such documents in the way the FBI did—from Charles Baroch and other informants on the research center staff. Of greater importance is the evidence that the CIA–Harvard connection was discussed and negotiated with President James B. Conant himself and had his approval. That fact has been one of the best kept of Harvard's academic secrets, but it is stunningly confirmed in a letter from Kluckhohn to Provost Buck on June 13, 1949. The problem was what to do with all the requests for information from various government agencies, which were swamping the research center:

> Naturally we want to be of service in every legitimate and reasonable way. But in some cases there has been needless duplication. . . . In other instances individuals have been sent to us who lacked even an elementary knowledge of Russian matters so that we have practically had to give an elementary course on Russia before we could get down to the actual business at hand. In view of all this *and in accord with previous conversations with you and Mr. Conant* [emphasis supplied], I arranged with Mr. Harrison Reynolds, the head of CIA for the New England area, that a directive be prepared whereby all representatives from the National Military Establishment, the State Department, and other government agencies would have to clear through the Boston office of CIA before requesting assistance from us. Exceptions are made in this directive for certain branches of the Air Force [from which the

research center was receiving considerable money], State Department, and the General Operations Research Office of the Army with which we have already had intensive and mutually satisfactory contacts. As soon as this directive has been approved by the National Security Council, Mr. Reynolds will ask for an appointment with you to present the document for your approval on the university side. . . . He and his staff have shown a general understanding of the academic research situation and of the special circumstances of a university.[41]

The answers to many questions with which we began now seem clear enough. We know what Harvard could offer the émigrés to enlist their indispensable cooperation in its studies for air force intelligence and other agencies: the hope, in some cases the promise, of release from the camps, money, jobs, protection from repatriation and possible prosecution, and possible admission to the United States with academic employment.

We know, too, that the intelligence aspect of the work of the Russian Research Center and the research aspect of its work cannot be distinguished. From the point of view of both the intelligence agencies and the university, they fortunately did not have to be.

The closeness of the relationship between intelligence operations and research helps to explain, moreover, why an agency like the FBI was so deeply interested in learning what was going on within the walls of the research center and who was there. The FBI was as much interested as when it investigated an agency of the government. What, after all, was the difference, when research grants to the university were the means by which the government paid for the subcontracting services it procured from the university?

Of course there were differences between the FBI and the CIA and the State Department. J. Edgar Hoover's notions of how to fight communism were not those of General George C. Marshall or Dean Acheson, and what sufficed to establish one's credentials as an anti-Communist, however satisfactory to the CIA or the State Department, was not necessarily satisfactory to the FBI. How to keep Hoover at bay and yet maintain cooperation with the State Department and the CIA was difficult. Harvard could not admit its cooperation without blowing its cover and that of the government agencies and, at the same time, exposing itself to the charge that it was violating accepted principles of academic autonomy.

Is there any other evidence that adds plausibility to this account of the intelligence agency–Harvard connection? Is the view of Harvard as defender of academic autonomy not history but an "official story," a tale that is told?

5. More on Harvard: Public Masks, Private Faces

WE NOW KNOW that Harvard had an institutional "arrangement" with the FBI and, at least so far as the Russian Research Center is concerned, with the CIA as well. The relationship with the intelligence agencies was sufficiently close for the FBI to consider talking directly to President Conant about getting information concerning the research center and other parts of Harvard. It is possible for the head of an organization not to know all the activities carried on by his subordinates, but it is also likely that some of Conant's subordinates had reason to feel that their cooperation with the intelligence agencies had his sympathetic understanding, even if not his open support. The statements to the FBI of a number of Conant's closest friends and associates, made during the security investigation at the time of his appointment as high commissioner to Germany, attest to the depth of Conant's feelings about the dangers of communism.

On January 9, 1953, Ogden Reid telephoned FBI Assistant Director Nichols. President and editor of the *New York Herald-Tribune*, Reid had played a major role in promoting Dwight D. Eisenhower's presidential candidacy. Reid advised Nichols that Herbert Philbrick, who had recently catapulted to prominence as an FBI undercover informant in New England, "was very suspicious of Conant. Reid thought that perhaps we should check our files and if there is evidence indicating any subversive connection with Conant, it should be made known to [President-elect Eisenhower]. I thanked Reid for calling this to our attention," Nichols told Clyde Tolson: "I frankly do not see that there is anything for us to do until we receive some request to investigate Conant, which I doubt we will receive." Hoover, however, scribbled on the bottom of Nichols's memorandum: "We have now received it." Secretary of State–designate John Foster Dulles had requested the usual security investigation; and Hoover responded by directing twenty-three FBI field offices to "conduct thorough investigation as to character, loyalty, reputation, associates, and qualifications of Conant."[1]

The Boston field office's January 19, 1953, report stated that "this Office has a file entitled, 'Listed Individuals not to be Contacted by Personnel of this Office.' This list was compiled of individuals who have demonstrated hostility to Bureau Agents or who are Communists or Communist sympathizers. Although Doctor Conant does not appear on this list, it does contain the names of twenty-one faculty members at Harvard University, who are not contacted by Agents doing investigations." SAC Boston pointed out, moreover, that Conant was listed in the pamphlet "Red-ucators at Harvard," published by the National Council for American Education.

None of the many persons whom the FBI interviewed doubted Conant's loyalty and staunch anticommunism. Some described him in terms suggesting that he set limits on the range of political beliefs and associations permitted to faculty members. For example:

> Mr. James R. Killion [*sic*], President, Massachusetts Institute of Technology, . . . stated that he regards Doctor Conant as a liberal in the sense that he has a strong belief in . . . freeing educational systems of political or governmental influence. . . . Conant was one of the first to express to [Killian] during World War II the opinion that the United States must inevitably oppose the Soviet Union and Communism as well as the Nazis. . . .
>
> Doctor Roger Irving Lee [member of the Harvard Corporation] . . . pointed out that Doctor Conant has described himself for many years as a liberal in that he was very strongly in favor of the principles of academic freedoms. Doctor Lee believes that the appointee is not as liberal at the present time as he was in the late 1930's in this regard.
>
> Mr. Donald Kirk David [dean of the Harvard Business School] . . . stated that Doctor Conant's opposition to Communism is almost violent in its strength. . . . Conant has many times told Doctor David that he believes that no university should have or keep on its staff a known Communist. . . . He also believes that the invocation of the Fifth Amendment by a faculty member constitutes grounds for dismissal of that faculty member.
>
> Mr. Charles A. Coolidge [member of the Harvard Corporation] . . . advised that the appointee has on several occasions declared his opposition to Communism. . . . After the Hitler-Stalin Pact . . . the Communists showed their true colors and since that time Mr. Conant's attitude, once relatively liberal, has undergone a complete reversal with respect to Communists and their beliefs. He is now utterly opposed to them. Mr. Coolidge stated that President Conant expressed to the

members of the Corporation his belief that the invocation of the Fifth Amendment by a faculty member constituted grounds for dismissal.[2]

Lee and Coolidge, members of the Harvard Corporation, suggest how Conant's beliefs possibly affected university policy. George V. Whitney, whom the FBI identified as a member of the Harvard Board of Overseers from 1932 to 1938 and again from 1947 to 1953, similarly described Conant's views. Conant, Whitney asserted,

> did not favor the retention of the University instructors who are members of the Communist Party, that he would favor the retention of those who had formerly been a member of the Communist Party but who had broken with that party; but that University instructors and professors should be allowed to explore Socialist and Communist doctrines so long as they did not openly advocate the overthrow of the government. . . . Conant had taken this stand apparently in the name of the doctrine of "academic freedom" and while the stand was not as strong as [Whitney] believes the situation warrants, he does not consider that this in any way reflects upon the loyalty of Dr. Conant to this country.

Princeton University President Harold W. Dodds believed that Conant would be in complete accord with the principle set forth by the Association of American Universities that communists should not be allowed to become university professors.

Washington University President Arthur H. Compton, an associate of Conant for more than thirty years, told the FBI that the Harvard president had no "immediate and direct connection" with the AAU statement, which was nonetheless "in accordance with Conant's attitude and thinking; he said that he based this belief on several comments made by Conant in his presence previous to the drafting of the statement." Compton then "voluntarily" added:

> Conant had been criticized for having had members of his faculty at Harvard University who have been either former members of the Communist Party, or who have been sympathetic with the Communist line of thinking. Mr. Compton said that he wished to state that in all such cases, it was his belief that Conant was aware of whatever affiliations with the Communist Party any of his faculty members might have had, but not through a direct knowledge. Mr. Compton went on to explain that Conant learned of the affiliations through investigation and only after being fully satisfied that all Communist affiliations on the part of any prospective faculty members had ceased, and there was no danger of renewed affiliation, did Conant allow any member of his faculty to be hired.[3]

How could Conant assert that no Communist should be appointed to a teaching position, learn of the affiliations of the faculty "through investigation," and still affirm that, so long as he was president of the university, "there will be no policy of inquiring into the political views of members of the staff"? Almost certainly the FBI conducted the investigations.

Aside from the evidence contained in the FBI documents, there is other evidence suggesting that those who worked with and for Conant were not without some justification in feeling that cooperation with intelligence agencies would have his approval. Did he set Harvard's course squarely against political interference in the universities, as many believed at the time and still believe? Did he really oppose investigations of faculty members, as he said—or was he perhaps even deliberately misleading on that score?

Conant's 1970 autobiography, *My Several Lives,* is an official story— formal and concerned with presenting the impression of himself and analysis of events that he wanted others to believe. What happens when his "official story" is confronted with contemporary evidence? Fortunately, some such evidence is available, and it is possible to use it to confront the Conant of the official story.

Two collections of documents are of particular interest because they deal with issues of special, even crucial, importance in the events of the 1940s and 1950s and involve actors in close association with Conant.

First is the Grenville Clark Collection at Dartmouth College. Clark, one of the most distinguished leaders of the American bar in the twentieth century and for more than fifty years—as undergraduate, law school student, overseer, member of the corporation—a devoted and dedicated Harvard man, did not leave his enormous collection of papers to Harvard because of a conflict with the university that led to a lawsuit charging breach of faith in the university's handling of the bequest that gave it the Arnold Arboretum. Conant regarded his lawsuit as "dirty pool." Instead of leaving his papers to Harvard, Clark left them to his children, who deposited them at Dartmouth, in a "shape so that they would become available to researchers."[4]

The contrast between the official Conant of his autobiography and the Conant of his correspondence antedates the events that most concern us and therefore throws light on Conant's later behavior and attitudes.

In his autobiography Conant writes proudly about Harvard's reception of German refugee professors:

> As the true nature of the new government [of Hitler] became clear, more and more German scholars had sought refuge in the United States. By 1940 we filled a number of prominent positions at Harvard with distinguished refugees.

That is the Conant of 1970. What of the earlier Conant?

On October 9, 1933, Stephen Duggan, secretary of the Emergency Committee in Aid of Displaced German Scholars, wrote recently elected President Conant that he had offered sixteen leading American universities $2,000 per year for two years in partial payment of the salaries of displaced German scholars who would be invited as honorary professors. Fifteen universities had accepted the offer; Harvard, five months later, had not officially even acknowledged it. Duggan took up the matter with some members of the Harvard faculty, who in turn discussed it with members of the corporation and with Conant—still no acknowledgment. Duggan wanted to know Harvard's intentions. A few weeks later, Grenville Clark wrote to Conant about a recent telephone conversation with Judge Julian W. Mack, a former Harvard overseer. At Mack's suggestion Clark had spoken to Dr. Alfred Cohn of the Rockefeller Institute, who told him that there were more than a thousand "real scholars (Jews and 'liberals') who have been exiled" and who were available for appointment "without cost to the universities." He wrote Conant that President Lowell had earlier been told about the matter but had done nothing; Conant had said he might bring it up at a corporation meeting. Conant apologized to Duggan for not having acted earlier and promised that he would bring the offer to the corporation within two weeks. On October 30 he wrote Duggan that the offer had been turned down: "I trust that the delay in coming to this decision will not too greatly inconvenience your Committee."

The corporation's decision had Conant's endorsement. On November 14, 1933, he wrote Clark, enclosing copies of his correspondence with Duggan: "My own letters to Mr. Duggan are noncommittal. I felt it was very unwise to argue my position in writing":

> I feel that people outside the University like Judge Mack are very apt to mix up charity and education, but of course I should be the last person to tell him this bluntly. The question of fitting many distinguished men into an academic community is a difficult one, and I have not seen many men on the list of displaced scholars whom I thought we could use at Harvard. In Chemistry I am very familiar with the situation and can claim competence. A large number of the distinguished German chemists were Jews. . . . I have not heard of any displaced one whom we could use satisfactorily in the Chemistry Department. . . . If we fill the important positions in our universities with imported people of middle age, we are striking a blow at the prospects of every young man in that branch of academic life.

Conant was telling this to Clark in case he "should want . . . ammunition in attempting to defend my position."

Harvard did indeed accept refugee professors ultimately, but the

Conant of 1970 who wrote proudly of the fact was not the Conant of the early 1930s who called them "imported people of middle age."[5]

Of all the services that Grenville Clark performed for Conant personally and for Harvard during his many years on the corporation, none was more notable, and none more applauded, than the letter he wrote in May 1949 on behalf of Conant and the university to Frank B. Ober, the Harvard Law School alumnus who had begun a public campaign to have alumni end financial contributions to the university until radical professors—he mentioned Harlow Shapley and John Ciardi specifically—were fired. Ober, a former president of the Maryland Bar Association, had appointed a committee of legislators, lawyers, and laypeople to recommend legislation to deal with the Communist threat. Its recommendations, known as the Ober Law when adopted by the state of Maryland, provided for loyalty oaths, declared the Communist Party illegal, and the like. Ober wrote to Conant about his campaign and the reasons for it; Conant asked Grenville Clark to answer Ober's letter. In his autobiography Conant deals with the matter at some length.

It is discussed in a chapter entitled "Heresy or Subversion?" About that title Conant says: "The title of this chapter might well be 'in defense of academic freedom.' " He was less sure now about the correctness of his earlier views on academic freedom. Even then he had taken the position that the Massachusetts loyalty oath of 1935 had to be signed by the Harvard faculty as long as it was the law. He had opposed the effort to repeal the law in 1936 because not enough time had elapsed since its passage. On both issues he had been opposed by Clark. What seems to have been decisive in convincing him that no Communists should be permitted to teach was a 1947 article in *Foreign Affairs* by Henry L. Stimson, who wrote that "those who now choose to travel in company with American Communists are very clearly either knaves or fools. . . . Are either to be tolerated in an academic community?" When Clark answered Ober, "I [Conant] was delighted to have such a powerful brief on behalf of academic freedom placed before the graduates of the university. Nevertheless a new issue, namely the nature of Communism, had not been explored. Ober, in his reply to Clark, pointed to this fact."

During the debate the Educational Policies Commission (EPC), of which Conant was a member, issued its statement, "American Education and International Tensions," which took the position that Communists should not be employed as teachers. Conant was embarrassed: "The accident of the dates of publication of the Educational Policies Commission statement and the Ober-Clark correspondence had placed me in an almost indefensible position. The charge of inconsistency was not easily answered." He attempted to explain his attitude to a group of alumni before commencement in 1949. He said then that, with the single exception of Communists, "a professor's political ties . . . are of no concern to the University. . . . As long as I am president of the University, I can assure you there will be no policy of inquiry into the political views of members of the staff." The reason for making an exception of Communists was clear enough: "This is not a question of heresy; this is a question of a conspiracy which can only be likened to that of a group of spies and saboteurs in an enemy country in time of war." Ober had come to "exactly the same conclusion." In his first letter to Conant, he had argued that communism was not a political movement but a criminal conspiracy. In his second letter, he had applauded the EPC statement and expressed his belief that Harvard would now implement that policy. Conant relied on Clark "to rescue me from my troubles." Clark had written to Ober:

> You want to discipline any teacher if, after hearing, "reasonable grounds on all the evidence" are found to doubt his "loyalty." These are slippery terms.
> I affirm again that your plan implies an intensive system of detection and trial. Nothing of this character will happen under Mr. Conant. There will be no harassment of professors. . . . There will be no apparatus of inquiry. . . . I know these to be Mr. Conant's firm convictions.

Conant concludes: "I could not have expressed them as well myself."[6]

Conant's problem was easy to state, but hard to solve: how to disassociate himself publicly from Ober, with whose views he in large part agreed. An examination of his correspondence with Clark, and that of Clark with others—especially Zechariah Chafee, Jr., the noted First Amendment authority at the Harvard Law School—suggests some possible answers to Conant's vexing problem and raises other questions.

Was Clark aware that, as Conant admitted in 1970, he was being used to pull Conant's chestnuts out of the fire? Did he know that Conant did not fully agree with his answer to Ober, that, in some fundamentals, he agreed with Ober? Did Chafee share Clark's view of the situation or Conant's? The nagging possibility exists that the reason Conant "could not have expressed" his "firm convictions . . . as well" as Clark did was that he did not have those convictions, though he was delighted to accept credit for having them. If that is so, it tells us a great deal about the internal academic context of the intelligence agency–Harvard "arrangement."

On April 26, 1949, Ober wrote Conant about two recent events: (1) Professor John Ciardi had spoken at a Progressive Party rally to raise funds to oppose the Ober Bill in the Maryland legislature; (2) Professor Harlow Shapley was chairman of a peace rally at the Waldorf-Astoria Hotel in New York City. Harvard would not permit its professors to remain on the payroll if they attended conferences encouraging "other types of conspiracies looking toward other crimes. . . . Why then the

distinction because the conspiracy is directed toward the forcible overthrow of our government?" Until corrective action was taken, he would
not contribute to the Harvard Law School Fund. Within a few days,
Conant sought Clark's assistance. "My correspondent from Baltimore,
Mr. Ober, is somewhat of a special case," he wrote. "He is the author
and proponent of a bad piece of legislation which has recently passed in
Maryland. It may well be that he is planning to push the crusade into
other states. Anything he can attach to the signature of the President of
Harvard might well be used in an unscrupulous way against us. On the
other hand, a forceful brief from you as one of the outstanding leaders
of his profession might make him stop, look and listen. Would you like
to take on the job?" He ended by suggesting that Clark discuss the matter at the corporation dinner that evening with William Marbury, a
member of the corporation and a prominent Maryland attorney. Two
days later, on May 11, 1949, Conant informed Ober that he had asked
Clark to write to him in view of the fact that Ober's "comments go to
the heart of the nature of a university and have broad implications. . . .
I am sure you will be interested in his account of the history and significance of the traditional Harvard policy." On this point he stood with
President Lowell, who in his annual report of 1916–17 had written:

> There is no middle ground. Either the university assumes full respon-
> sibility for permitting its professors to express certain opinions in pub-
> lic, or it assumes no responsibility whatever, and leaves them to be
> dealt with like other citizens by the public authorities according to the
> laws of the land.[7]

The Ober affair must have been much on Conant's mind. Zechariah
Chafee, Jr., wrote to Clark about a comment Conant had made to him
at the close of the Law School faculty meeting on May 10: "He thought
it would be unwise for me to write to Ober, because Frank already has
me labeled and what I say would be of little influence." But he agreed
with Conant's suggestion "that I try to learn from somebody in Baltimore who could reach Frank. Mr. Conant suggested such people as the
president of Inland Steel. I am not sure how far I have got with this
inquiry but I thought that I would write Frank's partner, Williams, A.B.
1912 and LL.B. 1915 whom I know very well. Enclosed is a copy of my
letter for your files and the President has a copy." In the next few days,
Clark was in touch with people in connection with the letter he was
writing on Conant's behalf. To Conant himself he wrote that Marbury
and Henry Shattuck, another corporation member, had seen copies of
his proposed draft and commented on it, and that one of Marbury's
suggestions was made "in view of a talk he had with Ober. . . . I would
like to get your comment on the general structure and ideas before I

revamp it," he told Conant. There is no evidence that Conant recommended any changes.[8]

Chafee was as good as his word. He wrote to his friend and Ober's law partner, Robert W. Williams:

> What is happening to my friend, class-mate, and in-a-way relation Frank Ober? The other day he sent the President—Conant not Truman—the most extraordinary letter I've ever seen.
>
> He says he isn't going to give any money to build dormitories for law students because an English professor made a speech in Baltimore and an astronomer presided at a meeting in New York. . . .
>
> Of course we need all the help for those dormitories we can get. . . . I'm sorry not to receive the gift he'd naturally make.
>
> But I'm a lot more worried about Frank than I am about the School's losing a few hundred. Is he letting this Anti-Communist Commission of his capture his whole personality the way Captain Ahab in *Moby Dick* let the White Whale he was chasing drive every other thought and emotion out of his life? Frank's letter looks as if he were losing all sense of proportion.

Chafee attempted to show Williams the dangers involved in Ober's view that communism was a criminal conspiracy and the injustice to Ciardi and Shapley if Harvard were to fire them, as Ober wanted, on the grounds of their associations. He was concerned especially with Ober's feeling that

> professors should be disciplined . . . no matter if they cannot "be actually proved guilty of a crime." Reasonable grounds to doubt his loyalty should disqualify him. The colleges should "police themselves." Every professor's contract should contain a condition "to avoid aiding and abetting sedition." Now, *committing* sedition is a pretty vague offense, but "aiding sedition" could mean anything which anybody in authority at a university happened to dislike. . . .
>
> A university such as Frank desires would be either a hell or a bunch of stuffed-shirts.

He appealed to Williams for help in influencing Ober: "What I most want you to tell me is—who can 'get to him'? Has he any heroes, any Harvard or Princeton men whose achievements he admires, who could perhaps persuade him to stick to Communists and the practice of law, and leave the colleges and the universities to save their own souls in their own way. . . . In the city where the first president of Hopkins took Gildersleeve into a classroom and said, 'Now radiate,' the zeal of Mohammed has no place."

Chafee had to notify Clark that Williams was of no help; in fact, Williams agreed with Ober: "We cannot expect any help from this quarter," Williams felt that the real cause of Ober's concern, and of his own, was that "the attitude and the tolerance of Shapley to the aims of the Communists becomes in the mind of the world the attitude of Harvard University."[9]

On May 27 Clark answered Ober. Ober stood in sharp contrast to Harvard's "conviction and tradition" as expressed in official statements of Presidents Eliot, Lowell, and Conant and as acted upon in the famous incidents involving Chafee's position on the Abrams sedition case of 1920 and Harold J. Laski's on the Boston police strike of 1919. He suggested that Ober had not thought through the implications of his own position; these would necessarily include surveillance of faculty and students: "And how could that be done without a system of student and other informers,—the classic and necessary method of watching for 'subversive' utterances?" All of this he rejected. He ended by referring to the relation between financial contributions and the principle of "adherence to free expression." Did the university gain or lose money by maintaining its tradition?

> While that is an intriguing question, it is not the real one. For whether the policy gains money, or loses it, Harvard, in order to *be* Harvard, has to hew to the line. That is what Mr. Eliot meant, I am sure, when he said, in 1869, that while a university "must be rich" it must "above all" be free. That choice is as clear today as 80 years ago. . . . There is a deep-rooted tradition at Harvard utterly opposed to your views,—a tradition that must and will be upheld as long as Harvard remains true to herself.[10]

The letters were published in the *Harvard Alumni Bulletin* at the end of June 1949. By that time the EPC statement denying Communists the right to teach, which Conant had signed as a member of the commission, had been issued. Chafee and Clark were dismayed. "I regret very much Mr. Conant's joining in the statement by university presidents," Chafee wrote. "It will be interpreted with a very much wider scope than he intended. Thus it was meant to apply only to schools and yet Ober already construes it to apply to universities including Harvard." Clark replied: "Yes, I was sorry for Conant's joining that statement. I was [not] consulted or informed until it was a *fait accompli.*" But Ober was delighted. He took pleasure in the fact that "Mr. Conant's joinder in a splendid public statement on Communist teachers today gives the reassurance I was seeking—that Harvard is alive to that menace. Appropriate steps to implement that policy are now in order."[11]

It is likely that Ober's reading of Conant was more accurate than Chafee's and Clark's. If Chafee and Clark were taken by surprise at Conant's endorsement of the position of the Educational Policy Commission, they might well have been overwhelmed by Conant's reaction to Chafee's Phi Beta Kappa oration at Harvard on June 20, 1949. Chafee's talk, "Freedom and Fear," dealt with the legal and constitutional defects of the Mundt-Nixon Bill, an extreme example of Cold War antisubversion legislation, which he vehemently opposed. It came at a time when Harvard and other universities were considering how to respond to a demand from Congressman John Wood of the House Un-American Activities Committee to make course reading lists available to the committee. Both Clark and Chafee wanted Harvard to refuse to comply; Clark called for legal advice from former U.S. senator Edward Burke, who agreed with them. As Chafee wrote Clark:

> Yours of June 1st . . . leads me to hope that we shall fight them on the beaches. I was rather disturbed that [Dean] Griswold thought that we ought to comply with a summons in case it cannot be staved off by negotiations. My own feeling is that we should not yield an inch. It is the first step which counts. Once colleges and universities start complying at all with this extraordinary request the ranks of scholarship will be broken and it will be very hard to re-form them on another line when the authors of the books or the professors who use them are summoned to explain particular pages, etc.

Clark wanted Chafee to take special pains with his Phi Beta Kappa lecture. The platform was exactly right, and besides, "the subject is certainly right at its peak." The day on which Chafee spoke, June 20, 1949, was the day on which the Clark-Ober correspondence was released. Conant was in the audience. The talk was well received, but Conant expressed reservations as he and Chafee walked together after the meeting. He felt that Chafee had downplayed the Communist threat. Later that same day he wrote to Chafee, "following up an argument of this noon as we walked around the Yard." He presented evidence to convince Chafee of the imminent danger of communism: (1) the testimony of those who had been fairly closely associated with communism; (2) his own experience in wartime, when he "knew something of the espionage work of Party members"; (3) the record of the recent spy case in Canada; and (4) statements of Party doctrine in which "it is frankly declared that the ethics of war are the prevailing ones vis-à-vis the bourgeois on the one hand and the Party on the other." And then came the revelation of his position on Ober, of which Chafee and Clark had not been aware:

> As I said before, it seems to me you can admit the validity of my position which on one point is identical with Mr. Ober's, or at least say I might be right, and still maintain with force all the excellent things you said.

He congratulated Chafee for "a ninety percent excellent speech."[12]

That Zechariah Chafee cooperated with Clark in the refutation of Ober, in fending off the House Un-American Activities Committee's attempt to obtain course reading lists, and in other matters as well, is not surprising. He had been, after all, the most outspoken advocate of First Amendment rights on the Harvard Law School faculty at least since the time of the Abrams case, and he was often combative in asserting those rights. Nor was he easily embarrassed, as some of his colleagues were, at the company he kept in waging his political battles. He wrote his friends Senators Robert A. Taft and Owen Brewster soliciting their help in opposing various versions of the Mundt-Nixon Bill and the House Un-American Activities Committee. As he wrote to his classmate, Senator Brewster:

> Off the record . . . I am saddened by your statement backing up Senator McCarthy. . . . McCarthy and his kind are not really aiming at extremists but at the honest expression of views on public questions when those views are disliked by McCarthy and the others. . . . Whether one agrees with Henry Wallace or Mathissen [*sic*] or Shapley or Lattimore is immaterial. It is a vital element in the life of the nation that men should be able to express their opinions without being treated as traitors and outlaws. . . . I once praised you publicly as that rare thing—a politician with brains. Yet McCarthy's policy makes brains *ipso facto* proof of disloyalty. . . . Do think this over. The dangers from communists in this country are as nothing compared to the dangers from intolerance and rigidity of thought.

His young Harvard colleague Arthur M. Schlesinger, Jr., warned him of his dangerous associates on the National Committee to Defeat the Mundt Bill. "I feel you may not know about the nature of the organization," he wrote Chafee. It "is clearly a Communist controlled outfit. Its chairman, Jerry O'Connell, has been a faithful fellow-traveler. The list of sponsors includes such people as Elmer Benson, F. O. Matthiessen, Grant Oakes, O. John Rogge, Frederick Schuman, Dr. Harry F. Ward—all of whom have been repeatedly identified with party line activities." He advised Chafee to fight the Mundt-Nixon Bill through the American Civil Liberties Union and Americans for Democratic Action, and he suggested that Chafee check with Roger Baldwin and Joseph Rauh. Within a few days, Chafee received letters from both. "I hate to see genuine believers in democracy utilized by un-democratic groups," Rauh wrote. "I know you want to support a good cause," Baldwin said, "but this is, I am sure, the wrong company."

Chafee was not dissuaded. "Of course I do not know many" of the members of the committee, he wrote Schlesinger, "but I do know and admire Durr and Houston, Rogge is a former government official, and Kane and Ward fought some good fights with me thirty years ago. . . . I do not find in your letter any statement that any of these men is a criminal, even under the ridiculous terms of the Smith Act. You just don't like the ideas of some of them and very likely I shouldn't like them either." He would not accept Schlesinger's invitation to withdraw from the committee:

> These people were the first in the field to write me and I felt it my duty to throw in my lot with a group on the spot which would do its best to kill these measures. I would even ally myself with an anti-vivisectionist to fight these bills. . . .
>
> If some other group had asked me at the same time, then I would have made a choice. . . . All the people who have written me since, including yourself, seem much more stirred up by my associations with this Committee than they are by the Mundt Bills.

He wrote Rauh and Baldwin in the same vein.[13]

Given Chafee's record on civil liberties and the boldness with which he spoke out, it is somewhat surprising that he joined his Law School colleague Arthur Sutherland in writing to the *Harvard Crimson* on January 8, 1953, a letter on the use of the Fifth Amendment that was seen by many faculty members and university administrators as requiring full cooperation with congressional investigating committees and other civic authorities. Why did Chafee write such a letter? Did he in fact write it? Did he have occasion later to regret his action? Where did the idea of the letter originate? The search for answers tells us something about the Harvard of the 1950s, above all, the contrast between official statements and offstage acts.

On December 8, 1952, Harvard corporation member William Marbury, whom we encountered in connection with the Ober affair, wrote to Conant expressing his worry about the embarrassment a professor might cause the university by using the Fifth Amendment. On December 29, 1952, he wrote to Chafee about the same matter. "It seems to me that there is real danger that the academic profession may . . . be about to inflict unnecessary wounds upon itself. . . . You more than any other man can help prevent this." His fear was that widespread use of the Fifth Amendment would confirm the belief "that the teaching profession is harboring active participants in a conspiracy to overthrow our government by force and violence. . . . The consequences to academic freedom seem to me to be very dismal to contemplate." His point was that

> unless a witness has actually participated in criminally subversive actions, it makes no sense whatsoever for him to plead his privilege. Of course, evidence may tend to incriminate the innocent but I have difficulty in seeing the application of that principle to these investigations. Present membership in the Communist Party may well be incriminating in the light of the general understanding we all now have of the

nature and purposes of that organization, but I do not understand that past membership can be so. . . . For this reason it is difficult for me to see why any witness who is not now a member of the Communist Party would be incriminated by answering questions on that subject. Similarly I do not see that a witness gains anything by declining to answer questions as to membership in organizations which have been branded as subversive.

He suggested the possibility, citing the Hiss and Lattimore cases, that refusal to answer would at least eliminate the possibility of a charge of perjury. That, too, he rejected: "I am frank to say that this strikes me as a counsel of despair. To refuse to deny a crime for fear of prosecution for perjury is to admit that other evidence of the crime is so strong that the denial will not be believed. In the Hiss case, the perjury prosecution would never have been undertaken without the presence of very strong documentary evidence. Unless similar evidence is produced against Lattimore, the case against him will inevitably collapse."

He argued, too, that the use of the Fifth Amendment "in order to avoid informing against others" was impermissible. That would be an abuse of the privilege against self-incrimination, "and the result would be that the witness would be salving his conscience at the expense of the institution with which he is associated." He was approaching Chafee with a specific proposal in mind. Chafee should make clear his disapproval of "the growing tendency" among faculty members to use the Fifth Amendment:

> Should those who refuse to answer be called before some academic tribunal? If so, how should it be constituted? Should an investigation be conducted? If so, by whom? If investigations are proper in these cases, why not investigate other members of the faculty whose activities give rise to suspicion of disloyalty?
> I, for one, do not want to face these questions if it can possibly be avoided and I believe that one way to avoid it is to have men like yourself point out that there is no need to resort to such a desperate expedient as is involved in refusal to answer questions on the ground that the answers do tend to incriminate the witness.

Chafee made a number of marginal comments on Marbury's letter to him of December 29. They suggest something less than full approval of the position Marbury was proposing.

Next to the third paragraph of Marbury's letter—the one beginning ". . . unless a witness has actually participated in criminally subversive actions, it makes no sense whatsoever for him to plead his privilege"— Chafee drew a line and wrote "LAW?" Alongside the section in which Marbury argued that past membership in the Communist Party is not incriminating, Chafee drew a line and wrote "Act of 1940 says it is if within S." Where Marbury wrote that the perjury case against Lattimore will "inevitably collapse" without strong documentary evidence, Chafee underlined "inevitably collapse" and wrote in the margin, "Wish I thought so." Alongside the next-to-last paragraph, in which Marbury lists the possible courses of action trustees might take if faced by recalcitrant witnesses, Chafee wrote of his recommendations, "This is bad." Elsewhere he distinguished in the margin of the letter between matters of "Policy" and matters of "Law." [14]

If Chafee, as has been said, wrote on January 3, 1953, agreeing with Marbury, then something must have happened between the time he read Marbury's letter of December 29 and January 3. We do not know exactly what led to Chafee's apparent change of mind, but we do know that he consulted with his Law School colleague Professor Arthur Sutherland and that they both signed a letter in the *Harvard Crimson* of January 8, 1953, in which the essence of Marbury's position was accepted:

> The citizen . . . has no option to say, "I do not approve of this Grand Jury or that Congressional Committee; I dislike its members and its objects; therefore, I will not tell it what I know." He is [not] . . . justified in attempting political protest by standing silent when obligated to speak. . . . The Fifth Amendment grants no privilege to protect one's friends.

The publication of the Sutherland-Chafee letter unleashed a storm of comment. Hundreds of newspaper articles and editorials, statements by university administrators and public figures, and scores of letters are in Chafee's and Sutherland's papers at the Harvard Law School Library. A great many of the letters were favorable; a large number, especially from university presidents and deans, indicated their writers' relief at having laid out for them a course of action that seemed to satisfy their congressional critics and was at the same time endorsed by Chafee, a man with impeccable civil liberties credentials. Some expressed disappointment, even incredulity, at what seemed a total about-face on the part of Chafee. Chafee answered many of these letters. From these answers we know that the letter was for the most part written by Sutherland, though Chafee had read it and stood by it. As he wrote to Marbury on January 14, sending him a copy of the joint letter, "Most of the credit belongs to Sutherland, but we considered every word together and I thoroughly approve of it all." We know, too, that he was preparing to go abroad when the letter was published, and that before his departure he pledged $1,000 to Sutherland so that, if required, Sutherland and other members of the faculty might "obtain the services of a lawyer to advise members of the Harvard faculty who are concerned in a possible congressional investigation." [15] In explaining his reasons for signing the letter, he seemed at times to be embarrassed by the fact that it was being given wider application than he had intended. He suggested limits to its applicability. Perhaps his most important effort to suggest those limits was a lengthy letter to the vice-chancellor of the University of Pittsburgh; the Sutherland-Chafee letter "was intended only as advice to witnesses before legislative committees about their legal rights. It was not a discussion as to what would be desirable educational policy on the part of the authorities of the institution when one of its professors claims his constitutional privilege to remain silent." Without referring to specific cases in which his position had been invoked by a number of universities as legal justification for dismissing silent professors, Chafee made clear that he disapproved of that policy:

> Speaking only for myself, I feel that the legal boundary surrounding the constitutional rights of a professorial witnesses ought not to have any decisive effect on the policy of the college or university toward such a witness. Each case ought to be decided by the educational authorities on its individual merits. The basic question is whether the man is a good teacher. Of course, high moral character is one of the elements of a good teacher. Still, a man can sometimes get into difficulties with the law and yet be a man of high moral character. Two examples of this statement are Socrates and a man who parks his car on the wrong side of the street.

He asked if a university president could refuse to tell an investigating committee what a faculty member had said in confidence about that faculty member's refusal to answer all questions. The president's refusal entailed "the risk of going to jail for contempt. Indeed, the spectacle of a university president behind bars for contempt of court would be a very great contribution to liberty. It might put a stop to the hysteria from which we are now suffering."

He was pleased that in the cases at Harvard that had arisen while he was in Europe, no one with a permanent appointment was dismissed. But he disagreed "with that portion of the reasoning of the Corporation in which it described the claim of privilege as 'grave misconduct.' As one who has sworn allegiance to the Constitution, I think this is a very inappropriate phrase to apply to the use of a right given by the Constitution."

What ought to be a university's policy toward, say, a faculty member who persisted in refusing to answer questions on the grounds of the Fifth Amendment and served a six-month sentence for contempt:

> Does this make him automatically unfit to teach? Or should the university get the benefit of his great abilities and of a character which has been unimpeachable apart from this criminal proceeding . . . ? I should not excoriate the educational authorities who discharged Mr. A., but I

should honor those who decided to keep him. . . . I am by no means sure that there is a duty to disclose political crimes and dangerous thoughts, which are certainly close to being protected by the First Amendment even if the Supreme Court holds they fall outside it. The desire to shield a friend from a detestable kind of attack is not inconsistent with high moral character.[16]

He was more blunt in a letter to the secretary of the College of Wooster, who had written for a copy of the Sutherland-Chafee letter. Chafee sent him one and added a lengthy cautionary note. He and Sutherland were discussing in that letter only the legal rights of the witness:

> Yet this is a widely ramifying subject, which involves consideration of ethics, academic policy, employer policy, decent standards for investigating committees, etc. in addition to pure law. Mr. Sutherland and I were discussing pure law and nothing more.
>
> A man has a legal right to wear a sweater to a formal dinner party, but he ought not to do so just the same. Sometimes it seems unwise to me for a witness to stand on his legal rights and sometimes it seems very unwise and undesirable for his employer, especially a university, to penalize him for going outside his legal rights.

He had long wanted to write a "well-rounded discussion of the privilege of self-incrimination"—something that the Sutherland-Chafee letter was not—which would "deal with the legal rights of the witness, considerations of wisdom that he ought to think about, standards of decency on the part of the questioning tribunal, and standards by which universities, employers, and the public ought to judge the witness who keeps silent both inside and outside his constitutional rights." He added ruefully:

> Meanwhile I keep running against the troublesome fact that a discussion of one aspect of the subject is taken by readers to be an opinion on other aspects, which I did not intend at all to treat. Thus the letter of Sutherland and me has been used to my great regret by some universities as a reason for discharging professors who remain silent outside their constitutional rights, perhaps to protect friends or to avoid a perjury prosecution.[17]

We know a great deal about Zechariah Chafee. What do we know about Arthur Sutherland, the main author of the Sutherland-Chafee letter? Not enough to solve our most interesting riddle—how did he get involved in the writing of the letter in the first place? Chafee came to regret the letter, but Sutherland, judging from his correspondence, never had second thoughts. That Sutherland was no Chafee can be seen in the different views of the two men held by the FBI.

Chafee's FBI dossier began in the early 1920s, when, as a result of his activities in the Abrams case and his protests against the Palmer raids, records began to be kept on his "Communist activities" and he was referred to as a "security matter." He attracted the attention of J. Edgar Hoover, then head of the General Intelligence Division of the Bureau of Investigation, because he had succeeded in getting Felix Frankfurter, Dean Roscoe Pound, Francis B. Sayre, President Wilson's son-in-law and a Harvard law professor, and Edward B. Adams, Harvard Law School librarian, to join with him in asking Wilson for amnesty for Abrams. Hoover ordered an investigation of all five of the men and information on them from U.S. military intelligence. An FBI agent was sent to Providence to see what embarrassing facts might be dug up concerning Chafee's undergraduate activities at Brown University. The Brown authorities cooperated, but the investigation disclosed only that he came from a "very wealthy family" and that none of his relatives could be linked with radical organizations. He never escaped—not that he sought to—the penetrating eye of the FBI. His dossier included a number of his articles, including his Phi Beta Kappa oration, memorandums on his involvement with the Free Earl Browder Committee, references to his work on the Bill of Rights Committee of the American Bar Association, and newspaper clippings on his activities at the United Nations on human rights (concerning his statement that Americans should have complete freedom to study and discuss communism, Hoover noted: "What an expert for the U.N. to select!—H."). One memorandum he wrote in 1944 produced from Hoover himself what Chafee called "the nastiest letter I ever received in my life." The dossier ends in early February 1957, when SAC Boston sent FBI headquarters a number of newspaper obituaries with a note that the Zechariah Chafee file could now be completed.[18]

It was quite otherwise with Sutherland. His FBI file is heavily expurgated, but what remains is largely complimentary, certainly far different from the Chafee file. On March 9, 1953, SAC Boston notified FBI headquarters that Arthur E. Sutherland had been appointed chairman of a committee to provide legal advice to Harvard faculty members involved in congressional investigations of "alleged subversive activities" at Harvard. A three-page memorandum on Sutherland was appended. It contained quotations from a speech by Sutherland on March 17, 1951, at Springfield College as reported in the *Springfield Republican* on "the evil expansion of Russian imperialism." The FBI report also contained references to a number of *Harvard Crimson* articles on Sutherland. On September 14, 1953, Hoover sent a memorandum to D. M. Ladd asking for information about Samuel A. Stouffer and Sutherland; he had had a conversation with Clifford Case, president of the Fund for the Republic, who told him that Sutherland was doing research on the Communist Party, and Stouffer on public reaction to "security measures," for the fund.

More than a year later Hoover was still expressing interest in Sutherland's connection with the Fund for the Republic, in part because Sutherland himself had approached the FBI. On March 30, 1954, F. J. Baumgardner sent a memo to A. H. Belmont, stating that the Boston FBI office had been approached by Sutherland, "whose relationship with the Boston Office is cordial and cooperative." Sutherland wanted to know "whether the Bureau could make available certain specifically requested material in conjunction with a project of the Fund for the Republic. Sutherland said that he would gladly discuss this project at the convenience of the Bureau officials":

> He feels too many individuals in the academic field have been "softhearted and softheaded" about Communism and have been misled by Communist propaganda. . . . A research work which contains the actual record of Communist activities, one which is scholarly and factual and which will be available to scholars everywhere, represents an effective method of proving to these scholars their approach to Communism has been childish. Sutherland advised that it is the aim of the Fund for the Republic to make such a record available.

Baumgardner added that an earlier memorandum on Sutherland "reflected that we had never conducted an investigation of him." He recommended that no change be made in the bureau's policy that "precludes us from taking any part in a project of this nature," but that the bureau consider providing him with material "in the event he has a specific request to make." Clyde Tolson noted: "I agree. We can't open up files to him." Hoover added: "I concur. While Sutherland may be alright and sound I have grave doubts as to final outcome of the report since it would have to be cleared by Ford Foundation."

The Fund for the Republic study bothered Hoover. In October 1955 he requested a summary of information on Sutherland and his associates on the study of communism. There had been no FBI investigation of them, he was told; Sutherland "has been very cooperative with our Boston Office in past on applicant and related matters and our relations with him at all times have been most cordial." [19]

Sutherland had been appointed to a committee to give legal advice to Harvard professors entangled in congressional investigations. On June 15, 1953, SAC Boston sent FBI headquarters copies of a blind memorandum "having a bearing on the events leading" to interviews with two subjects on May 21, 1953. That memorandum, from which the names of the two subjects have been deleted by the FBI, states that efforts to interview them had met with resistance. On May 20, 1953, the Boston

FBI office had been contacted by Arthur Sutherland, their legal representative, who wanted to know if it was necessary for them to go through with the FBI interviews in light of the fact that the subpoenas for them to testify before the House Un-American Activities Committee had been vacated. But Sutherland "stated he was very desirous of having the [names deleted] interviewed for clarification purposes and he arranged for the interviews on the afternoon of May 21, 1953." Attached to that memorandum is another one, dated May 20, 1953, from a special agent in the Boston office to SAC Boston, concerning Sutherland and the interviews:

> Sutherland inquired of our interest in [name deleted] and I informed him this Bureau was attempting to prove or disprove allegations made against [half line deleted]. . . . He expressed the opinion there wasn't much basis to the allegations . . . and then stated he would contact [name deleted] to see if [word deleted; probably "they"] would consent to an interview.

Sutherland called back to say his clients "would gladly consent to the interview." They "have no intention of hiding behind the fifth amendment and were perfectly willing to answer any question propounded to [word deleted, probably "them"] . . . the questioning to take place in Sutherland's presence." The records on Sutherland were checked; no case file was found.

The FBI has deleted the names of Sutherland's clients, but we know who they were and what was said at the interviews from documents in the Sutherland Papers at the Harvard Law School library. Those documents cast more than a fitful light on the atmosphere of the 1950s. They also suggest a degree of cooperation between Harvard and the intelligence agencies in the making of faculty appointments that is surprising for what it reveals of the abdication of university autonomy.

The two whose names have been deleted from the FBI documents were Roman Jakobson, distinguished professor of Slavic languages and literature at Harvard, and his wife. On April 23, 1953, Jakobson wrote to Sutherland to give him information about his past and present political beliefs and activities: "I have never been and never will be a member, sympathizer or fellow traveller of the communist party. . . . I have never agreed with Marxism and have never belonged to any Socialist group." He had been a member of the Russian Constitutional Democratic Party and had escaped to Prague in 1920, where he remained for nineteen years. He had "fully informed" the Justice Department about his two decades in Czechoslovakia before having received American citizenship. His information was supplemented by detailed confirmation from two leading Czech statesmen, who attested to his anti-Nazi and anti-Communist convictions. In Copenhagen, Oslo, and Uppsala, where he lived after the German occupation of Czechoslovakia, he continued both his anti-Nazi and anti-Communist activities. For six years he had taught at Columbia University; in 1949 he had come to Harvard. Jakobson quoted from what he called "the official statement made by the head of the Department, Professor Michael Karpovich, leader of the Russian anti-communist emigrants in America." To whom that official statement was made is not clear, but it was probably the Department of Justice. In any case, Karpovich's statement is astonishing for its admission that Harvard's standard policy was to investigate the loyalty of non-citizens who were being considered for faculty appointments. Harvard has always insisted that scholarly merit was the sole consideration in making appointments. Karpovich's admission that a loyalty check was conducted, in the case of noncitizens at least, suggests the possibility that it was done in the case of citizens as well—loyalty, after all, is loy-alty—but the academic world and the world at large did not know be-cause the official story was one thing and the secret policy quite another. Karpovich's report, quoted by Jakobson, is as follows:

> Dr. Roman Jakobson has been a Professor of Slavic Languages and Literatures at Harvard University since July 1, 1949. At present he holds the specially endowed Samuel H. Cross Chair of Slavic Languages and Literatures.
>
> Before inviting Professor Jakobson to join its Faculty, Harvard University had made many inquiries as to his loyalty to this country and its government—a procedure that is always followed in cases where the appointment of a man who is not an American citizen is involved.
>
> Professor Jakobson's election to the chair at Harvard took place only after the University administration was fully satisfied that there was nothing in Professor Jakobson's record that would permit any doubts as to his loyalty.
>
> As Chairman of the Slavic Department . . . in close and constant contact with the members of the Department, I can testify that these preliminary findings have been fully confirmed by Professor Jakobson's personal behavior and academic activities since he became a member of the Harvard teaching staff.
>
> I wish to add that personally I had known Professor Jakobson for many years before he became my colleague at Harvard and that it never occurred to me that he could be suspected of any subversive activities or tendencies. On the contrary, I always knew him to be a determined opponent of Communism or any other totalitarian ideology.

Sutherland arranged for counsel for Jakobson in Washington; after a meeting among counsel, Jakobson, and staff members of the House Un-American Activities Committee, the subpoena for Jakobson was withdrawn.

That ended Jakobson's troubles with the committee, but not with the FBI. We know that Sutherland had agreed to the interview with the

Jakobsons to clarify matters; he also guaranteed that they would not use the Fifth Amendment. On May 25, 1953, Jakobson sent a lengthy report of the interview to Sutherland:

> When on May 20 Mr. Sullivan from the Boston FBI asked Mrs. Jakobson and myself over the telephone to visit him at the FBI Office, I immediately informed you and asked that you propose to Mr. Sullivan to meet us in your office and in your presence. Since they insisted on speaking with us without witnesses, I accepted their visit at your instigation.

The two agents, both named Sullivan, interviewed him at his apartment on May 21 to "clarify" a new allegation. They were not put off by Jakobson's insistence that all questions about his politics had been satisfactorily answered when he was cleared in October 1952 and received citizenship on November 17, 1952. Notwithstanding the fact that the whole matter was in his Department of Justice file, "they insisted on having the questions answered again and, following your advice, I complied." The FBI was interested in possible connections with Gerhart Eisler, Alger Hiss, and Soviet journalist Ilya Ehrenbourg, and Jakobson's occupancy of the Masaryk Chair at Columbia and his relation with Professor Ernest Simmons there. Had he been contacted in the summer of 1950 by Czech and Russian officials and "asked by some of them to spy against the United States"? Whom had he recommended for teaching positions—possibly Dr. Cizovsky at Harvard, or "the member of the Communist Party [anthropologist Morris] Swadesh for as professorial post at Columbia"? And what about his "personal relations with Professor André Martinet, head of the Department of Linguistics at Columbia University, whom I have known some twenty years and who is poles away from political questions in general"? Jakobson was sure that one of his calumniators was Roman Smal-Stocki, a Ukrainian DP at Marquette College, whose "praises for Nazi social science in his book published in Leipzig in 1952" had drawn a rebuke from the Jesuit journal *America* and the *Review of Politics*. Sutherland reported to Provost Buck about the matter; although he felt the FBI agents had no right to interview Jakobson, "it [was] probably a good move to do it." He attached to his letter to Buck a copy of Jakobson's report to him.[20]

Whoever was responsible for the appointment of Sutherland to the committee to offer legal advice to Harvard professors facing difficulties with investigating committees had abundant evidence of his views on the use of the Fifth Amendment. Did Chafee know how deep Sutherland's feelings ran? In the summer of 1953, Sutherland was retained as counsel for Professor Philip Morrison, a Cornell physicist on leave at MIT, who had been subpoenaed by the Jenner Senate Internal Security Committee. Wanting to placate the authorities at Cornell, Morrison decided not to use any of the attorneys associated with the "unfriendly witnesses"; instead, he chose Sutherland, "a staunchly Republican law professor at Harvard, recently from Cornell." Despite Sutherland's warnings not to do so, Morrison decided to use what was called the "diminished Fifth"—he would talk about himself but not about others, precisely what the Sutherland-Chafee letter had urged against. He recognized the legal risks he was running but felt that, given his past difficulties with the Cornell administration, invoking the Fifth Amendment would cost him his job.[21]

Sutherland's attitude toward the Fifth Amendment and his connection with the project on the study of communism by the Fund for the Republic called him to the attention of both the FBI and the American Committee for Cultural Freedom (ACCF). The relationship between the ACCF and the fund in connection with the Sutherland study throws light on the conflicting strategies toward McCarthyism that developed in the universities.

On March 1, 1954, Sol Stein, executive director of the ACCF, sent Sutherland a copy of a memorandum the ACCF had sent to Clifford Case, president of the fund. It was the follow-up of a conversation the ACCF had had with Sutherland "and his group" on February 4 on the abuse of the Fifth Amendment. The ACCF outlined the specific problems to be studied, suggested how the findings should be publicized, submitted a detailed budget, and recommended "Mr. Alan Westin as one of the researchers" for Sutherland.[22]

Later that same month, the ACCF sent Sutherland a detailed twenty-nine-page memorandum on the history of communism in the United States. Stein was anxious to get the reactions of Sutherland's group because two histories of the Communist Party being written by Irving Howe and Theodore Draper "will be largely impressionistic rather than detailed and scholarly, and they will have the special biases of their authors." The preparation of those books "makes it that much more urgent that a thorough and objective history be undertaken soon." It was a timely task, since most of the men who made—and opposed—the Communist movement were still alive. It would show "a story of machination, intrigue, and conspiracy which must be carefully recorded . . . as objectively as scholarship permits." The main consultant to the research staff would be Bertram D. Wolfe, "the chief ideological advisor on Communism to the U.S. Information Agency"; general policy guidance would be in the hands of the ACCF Administrative Committee—Daniel Bell, then labor editor of *Fortune*, chairman; S. M. Levitas, executive editor of the *New Leader*; Arnold Beichman of the International Confederation of Free Trade Unions; history professor Hans Kohn of CCNY; and philosophy professor Sidney Hook of New York University. The estimated cost of the project was $192,655.24.[23]

On March 25, 1954, Sutherland wrote to Clifford Case emphasizing the importance of the selection of highly competent people to carry out the research and do the writing. The studies of communism proposed by the ACCF "seem admirable to me, and I think they would achieve, when well-executed, most of the good which the history of the Communist Party proposed by our committee would accomplish. . . . Accordingly, the American Committee's proposals should I think be considered by the Fund for the Republic with a general favorable attitude." He had one reservation—what were the names and qualifications of those who would actually do the work? "If the Fund for the Republic feels so inclined, it might criticize the proposals on the ground that the emphasis is too largely on the overhead and too little on the actual prosecution of the work."[24]

Sutherland handled the case of social relations professor Samuel A. Stouffer as well as that of Jakobson. On August 20, 1953, Stouffer had received a letter from the Eastern Industrial Personnel Security Board informing him that its Screening Division would deny consent for his employment on any classified military contacts. At that time he was a consultant on a special classified research contract at George Washington University under the Department of the Army. The reasons for denying consent to his employment were that he was a "close and sympathetic associate of members of organizations cited by the Attorney General . . . as subversive, and of persons who have participated in the activities of such organizations and of organizations established as a front for subversive organizations"—Gordon W. Allport, Talcott Parsons, and Jerome Bruner of Harvard; Dorwin Cartwright of the University of Michigan; William F. Ogburn of the University of Chicago; and a graduate student in the Department of Social Relations at Harvard. In addition, he had sporadic relations with Harlow Shapley and Bart J. Bok of the Astronomy Department and Kirtley Mather of the Geology Department. He informed McGeorge Bundy, dean of the Faculty of Arts and Sciences, that "I neither sympathize with nor sympathetically associate with communists or subversives of any kind, that I have never been a member of the Communist Party [nor] a member of any organization whatsoever on the Attorney General's list. I have never refused to answer any questions asked by any governmental body, either by invoking the Fifth Amendment or on any other ground, and have no intention of refusing to disclose any information that I may be called on to furnish. I am and have been for many years a Republican in politics." Under the circumstances, he would appeal the decision. He also wrote to Clifford Case, proposing to resign as chairman of the Fund for the Republic's special committee on a survey of public opinion on the Communist threat in the United States in order to save the fund from embarrassment. He informed Case of his decision to appeal:

I view the prospects of the appeal with serenity, because there is no possible ground even for a trace of suspicion when the facts are all made clear. In a less critical period, all this might even be faintly amusing. But we are going through dangerous times in which our Government must uncover and root out the Communist conspiracy wherever it exists, and in the process some mistakes are bound to be made.

The danger was that "we reach the point where nobody is safe from embarrassment." The appeal was to be a private hearing, presumably not to be publicized, but "unless appeals such as mine are successful, any professor in any major university, no matter how circumspect his behavior or conservative his beliefs, would be similarly vulnerable."

Stouffer's position was to deny the charges, not to challenge the procedures. That was also Sutherland's position. At the appeal hearing in New York on March 1, 1952, Stouffer produced a number of witnesses and affiants to establish the fact, as he told Bundy, "that the environment of Harvard in general, and the Department of Social Relations in particular, is wholesome and patriotic, and one in which a consultant to the Armed Forces can live without compromising security. . . . The keynote was complete candor." Sutherland argued that the evidence demonstrated Stouffer's "complete candor and frankness"; his "long experience in the handling of classified matters, and his discretion, patriotism, and high ability of which the United States stands in the greatest of need"; and his "great usefulness to the government." In his oral testimony, Allport "conceded that in the past he had been from time to time misled by appeals that he support this, that, or the other charitably-named cause. He stated that today he would be much more suspicious and cautious about the types of committees or associations" on the attorney general's list. The lecture notes produced by Father Theodore V. Purcell, S.J., who "as the author of a recent book dealing with Communist infiltration in labor unions . . . knows an anti-Communist when he sees one," demonstrated that "Allport's teaching, like that of Parsons, is unmistakably anti-Communist in direction." Stouffer's lectures "even in a technical course in statistics, could not be construed as other than anti-Communist in character." Sutherland wrote that Stouffer firmly believed that security clearance should be granted "only when clearly consistent with the interests of national security." The witnesses were of one mind as to his "reliability, . . . his complete lack of any tinge of disloyalty or subversion, or even of leftist sentiment, and . . . his long experience and proved discretion in the handling of classified material." The case was won; Stouffer was cleared by the Eastern Industrial Personnel Security Board. McGeorge Bundy sent Sutherland a letter of congratulations and gratitude.[25]

We still do not know how the Fifth Amendment letter of Sutherland

and Chafee was arranged. We do not know, either, why President Conant, at the very time he was asking Grenville Clark to answer Frank Ober, did not tell Clark about the degree to which he approved of Ober's position. Under the circumstances, Stouffer's statement to McGeorge Bundy that the "keynote" of his hearing "was complete candor" has a certain irony. No doubt Stouffer was completely candid. Were the Harvard authorities? Was Sutherland? On the matter of candor, compare the ringing conclusion of Lipset's study of education and politics at Harvard:

> As McGeorge Bundy once explained of Harvard, "the extraordinary freedom . . . was sustained . . . more by the universal commitment to the ideal of excellence," than by anything else—

with the chilling report of SAC Boston to Director Hoover:

> It is noted that as a result of [half line deleted] on this date, arrangements have been completed for a most cooperative and understanding association between the Bureau and Harvard University.[26]

The contrast between the two statements provides another illustration of what we have already so often encountered—the discrepancy between official statements, publicly proclaimed, and actual policy, privately pursued.

The complexity of the political situation can be gauged from the fact that even opponents of the Conant position felt constrained to carry on their battle in private and to pretend, in fact, that no battle at all was taking place. Warfare was less politics by other means than it was sub rosa politics. Even so conscientious a defender of academic freedom and so valiant an opponent of the Conant policy as law professor Mark Howe was unable or unwilling to carry the fight beyond the limits of "quiet diplomacy."

On January 7, 1953, he wrote to Conant objecting to Harvard's policy concerning congressional investigations. That policy, he argued, would "dissociate the university from the efforts of its faculty members to discover the answers to the pressing problems of our time and as citizens to express freely their opinions." The Harvard policy accepted the notion that "inquiry and expression involve unacceptable risks" and would lead the public to believe that universities regret the "indiscreet efforts" of scholar-citizens to discover and proclaim the truth. Faculty members would feel that the university "regrets their occasional proclivity to assume the responsibilities of articulate citizens." The young teacher "can no longer afford to be an energetic citizen"; the risks "come no less . . . from the obscure excesses of Senator McCarthy than from the cautious proprieties of the universities which, acting on the advice of public relations and legal counsel, have been persuaded, apparently, that the tranquillity of an orthodox faculty is preferable to the ferment of dissent and questioning. If the universities express no concern that Congress looks upon teachers as citizens who should be silent partners in the democratic venture, the teachers not unnaturally will assume that professional advancement is to be achieved by discretion rather than by valor."

And yet, certain as he was of the weakness of the Harvard position, Howe nevertheless helped organize a tribute by the Harvard chapter of the American Association of University Professors (AAUP) for its defense of academic freedom. Had Harvard "not insisted on following the traditional American procedures of fair hearing, of adequate deliberation and of just decision," the chairman of the meeting said, "there can be little doubt that other universities would also have surrendered their rights as free institutions and that the United States would have taken a long and irretrievable step toward that form of society to which Americans are most bitterly opposed—the form of society in which the things of the mind and spirit are regulated by the central state." Howe and Kingman Brewster, who later became president of Yale University, wrote the citations for five individuals especially singled out for honors. Among them were Paul H. Buck, who was an FBI informant and who, with Conant, cleared the way for CIA involvement in the Russian Research Center; senior corporation member Charles A. Coolidge, who wrote to Professor Helen Deane Markham when she was under congressional committee attack that "what bothers us is how we can distinguish your case from a person who is more valuable to the party if not technically a member"—damned if you are a member and doubly damned if you are not; and President Nathan M. Pusey, who met the "situation with a serene and quiet courage which did as much as the earlier acts of specific decision to affirm the continuing integrity of the University."[27]

There is no reason to suppose that Howe and others like him condoned the actions of Conant, Buck, Pusey, and others, or even that they knew of them all. The point is that the strategy they followed allowed the Conants to keep the initiative. The academic world assumed that Harvard did as Harvard said. So long as even those who knew better did not break the silence, the Harvard authorities could say what they pleased and do what they wanted.

6. Henry Kissinger and William Yandell Elliott: Mail-tampering, etc.

I DID NOT request the FBI document concerning Henry Kissinger that I am about to discuss. I did not know it existed. It simply showed up in a large collection of Harvard materials. Nor do I know why the FBI left Kissinger's name undeleted. Serendipitously, the document suggests much about Kissinger and about the activities in the secret intelligence services of so many leading political and academic figures early in their careers.

In chapter 7 of *White House Years*, "The Agony of Viet Nam," Henry Kissinger writes on his and President Nixon's outrage over leaks to the press about air strikes in Cambodia. "The conviction that such leaks were needlessly jeopardizing American lives, which I shared," he writes, "caused the President to consult the Attorney General and the Director of the FBI about remedial measures. J. Edgar Hoover recommended wiretaps. . . . The Attorney General affirmed their legality. Nixon ordered them carried out on the basis of explicit criteria of which access to or unauthorized use of classified information was the principal one. I went along with what I had no reason to doubt was legal and established practice in these circumstances, pursued, so we were told, with greater energy and fewer safeguards in previous administrations."[1]

Kissinger later had second thoughts: "I believe now that the more stringent safeguards applied to national security wiretapping since that time reflect an even more fundamental national interest."[2]

Kissinger's account in his memoirs suggests that his acquiescence in wiretapping was a onetime expediency, impelled by concern for saving

American lives and by the arguments of Hoover, John Mitchell, and Nixon that the taps were "legal and established practice." He would not find these arguments as compelling now as he did then, he concludes.

An FBI document gives us reason to believe that this was not the first time Kissinger was involved in the secret scrutiny of associates. And earlier, he did not have the assurance of Hoover, Mitchell, and Nixon as to the legality of his action.

The document reveals that Kissinger volunteered information to the FBI obtained by opening other people's mail when he was a member of the Harvard University faculty in the 1950s. Tampering with the mails is punishable by a fine of up to $2,000, or imprisonment up to five years.[3]

The text of the FBI report from SAC Boston to the Director, July 15, 1953, begins:

> On Friday morning, July 10, 1953, the Boston Division was in receipt of a telephonic communication from HENRY ALFRED KISSINGER who identified himself as a teacher at Harvard University, Cambridge, Massachusetts. Mr. KISSINGER stated that he had information of interest to this Bureau and requested an agent contact him that afternoon. SA [name deleted] of the Boston Division interviewed KISSINGER at 1:45 p.m. on July 10, 1953 and obtained the following information: HENRY ALFRED KISSINGER is a teaching-fellow in Government at Harvard University as well as Executive Director of the Summer School, International Seminar and Editor of "Confluence," an international forum. KISSINGER, who has his office at 10 Weld Hall, Harvard University and who resides at 59 Frost Street, Cambridge, Massachusetts, stated that the Harvard Summer School, International Seminar, has been set up through private sources to provide an opportunity for individuals from abroad to discuss the nature of present-day problems with their contemporaries with [sic] other European and Asian countries and in the United States. The Harvard International Seminar assumes all the expenses of its participants including transportation to and from their homes, room, board, tuition, and an adequate allowance for personal expenses.

It then describes the program of the International Seminar and attaches material provided by Kissinger.

> KISSINGER stated he has jurisdiction in the naming of these individuals to attend the Seminar.
>
> On July 10, 1953, there arrived at his office approximately 40 letters addressed to all individuals slated to appear at the Seminar. These letters were postmarked Providence, Rhode Island, and dated 6:30 p.m., July 9, 1953. According to KISSINGER, all the letters gave evidence they had been typed on the same typewriter. He opened one such letter addressed to [name deleted] who, as of July 10, 1953, had not appeared at the Seminar session. Enclosed in an inner envelope was an eight-

page flyer captioned, "A Few Grains of Truth." The flyer, in general, was highly critical of the American atom bomb project. . . . KISSINGER stated he did not know how the unknown individual or individuals who had forwarded these flyers to members of the Seminar had obtained the list of its members.

He did, however, inform the FBI of "five general sources" that could identify the seminar participants: (1) newspapers that had been given press releases about the seminar; (2) guest speakers invited to address the seminar; (3) persons asked to "extend hospitality" and provide "weekend relaxation" to the students; (4) former Massachusetts governor Robert Bradford, who suggested several of the guest speakers; (5) the staff of the *Harvard Crimson*, the undergraduate newspaper.

KISSINGER stated that the flyer on the surface appears to be well written and no doubt will cause some discussion in meetings of the Seminar. He stated that he intends to show no alarm, whatsoever, concerning the article and will "play it down" in his discussions. . . .

He promised to provide to the Boston Division any additional information at similar attempts to provide this type of literature to participants in the Seminar.

KISSINGER identified himself as an individual who is strongly sympathetic to the FBI and added he is now employed as a Consultant to the U.S. Army and is a former CIC [Counter-Intelligence Corps] Agent who, approximately in mid August 1953, will engage in a two-week tour of duty for his CIC detachment. . . .

KISSINGER noted that four copies of the flyer had been enclosed in the letter to the Seminar participant and presumed that the person who wrote the letters meant the Seminar participant to distribute the flyer.

Boston will take no additional action in this matter unless called back by KISSINGER. Steps will be taken, however, to make KISSINGER a Confidential Source of this Division.

Written in longhand at the end of the memorandum is the notation "Being handled separately."

This report raises a number of important questions, on some of which Kissinger himself and his associates later commented.

Did Kissinger succeed in determining who leaked the names of the seminar participants? If so, did he inform the FBI? What methods did he use in plumbing for the leak? Did Kissinger serve as a "Confidential Source" for the FBI? If so, when did his service terminate, or did it ever terminate? Perhaps, as in the episode described in the memorandum, he preferred to work voluntarily.

Additional questions: Did Kissinger's students know that in speaking to him they were speaking to a "former CIC agent" still engaged in intelligence activity? Did Kissinger's colleagues on the Harvard faculty know it? Did his employees? Did the authorities at Harvard University? If so, did they approve of his activities, or did they regard them as matters over which they had no control?

When *The Nation*, in which this document first appeared, put these questions to Kissinger, his associate William Hyland said that Kissinger refused to confirm or deny the report: "The implication of these questions is ridiculous and contemptible." A week later, Hyland changed his story—or rather Kissinger's story. Kissinger now claimed he "did not open anyone's mail" but had received a copy of the flyer from "a number of participants" who showed him their letters. He added that he "does not recollect" calling the FBI and that, besides, the FBI would never release such a document about him to anyone else because the Freedom of Information Act permits the release of documents on a specific person to that person alone.[4]

When Kissinger claimed that he did not open the mail of his students nor remember going to the FBI, he had already had considerable experience denying such activities. He denied knowing anything about the wiretapping of members of his staff, for example, despite having participated in the discussions that led to the tapping and having given J. Edgar Hoover the names of those to be tapped. He denied to the Senate Foreign Relations Committee that he knew David Young was a "plumber" working on security and news leaks, but he told the Senate Armed Services Committee that he had listened to the tape of an interview conducted by Young concerning the theft of documents from Kissinger's office. When he said that the "implication" of the questions raised by his opening of letters addressed to others was "ridiculous and contemptible," he was standing on the same high ground he took at his famous press conference in Salzburg in 1973, when again he denied knowing anything about wiretapping: "This is a question of my honor. I have attempted, however inadequate, to set some standards in my public life. If I cannot set those standards, I do not wish to be in public life."[5]

Kissinger is quite incorrect when he says that the FBI would never release such a memorandum about him because the Freedom of Information Act permits the release of records on a specific person to that person alone. *The Nation* requested a copy of the FBI memorandum of July 15, 1953, after I received it, and got it. And I have more than one copy of that memorandum, each of which was filed under a caption relating to Harvard University. If there are additional copies of the memorandum in Kissinger's personal FBI file I have not seen them, for I have never requested documents from his file. Kissinger must know that the FBI was assiduous in collecting and storing information, and that information relating to him was filed under captions other than his own name. Perhaps that is the price one pays for being truly a mover and shaker, rather than merely a private person.

Additional material relating to this episode appears in two memoranda, dated September 1, 1953, and May 7, 1954, from J. Edgar Hoover to the director of the Central Intelligence Agency. They are captioned "Harvard Students Seminar for Political Relations/Security Matter—C" and "International Seminar Harvard Summer School, 1953/Internal Security—C." It is not clear why a matter concerning the relatively trivial Harvard Summer School needed to be brought to the personal attention of the director of the CIA by the director of the FBI. Perhaps Kissinger was the subject of interest, rather than the Summer School.

But the surmise that Kissinger was not fully candid in his description of the letter-opening episode does not depend on our knowledge that he was not fully candid about the later wiretapping episode. More documents in response to FOIA requests have been provided by the FBI since the publication of the July 15, 1953, memorandum and Kissinger's denial.

Kissinger's claim not to remember calling the FBI is ambiguous. Did he mean that he does not remember calling the FBI to report his having opened the mail of his students? Did he mean that he does not remember ever having called the FBI, then or later? Did he mean that he does not remember the FBI's having been in touch with him? The FBI documents released after Kissinger's memory lapse show that the agency's relationship with him was not of the "Don't call me I'll call you" kind, but of the "Let's call each other" kind. The case began with the memorandum to the director of July 15, reporting Kissinger's phone call and interview of July 10, and it lasted at least until May 7, 1954, by which time the State Department had been drawn into the affair, the CIA was receiving copies of FBI reports, and the investigation had spread beyond Harvard. Kissinger knew what was going on and cooperated in the investigation.

===

Two heavily censored FBI memorandums of July 21 and July 24, 1953, captioned "Harvard Student Seminar for Political Relations/Information Concerning Security Matters," deal with the matter. Despite the censorship, it is possible to learn at least something of their content from the replies to them and from other documents. On August 13, 1953, for example, Hoover sent a telegram to the Boston office of the FBI referring to the memorandum of July 24: "If reply has not been submitted, advise immediately of your interview with Kissinger and the other data requested on page two of the Bulet [bureau letter]." In fact, the Boston office had already responded to the memorandum of July 24, 1953. On August 7, 1953, SAC Boston reported to Hoover that his instructions "in regard to information furnished by Mr. Kessinger [*sic*]" had been carried out; Kissinger had been interviewed that very day "to establish the identities of the sources furnishing the subversive literature to the Seminar students." At that interview, which must have been at least the second Kissinger had with the FBI on the subject, he "stated that . . . it would appear that the individuals mailing the literature had access to a list of proposed foreign Seminar participants. . . . It was Mr. Kessinger's [*sic*] opinion that this literature was mailed by an individual affiliated in some manner with Harvard University and was utilizing these foreign students as an outlet for subversive propaganda." SAC Boston outlined the steps that would be taken to track down those who had access to the names of the students, including maintaining "close contact with Mr. Kessinger [*sic*] for any pertinent information developed in this matter" and checking on Kissinger's clerical staff: "In this regard Mr. Kessinger [*sic*] volunteered the information that he has three female clerical employees, only one of which has been cleared for top secret classifications."

On this matter, Kissinger was as good as his word and the FBI as good as its. A lengthy FBI report of November 27, 1953, contains, among other information, the full roster of administrative staff, faculty, and students as provided by Kissinger. The students did not know that their names were being provided to the FBI by Kissinger, nor that the FBI would investigate them. Kissinger's list contains the names of forty persons from nineteen countries, including that of someone who later became prime minister of his country.

The FBI files were checked on each of the participants, further investigation was made to determine the origins of the pamphlet "A Few Grains of Truth," clues were tracked down in Providence and Newport, and Boston informants familiar with Communist activities at Harvard University were interviewed—to no avail. The source of the leak was never discovered.

But the episode did have some consequences for the FBI and probably for Kissinger. As to the FBI: Hoover himself wrote at the bottom of an FBI memorandum of July 21, 1953, dealing with the seminar, "This is an amazing project. H.," and he sent letters to the State Department and the CIA reporting on the FBI investigation. A letter of November 23, 1955, from the State Department to the FBI, is attached to a letter from one of the seminar students discussing some of the "critics" of American policy among the students. The "two foremost critics and detractors of this country" were George Chetwynd, "a member of the British Labor Parliament [*sic*]" and Rajagopal Naidu, a member of the Indian parliament. But there were also Father Calvez, a "French clergyman who especially advocated admission of Red China" to the UN and "economic aid without political concessions"; Harris Sitompel of Indonesia; Kikuji Ito of Japan; and others. On one occasion Professor William Yandell Elliott, director of the Summer School and Kissinger's chief patron at Harvard, "argued with and criticized in particular the activities of one George Chetwynd." Dutifully, the FBI checked its records for information on Ito, Sitompel, Chetwynd, and others.

The additional documents provided by the FBI raise new questions. Kissinger volunteered to the FBI the information that of his three "female clerical employees, only one . . . has been cleared for top secret classifications." Why should any Harvard clerical employee need security clearance at all, let alone top secret clearance, unless, of course, the nature of the employer's work demanded it? At the time of the letter-opening episode, Kissinger was only an assistant professor. What was there about his work that required three clerical employees (how many full professors had even one?), one of whom had "top secret" clearance? If there was something about his work that required his clerical employees to have such clearance, who, aside from his superiors, knew it? Did his colleagues? Did his students? Did the Harvard administration? And who paid for his clerical staff? Did the money come from the Harvard administration? Or did it come from grants—from which agencies and for what purposes?

More questions: The State Department memo to the FBI of November 23, 1955, shows that it knew a great deal about discussions in the seminar room. Who was the informant? The student who visited the State Department? If so, did the student act alone or with the knowledge of those who ran the program? Was it someone on the seminar staff? Was it Kissinger?

Mentioned in a number of the FBI documents as director of the Harvard Summer School and highly important in the operation of the International Seminar was William Yandell Elliott, professor of government at Harvard. The *Harvard Crimson*, commenting on the letter-opening incident after *The Nation's* article appeared, speculated that Kissinger was so close to Elliott that "if Kissinger consulted with anyone before notifying the FBI, Elliott would have been the man." It checked with Elliott's widow and children and with members of the staff, but all it was able to turn up was the statement of Marguerite Hildebrand, executive secretary of the Summer School, that Kissinger always kept Elliott informed of the seminar's progress and problems.[6] Those who knew both men at Harvard and have written about Kissinger's early years attest to the closeness of their relationship and agree that Elliott, if he had been told about Kissinger's approach to the FBI, would have approved.

David Landau, for one, writes that Kissinger, as Elliott's protégé, founded and directed the International Seminar and the journal *Confluence*. When Hamilton Fish Armstrong, editor of *Foreign Affairs*, was looking for a replacement in the winter of 1954–55, "reflexively" he "turned to Harvard. . . . Kissinger was heartily recommended for the post by Elliott," but even "more crucial recommendations came from" two other friends of Kissinger, Arthur M. Schlesinger, Jr., and Mc-George Bundy. Stephen R. Graubard, who worked with Kissinger in the seminar, confirms the closeness of the relation with Elliott, who had been Kissinger's tutor. They began to make plans for the seminar in early 1951: "Elliott's position as Director of the Harvard Summer School made the experiment possible; Kissinger's personal involvement gave form and substance to the idea." As to the founding of *Confluence* in 1952, "again, William Elliott, in his capacity as Director of the Harvard Summer School, stood behind the effort."[7]

The close relationship between Elliott, Kissinger's mentor, and the FBI—as well as the CIA and the State Department—need not be inferred from statements of their associates. It can be seen directly in the FBI documents themselves. They show the FBI to have been as assiduous in cultivating Elliott as Elliott was in currying favor with the FBI. They are important because they cast light not only on what went into the care and feeding of the young Kissinger but on the university–intelligence agency complex.

Elliott had already served with a number of government agencies, both full-time and as a consultant, when, on October 3, 1949, the CIA requested that the FBI investigate him in connection with a position for which he was being considered. He was in due course appointed to that position—consultant to Frank Wisner, deputy CIA director for plans (secret operations)—and later to consultantships at the Office of Defense Mobilization and the State Department. The FBI did field investigations of Elliott in Boston, Washington, New York, Tennessee, California, and elsewhere, and found no seriously derogatory information. It did find, however, in an earlier report dated April 26, 1944, from a "reliable unidentified source" reporting to another agency, some interesting information about Elliott:

> Locally, at Harvard he is known deservedly as a brilliant philosopher, dealing in the most nebulous of phraseology and able, nevertheless, to make the most complicated and abstruse impracticalities sound reasonable and even sensible. . . . His lectures and his courses are notorious among the Harvard students for their complete lack of organization, incongruity and disorderliness. However, his public lectures are often brilliant . . . and he is particularly popular with ladies' organizations, luncheon meetings, etc. . . . With his faculty colleagues in the department of Government, Professor Elliott has never been popular due to his strong tendency to monopolize the floor and to maneuver administrative affairs in such a way as to place authority in his own hands and in those of his junior friends. He is adept at securing the services of other people and at disappearing when the hard ground work needs to be done. . . . He is regarded by those who know him well as an expert organizer of other people's affairs, particularly in fields of which he

> knows practically nothing. . . . His war experiences [World War I] often
> form the subject of his classroom lectures which also show a decided
> tendency to enhance the importance of his participation in any affair in
> which he has participated in any degree.

These sentences are marked "Delete" or "Delete entire page." However, not deleted was the information that in testimony in 1948 before
the House Committee on Un-American Activities, Elliott, appearing as
an expert witness, "gave an analysis of the Communist Party activities
and history" and "also rendered an expert opinion in which he concluded that a Communist Party in the United States of America should
be made illegal."[8]

Elliot's testimony before the House Un-American Activities Committee, cited approvingly by the FBI, ran counter to the advice given him
by Zechariah Chafee, Jr. Elliott had written Chafee what he intended
to say. Chafee's reply was polite, cool, and devastating. He thought Elliott was wasting his time talking about matters of constitutionality to
the "Un-American Committee, which is the only right name for the
absurd group." Rather, "you would be much more useful if you prepared a statement which would give the committee a different sort of
enlightenment badly needed by them. . . . I would leave constitutionality to lawyers in the court room, and give the legislature the benefit of
your personal studies and your personal experience in the actual business of government." He suggested that Elliott ask about the propriety
of proscribing any party that complies with the election laws and about
the effect of loyalty oaths and investigations on the recruitment of scholars to government service. He wanted Elliott to ask whether the disclo-
sures of the committee should be subject to libel laws, and whether the
FBI maintains files on members of Congress: "Isn't it about time for the
Un-American Committee to wind up its affairs . . .?"[9]

Elliott did not ask the suggested questions.

The FBI was interested in another activity of Elliott's: a program to
educate high school and college students in "international communism
as a global menace." When Elliott announced that his group—the Committee on American Education and Communism—had received a grant
of $12,500 from the Richardson Foundation of New York, the officers
of the committee and the foundation were checked against FBI files.[10]
"No investigation or derogatory information " was found.

Long before, Elliott had won a solid place in the affections of the
FBI. According to an office memorandum from A. H. Belmont to D. M.
Ladd on December 4, 1952, the Boston office had on August 23, 1951,
notified headquarters that Elliott

> has been frequently contacted by that Office in connection with appli-
> cant and loyalty inquiries and has always been found to be an outspo-

ken critic of Communism, the Soviet Union and its satellites. Professor Elliott had frequently expressed his complete understanding and appreciation of the work and problems of the Bureau. . . . He had, at all times, displayed a most friendly and cooperative attitude and was an established contact of reliability of the Boston Office.

He obviously did not confine his contacts to the Boston office of the FBI. He called the attention of FBI official W. C. Sullivan to the dangerous activities of Senator J. William Fulbright and to his "concern over the group of Harvard professors who in an open letter on May 10, 1961, criticized the Administration's action against Cuba." Elliott was sent the results of the FBI investigation relating to the open letter, together with information on the Fair Play for Cuba Committee, the July 16 Movement, the Socialist Workers Party, the Non-Violent Committee for Cuban Independence, and "other groups similar to 'Cuba Protest Committee.' " Earlier, Vice-President Nixon had made Elliott a member of a committee of twenty to give him advice on a number of issues; the FBI once again gave Elliott a clean bill of political health.[11]

The FBI did more than give Elliott, who hardly needed it, a clean bill of health. It had an active plan to put him to work, developed by William C. Sullivan, the real architect of the famous Tom Charles Huston Plan (developed in the Nixon administration to expand greatly the federal political surveillance system) and the mastermind behind the program of "black-box" illegal break-ins and thefts, who became head of the FBI Domestic Intelligence Division in 1961 before being fired by Hoover.[12] Sullivan had met Elliott on the lecture circuit and been impressed by him. It occurred to him that the bureau could take advantage of Elliott's academic credentials by asking him to write an article "to the effect that liberals . . . should come to realize that the FBI is the foremost bulwark that permits them to be liberals and guarantees them the right to be liberals." During an interview at the State Department concerning Cyrus Eaton, the financier and founder of the Pugwash Conference, Elliott expressed interest in doing the article:

> He commented that he would like to include . . . the idea that was conveyed to him by the former Chancellor of Germany [probably Heinrich Bruening, who for a time was on the Harvard faculty] that Hitler and his Nazis came into power because the courts in Germany bent over backwards to protect the rights of individuals and special groups at the expense of the majority, the people of Germany. Elliott said that this Chancellor felt that this was the way the U.S. would go; that the courts in their over-emphasis on individual rights would be blind to the good of all. Elliott . . . felt that the Supreme Court was going in this direction and we listen too much to the pleas of minority groups.

Elliott was alarmed that "communist writers in the film and TV industry" were being rehired and that law enforcement officers were portrayed as "sadistic . . . as contrasted to the poor criminal who has had a raw deal." The FBI liked what it heard: "He is definitely and without question pro-FBI and pro the things that the FBI stands for. He is a little hard to pin down because he has so many and varied theories, ideas and policies that he would like to see considered or affected. Underneath it all his basic thinking appears to be sound."

And the FBI liked what it read as well as what it heard. Elliott forwarded a reprint of an article he had written in the summer 1958 issue of *Orbis*, a quarterly journal of public affairs published by the Foreign Policy Research Institute of the University of Pennsylvania, entitled "Proposal for a North Atlantic Round Table for Freedom." He inscribed it: "For J. Edgar Hoover—one of the grandest true Americans, with the respects of W. Y. E." Only quotations from it can do justice to the quality of mind that won approval from the CIA, the FBI, the State Department—and Harvard University and Henry Kissinger.

The article, an expansion of a proposal he had made to the Bruges Conference on the North Atlantic Community in September 1957, addressed the question of the political and ideological unity needed to oppose Soviet totalitarianism. The crisis was one of political leadership: "Statesmen in the democracies . . . can seldom rise much higher than the level of the response which they can elicit from the electorates to which they are responsible. . . . This leveling tendency of democracy . . . destroys the remnants of an aristocratic tradition which cherishes excellence and invites recognition of superiority." What we need are "epic symbols to imitate, such as embody the epic virtues of Western civilization which are part of our tradition."

The most useful of these "epic symbols" is "the legendary Arthurian Round Table," which

> embodied the great tradition of chivalry, the protection of the weak by the strong, the maintenance of freedom, the rule of law and the great Christian virtues which rendered men gentle in strength, magnanimous in power and stern in duty. Only in the West could the concept of womanhood be raised to the position that chivalry assigned to it; and only in the West has this produced the combination of the helpmate with the inspirer of men. Chivalry was strong enough to hold the West against Hun and Moslem. Wisdom and dedication must be joined in any modern version able to rescue humanity from slavery or destruction.

At the start, "ten outstanding Companions of a Round Table for Freedom would be selected by an International Institute, beginning with the North Atlantic countries, supported by . . . the Rockefeller, Ford and Mellon Foundations. . . ." Bowing to tradition: "An adequate staff should be furnished to permit each Companion to have a 'squire who would assist him in his labors.' "

We can only guess at J. Edgar Hoover's reaction to Elliott's passionate conclusion:

> The Round Table of Arthurian legend has its counterpart in the symbolism that Wagner used for *Parsifal*, and finds another and less limited reflection in the common Christian chivalry that is reflected in the *Chanson de Roland* and in *El Cid* and many another epic of the West, including Shakespeare's great epic of Britain in the Chronicle Plays. An Atlantic Round Table for Freedom . . . would call on its Companions, and on all others who would be like them, to accept a knightly duty and to share in a great and common task.[13]

But we need not guess at Sullivan's reaction. He was worried by Elliott's apparent reluctance to get down to writing the article about the FBI Sullivan really wanted. He met with Elliott on March 27, 1959, to consider the points that were to be emphasized, among them:

> Informants are a useful and valuable part of any internal security or national defense program and liberals and intellectuals need to face reality and recognize this. . . . It is in the interest of all intellectuals and liberals that they cooperate fully with the FBI if they are to continue to enjoy the freedoms which make their academic interest possible.

On June 11 he sent a memorandum providing information Elliott would need for the article Sullivan still hoped to get from him. Elliott was interested in knighthood, chivalry, and lofty ideals. Sullivan was interested in pedestrian matters like wiretaps, informers, and the implications of membership in the Communist Party: "There are some who attempt to depict the FBI as a Gestapo-type cloak-and-dagger agency whose furtive snooping and prying techniques menace the privacy of every individual in the Nation. The claim is laughable for those who know the facts." The facts were that wiretapping was limited and strictly controlled; so was the use of informants. The country was in a struggle between "the forces of good and evil, represented on the one hand by the FBI and on the other by the Communist Party." Why did so many still fail to recognize this fact? "The answer, of course, stems from the inability of many to distinguish the difference between heresy and conspiracy." The FBI is "one of the strongest weapons in our arsenal not only because it has waged a relentless fight against Communism through the years but also because it has become a dynamic force in our society upholding the individual liberties Communism would destroy."[14]

Elliott probably never produced the document the FBI hoped to get from him. Perhaps the informant of 1944 was right when he said Elliott was "adept at securing the services of other people and at disappearing when the hard groundwork needs to be done." Based on the evidence we have seen, Elliott's article—had he produced one—could not possibly have had the impact of his less formal work, such as paving the way for the entrance of Henry Kissinger into the government. Kissinger scholars agree that the network of connections he made through the International Seminar was of great significance for his career. Through the International Seminar and *Confluence*, David Landau writes, "Kissinger developed a vast network of personal acquaintances and contacts which proved invaluable in the progression of his own career." Kissinger's friend Stephen Graubard agrees: "After only a few years, Kissinger's network of foreign friends—persons in the prime of their political and professional lives—was unrivaled. No American could boast acquaintance with a more diverse group of European and Asian intellectuals. . . ." Perhaps Thomas Schelling, Kissinger's colleague at Harvard, put it most succinctly: "Henry collected a repertory of people. I don't think it was altruism."[15]

But if it was not altruism, what was it? To have a network of friends and associates is one thing; to open their mail and tap their telephones is quite another, unless, of course, usefulness is defined not only as what a friend can do for you, but what you can do to a friend. It is likely that Seymour Hersh comes close to hitting the bull's eye when he writes: "Proving his loyalty remained an obsession for Kissinger in the Nixon White House"—as it was earlier and as it has remained. William Yandell Elliott may have been quixotic in his search for chivalry in a world from which knights without fear and without reproach had vanished, but he was as shrewd in detecting the truth about Kissinger as Kissinger was in detecting the truth about him.[16]

7. William F. Buckley, Jr.: The FBI Informer as Yale Intellectual

AMONG THE HARVARD documents in the FBI file were a number that dealt with the *Harvard Crimson,* the undergraduate student newspaper. The FBI was worried in 1949 that the editors of the *Crimson* were on the verge of exposing a relationship between the FBI and Yale University through which, secretly, information was made available about students and faculty members. My concern with uncovering the details of Yale–FBI cooperation was not made easier by the fact the the names of some of the key figures in the relationship—including that of a person described as "liaison officer, Yale University"—were blacked out of the documents. Eventually, I was to discover that the "liaison officer" was Harry B. Fisher, an undercover employee of Yale University for twenty-five years, whose last fifteen years of service were devoted mainly to political surveillance. One of the names not blacked out was that of William F. Buckley, Jr., editor of the *Yale Daily News.* Buckley had not yet written *God and Man at Yale,* and he was, of course, less notable than he was to become. But he had already attracted the attention of the Yale administration, and the service he performed for both the Yale and FBI authorities in damping down a potentially explosive situation earned him the gratitude of both masters. But what exactly had he done? The Yale–FBI relationship was temporarily put aside in favor of Buckley-hunting.

    William F. Buckley, Jr., was aware that some readers of the account of his four-year undergraduate pilgrimage might find it egocentric; he was at pains, therefore, to point out that what might appear to be exces-

sive concern with self was really required by candor and the need to
base his account on what he knew and what he had done:

> I must ask indulgence for the frequent references in the text to myself
> and my personal experiences at Yale. If there were a way out, I should
> willingly have taken it. But a great deal of the material that I have
> summoned, and of the insights that I have received, have been a result
> of personal experiences. To avoid mention of these would be not only
> coy, but restrictive. For these reasons I ask patience; and further, I ap-
> proach my thesis with profound humility and with the desperate hope
> that even those who disagree emphatically will acknowledge that I could
> have no motive other than a devotion to Yale, a recognition of Yale's
> importance, and a deep concern for the future of our country.[1]

Modesty, which he would have preferred, had to be sacrificed for
completeness. But did Buckley give his complete record? It is now clear
that, while Buckley could not find God at Yale, about which he was
talkative, he did find J. Edgar Hoover, about whom he was reticent.

On May 25, 1949, the *Harvard Crimson* published the first of three
articles by John G. Simon, Burton S. Glinn, and David E. Lilienthal,
Jr., on the state of academic freedom in American universities. Accompanying the third of these articles, on May 27, 1949, was an editorial
that discussed the effect of the "anti-Communist crusade" on teaching:

> This cannot be measured in dismissals alone, for the young men black-
> balled by college administrations under pressure will be the greatest
> loss to education. . . .
>
> There is only one way to assure a solution of the problem. Univer-
> sity administrators, from assistant deans and department chairmen up
> through university presidents, must be prepared to show the greatest
> integrity and personal courage to protect the freedom of their teach-
> ers. . . .
>
> A university can afford to remove itself from our social fabric to
> protect those who search in any manner for the truth in any form. It
> must do so to justify its existence, for a school which lacks freedom to
> inquire into the nature of truth does not deserve the title of university.

We can only guess at how grating these sentiments must have sounded
to the FBI, but there is no need to guess at its reaction to two *Crimson*
articles by William S. Fairfield, the paper's former managing editor, in
the issue of June 4, 1949. From the FBI office in Boston, to the FBI
office and Yale University in New Haven, to Washington headquarters,
including Hoover himself, the response was instant, and echoes were
still rumbling four years later.

Under the headline "Stringent Loyalty Checks at Yale Keep Teachers Tense," Fairfield reported that FBI activity at Yale included "eight

or so agents" who "wander in and out of of Provost Edgar S. Furniss' office every day," plus "several undercover agents and general informants." The FBI was influencing academic appointments by providing reports on teachers to the Yale administration. Fairfield quoted Furniss as saying that "accepting any such report is neither a university practice nor policy," but also that he would oppose any appointment "if the fact that the man was a Communist 'came to my attention.'" In a second article, Fairfield reported that younger members of the Yale faculty were frightened. On the one hand was the stated policy of the Yale Corporation and President Charles Seymour that no Communist would be appointed to the faculty; on the other hand were Seymour's statement that there would be no witch-hunts and Provost Furniss's that accepting "secret reports" from the FBI or elsewhere was not Yale's "policy nor practice." How would the corporation implement its policy? "There is no satisfactory answer to that question."

Fairfield also mentioned "two definite cases and a third probable case in which the FBI has gone beyond official FBI policy in influencing Yale academic and political activities." The first involved physics professor Henry Margenau, who was reported as having been castigated by an FBI agent for speaking at a meeting of the New Haven Youth Movement: "So now he calls the New Haven FBI office every time he has doubts about a group which has asked him to speak."

The second case involved a controversy over the appointment as instructor in philosophy of Dr. Robert S. Cohen, a young philosopher and physicist. Fairfield reported that Cohen had been unanimously recommended by the Philosophy Department and by the Yale College faculty for the appointment, and that the Prudential Committee of the Yale Corporation had rejected the nomination on the basis of information provided by an informant concerning Cohen's political activities. Both Provost Furniss and Yale College Dean William C. Du Vane felt that the informant was trustworthy and acknowledged he "had some connection with the FBI, or at least with a thoroughly systematized investigatory body." After considerable protest by members of the Yale faculty and others, Cohen's rejection was reversed and the appointment was made. In the third case, Provost Furniss was quoted as having rebuked "one of the FBI's many liaison men" at Yale for having threatened a faculty member.

On June 10, 1949, J. Edgar Hoover wrote to Sedgwick W. Green, managing editor of the *Crimson* (now Congressman Bill Green of New York), calling Fairfield's references to the FBI "inaccurate, distorted and untrue." Hoover denied that FBI agents "wander in and out of" the Yale provost's office every day and that "there are several undercover agents and general informants" for every known agent. Files had not been "opened to Yale or any other educational institutions," nor had the FBI investigated "applicants for teaching positions in Yale or any other college or university." Hoover also claimed that two people mentioned in Fairfield's study "have advised that they were misquoted."

Hoover's letter was printed in the *Crimson* of June 21, 1949, together with an answer from Fairfield. Fairfield stuck to his guns. His article was based on information from about thirty people at Yale; Hoover had not refuted his charge that the FBI was influencing academic and political activities at Yale: "*The Crimson* had hoped that Mr. Hoover would severely spank his errant agents, not rush to their defense."

The FBI brought in reinforcements.

On September 28, 1949, J. J. Gleason, SAC New Haven, wrote to the director (Attention: Assistant Director L. B. Nichols) referring to earlier telephone calls between himself and Nichols about an article to appear in the *Yale Daily News* dealing with the *Crimson* story of June 4. He had been told on September 20 by David Ralston, a reporter for the *Yale Daily News,* that the paper was going to run a story about the "Harvard Crimson article relative to FBI activities at Yale. I was able to elicit from him that the article was to contain mainly an interview with Professor Robert S. Cohen, whose *identity is known to the Bureau,* and that the trend of the article would be somewhere between the stand taken by The Crimson and Cohen's statements. Mr. Ralston further stated that the News was to carry an editorial but he was unaware of the nature of the editorial." Gleason continued:

> I immediately contacted Mr. H. B. Fisher, Liaison Officer at Yale University, and advised him of the call from Ralston. Mr. Fisher stated that he would advise me as to what was transpiring at the University in this matter. He subsequently informed me that through the assistance of Mr. Carl Lohmann, Secretary of the University, and Provost Edgar S. Furniss, efforts were being made by University officials to have the story killed. . . . On Thursday, September 22, 1949, I was advised that no material would be used in the Daily News relative to the Harvard Crimson article.
>
> Meanwhile, Mr. William F. Buckley, Jr., who is presently the student head of the Yale Daily News, contacted me for the purpose of having a discussion of the article which appeared in the Harvard Crimson, particularly relating to Professor Cohen's statements and the position of the FBI.

Gleason was authorized by Assistant Director Nichols to tell Buckley that at no time had the FBI conducted an investigation of Cohen and to give Buckley a copy of J. Edgar Hoover's letter of June 10 to the *Crimson.* During his discussion with Buckley, Gleason reported, he showed Buckley a copy of Hoover's letter (Buckley's contact with FBI agent Gleason could not, therefore, have been a mere telephone call). Buckley told Gleason "that he had changed his mind considerably about the matter and was now of the opinion that the articles appearing in the

Harvard Crimson were vicious and insidious in addition to being journalistically poor and that in his opinion the FBI had been maligned. He stated that in the event the Harvard Crimson carries further articles that are derogatory to the FBI's position at Yale that the Daily News at Yale will publicly clarify our position in connection with the University's activities."

Gleason appended two letters, one from Provost Furniss, the other from Buckley. Furniss denied he had told the *Crimson* that the FBI "was engaged in investigating the loyalty of the members of the Yale faculty." Gleason wrote that he was keeping a copy of Furniss's letter in the FBI office and was awaiting a similar denial from Professor Margenau. Furniss's letter to Gleason is dated September 22, 1949. Hoover's letter to the *Crimson* stating that both Furniss and Margenau had denied the statements attributed to them by the *Crimson* is dated June 10, 1949, more than three months earlier.

Buckley's letter to Gleason (dated September 27, 1949) reads as follows:

> As you know, there is an extraordinary amount of misunderstanding not only in some parts of the United States, but also here at Yale in regard to the precise roll [*sic*] of the FBI. This was highlighted on a local level when the Crimson editors made their preposterous charges against your department last June. It is also clear to me that several members of the undergraduate body and a number of faculty members constantly insinuate that the FBI is neglecting its proper function and is given more and more to prying into private affairs. The most ludicrous charge, of course, is that the FBI is a potential Gestapo.
>
> I am extremely anxious to facilitate . . . a meeting between yourself and various members of the faculty and of the undergraduate body in order that you may outline to them the actual roll [*sic*] of the FBI in the state and community levels.

Buckley's proposal was taken seriously. Nichols wrote on Gleason's letter: "I recomend [*sic*] we do this but feel someone from Washington should handle with Gleason making introduction." To which someone else—perhaps Clyde Tolson, Hoover's assistant, or Hoover himself—has added the comment: "I suggest Nichols do this."

On October 3, 1949, SAC Gleason again wrote to the director. Buckley had informed him that on September 28 he had received a telephone call from John G. Simon, president of the *Crimson*. Buckley "thought that this office would be interested":

> Mr. Buckley stated that Simon advised him that he was in receipt of a communication from New Haven, the author of which he did not care to divulge, which stated that the Yale Daily News was all set to run an article supporting the Harvard Crimson's exposé of the FBI of June 4,

1949, whereupon Buckley received a telephone call from me and at a meeting . . . I intimidated Buckley to the extent that the article was killed.

Mr. Buckley advised me that he told Simon that the story in the letter from New Haven was as preposterous as the story carried in the Harvard Crimson on June 4th; that as a matter of fact the story to be carried in the News was killed prior to any contact I had with Buckley and that Buckley had called me and invited me to lunch.

Buckley told Gleason that Simon had found the communication from New Haven "a little irregular" and was calling for verification. Further, Buckley had told Simon that he would be glad to meet with him in New Haven within ten days "to point out to him the errors as he knew them in such false accusations against the FBI." Gleason added:

This situation is obviously delicate and I intend to furnish Buckley no more information than was approved by the Bureau as indicated in my letter of September 28th, 1949; further, any contact had with him will be as a result of his calling me. In the event John G. Simon calls at this office during his stay in New Haven, I will tell him nothing unless advised to the contrary by the Bureau. I did advise Buckley that I would be interested in the author of the communication to John G. Simon.

On October 7 Gleason sent FBI headquarters a letter he had received from Professor Margenau denying statements attributed to him in the *Crimson* article of June 4:

The activities of the F.B.I. on this campus . . . were tactful, reasonable, and circumspect. . . . I feel that you should be informed of this.

Like Furniss's letter, Margenau's was dated October 7, well after J. Edgar Hoover's claim on June 10 that he had such statements.

The letters from Furniss and Margenau were clearly felt by the FBI to be important to its defense. On October 10 Nichols wrote to Clyde Tolson, sending him a copy of Margenau's letter:

Immediately after the appearance of the Harvard Crimson story Margenau called the office and was very angry and denied that he had even talked to the author. His letter now states that he talked to the author but was misquoted.

The FBI had already made use of Furniss's letter. Furniss had suggested that the FBI could claim to have written denials of the *Crimson* article and release his letter if necessary. Nichols had sent it to Roger Baldwin of the American Civil Liberties Union. It served its purpose: to stop ACLU criticism of FBI activities at Yale.

In the meantime, the FBI had accepted Buckley's proposal for a meeting at Yale. It was held on October 24, 1949. On October 25 Nichols, the main FBI spokesman at the meeting, reported to Tolson that Buckley opened the meeting with a reference to the *Crimson* article, the accuracy of which both he and Hoover denied. Two persons mentioned in the article denied the statements attributed to them. Further, "the philosophy instructor could not have been reported on by the FBI for the simple reason that the FBI had never investigated him."

Professors Fowler Harper and Fred Rodell were easily handled. Rodell asked about

> current rumors in Washington that the FBI had files on Congressmen. I branded this as a lie and told him that we were not unmindful that there was gossip to this effect but that the gossip remained in the minds of individuals and defied him to cite one single instance.

Professor Willmoore Kendall of the Political Science Department tried to be helpful by supporting the Bureau's position that it kept no files on members of congress.

One student wanted to know if it were proper to ask if one "read the Nation." When Nichols said, "No," the student answered that Agent Murphy had recently asked him this question. Nichols wanted to see the student to arrange a meeting with him and Murphy.

Nichols did meet with the young man, "who outlined that maybe the Agent was within" his "rights in asking the question." Nichols "told him that in that event he should have so stated on the floor, but that now we had to look into the matter." It was looked into the next day:

> Murphy, when questioned by SAC Gleason this morning, said that he knows it is against the rules to ask this question and that he did not ask such a question. The whole problem did come up as to the type of literature the student, whose name is Allen Scher, received. J. Gordon Logue, the student who raised the question from the floor, told me that he had roomed with Scher; that Scher had sent off for literature pertaining to Communist groups. Investigative reports show that Scher used a different name and in the interview by Murphy with Logue, Logue pointed out that he used this name so that his correct name would not get on any Communist lists. Logue [said] that it was his word against Murphy's word and that Murphy said he did not ask the question, so he did not ask the question.
>
> Gleason states, after talking with Murphy and reviewing the file, he is convinced Murphy did not ask the question. . . . Logue, being temperamental . . . and very much upset over the comment he made, should now be called to the office and Murphy should confront him. I think this will end satisfactorily.

The memorandum ends with a statement about Buckley:

I was very much impressed with William Buckley, editor of the Yale Daily News. I have a very definite feeling that we will hear from this young man in years to come. I would say very definitely that he is pro-FBI. I invited him to visit the Bureau and told him I would like for him to meet the Director. . . . I also got quite a kick out of the fact that he apparently had members of the Daily News staff spotted around the audience because he reported that a reporter from the Harvard Crimson was present and that as the reporter . . . would make notes his men would jostle him.

A day later, on October 26, 1949, Buckley wrote Nichols promising him a copy of the transcript of the proceedings as soon as it was available and enclosing a copy of the *Yale Daily News* article on the meeting and a copy of a letter he had written to Hoover:

I don't think you can possibly realize the good that was done here last night by the open forum at which Mr. Nichols and Mr. Gleason answered questions on F.B.I. policy. . . .

A straightforward and honest appraisal of Mr. Nichols . . . leads me to comment that he is one of the most able men I have ever seen at work on a platform. His patent honesty, his wealth of information, his manifest devotion to his organization and to the law of the land elicited highly laudatory comments from men as cynical as Professors Rodell and Harper.

Enclosed with Buckley's letter is a blind (unsigned) copy of another letter by Buckley, dated October 26, 1949, to John G. Simon, president of the *Harvard Crimson:*

I regret extremely that you did not have the opportunity to check in here as you anticipated doing several weeks ago when I spoke to you over the phone.

You may have heard from one of your reporters who attended the F.B.I. conference Monday night the nature of the meeting and the satisfaction of the audience that insofar as the F.B.I. was concerned William Fairfield simply did not know the facts or else did not care to state them accurately. . . .

I speak earnestly because a fantastic amount of damage was caused by Fairfield's irresponsibility, witness for example, the indictment of the F.B.I. by the Civil Liberties Union as a result of the Crimson article. You must know by now, I assume, that the ACLU will withdraw its charges on the basis of its own investigation into F.B.I. activity at Yale. . . .

I do feel that it is your duty, as well as mine, to exercise every possible control over outright misrepresentation. . . . I feel that objectivity was lacking in your reply to Mr. Hoover's letter late in June.

On October 28 Hoover answered:

> I do want you to know how deeply I appreciate the objective manner in which you handled the conference and your kind observations for the Bureau's representatives who participated. It was most considerate of you to set forth . . . the position of the Bureau on the all important matter of the preservation of our freedoms. . . .
>
> I think that through your efforts considerable progress had been made toward dissipating any erroneous ideas. If at any time in the future any question should arise pertaining to the FBI's activities I sincerely trust you will not hesitate to communicate with us.

The *Crimson* was not persuaded that its report had been inaccurate. On October 26, 1949, it reported that the two FBI speakers at the Yale meeting, while admitting "the existence of 'liaison men' on the Yale campus as sources of information on people being 'checked,' " repeated earlier FBI denials that undercover agents "have infiltrated into the nation's universities." The *Crimson* referred to Hoover's letter of June 10 denying that the FBI had agents at Yale.

So long as the *Crimson* was unrepentant, the FBI remained concerned. On October 27 the Boston office teletyped Washington the verbatim text of the *Crimson* article. And clearly Hoover himself was still concerned. On November 2, 1949, Nichols sent a memorandum to Tolson about Robert S. Cohen:

> You are advised that we have never investigated him.
>
> Cohen was the instructor in the Philosophy Department referred to in the Harvard Crimson article who was accused by the Yale authorities of being a Communist, that the information came from an informed source and then, in a very snide manner, the Harvard Crimson indicated that it came from no one else but the FBI.
>
> At the forum on October 24, this question came up. It was answered by the statement we had furnished no information on Cohen to Yale. This is 100% accurate. . . . We had not furnished any information to Yale for the simple reason that we had never investigated Cohen.

The fourth paragraph of this memorandum has been entirely inked out "to protect the name and information concerning the activities pertaining to an individual, which if released, would reveal an investigative interest by the FBI in that individual."

The FBI continued to interest itself in the matter; so did Buckley. On November 10, 1949, the New Haven FBI office sent a memorandum to the director, enclosing a blind copy of a second letter, dated October 31, 1949, from Buckley to Simon.

The blind copy of Buckley's letter begins with a rueful admission that while he remembers the *Crimson* article of June 4, he can find no copy of it at his office. He continues:

> I deeply regret that you should not interpret the FBI conference and the facts I related to you over the telephone as clear refutation of that part of the Fairfield story that dealt with the FBI at Yale. . . . Fairfield erred in the following general particulars:
>
> 1) Professor Margenau was not approached by the FBI, and was not told to communicate with the FBI before making any public speaking engagements. . . . Our source is Professor Margenau who came close to calling Fairfield "grossly irresponsible" in a statement he prepared . . . last June. The university prevailed upon him to send out the statement. [Did the university prevail upon Margenau to send out the statement, as Buckley claims here? Or did the FBI, as Gleason said in his memo to Nichols of September 28?]
>
> 2) Professor Furniss, a gentleman of unquestioned probity, denies categorically alleged statement to the effect that "those gumshoes come in and out of here everyday." In fact, he asserts that "gumshoes" was never part of his vocabulary.
>
> 3) There is no evidence whatever of FBI interference at Yale. The Bureau is consulted only in cases of appointment to the nuclear fisson [*sic*] project which is going on at Yale. . . .
>
> 4) The Liaison agents which Mr. Fairfield leads us to believe swarm over the Yale Campus are non-existent. . . .
>
> 5) I have personal knowledge as to the "informants" against Mr. Cohen, but this information, as you must readily realize, is confidential. I can give you my word that this information did not come from the FBI which does not even have a file on Cohen, and which would certainly not break an established policy purely to accommodate the Yale Administration. . . .
>
> I am sorry that you did not have a representative at the FBI Conference, but am at the same time surprised because I was accosted after the meeting by a student who claimed to represent you. I spent some time with him, and had hoped that he had relayed all to you. . . .
>
> I cannot put my finger on the ACLU report because I got notice of it from Mr. Nichols. I suggest you contact their office in New York for further details.

The FBI could worry the bone, but not let it go. On April 12, 1950, nearly a full year after the *Crimson* story and nearly five months after the Yale meeting, Nichols belatedly sent Tolson copies of the *Yale Daily News* of October 25 and 26, 1949, with stories about the Yale forum and a letter to the editor from Robert S. Cohen, "pointing out that the public concern over current American 'loyalty' investigations should not, in his opinion, be stilled." On May 3, 1950, M. A. Jones of the Washington FBI office sent Nichols a memorandum on "John G. Simon, Harvard University," with a letter by Simon to the *New York Times Magazine,*

April 30, 1950, which questioned the authorities cited by Hoover as establishing policy on wiretapping:

> John G. Simon is believed identical with John G. Simon who, as President of Harvard Crimson, was party to the Harvard Crimson, June 4, 1949, story "FBI's Activities Spread Fear at Yale" which alleged the FBI attempted to influence academic and political activities at Yale.
>
> Since Simon refused to "back up" even after you appeared on the Yale panel forum October 24, 1949, it is recommended that no action be taken in answer to Simon.

In this matter, as in many others, the FBI had a long memory. On December 11, 1953, Nichols sent Tolson a memorandum informing him that he had just been advised that the *Harvard Crimson* had that day run a story by William Beecher containing statements from a number of members of the Harvard faculty concerning the Harry Dexter White "espionage" case. The most outspoken in his disapproval was assistant professor of government Charles R. Cherrington. "We will . . . run a file check on Cherrington and Beecher," Nichols wrote. The FBI probably checked its files for information on Cherrington and Beecher, the student reporter, but without doubt it did check its files on the *Crimson*. On December 16, 1953, M. A. Jones sent a memorandum to Nichols captioned "Derogatory Article in the Harvard Crimson issue of December 11, 1953," with a summary of the information contained in the FBI files on the *Crimson*.[2]

There are reasons to be skeptical about statements in FBI documents: Were they written to make a record, to protect the agent or the bureau, to save an institution or an individual from the embarrassment that might result if an association with the bureau were revealed? In this case, the Buckley of the documents looks very much in training to become the Buckley of later years. And the information contained in these documents—dealing not only with events but with the assumptions and values of those who participated in those events—tells us much about history as well as biography, the general as well as the particular, the idiosyncrasies of Buckley and Hoover and Furniss, but also the relationships that controlled the traffic between the intelligence agencies and the universities.

What is wrong with arranging a meeting to clarify the role of the FBI at Yale—and with keeping secret the role of the FBI and of the Yale administration in organizing the meeting? And if a Yale man jostles the arm of a Harvard man who is taking notes—well, when was Frank Merriwell last taken seriously? What is wrong with sending blind copies of one's own letters to the FBI? What is wrong with not printing letters to the editor that contradict the editor and informing the FBI—though not

the author of the letter—of what one has done? What is wrong with
telling the FBI about phone conversations with fellow students—and not
telling the students? Nothing, if one feels that at all costs Yale—and the
country—must be protected against the menace of communism. The
drummer Buckley was marching to was God himself, and compared to
the sound of celestial music all other sounds are discord.

But since there is history as well as biography in this tale, its significance is not limited to Buckley himself.

First, Buckley and Hoover were not the only actors on the scene;
there were the Yale authorities as well. The relationship between Yale
and the FBI, as set forth in these documents, was institutionalized to the
extent that a "liaison officer" operated between the two. How was he
appointed? To whom did he report? What was the function of the "liaison officer"? Was it carried on behind the backs of the faculty and
students?

Second, it was a reporter for the *Yale Daily News* who first called the
FBI office in New Haven to alert it to the forthcoming story about the
Crimson article. Was the reporter an FBI informant? If so, how common
was the practice of student informing? Was it done with the knowledge
of the university authorities? Was the student paid for his information?
Was his experience helpful to his postcollege career? Did editor Buckley
know about what reporter Ralston had done?

Third, what are the implications of SAC Gleason's disclosure that
both the secretary and the provost of the university were making efforts
"to have the story killed"? Was this only the agent's boast? Or was it
true? And if it was true, why was Yale trying to have the story killed—
because its relationship with the FBI would be embarrassing if disclosed? Had the Yale authorities acted on other occasions to prevent
facts about Yale and the FBI from becoming known? Had the Yale authorities been able to influence editorial decisions in regimes before
Buckley's, or was there some quality that made him an especially likely
collaborator? SAC Gleason reported that the "liaison officer" advised
him "that no material would be used in the *Yale Daily News*." Had an
informant told the officer of Buckley's decision to kill the story? If so,
who was the informant—Buckley, Ralston, or someone else? Or was it
because some Yale authority had so instructed the editor?

Fourth, were the written denials by Provost Furniss and Professor
Margenau voluntary, or were they the result of subtle or crude coercion?
Several months elapsed between the time Hoover wrote the *Crimson*
that he had received these denials and the time Furniss and Margenau
wrote their letters. What was happening between the FBI and them during that time? If the letters were truly voluntary, had the *Crimson* reporter simply made up the "thirty" interviews on which his story was
based? Or was the real story the climate of fear that led many to believe
that their careers at Yale involved political considerations and FBI investigations?

Fifth, there is the matter of the ethics of Buckley's sending blind copies of his letters to the FBI along with reports of his telephone conversations with his counterpart on the *Crimson.* John G. Simon, now a Yale Law School professor, has told me he did not know that copies of Buckley's letters to him had been sent to the FBI. Buckley had refused to publish a letter he had written to the *Yale Daily News* concerning the *Crimson* story. At no time did he know that reports of his telephone conversations had been made available to the FBI. If the practice of sending copies of one's letters to the FBI was really innocent, then why a blind rather than an acknowledged copy? Buckley's reporting to the FBI did less to damage Professor Simon than to enhance Buckley's reputation with the FBI as an eager informer. Given the young Buckley's concern with moral inquiry, his behavior, while less than shattering in its consequences, is nonetheless interesting for the light it sheds on ethical behavior.

Sixth, Nichols replied to Professor Fred Rodell's reference to rumors that the FBI kept files on members of Congress: "I branded this as a lie." The rumor was not a lie; Nichol's statement was a lie. How many other lies did Nichols tell during the Yale meeting? The FBI repeatedly denied ever having conducted "an investigation" of Professor Robert S. Cohen, though it admitted that Cohen was "known" to the bureau—a code word for having a file on someone. The denial of "an investigation" was an FBI subterfuge that Buckley endorsed. Did he know that it was a subterfuge, or was he simply perfectly willing to make the statement to prove to the FBI how agreeable he could be?

But the most important question is: Why were both the FBI and Yale so extraordinarily sensitive to what was, after all, only an article in an undergraduate newspaper, and so assiduous in denying that any relationship existed between them? Like Chicken Little, they acted as if the sky had fallen down—or was about to. If the news had leaked, the country would have learned that a political purge of the universities was under way by 1949, and that it was being conducted by university authorities as well as by the FBI.

＝＝＝

Buckley replied to my article in *The Nation* with a letter to the editor. Of the questions I had asked, he confronted only two: (1) He had indeed sent blind copies of his letters to Louis B. Nichols of the FBI: "I send blind copies of letters I write half the time, usually to friends who I suspect would be interested." (2) He would not consider apologizing for the lie Nichols told about not keeping FBI files on members of Congress because Nichols might not have known he was lying. He feels "no obligation to apologize for other people's lies"; besides, files should be kept on congressmen if they are suspected of illegal activity.

Additional FBI documents enlarge the role Buckley played in the affair. The anguish he expressed in *God and Man at Yale* over having to forego modesty in the interest of candor—"to avoid mention of [personal experiences] would be not only coy, but restrictive"—seems even less authentic in the light of the new documentation.

It now appears that the forum Buckley chaired had been carefully orchestrated in advance—even to changing the panel of speakers to conform to the wishes of the FBI and providing the FBI spokesmen with a list of questions in advance: "I had previously told [SAC] Gleason to suggest to Mr. Buckley that they send a list of any questions he would like to have answered. Buckley will send a list."[3] Writer Bernard DeVoto and law professor Thomas Emerson were to have been panelists, but Hoover objected: "Absolutely no. I learned long ago not to enter into a wrestling match with skunks," he wrote on Nichols's memo of October 12, 1949. On October 12 Buckley called Nichols to make final arrangements for the forum. DeVoto would be scrapped: "Buckley stated that . . . DeVoto was a Harvard man and would probably deliberately endeavor to use such an opportunity to smear Yale. He stated that Emerson was the last person invited and that they would withdraw the invitation. . . . These were his words which he volunteered, 'that Emerson had forfeited his right to be heard or to ask questions on the ground he has already proven his dishonesty.' I did not comment on this."

Nichols told Tolson that "Buckley stated he would act as moderator of the meeting, he would rule out any statement which was a criticism of the Bureau, that there would be no argumentation, that the Bureau's representatives would merely answer questions, that he would make it clear that the questions would have to fit any framework that we specified and that we would be the sole judge as to whether it would be proper to answer a question, that he would make this clear at the outset."

That same day—October 12, 1949—Buckley called Nichols: "He stated that he had been waging a campaign on the Yale Campus to undermine 3 or 4 people up there who are campaigning against the FBI, that when he learned I was going to come up he assumed that the Bureau desired to really launch an all-out offensive."

On October 14, 1949, Buckley wrote Professor Fowler Harper, whom he had described to Nichols as "a typical intellectual who fumbles around and who would not make a good impression at all,"[4] telling him of the ground rules for the forum: "It is vital that you send me immediately any specific questions concerning FBI policy which you contemplate asking. The FBI may need to search through their files in order to answer informatively. . . . It is naturally impossible for them to anticipate any question you might ask. . . . Again, you are reminded that this forum is not a debate, but rather an opportunity for you and members of the audience to ask questions about FBI policy at Yale and on the national scene."[5]

We know that Hoover and the FBI appreciated Buckley's help in arranging the forum and explaining the role of the FBI. "This is a classic," Hoover wrote about Buckley's editorial, "Hats Off to the FBI," in the October 25, 1949, issue of the *Yale Daily News.*[6] Indeed, Hoover was so pleased with Buckley's editorial that he sent a copy of it to Roger Baldwin, director of the American Civil Liberties Union, with whom he had had a "recent correspondence pertaining to the FBI's intrusion into the field of academic freedom." In Hoover's opinion, Buckley's editorial about the Yale conference disposed of the issue.[7] We know that the FBI used Provost Furniss's denial of the *Crimson* story to calm ACLU fears about the FBI.[8] But we now know that Buckley's cooperation went beyond making the arrangements for the meeting. It included his involvement in the FBI's denial that it asked questions about reading *The Nation.*

The Yale law student who asked if it was proper for the FBI to inquire into whether a person was a reader of *The Nation* was identified in the FBI documents as J. Gordon Logue, "brother of Edward Logue, who is presently the legal adviser to Governor Chester Bowles of Connecticut."[9] He was summoned to FBI headquarters to confront the FBI agent who had allegedly asked the question. Logue insisted the question had been asked; the agent denied it. Once again, Gleason thought of using the good offices of Buckley. On October 24 he wrote Hoover:

> There is a possibility that a satisfactory solution to this matter for both the Bureau and Logue would be . . . for Logue to write a letter to the Yale Daily News advising that he has checked into the matter; the Bureau has also checked into the matter; Logue has talked to Murphy again and Murphy denies that any discussion took place relative to "The Nation" whatsoever; Logue still insists that the conversation took place, but . . . he has now concluded that such a question would be relevant in the investigation as he now understands it and that he has determined that the matter was handled on a high plane by the FBI.

Nichols agreed: "I think the thing for me to do is write Buckley a letter," he wrote Tolson on November 4. "Such a letter is attached. I suggest Gleason deliver it to Buckley and get over the point that the issue is now closed." Hoover also agreed. He sent Nichols's letter to Buckley to the New Haven FBI office with instructions that it be delivered to Buckley. "It is not believed that it is necessary to make public the contents of the attached letter; however, it is felt Mr. Buckley should have this should any further question arise."[10]

That the real point of the episode was the relationship between the FBI and Yale—a relationship in which Buckley's role, though deeply appreciated, was to run errands—is made clear in the letter of October 27, 1949, to Hoover from H. B. Fisher, "Liaison Officer, Yale University, Box 1111, Yale Station." Fisher assured Hoover that the two FBI representatives at Buckley's forum had met "the onslaughts of . . . Fowler

Harper and Fred Rodell, two notorious antagonists and avowed enemies of the FBI and its loyalty investigations. Both of these men, as I had said many times, are dangerous individuals." As to Buckley:

> Bill Buckley, the Chairman of the Yale Daily News, one of the finest characters on the Yale campus in many years among students, has been very cool and very sincere through this whole matter. . . . Mr. Buckley had the summer months to lay plans for and do some exploring in answer to the Crimson article and when he returned to the campus this fall he . . . came straightwith to the New Haven Field Office for frank interviews with Mr. Gleason, then went straightwith to the administrative heads of this university, and included among this group was myself. Mr. Buckley and I had a long extended luncheon interview. . . . After the luncheon session . . . Mr. Buckley wrote me a little note from which I quote the last paragraph—
>> "I enjoyed extremely talking with you and confess myself a confirmed admirer of your record."
> This, of course, includes the record of the Bureau in our mutual relationships and problems and also Mr. Buckley's growing admiration for Yale University in meeting all of these issues by having such an animal as am I in this position.

Hoover was grateful to Fisher and Buckley. He wrote Fisher on November 3, 1949, that he hoped "the FBI will always be deserving of the confidence and support reflected in the editorial 'Hats Off To The FBI' which appeared in the Yale Daily News."

Buckley's reluctance to discuss his role in this episode is perhaps less related to modesty than to other considerations. Revelation of what he did would not have been incriminating, only, to some, shameful. Even more, it would have provided a basis for genuine, not false, modesty on Buckley's part, for he would have been seen to be mainly a runner between the main performers—Yale University and the FBI. The question I raised earlier remains: Why were both the FBI and Yale University so extraordinarily sensitive to what was, after all, only an article in an undergraduate newspaper and so assiduous in denying that any relationship existed between them? For Buckley to admit what he did would be to prove the existence of that relationship. He did indeed sacrifice modesty, but not for candor.

Pursuing the lead that Yale University had on its staff a "liaison officer" to the FBI, H. B. Fisher, I requested permission to do research in the archives of the university. The William F. Buckley, Jr., papers have been given to Yale and are in Sterling Library. Most of them are closed to the public; only a few boxes—described in the catalogue as relating to the writing and publication of *God and Man at Yale*—are open to scholars. These documents permit us to see more deeply into Buckley and learn what he and the FBI found in each other, and to probe into a fundamental question of the politics and culture of our time—why so many of our current political and academic leaders have had experience in government intelligence agencies. Finally, even the few Buckley papers that are now available make clear that the rage for secrecy so characteristic of the intelligence agencies is no less characteristic of the private persons who collaborate with them.

On November 2, 1981, the Securities and Exchange Commission and the Catawba Corporation, an oil, gas, and financial consulting firm founded by William F. Buckley, Sr., shortly after World War II and 98 percent owned by the Buckley family, entered into a consent agreement under which the Catawba Corporation and some associates agreed to make payments and relinquish royalties totaling more than $800,000 for financial irregularities from 1969 to 1980.

According to the *New York Times* of November 3, 1981, Catawba, John W. Buckley, its president, and several associates made "untrue statements of material facts concerning transactions that benefited the company." Several companies with close associations to Catawba paid for the upkeep of the Buckley family estate in Sharon, Connecticut, as part of their corporate expenses.

Catawba is known as an oil and gas exploration company, but at least at one time it had an interest in publishing. It made an agreement, dated September 1, 1951, with William F. Buckley, Jr., of Sharon, Connecticut, "hereinafter called the Author," signed by John W. Buckley, president, and William F. Buckley, Jr.

Clauses 1 and 2 transfer from the Author to Catawba all the Author's rights to "a work hitherto not published in the United States of America in book form, now entitled *God and Man at Yale*," as those rights were set out in the agreement of August 1, 1951, between the Author and the Henry Regnery Co., publisher of the book.

Clause 3 directs Catawba to pay immediately to the Author the sum of $6,000 as reimbursement for costs and expenses in writing the book.

Clause 4 commits Catawba to pay Regnery $10,000—$5,000 on or before September 1, 1951; $5,000 on or before October 1, 1951—which sum, under the contract between Regnery and Buckley, is to be "expended exclusively in promoting the sales and dissemination of the book."

Clause 5 gives Buckley the right, "if requested," to continue to receive payments from Regnery or to join with Catawba in arranging that such payments "be made directly to the Company [Catawba] or its designee." All payments received by Buckley from Regnery will be "promptly" turned over to Catawba. Whenever Catawba realizes "from the sale and disposition of the Work or from whatever source a return on its initial investment of Sixteen Thousand Dollars," it will then pay to Buckley one-third of the gross proceeds thereafter received from Regnery, plus 50 percent of the gross proceeds received from any other sources in connection with the sale or disposition of the book.

Clause 6 commits the Author, at Catawba's request, to spend "a reasonable amount of time" on lectures and other appearances on behalf of the book, expenses reimbursed.

Clauses 8 and 9 discuss the duration of the agreement and its binding quality.

Clause 7 is the most interesting, in the light of Buckley's concern with candor:

> The Author will not under any circumstances, unless permitted to do so by the Company, divulge, reveal, or publish the actual ownership of the Work but will at all times, unless agreed to otherwise, hold himself forth as the Author and owner of said Work.

Did Catawba's insistence that its ownership of the book not be revealed and that Buckley "hold himself forth as the . . . owner" stem from awareness that the publication of the manuscript was more like that of a vanity press book than of one that must make its way by its own merits? Catawba was involved at the time in negotiations with Regnery over the purchase of stock in the publishing company; public knowledge of the details might have affected not only the academic reputation of the book, but Catawba's tax liabilities and other financial aspects of the deal.

A memorandum to "Billie" from "Father," dated June 25, 1952, shows that the Buckley family was considering additional investments in Regnery: "I had a long talk with Mr. Regnery yesterday and went into the matter of the investment by the Children in his Company. I told him that I would not have any objection to the Children putting $25,000 in his Company and taking preferred or common stock but . . . for the time being you yourself should not join in the investment, having in view the possible formation of the committee that we have discussed so often and which might boost his Company's textbook." Letters among Regnery and William F. Buckley father and son in July 1952 show a continuation of negotiations and more than a minimal interest on young Buckley's part:

> I am of the opinion that an investment in common stock would be more satisfactory all the way around. As you know, I have boundless faith in your enterprise, and even if it should founder, we should be left with a residue of good feeling at having contributed to the promotion of our ideology. I shall talk with Jimmy and John in the next few days, and our trustee should return from his vacation within a week. I promise to start the wheels rolling as soon as I can.[11]

Regnery was amenable to the idea of selling common stock to the Buckleys, though a different solution had been suggested. If "you would prefer to have common stock," he wrote to the senior Buckley on July 15, 1952, "I would sell some of my own stock and then after a few months reinvest the proceeds in the company. I would, as a matter of fact, very much prefer it if you would be willing to take common stock since I would welcome the active participation of Bill in our affairs." Ideology and finance were never far apart, either in Regnery's or Buckley's mind. "I think that I will be successful in raising the $100,000 or so I need, and it means very much to me that you are willing to participate," Regnery wrote on July 24, 1952:

> General Wood [once of the America First Committee] will come through, and Ed Webster [of Kidder, Peabody] promised to do something. I also got a very friendly reception last week from Sterling Morton. . . . It will look like the America First Committee all over again. There are three more America Firsters I shall probably call on after I get back— Douglas Stuart, Sanford Otis, and H. L. Stuart.[12]

A few days later Regnery repeated his gratitude for young Buckley's willingness to accept common stock. He was also more explicit about the expanded role of young Buckley in the company:

> I would also like to increase the size of our Board of Directors. Would you be willing to become a Director? I would like to ask Welch [Robert H. W. Welch, Jr., of the John Birch Society] to become a director, and possibly Whittaker Chambers, who has had enormous editorial experience. There is a man in New York, whom I met at the [Republican] convention, named William J. Casey, who could be of considerable help also, but I want to find out more about him. He is a lawyer, was in the OSS during the war, and publishes several Tax letters, on which he has made quite a lot of money. He seems very intelligent to me, has sound ideas, and knows his way around. He came out at his own expense to help Taft.[13]

Young Buckley was delighted to serve as a director. As to stock ownership, "Father is anxious to know what difference in the number of shares of common stock we would be entitled to if we bought common stock outright as compared to buying notes convertible into common stock at our option at some later date." [14] By October 1952 William F. Buckley, Sr., had bought $25,000 of common stock from Regnery.

Whether the Buckley investment in the Regnery firm produced a profit we do not know, but it is probable that concern with profits was a secondary consideration. The Buckleys were investing in a social system even more than they were in a company. On January 5, 1953, Henry Regnery, in a lengthy "general statement concerning the History and

Purposes" of the company, described why the company should be attractive to the Buckleys: "If atheism, collectivism, and positivism represent the present orthodox position of the 'modern' intellectual, then we have been very unorthodox. . . . The position we have consciously tried to represent, is at least indicated in a general way in the following six 'canons' of conservatism . . .":

1. Belief that a divine intent marks society as well as conscience. . . .
2. Affection for the proliferating variety and mystery of traditional life, as distinguished from the narrowing uniformity and equalitarianism and utilitarian aims of most radical systems.
3. Conviction that civilized society requires orders and classes. . . .
4. Persuasion that property and freedom are inseparably connected, and that excessive levelling is not economic progress.
5. Faith in prescription and distrust of "sophisters and calculators." . . .
6. Recognition that change and reform are not identical, and that innovation is a devouring conflagration more often than it is a torch or progress.[15]

It was a creed to which the Buckleys could subscribe without reservation, and it was sweetened by assurances of fiscal stability: $10,735.14 in royalties for young Bill for the fiscal year ending June 30, 1952, and arrangements with some organizations "which have tax exemptions to 'accept contributions' which would be used to place Regnery books in libraries."[16]

The few Buckley papers now open to the public are studded with references to interesting circumstances in the publication of *God and Man*.

A memorandum written by William F. Buckley, Sr., "regarding data that may be used in part in writing an article on 'God and Man at Yale,' " lists twenty-two categories of material thought to be useful in publicizing the book. These included "Some Data and Reflections on the Yale Smear"; "Smear on Religious Grounds"; "Smear by Virginia Kirkus Bookshop Service"; "Billie's Answer to Bundy, and Bulletin of Maryland Minute Women"; "Defensive Steps by Yale"; "Regarding People Who Would Help in the Preparation of Articles"; "Billie's Editorials While He Was Chairman of the Yale Daily News"; "A memorandum will be forthcoming on a degree by Yale to one of the professors at the University of California who refused to take an oath—and has several subversive affiliations." (Buckley is referring to the psychologist Edward C. Tolman.) Among those present at the dinner honoring Buckley on the publication of the book at the University Club on October 22, 1951, were Merwin K. Hart, Joseph P. Kamp, Alfred Kohlberg, Dr. J. B. Matthews, and Dr. Edward A. Rumely.[17]

The mobilization to command attention and sell copies, directed more from Sharon, Connecticut, and New York City than from publication headquarters in Chicago, was based in large part on the senior Buckley's connections. "We have sent seventy-five copies to your father's office, plus your six editorial copies," Regnery wrote Buckley on September 29, 1951. "Your father asked us to send an additional thirty. . . . The publication party is to be at Sherry's. . . . I have sent our list to your father, and we will send him thirty-five invitations next Monday."

Quite dissimilar people wrote to Buckley in praise of *God and Man,* influenced by concerns they felt they shared with him. Admiral Louis L. Strauss, who had just been given a copy of the book by former president Herbert Hoover, was worried about "the growing tendency to abuse the doctrine of 'academic freedom.' . . . I hope and believe that your book will start a healthy ferment." William Rhodes Castle, the former diplomat, told Buckley about a letter he had just received from Yale President Charles Seymour, complaining that Buckley had distorted the position of Yale and could have been more helpful to his own cause, which was also Seymour's. Seymour wrote:

> I knew Bill very well as a Yale undergraduate and had many long discussions with him. He has, of course, hit on the two vital issues: religion and the American Way of Life. . . . In his attack upon existing conditions (not entirely without justification) he disregards what has been done to improve them. For example, the last two gifts I got for Yale in my administration were half a million for the teaching of religion on the undergraduate level; and a half a million for American studies also on the undergraduate level. . . . I wish that instead of his destructive criticism Bill had come out to say: More power to this movement to strengthen Religion and Americanism: who is going to help?

Gilbert M. Tucker, president of the Association for Economic Justice, who wanted to meet with Buckley, had some practical advice for him, now that Buckley was in Mexico:

> Do you know the Doctor's Club? It is a perfectly delightful place to stay, not very far from Mexico City. . . . Theoretically, it is open to club members and their guests, but if you will mention my name if you should go there, you will be more than welcome, that is unless you have a big hook nose and insist on Kosher food. Some of our Jewish brethren are not welcome there.

Ada P. McCormick of Chicago bought a thousand copies of *God and Man.* Her family had given large sums of money to Radcliffe, Vassar, and Yale, she wrote to the elder Buckley: "It is probable that your boy will stand next to Willard Gibbs as two Yale graduates separated in time but not in intelligence contributing the most vital studies on unrealized relationships." [18]

The actor Adolphe Menjou wrote to Buckley on December 14, 1951:

I took it upon myself to contact Elton Hoyt of Cleveland and F. K. Weyerhaeuser of St. Paul in an effort to get a group of Yale men of importance together to oust Emerson, Haber and Fowler from the Law School. I believe that some action will be taken. . . . Am also organizing a group of my own alumni to oust from Cornell Phillip Morrison. The discharge of John S. Service from the state department is very encouraging. Next is Jessup and then the king [Acheson] himself. Am doing all I can to further the sales of your book.[19]

Human Events, which published some of Buckley's earliest articles, agreed to withdraw an advertisement for *God and Man* because it contained a quotation from a review by the Rev. George G. Higgins, assistant director of the National Catholic Welfare Council, which left the impression that Father Higgins's review had been favorable. The publication of an "isolated excerpt from the review cannot possibly be characterized as anything but dishonest," Father Higgins protested. Frank Chodorov, associate editor of *Human Events,* claimed that he had been something of a midwife at the birth of Buckley's book. "Bill is my find," he wrote to a correspondent. "I mean Bill Jr. He was writing his book on Yale when I met him. I read the MS., did a little scrubbing on it, got Regnery to read it. Then I got him into *The Freeman* and into *Human Events.* . . . He's on his way to Mexico, but he promised to write and write and write."[20]

The Buckley family's involvement with Mexico began not long after the turn of the century, and young Bill spent the year 1952 there, during which, as we now know, he worked for the CIA. E. Howard Hunt, who later came to prominence in the Watergate affair, was his case officer.[21] We do not know all that Buckley did in Mexico, but we do know that he was assigned to follow the student movement and that he organized an import-export business as a cover. There is a possible clue about other activities in a letter to him in Mexico from John Davenport, editor of *Barron's.* Sandwiched between a discussion of the philosophical foundations of *God and Man at Yale* and practical advice on how to promote the book is an offer of a writing assignment:

I wonder whether there is not a first class story you could do for us on PEMEX, the Mexican government oil company. . . . It would give us a chance to briefly review most of what has happened since Mexico's decision to "nationalize" and dispossess private capital. Talking with Eugene Holman of Standard Oil the other day re Iran he got on the subject of Mexico, and pointed out that without much question nationalization has slowed Mexico's oil development. . . . What are the lessons if any? The Iran thing gives you . . . a peg for the articles.[22]

Buckley at Yale became an informant for the FBI and a covert agent for the CIA, and went on to endorse political murder, as witness his commendation of the efficiency with which the Argentine military junta "acquiesced in kidnappings, torture, and executions of those suspected of conniving with [the terrorists]." He proposed creation of an international antiterrorist organization to apply the Argentine method to produce "the extinction of a species" by killing them.[23]

There is a consistency to Buckley's life; it has few of the unexpected twists and turns that plague—or bless—the lives of most. When William James wrote that at the end of a lifetime of choices that lead to different roads one looks back and cannot even recognize the selves one killed along the way, he could not have been thinking of someone like Buckley, for whom there has been no metamorphosis, only stasis. Perhaps that is because the care and feeding of William F. Buckley, Jr., under the direction of William F. Buckley, Sr., was less that of a member of a family than that of a member of a bureaucratic organization. The training provided by the senior Buckley was at certain points reinforced by Yale University, but not the Yale of Dr. Gesell or Dr. Spock, who were more concerned with what came out of the child than with what was put in.

We cannot provide a full-scale review of the life of William F. Buckley, Sr., but it is appropriate to give at least a summary, which can help us answer some of the questions we asked at the start. Why have so many intellectuals put themselves at the service of the intelligence agencies? What was there about Yale that led Buckley to find J. Edgar Hoover? What aspects of American culture—deriving from family, from education, from wherever—nourish the Manichean view of the world that subordinates all judgments to the struggle between Light and Darkness?

Fortunately there are sources that can help construct an account of the life of William F. Buckley, Sr. These are limited but provide a more complete version than those written by his children and by the junior Buckley's quasi-official biographer.[24] These are FBI dossiers, his own and that of A. Bruce Bielaski, head of the Bureau of Investigation—the predecessor of the Federal Bureau of Investigation during World War I—the papers at the University of New Mexico of Secretary of the Interior Albert Fall, Buckley's close political associate who was jailed for his involvement in the Teapot Dome scandal, and those of Buckley himself in the library of the University of Texas—volume after volume of letters, notebooks, memorandums, newspaper clippings, and miscellanea. From the documents emerges a picture of a man of boundless energy, utterly absorbed in the proper training of his children, and capable of the most subtle and surreptitious to the crudest maneuvering in pursuit of a passion that possessed him—the return of his properties in Mexico. The full-scale biography—deserved by its subject and needed by its audience—would throw light on matters both contemporary and historical: the role of ideology in the formation of foreign policy; the sabotage of official policy by disaffected officials and their supporters; the illegal provision of money and munitions to groups eager to overthrow the government of their own country to please their patrons north of the Rio Grande; the presentation of false testimony to Congress, often with the support of legislators opposed to official policy; the mobilization of public opinion through manipulation of the press and the co-optation of "private" organizations. Only a few of the high points of his career—which throw considerable light on the creation of William F. Buckley, Jr.—will be mentioned here.

Buckley opened a law office in Tampico, Mexico, in 1912. His brothers handled the legal business; he concentrated on investments, especially in oil and real estate, and cultivated the political connections that provided security for his financial transactions. These led to active political dealing on his own part—opposition to economic, political, and social policies of the Mexican revolution, to the foreign policy of the Wilson administration, which opposed armed intervention in Mexico, and to the growing tendency on the part of the largest foreign companies and bond-holders to seek an accommodation with the Mexican government. In 1921 he was arrested and deported for having supported armed uprisings against the Mexican government.

Before that, as head of the "Murray Hill Group" in New York City he provided witnesses for the subcommittee investigating Mexican Affairs, chaired by his friend Senator Albert Fall, wrote their testimony, helped devise the subcommittee's strategy to prepare the ground for armed intervention by presenting Mexican officials as agents of Kaiser Wilhelm or, more often, as creatures of the Russian revolution (in some of the Murray Hill Group's memorandums, the Mexican revolution is seen as the work of Jewish financiers and the Elders of Zion), and by continual lobbying with Catholic organizations in the United States and with the Vatican. In January 1921 he formed the American Association of Mexico, in opposition to the National Association for the Protection of American Rights in Mexico, which, he felt, was willing to grant recognition to Mexico and sell out the interests of the small oil producers. How could "patriotic Americans," he asked Senator Fall, "advocate the recognition of a government in Mexico . . . under which Americans are placed in the same category as Japanese in California"?[25]

Buckley seemed to play no favorites in his choice of a leader of the antigovernment military forces; his concern was to require the opposition groups to forge the political unity that would result in unified military operations in the field. There were to be no more "conversations, flirtations and whisperings."[26] With time, he came to favor General Esteban Cantu, former governor of Lower California, who was the recipient of military and financial aid from both private persons and government officials in the United States. Seven years before his expulsion from Mexico on November 29, 1921, Buckley wrote a "Plan for the

Establishment of a National Administration in Mexico," which made clear that his program depended on receiving the support of key officials in the United States. For years after his expulsion he continued his activities; he supported the Cristero rebellion, lobbied for funds from financier Nicholas Brady, and seems to have been secretly involved in one of the more bizarre episodes of twentieth-century American diplomatic history, the faked kidnapping of A. Bruce Bielaski, the World War I director of the Bureau of Investigation, near Cuernavaca.[27]

Scores of newspaper clippings in the Buckley files deal with the alleged kidnapping of Bielaski, which occurred at a time when it appeared that some kind of arrangement might be worked out between the Mexican and U.S. governments over the oil expropriation and debt default issues. Nothing could have been better calculated to prove that Mexico was out of control, that the government of President Alvaro Obregón—a mixture of revolutionary zeal and corruption—was unable to discipline its own people.

Bielaski, who was in Mexico on business for a New York oil engineering company, was allegedly kidnapped and held for ransom by bandits; speculation in the North American press about his kidnappers ranged from typical south-of-the-border brigands, to the government itself, to radicals from the United States, Russia, Italy, and elsewhere, smarting from the defeats inflicted on them when Bielaski directed the Bureau of Investigation. At first none doubted the authenticity of the kidnapping, even when it was revealed that some of those allegedly kidnapped with Bielaski were connected with Tijuana gambling interests supporting rebellious General Cantu, and that—in the face of the most harrowing difficulties—Bielaski had escaped without ransom being paid. Later, suspicions developed that the episode was a hoax. According to the *New York American* of June 29, 1922, the Bielaski kidnapping and dozens more in Tampico "resulted from a conspiracy conceived in this country to prevent recognition of the Obregón government. . . . The conspirators included an official of an oil company doing business in Mexico and two well-known gamblers and sporting characters."

Was the *New York American* story based on anything more than mere gossip? Could William F. Buckley, Sr., have been associated with Bielaski in the episode? Quite possibly. Buckley and Bielaski were both closely associated with Senator Fall, both had strong interests in Mexico, both worked with the Murray Hill Group, of which Buckley was unofficial director—and it is at least suggestive that the Buckley papers show that he followed the case with great assiduousness. Most telling is a heavily censored document in Bielaski's own FBI dossier. That dossier is incomplete. The FBI is not likely to provide full information on one of its own directors, even when it is clear that that director—for reasons not explicitly stated—is persona non grata with the agency. On January 19, 1953, FBI official A. H. Belmont, in a memorandum to Assistant

Director D. M. Ladd summarizing the Bielaski file, refers to the kidnapping as having been "allegedly instigated by Bielaski." Why "allegedly"? On July 6, 1922, Charles T. Allen, a U.S. manufacturers' and exporters' representative in Mexico City, wrote to William J. Burns, successor to Bielaski as head of the Bureau of Investigation, notifying him of the widespread belief that Bielaski "never was kidnapped or held for ransom but that he pretended all of this." The belief was growing in Mexico that "no kidnapping took place at all and that this was a pretext only to disturb the work of Mr. de la Huerta [representative of the Obregón government] in the United States, it being plain that only very little was needed in order that the American Government would recognize [the Mexican] government." Allen agreed with the newspaper *Universal* that Bielaski was selected for the job. "Since . . . Bielaski was for a long time the chief of the Secret Service . . . he was accepted in the United States as the most skillful individual and commissioned by the enemies of Mexico to let himself be kidnapped in order that the work of [de la Huerta] be disturbed."

On July 17, Director Burns answered Allen:

> The general trend of opinion here is just as you expressed it in your letter and the hope of all good citizens here is that if he is found guilty and if he is that he be sent to the penitentiary for a good long term which he would rightfully deserve. . . . I don't know of anything more dastardly if what many people claim is true, namely that these men sought to bring about trouble between Mexico and the United States.

On August 10, 1922, someone whose initials are indecipherable sent Director Burns a memorandum on the case, alleging that Bielaski and "two well-known gamblers and sporting characters in the United States and Mexico" had entered into a conspiracy to bring about the kidnapping to prevent the recognition of the Obregón government by the United States. "Letters, correspondence, and other documentary evidence confirming the existence of the conspiracy," he wrote Burns, could be obtained at the offices of certain banks in New York and Mexico (their names have been blacked out by the FBI) and from the files of Bielaski, Felix Diaz, Chester Crowell, Thomas B. Lee of the Petroleum Producers Association, and William F. Buckley, Sr.[28]

———

Why have so many prominent political and academic figures in the United States had experience in the intelligence agencies? Individual cases suggest different reasons, but there can be little doubt as to the influence of family in the case of William F. Buckley, Jr. He had to go no further than his father to learn to be cooperative with the intelligence agencies—openly and surreptitiously. The relationship between William F. Buckley, Jr., and E. Howard Hunt, Buckley's chief in the CIA and a major actor in the Watergate break-in, is reminiscent of his father's relationship with Bruce Bielaski.

How did Yale University reinforce Buckley's parental guidance? For the two Buckleys, Mexico provided a focus for both what they were fighting for and struggling against, just as Yale University did. The combination of Mexico and Yale, or, more precisely, the idea of Yale as the salvation of Mexico, has been a curious motif of twentieth-century history. In 1929 a group of Yale alumni decided that the University of Mexico needed a U.S.–style football team, coached by an Eli, to teach high ideals of the "American sort" to Mexican youth. Ten Yale alumni, including Arthur Bliss Lane, first secretary at the U.S. Embassy, gave $500 each, and Reginald Root (Yale, 1926) went as coach. Lane tried to convince the university to subsidize the coaching enterprise. James Rockwell Sheffield, a Yale alumnus who was U.S. ambassador to Mexico, was depressed by the country. He wrote to Columbia President Nicholas Murray Butler in 1926: "There is very little white blood in the cabinet. . . . Calles is Armenian and Indian; Leon almost wholly Indian and an amateur bullfighter; Saenz the Foreign Minister is Jew and Indian; Morones more white blood but not the better for it; Amaro, Secretary of War, a pure-blooded Indian and very cruel." The Mexicans were "barbarians who needed to be taken over and civilized by sons of 'Mother Yale.' " It could be done. He wrote Yale professor William Lyon Phelps: "Somewhere within us all dear Mother Yale had planted that spirit of struggle against odds shown in the last half of the Pennsylvania game and throughout the Army game [,] . . . shown in the race at New London last June against a very fine Harvard crew one and one-half lengths in the lead with more than a third of the course covered. I do not know just what it is but that it exists there can be no doubt and I hope I have accumulated enough of it to carry me through down here." He yearned for class reunions so that he might leave the Mexican purgatory and "revel with the good chaps at the Tomb of Skull and Bones."[29] The difference between Sheffield and the Buckleys was that they took Mexico more seriously than he did and Yale less seriously. That is, they took education at Yale less seriously. It is possible that they took other aspects of the Yale experience—like revelry "with the good chaps at the Tomb of Skull and Bones"—at least as seriously as Sheffield did:

> Take a look at that hulking sepulcher over there. . . . It's the citadel of Skull and Bones, the most powerful of all secret societies in the strange Yale secret-society system. . . .
>
> You could ask Averell Harriman whether there's really a sarcophagus in the basement and whether he and young Henry Stimson and young Henry Luce lay down naked in that coffin and spilled the secrets of their adolescent sex life to fourteen fellow Bonesmen. . . . You could ask McGeorge Bundy if he wrestled naked in a mud pile as part of his initiation and how it compared with a later quagmire into which he

eagerly plunged. You could ask Bill Bundy or Bill Buckley, both of whom went into the CIA after leaving Bones—or George Bush, who ran the CIA—whether their Skull and Bones experience was useful training for the clandestine trade.[30]

You could ask, but they would not tell. The search for some things that are never found—like God at Yale—can be described fully. The finding of some things—like the FBI at Yale or the support of armed rebellion in Mexico—will not be described at all.[31]

The full account of how Yale, or any university, defined its mission—the molding of an influential and desirable social type, as well as the production and dissemination of knowledge—has rarely been told by those who have been the major recipients of its beneficence. Their concern has been to conceal rather than to reveal. But paradoxically, even concealment requires the production of records—this must never be recorded, one document says; you must deny what the records show, says another; you will produce the documents we need to make our case, says a third, giving carte blanche to deception. The search for documents may, therefore, allow a glimpse of what we are not supposed to see. Do such documents at Yale show us only the Buckleys and a few other notables, or do they present a wider picture of an institution in which the notables and others are trained to display their talents on the broadest stage?

8. H. B. Fisher and Yale University, 1927–1952: Ivy-covered Surveillance

How DID I learn that Yale University had on its staff a liaison officer with the FBI named Harry B. Fisher? An FBI memorandum concerning Buckley, from SAC New Haven to the director, September 28, 1949, refers to "[named deleted], Liaison Officer at Yale University." The phrase suggests that relations between the FBI and Yale were so formalized that a special office—that of "Liaison Officer"—had been created to handle them. It was impossible to determine from the text of the memorandum whether the deleted name was that of an FBI employee who had liaison responsibilities with Yale or that of a Yale employee who had liaison responsibilities with the FBI. The answer to that question was obviously important, but there was no way to answer it. And yet there was—by accident. In response to a suit to compel the FBI to provide unedited copies of all documents requested, the Department of Justice, in an effort to show the court how responsive it had been, submitted copies of all the documents the FBI had sent. The name deleted from the copy sent to me was not deleted from the court's. The phrase read "H. B. Fisher, Liaison Officer at Yale University." But who was H. B. Fisher? None of the histories of Yale and none of the published records of the university contained references to him. Yale gave me permission to examine its archives, where I found documents dealing with this episode of surveillance and political espionage.

In 1927 Yale University secretly established an administrative apparatus for carrying out certain parietal functions. By the outbreak of World War II, that apparatus, still secret, was performing essentially political

179

functions. Why in 1927 did Yale see its problems as mainly parietal? Fifteen years later, what led Yale to feel that its problems were political? Who, indeed, determined its agenda—the Yale authorities acting autonomously, or the Yale authorities in cooperation with government agencies and private citizens?

In his 1949–50 report to the Yale University Deans' Committee on Social Research, H. B. Fisher, identified in the report as "Liaison Officer, Yale University," called attention to a number of important dates in the history of the Social Research Committee:

> On [January 2, 1927] the first Program Session of the Social Research Committee was held during which an active Research Program was launched. . . .
>
> Following this meeting . . . I placed two of my own Agents together with one from the Federal Narcotic Bureau and one from the Washington Prohibition Bureau with special assignment in the College Highway area of Connecticut and Massachusetts. These men worked entirely under-cover with my New York City Office and that of Mr. Emory R. Buckner, the United States Attorney, 2nd Federal District, New York. I had been associated with Mr. Buckner in an Undercover Program for two and onehalf [sic] years. . . .
>
> January 10, 1927, while still associated with Mr. Buckner in New York, I placed eight additional Agents in Connecticut. . . .
>
> On . . . [February 1, 1927] I filed my resignation with Mr. Buckner, taking effect March 1st, 1927. . . .
>
> March 28 or 29, 1927, Dean Clarence W. Mendell, Dean P. T. Walden of Yale University, and Dean Nicholson of Wesleyan University accompanied me to Washington, where we had ten or twelve busy hours of conferences with the Attorney General, the Head of the Prohibition Enforcement Administration, the Head of the Federal Narcotic Bureau, and the Assistant Attorney General handling each of these three Divisions. . . .
>
> Mr. Chief Justice Taft and the U.S. Attorney General asked me to come to Washington several times soon after this for conferences on the future set up [of the U.S. Circuit Court] in Connecticut.

The early years of the Social Research Committee focused on "attempted black-mail, indecent pictures, homosexuals, liquor drops and girl drops within the campus buildings, etc., etc. NEVER A DULL MOMENT." Through his new "contacts with Roadhouses, Taxi Drivers, Houses of Prostitution, and Pimps" and his old contacts dating back to his service in New York with Buckner, Fisher began to investigate the "White Slave Ring."

But all that changed on December 7, 1941, with the attack on Pearl Harbor. Not that "V.D. Control" and "Vice Problems" ceased to be important; other matters became more important, especially cooperation with federal investigative agencies:

Scarcely a week passes that I am not called . . . from Maine to California and Washington to Florida for information regarding some investigation, and . . . on every tongue is a word of sincere praise for the splendid records kept by Yale and further for the splendid way Yale University is cooperating. . . .

I am deeply and truly thankful for the years I have shared with all of you in the ONE AND ONLY RESEARCH PROGRAM OF ITS KIND IN THE U.S.A. I am confident that the day will come when every large University will follow much the same program as you have followed and will recruit for such service men trained by one or more of these Federal Agencies such as the F.B.I. or the Central Intelligence Administration [*sic*]. Such men would be invaluable in Public Relations fields, Intelligence Directors in Security Posts [*sic*]. The New World we are now forging will require such a POST in every American University.

A university administrative agency, established to deal with classic parietal issues—drinking, drugs, sexual relations—had come to devote most of its attention to cooperating with federal investigative agencies on other matters. Was the shift in goals the result of consideration by the university authorities? How was it accomplished, and who was involved in the decision to establish the Committee on Social Research and to alter its functions? But first, who was H. B. Fisher and where did he come from? No history of Yale mentions Fisher, a Yale employee for a quarter of a century, or the committee, nor are they referred to in any printed table of organization of the university. The only references to them are scattered through the manuscript papers of a few high university officials—presidents, deans, provosts, secretaries of the Yale Corporation.[1]

What is most striking in the little that is known of Harry B. Fisher is his dedication to Christian morality. His brother, Frederick B. Fisher, at one time reputed to be the youngest bishop in the Methodist Episcopal Church, was especially concerned with the propagation of Christianity in India, where he had been Bishop of Calcutta, and with the active participation of religious organizations in political and social affairs. He was the first director of the Industrial Relations Department of the Interchurch World Movement, formed in the summer of 1919 partly to offset what some feared to be growing Catholic support for the labor movement. Bishop Fisher strongly advocated the use of ministers as arbitrators in strikes and other social conflicts and the use of church influence to force acceptance of such arbitration. By the 1920s enforcement of the Volstead Law and the struggle against the moral corruption that was both cause and consequence of the failure to enforce the law had come to be the major concern of the Fisher brothers, Frederick B. and Harry B.

By January 1927 Harry B. Fisher, also a minister in the Methodist

Episcopal Church, had had more than two years of experience as an associate of Emory Buckner, U.S. attorney for the Southern District of New York. Buckner, partner in a distinguished New York law firm with Elihu Root, Jr., and Grenville Clark, had been involved in investigating the connection between law enforcement and political corruption since 1911, when, as a young lawyer in the office of District Attorney Charles Whitman, he had discussed the links between corruption and prostitution with John D. Rockefeller, Jr., and some of his associates: Abraham Flexner, Jerome Green, and City Commissioner of Accounts Raymond B. Fosdick. In 1913, following the state Lexow investigation, Buckner became associated with the New York City Aldermanic Committee to investigate vice and police corruption. He arranged for members of the City Club and Citizens Union to supply unpaid investigators for his staff. When in 1925 he was appointed U.S. attorney, therefore, he already had precedent for appointing private citizens as investigators—and he found a willing, even eager, collaborator in Harry B. Fisher.[2] This was neither the first time nor the last in American history that political and moral zealousness provided mutual reinforcement.

On September 1, 1925, the New York Civic League opened a headquarters in New York City under the direction of the Rev. Harry B. Fisher. The league, after a sixteen-year crusade against "everything that injures the morals of the people, such as the white slave traffic; the dope traffic; immoral conditions in traveling carnivals, circuses, theatres and agricultural fairs; gambling, illegal liquor selling, obscene books and magazines; Sabbath desecration and political corruption," appointed Fisher director, "largely [as] the result of [the] urgent appeal . . . for more help" from Buckner and J. A. Foster, Prohibition director for New York City. Buckner wanted to increase the effectiveness of Prohibition law enforcement by the co-optation of a "private" organization into the government's police apparatus: "The only limit of your assistance to us," he told the Civic League, "will be the amount of money your League will be able to put into this work, especially in sending out expert investigators to secure evidence of law violations on which we can apply the padlock." The Civic League was eager to be co-opted, for it saw in co-optation a mechanism for the establishment of its moral imperium.

Harry B. Fisher lectured widely to church, civic, and youth groups, testified at grand jury investigations of gambling, and participated in raids to padlock premises where violations of the liquor laws were suspected. The New York Civic League fought for Prohibition and against corruption on both the political and judicial fronts. The work of the league and its metropolitan secretary was gratefully acknowledged by Buckner: "I wish to thank you for the very great assistance you have rendered me in securing evidence against important and defiant violators of the Prohibition law," he wrote the league on February 23, 1926. He asked for "additional expert investigators of high character and unquestionable integrity" to work under the direct supervision of Harry B. Fisher, who had been of such great assistance during the past year.

From September 1, 1925, to March 1, 1926, investigators of the New York Civic League, under Fisher's direction, provided the evidence for the padlocking of twenty-one "elite night clubs" in New York City, fifty-five elite clubs elsewhere, forty-one "smaller clubs, restaurants, wineries, and saloons," and twenty-eight places in counties and cities outside New York.[3]

Such was the man called to Yale in 1927. By profession a minister, of stern moral purpose but hardly a cloistered cleric, Fisher sought to establish a social order that incarnated a particular moral code. A soldier of the Lord, he was convinced he stood at Armageddon. Just what it was that brought Yale and Fisher together we do not know. It is possible, as Fisher intimates in his report for 1949–50, that Chief Justice Taft was the marriage broker; Taft had been a student and professor at Yale, was a member of the Yale Corporation, and combined a special interest in Yale with a special interest in law enforcement. It is also possible that the Yale-Fisher connection was the "logical" prescription that followed from a particular diagnosis of a social problem. On-campus drinking was serious; it was not a figment of the fevered imagination of the Yale authorities. What needs to be explained is, first, the relationship between how the fact of drinking was perceived and the solution adopted to handle it; and, second, how effortlessly parietal surveillance became political surveillance. The metaphor of vice as illness implied that moral improvement was a matter of public health; coercive means to obtain it were justified.

Whatever the mechanism that brought them together, Yale was ready for at least a liaison with Fisher, possibly a more lasting relationship.

To begin with, American colleges—even gentlemanly Ivy League colleges—were familiar with campus disorder. Fist-fights, window-smashing, theft, food riots, and sexual escapades were not infrequent campus occurrences in the late nineteenth century. At Yale mass riots broke out in the spring of 1919 over the issue of Prohibition; they often recurred at important football games and fraternity initiations and over such issues as compulsory chapel and the firing of popular professors.

Moreover, demographic, educational, and physical changes at Yale in the 1920s—including a major building program, the admission of new social groups to the student body, and the establishment of several professional schools—eroded the "single discipline . . . common traditions and common loyalty" of the older liberal arts college. In the past, Yale like many colleges, had relied upon the common outlook characteristic of the narrow social spectrum from which it drew its students to provide the order and decorum it desired; that moral discipline was reinforced by the religious beliefs and practices of the same narrow social spectrum. But the admission of new groups to the college and to the university created new problems. The authorities believed that disorder followed the admission of new social groups. The reestablishment of order, therefore, required the use of new methods. George W. Pierson, the historian of Yale, has described the problem as it appeared to Yale administrators in the 1920s:

> Then as the population multiplied, beliefs diversified, and new sciences were discovered, representatives of the rising interests inevitably pressed for admission. . . . The decline of religious fervor and chapel worship at Yale had been due in part to arrival of sons of the entrepreneurial class, but in particular to the multiplication of denominations, the rise of the Episcopalians, and then the admission of Catholics and Jews in some numbers starting in the 1880's and 1890's.

It was the responsibility of President James Rowland Angell to steer Yale through the dangerous waters of social and intellectual change. He could hardly be faulted for not having a foolproof program of educational reform to arrive at a safe harbor—who did? He was caught in a situation in which the solution he saw for some of the educational problems that engaged him—raising intellectual standards, developing graduate education—seemed to conflict with the solution he and others adopted for some of the social problems that plagued Yale. He was more aware of the implications of changes in the scientific disciplines than he was of the implications of social changes in the student body. Social changes produced problems that were more truly moral than educational; his solution, therefore, was not, in his own words, "purely intellectualistic." The "discovery and promulgation of truth" was not "the sole obligation even of the higher university." As Angell said, "you cannot get out of the ethical frame" that society "lays on the backs of its creatures." Mutual agreement that the stability of both college and country and the preservation of the character of the citizens of both rested upon the transformation of a moral code into a social structure led to the marriage of Yale and Fisher. More mundane considerations might also have added to their mutual attractiveness. In the 1920s Raymond B. Fosdick, an important figure in the movement that linked moral reform to public health and an associate of Fisher's superior, Emory Buckner, sat on a number of boards of Rockefeller philanthropies with President Angell. Understanding Yale's problems, Fosdick might well have mentioned Fisher—Buckner's employee—to Angell. Finally, in 1927 the use of police methods at Yale would not have struck the authorities as a shocking innovation. Its own police department, established in 1894, was probably the first in any American college. Now, in 1927, police power and morality would be joined; Harry B. Fisher was both confidential agent and clergyman.[4]

At the start, Fisher's duties combined enforcement of parietal rules at Yale and exposure of weaknesses in the administration of justice in the state of Connecticut. His report for 1949–50 perhaps exaggerated the closeness of his connection with Chief Justice Taft, but that he had such a connection and that Taft was concerned to help Yale are undeniable. "I saw Mr. Fisher yesterday," Taft wrote to President Angell on December 7, 1927, "and gave him an introduction to the Attorney General yesterday afternoon, so that he might explain . . . the very bad condition that exists in New Haven. . . . I mean to do as much as I can."[5]

As to parietal rules, Fisher kept a watchful eye on affairs at Yale and reported the results of his surveillance to his superiors, including President Angell. Concerning "Christmas Vacation Period Activities" in 1929 at Corbey Court, a Law School dormitory, Fisher wrote:

> [A] and another Law Student by the name of [B] [names deleted by S.D.] had two out of town school teachers with them in [A's] Apartment during the Christmas Vacation. These girls were there for immoral purposes. . . . My information places [B] as a member of the All Night party at the Court. This is the All Night Party reported to you by Dean Mendell . . . [C] and another student whose name I have been unable to get had two girls at the Court. . . . All four were every much under the influence of liquor.

Fraternity parties were especially closely watched. The smoker held by Phi Alpha Delta, a Law School fraternity, on March 15, 1929, was "most astonishingly WET. . . . About half of them became so drunk that they had to be taken out at some time during the evening." Fortunately, "there were no women connected with the party." The February 23, 1929, party given by Alpha Kappa Kappa, a Medical School fraternity, "included a number of Girls from the Medical School, Nurses School, and local and out of town girls. . . . The entire affair was one of a more or less drunken debauch." Fisher always took special pains to let his superiors know whether faculty members were present at the parties he had under surveillance. Concerning a "Faculty-Student BOOZ PARTY" held at the apartment of a medical student, for example, he gave Angell the names of two Medical School faculty members present and informed him that another party, to which faculty members would again be invited, would soon be held at the same apartment: "I would advise waiting for the second party thus getting some others from the Faculty. I think I can find out when this party is to be pulled off and you might pay them a visit."[6]

Fisher wanted to broaden the scope of his activities through the surveillance of women and a program, not uncommon in urban reform movements of the 1920s, for improved social hygiene. In his effort to win Angell's approval he had the support of Mrs. Bernice L. Corbin, wife of the distinguished law professor Arthur L. Corbin. Both Fisher and Mrs. Corbin felt that Yale might be embarrassed if the public knew of their program of cooperation with the New Haven authorities. The Yale-Fisher connection was very much under wraps. Fisher's official stationery gave no hint of it; his letterhead read simply "H. B. Fisher, Social Research, New Haven, Conn." and gave a post office box and telephone number not connected with the university. Nor, apparently, did he always see Angell in the president's office: "If you think best I could come to your home instead of to your office," he wrote to Angell in his request for an appointment to discuss "the Police Women's program" that he and Mrs. Corbin had broached to Angell.[7]

Discussion of that program—a combination of police surveillance and social welfare—dragged on for years. Fisher's interest was the expansion of his police activities; Mrs. Corbin's, improving the social environment at Yale. For both Fisher and Mrs. Corbin, cooperation with city government was a sine qua non. But with what branch of city government? The police department seemed the logical choice; besides, the new activity would put Yale in the vanguard of municipal police reform. In any case, the university would have to back the program completely if it wanted cooperation from the city. The university could demonstrate its support in a number of ways: by appointing Helen D. Pigeon, a graduate student in political science, to direct the program; by helping to obtain funds so that Mrs. Corbin would not have to continue to bear the brunt of financial support; by allowing Pigeon to write her doctoral dissertation on the program; by interesting the human relations group at Yale in the use of "patrol women on the streets"; and by getting financial support from "men of means." Prompt action was needed, since New York City had tried to lure "Miss Pigeon away from us with a salary of $6,000 per annum."[8]

Fisher and Mrs. Corbin met with Angell and succeeded in having him see Helen Pigeon and gaining at least his moral support for the program. Financial support was another, more difficult, matter. But Angell seems to have done what he could.[9] Edgar S. Furniss, dean of the Graduate School, inquired about Pigeon of the Department of Government. He found that though "she is considered a person of rather unusual ability," her department would not support her over other graduate students as a candidate for a fellowship; her "rather highly specialized interests and her peculiar background placed her at a disadvantage . . . with other first-rate graduate students, whose interests are more in line with the academic purposes of the School."[10]

Fisher's response to President Angell's request for more information concerning Miss Pigeon's financial requirements throws some light on what she was doing in the Yale Graduate School in the first place—and on Furniss's cryptic comment about "her peculiar background." Miss

Pigeon had already begun her work on October 1, 1929, under a two-year contract at $3,000 per year, a sum that had been borrowed. The financial problem simply had to be solved. Fisher wrote to Angell:

> I will not be able to do the kind of job I have longed to do here until some such program as this of Miss Pigeon's is launched and until I have my own contact men on the Campus Police.
>
> I am still confident we can find a group of friends somewhere among the parents of the lads now in the University who will help us launch the full program which Miss Pigeon came here to establish.[11]

"The full program which Miss Pigeon came here to establish"—Fisher's letter suggests that Miss Pigeon was engaged in police work before she had come to Yale for the purpose of establishing that program, and that payment for her work included, among other things, the fee for the two years of residence required for the Ph.D. Where did she come from? Did Fisher recruit her before she came to Yale or after? If before, how was it arranged that she be admitted to the Graduate School? The answers to these questions would shed light on what President Angell meant when he compared the importance of intellectual and social concerns, and would help explain the reticence of the Yale authorities—from President Angell down—to say anything specific about what she was doing at Yale. Details are hidden behind phrases like "her work" and "the program," but it is probable that surveillance and entrapment in the interest of morality were involved. Fisher had done such work for U.S. Attorney Buckner, and he was doing it now at Yale. It was, moreover, a fixed principle of the reform temper—going back at least as far as the Progressive period and seemingly confirmed by the program to combat vice in the vicinity of training camps during World War I—to look upon the struggle against liquor and prostitution as requiring methods of coercion and surveillance, including the use of policewomen, a newly emerging profession, to impose sanctions against offenders, to collect information on the connections between vice and politics, and to aid in the rehabilitation of prostitutes. Finally, the new "house system" at Yale gave planning for proper social arrangements as well as for buildings a new urgency. Proper social relations were the complement of proper buildings; Miss Pigeon was an architect of the former.[12]

That Fisher was not simply grabbing for more power behind the back of an administration that would have been in opposition had it been conscious of his maneuvering is strongly suggested by an exchange of letters between Dean Clarence W. Mendell and President Angell. Mendell wrote in support of Fisher's plea for funds to carry on Miss Pigeon's work:

> He understands perfectly that I cannot take any direct responsibility for the work which she does. At the same time I am interested in it to the

extent of letting you know that I believe that my work with Mr. Fisher
would be more effective if the program with regard to Miss Pigeon
could in any way be carried out.

Mendell and the Yale authorities clearly knew about Fisher and about
Miss Pigeon's "work." They simply felt they could not publicly admit
their knowledge. Angell thanked Mendell for his concern and agreed
with him: "About Miss Pigeon and her work. I am very keen to keep
this going, but I am at my wits [*sic*] end as to how we can finance it.
The good old alumni cow has been milked quite as much as it is at all
safe to do during the current year." Miss Pigeon's program seems to
have run afoul of the Depression, not of scruples.[13]

Angell did what he could to explore for solutions to the financial
problem—fellowships, contributions from philanthropic citizens, a fund-
raising committee "on which there should be at least one prominent
industrialist and one prominent banker and one prominent commercial
business man." He and Fisher were in complete agreement that confidentiality was required. President Angell: "I am aware of the danger of
enlarging a group of this kind, if it is to be kept at all within the bounds
of confidential procedure." Fisher:

> I should like to see such a group gotten together. You see the present
> group is the same group that sponsored my work when I first came on
> the job. It was felt that this group knew the value of strict confidence
> in matters of this type and could better launch the program and then
> reach out for that group of greater influence such as would insure its
> continuance.
>   . . . It has been necessary, of course, for me to stay in the back-
> ground. I have not felt that I could personally make any contacts other
> than those of the Deans' Committee,—Mr. Griswold, Mr. Aiken, Mr.
> Wear, and Dr. Coffin. I am naturally anxious to keep under cover in so
> far as local and State Politicians are concerned.[14]

Additional expedients were suggested. Miss Pigeon might be appointed as assistant dean in the Graduate School "to act as a sort of
Shepherdess [*sic*] over the 500 or so Women Students at the University."
That possibility had been discussed with Dean Mendell, but "all are
agreed that Miss Pigeon could do a much better job as the under-cover
director of such a program." The importance of the post could easily be
grasped by considering it in relation to the proposed women's dormitory
and the new Yale "house plan." "Miss Pigeon has assisted in the planning of such buildings both from the 'institutional' standpoint and from
the social and supervisional standpoint in many sections of the country,"
Fisher told Angell. She should be consulted in the planning of the new
dormitory. Angell passed on the suggestion to Dean Furniss and took
the occasion once again to emphasize the need for secrecy:

You know that we have been in contact for a couple of years or more—confidentially—with a Mr. H. B. Fisher, who has been assisting us in a good many problems affecting the general liquor and vice conditions in and about the campus and New Haven. . . . It has been suggested that possibly Miss Pigeon could be brought into connection with the administration of our general domestic facilities for women and that such an arrangement would allow us to exploit her services, in part for other kinds of work that we desire very much to have done. I should be glad if you would be willing to let Mr. Fisher talk confidentially . . . about the possibility of knitting Miss Pigeon in helpfully to any part of our program. It would all have to be quite confidential I am sure.[15]

Liquor and vice continued to be Fisher's main preoccupation through the 1930s. He wanted to expand his operations, including access to all private and public telephones on the campus and "having a contact man of my own on the Campus police."[16]

In other reports Fisher made clear why he needed contact men on the campus police. He also indicated that his work was made possible by "contacts" he already had with investigative agencies in Washington. "Wine, Women, Song, and Dope are the four winds that blow the flame of Social Disease," he wrote in 1936 to the Deans' Committee. The respect he had won from the Civil Service Commission and "certain persons" in the Treasury and Justice Departments had prevented the transfer of key government officials, "including the Special Agent in charge [of the FBI] at Hartford who held certain information most damaging to certain political circles which are known to you [Dean Mendell] and which I shall not mention further here."

There must have been in early 1935 some pressure to eliminate Fisher's program or at least to reduce his budget—possibly because of the Depression—but Dean Mendell declared his opposition directly to President Angell: "I shall personally consider it a major renunciation to give up Mr. H. B. Fisher. . . . He has established working relations with the Chief of Police which have been helpful to the situation in the College and in the City. . . . We are getting more than our money's worth." Two days later, transmitting Fisher's report for 1933–34 to Angell, Dean Mendell reiterated his support:

I am sending [Fisher's report] exactly as he made it. He maintains a rather vague style for he realizes that he is still, to a considerable extent, working under cover.

. . . The tangible part of Mr. Fisher's report might be made very melodramic [*sic*] but he does not believe in doing that.

. . . Except for him I am sure that we should have alarming conditions in Connecticut. His close friendship with Mr. [J. Edgar] Hoover in Washington also helped.[17]

Fisher's responses to the problems of "wine, women, song, and dope"—and Yale's—were classic, legitimized by apparent earlier success and by professional and educational authority. Moral reform and social welfare were a seamless web; ministry, social work, public health, and police work were professions equally concerned with the prevention of "social disease." How, then, could a line be drawn between the personal and the social, between private and public, between persuasion and coercion? The medical metaphor linked moral rehabilitation to social health and suggested the appropriateness of a variety of invasive procedures to guarantee the health of society. For the pioneer Boston settlement house leader Robert A. Woods, the New England Watch and Ward Society was "a sort of Moral Board of Health." The old idea of charity, sustaining the poor, the sick, the orphaned, and the aged, had given way to a larger conception—"to prevent . . . the moral diseases which lead to misery and crime." It was appropriate that the American Social Hygiene Association was formed from the merger, in 1914, of the American Federation for Sex Hygiene and the American Vigilance Society. Its first president, Charles W. Eliot of Harvard, the preeminent American educator of his time, added the weight of his enormous prestige to the identification of personal virtue and social health. Zealous participants in the antiprostitution movement supported procensorship campaigns. During World War I, the Watch and Ward Society was given power by the U.S. Commission on Training Camp Activities to protect moral standards in the vicinity of army camps. It was easy to move into politics.

John S. Sumner, successor to Anthony Comstock of the New York Vice Society, wrote in 1918:

> Just as we have the parlor Communist and the parlor Bolshevist in political life, so we have the parlor Bolshevist in literary and art circles, and they are just as great a menace. . . . While the governmental authorities are struggling against foreign ideas and their advocates regarding political attack, we have had the same conflict with foreign ideas calculated and intended to break down American standards of decency and morality.

His statement that political surveillance is the other face of moral surveillance was prophetic.[18]

Other times, other duties. Even before Pearl Harbor, Fisher, with the knowledge and approval of the Yale Deans' Committee to which he reported, broadened the functions of his office. To the traditional "general Student, Girl, Tavern, Road-House, [and] Health program" were now added the registration of aliens at the university and New Haven Hospital, "the compiling of further information" regarding noncitizens, and clearance investigations for all present and former faculty members and other personnel on behalf of the War, Navy, and State Departments and the FBI. "There are so many items of a confidential nature which cannot be given" in his reports, he informed the committee. Charles H. Warren, committee chairman and director of the Sheffield Scientific School, sent Fisher's 1944 report to Yale Treasurer T. W. Farnham for ultimate transmittal to President Charles Seymour:

> I am enclosing a brief report from "HB" [Fisher]. . . . The matter of avoiding details was gone into very thoroughly between Mr. Fisher and myself, and it appeared to both of us that it was unwise to put in writing any statement regarding detailed matters with which he has been concerned.
>
> Mr. Fisher has reported to me regularly throughout the past year at least once a month. . . . He has been extremely helpful in connection with registration of aliens connected with the University in any way and also in regard to clearing all members of the faculty who have volunteered their services to the government.[19]

Responding to pressure from government agencies to engage in activities that wartime conditions seemed to require, the Yale authorities adapted to new purposes an administrative system already in place. Extending it to new areas generated problems that had not been anticipated when the apparatus was created. The distinction between the administration of educational policy and the establishment of educational policy became blurred, with the result that values traditionally associated with academic freedom—like the right of faculties, not administrators, to appoint new faculty members—were compromised. That these values were being eroded became clearer with the passage of time. At Yale, as elsewhere, the way chosen by the administration to handle the problem was to keep it secret. It was not necessarily that the authorities eagerly went along with proposals to extend the scope of administrative power, though it is clear that many did approve the trend. Rather, they saw the need for security as more compelling than the academic tradition to which they claimed to be devoted, and they felt that security to be gravely threatened. Their policy of secrecy—dictated by their concern with security and possibly also by the fear of their own embarrassment if the public were to learn the contradiction between their claims and their behavior—made it difficult then or later to win over faculty, students, and alumni who might have supported an effort to maintain traditional academic freedoms. They could hardly have responded when they did not know that academic rights were in jeopardy. Indeed, even before the decade of the 1950s had begun, many were disarmed largely because they had been given reason to feel that the situation was well in hand.

Even scattered references to Fisher's activities and to Yale's policy regarding aliens are enough to document the blurring of the distinction between administrative powers and faculty rights. By late 1942 the office of the secretary had developed a printed form, always a sensitive indicator of increasing administrative activity, for maintaining a running record of government requests for information about students, alumni, and staff.[20] "Special investigations" of students, faculty, and staff had come to overshadow "our activities vital to . . . protecting our student body from the forces of organized vice," Fisher reported to his superiors in 1942.

More than four hundred special investigations were conducted for the FBI alone in 1942. Of those, sixty involved internal security, "any one of which could have been dynamite in untrained hands. Some of these subjects are still active in our University life and require a continual check to guard against any possible kick-back upon the University or the Government." Approximately twenty dealt with conscientious objectors, "a strange group, particularly since Pearl Harbor, yet a far too active group in contrast to the constructive all-out policy of the University. It is perhaps beyond our control, but I have wished many times that the University might establish a policy such as would automatically remove these Conscientious Objectors from our active student body." The most interesting of these investigations involved alumni who had gone into government service: "Dozens of times I have sat spellbound as some of these obscure men whose batting averages while in college were none too high have blossomed forth into both National and International figures."

As to the traditional activities, Fisher had investigated "around 76 girl cases" in 1942 and served on a government committee, with representatives of the FBI, concerned with venereal disease. His relations with the FBI were close.

Finally, he had been given—or assumed—a new responsibility, that of " 'Special Custodian' of the Enemy Aliens at the University. . . . As rapidly as possibly I am interviewing those listed as 'Enemy Aliens' or 'Men Without a Country' in our present list of students and faculty."

Dean Warren enclosed Fisher's report with a "Dear Charlie" letter to President Seymour. His endorsement suggests that Fisher's employment may have been a joint arrangement with the FBI, rather than an exclusively internal Yale affair:

> I am enclosing herewith confidential annual report of Mr. H. B. Fisher, *of the F.B.I.* [my emphasis]. He, of course, avoids specific details, but I think his report indicates how valuable his services have been to the University in many different ways. . . . His services have been quite invaluable and have saved us not only considerable annoyance, but actual trouble.[21]

Sometimes Fisher's references to his "clearing" of appointments through FBI files suggest that in pursuing his administrative tasks he crossed into faculty territory. "Also, I have cleared through the F.B.I. files certain research personnel and technicians employed by the several departments and laboratories of the University generally," he reported to his supervisory committee: "Particularly has this been done with reference to certain ones affiliated with the Institute of Human Relations in their several surveys being conducted under the National Research Council." [22]

In some cases, notably involving the employment of aliens, failure to be cleared meant withdrawal of the appointment.

On July 16, 1943, Provost Furniss was advised by the Yale Board of Admissions that the Japanese American Student Relocation Council had been notified that Yale had been added to the list of colleges deemed "undesirable for Japanese to attend" because it was the site of classified naval activities.[23] Fisher was delighted. Using not his own stationery but that of Secretary Lohmann's office, he wrote Lohmann on October 28, 1943:

> Referring to our conversation of this morning I would like to put down in black and white my own position in regard to Japanese students, namely, that it is my opinion Yale should earnestly seek to stay on the list of proscribed colleges and universities for the simple reason that we are in a defense area. . . . We should protect ourselves . . . by seeking to stay on the list of proscribed schools.[24]

In at least one such case, Fisher recommended rescinding an academic appointment.

On December 14, 1943, Fisher (now identified on his letterhead as "Liaison Officer, Yale University" with an official university address— P.O. Box 1111, Yale Station) notified Carl Lohmann that Kenneth K. Kurihara, a reader in economics, should be dismissed from the university. Kurihara had come to Yale as a teacher of Japanese; having resigned that position, he had, according to Fisher, no right to any other and was "no longer eligible for employment at Yale University for the 'Duration.' " Enemy aliens should not be permitted "access to other than 'contracted' employment." Lohmann attached to Fisher's letter two documents: a brief curriculum vitae of Kurihara, and the summary of a telephone conversation Lohmann had had with Elliott Dunlap Smith, chairman of the Economics Department and assistant to the president, which Lohmann had prepared for President Seymour. Kurihara had been employed by A. Whitney Griswold, professor of history, Seymour's successor as Yale president. When Griswold told him that "there was no place for him as an employee," he was sent to [Harold] Williamson for work as a reader in Economics." What Lohmann then wrote about Fisher is especially important in the light of the possibility that Fisher was perhaps as much an FBI man as a Yale man:

> About two weeks ago FBI Fisher called W[illiamson] and asked him to keep K[urihara] on while they were making their investigation. Then about two days ago F[isher] called W and said that the investigation was over, "You can let him go now." . . . No obligation to keep him, etc., etc. However, W feels that he will be put in a very embarrassing position to suddenly have to tell him that what he had previously said to him is not so.

Others on the Yale staff had no trouble at all in identifying Fisher as an FBI employee. Bernard Bloch of the Linguistics Department, sending on to Lohmann the forms supplied by Fisher that had to be filled out for all persons born in Japan or of Japanese parents, referred to *"Mr. Fisher of the F.B.I."* [emphasis supplied]. "Will you be so good as to see to it that these blanks are turned over to Mr. Fisher, since I do not know myself how to reach him?" [25]

Fisher's connection with government agencies—particularly the FBI—involved him in the establishment of the policy under which the files of the Alumni Office "and other confidential files of the various departments of the University" were opened to investigative agencies, government and private. He was the officer who administered the policy and kept the records of its enforcement. He was also placed in charge of compiling information on all aliens, "naturalized or otherwise," associated with Yale or applying for admission or employment: "Particularly shall it be necessary to take extreme care in the cases of 'Refugee Students' from Axis or Axis occupied countries, both in Europe and in the Pacific. Particular care must be taken in regard to a thorough check on all those students . . . whose parents are Japanese born. Even in the matter of transfer students from our own Pacific coast. It is urgent that your Agent check all such students before they are admitted to the University." [26]

Fisher did what he was supposed to do. One mimeographed form bearing his letterhead as liaison officer, a memorandum for the Office of Foreign Area Studies, states that "The application of [name deleted by S.D.] has been found not to be satisfactory by this office." To this Fisher has added: "My own investigation . . . makes it very clear that the University will run a very great risk by continuing the above-individual on its staff." Another memorandum to the Divinity School states that the "application of [name deleted by S.D.] has been rejected by this office." Was Fisher providing information to authorities who made the final decision, or did he have the power to reject applications for employment and admission? [27]

We know that he eagerly used what power he had to act and to make recommendations. Every report he wrote cites the growing number of investigations carried out for government agencies, particularly the FBI. Morality was now an also-ran. His report for 1943–44, for example, claims that the 1,073 investigations done for the FBI alone since Pearl Harbor "covered topical indices running all the way from Treason, Through Internal Security, White Slavery, Subversive Action, Espionage, to Illegal Use of U.S. Mail, together with numerous . . . Loyalty investigations." Most of these investigations "required the greatest care. Contacts for Special Agents [of the FBI] and introductions for them under many delicate situations have been secured."

In that report Fisher discussed two issues constantly repeated in later reports: the registration of applicants who were aliens or whose parents were born in a foreign country, and the increasing danger of Communist subversion. "I sincerely hope," he wrote, "that when World War *III* [emphasis in original] comes along all such alien personnel will be placed in uniform and maintained under strict Army and Navy regulations." He was alarmed by the "rather startling amount of 'Communist Activities and Communist Associations' among the families of certain applicants." These had increased "not only among 1st generation, but 2nd and 3rd generation families," and were "not limited to socalled immigrant families but . . . evident among old and established Yankee families as well."

His concern with political subversion led him to make recommendations about the admission of students just as it had about applications for employment. As "a Post War policy," he wrote in his report for 1944–45, "I wish we could organize a greater degree of 'investigative knowhow' among the Alumni sponsoring and checking applicants for admission to the University":

> In quite a number of instances I have discovered both the applicants and their families associated with Communist or Communist Front organizations. In other instances I have discovered the applicant's family active in other Anti American organizations, such as Nazi or Facist [sic] groups.
>
> I am not quite certain as to the method but I am certain that matters of this nature should be understood by those interested in the education of students of any Endowed University.

If Fisher had had free rein, political considerations probably would have affected employment policy, admissions, and research even more than they did. Though Yale had not gone as far as Fisher would have liked, it had gone far enough to win his approval:

> Every Federal Agency . . . has repeatedly stated that Yale University stands out alone both as to co-operation and sources of information from all other Colleges or Universities the country over.[28]

As we know, Yale used Fisher to solicit FBI cooperation in an effort to head off a potentially embarrassing exposé of Yale-FBI relations by the *Harvard Crimson.* He was a useful go-between. On September 17, 1950, SAC New Haven sent FBI headquarters the original and envelope of a letter sent to the Student Council of the Yale School of Medicine signed by Alexander Fuchs, an official of the Czechoslovak Student Council. "The Bureau will observe the peace theme throughout the attached letter," SAC New Haven wrote, and added, "Mr. H. B. Fisher, Liaison Officer, Yale University, made this letter available to the Bureau."

Episodes such as these, though important, were transitory. Other activities in which Fisher participated, less dramatic, were more important, for they had enduring institutional consequences. For example: Yale policy concerning access to its records. The policy that finally emerged was an amalgam of the interests of the university, the desires of investigating agencies (government and private), and the precedent of Fisher's own practices. On May 1, 1951, he wrote directly to SAC New Haven (with a copy to Yale Secretary Carl Lohmann) calling his attention to the proliferation of loyalty and security investigations at Yale, many of them conducted by private credit agencies and other businesses for companies under contract to the Atomic Energy Commission. A single credit agency, Bishops Service, Inc., of New York City, had made loyalty and security investigations of thirty-seven Yale students during the month of April 1951 alone. The number conducted by local New Haven agencies was even greater. The problem was, Fisher explained, that while the deans, masters, department chairmen, registrars, and professors at Yale were "perfectly willing to give one or two interviews regarding the loyalty and possibly security risk of students" to the one agency legally authorized to conduct such investigations—the FBI—they were not willing to grant multiple interviews, some with agencies totally unfamiliar to them: "I am merely reporting the above to you as the Liaison Officer at the University."

Fisher wrote again to SAC New Haven one week later:

> *My instructions to the Registrars at Yale* [emphasis supplied] are that under no circumstances are they to put in writing or give over the telephone any information to any such agencies or any such industries reflecting upon the "loyalty and security risk" of any student, former student or faculty member at Yale.

Did he have authority to give "instructions" to Yale registrars, or was this simply a boastful assertion of a power he did not really possess? In any case, his letter ended with a a threat to place the campus off-limits to investigators from private agencies. The FBI replied on June 1, 1951, in the form of an unsigned memorandum addressed to the attention of "Mr. H. B. Fisher, Liaison Officer": "It is not the FBI's responsibility to advise you and other officials at Yale University whether or not Yale University should continue to cooperate with the private concerns submitting requests to you in the course of their investigations."[29]

There were still other problems. The assistant to the president of Yale wanted a statement regarding cooperation with agents of military intelligence, who had complained that some of the college masters had refused to cooperate because of the policy of not giving information except to the FBI. He felt that "agents from any federal organization should probably get the same treatment that the FBI agents do," though restrictions should be placed on information given to "commercial outfits getting retail credit reports." Lohmann discussed the matter with Fisher, who told him that the military intelligence agents "were not permitted to ask for the information they hadn't received." Fisher's view was more restrictive—or more protective of the FBI monopoly in gathering information—than Yale's. Lohmann's directive to the deans and masters the following month announced that agents of the FBI and the intelligence services of the army, navy, air force, State Department, and Immigration Service were equally "entitled to receive full information about members of the University." Commercial credit agencies and private personnel service bureaus had no authority to conduct loyalty and security risk investigations.[30]

Fisher's time at Yale was drawing to a close. He had discussed retirement with Lohmann, and they had apparently agreed that he would leave at the end of the academic year 1951–52, which would mark his 25th anniversary as liaison officer and special representative of the Deans' Committee on Social Research. His approaching departure led him to thoughts of how he could finance his retirement, and these in turn to bittersweet memories about his relations with Yale. Year after year for a quarter of a century his Yale salary had not changed—$6,000 per year. His budget included items for auto and travel, investigations, telegraph, postage, and the like, but total annual expenditures had never gone much above $10,000. Since Pearl Harbor, expenditures had exceeded appropriations by $3,591.55, a deficit he had covered out of his own funds. The nest egg he had put aside for retirement in the South had been eaten up by rising costs and the need to repay bank loans he had made in order to meet the post–Pearl Harbor deficits of his office. He had turned down offers to do personal credit reports He was not eligible for retirement pay because his "job with the University was a contract job under Accounts Payable," and it was unclear whether he was eligible for social security benefits. Even Blue Cross had not been available to him until the past two years, when it was finally opened to the self-employed. Retirement would be possible only if he sold his home. Still, Yale might be able to help; reluctantly, Fisher asked if Yale would pick up the deficit:

> Do you think it would be possible for some sort of a "leave" to be granted whereby I might be able to get some of this money back? I realize this is probably asking "where I have no right to ask," but I have spent this money out of my own funds to do the job I have been set to do at the University.

The financial past was perhaps not quite as black as the $6,000 Yale annual salary might make it seem, for there are intimations in his final report that he may have received some compensation from the FBI. He wrote the Deans' Committee:

> I have decided to ease off the present policy of Bureau work as of March 1st, letting them get a head start on the setting up of a new schedule between now and June 30th. It will be a metter [*sic*] for them to start then (March 1st) while I am still around to help them make their needed contacts.

Did the "present policy of Bureau work" include compensation for Fisher? If it did, what was his status with the bureau—undercover special agent, or "confidential source" paid on a regular basis or by the piece of information he provided? If it did not, was his status with the bureau that of unpaid informant? But in that case, why should Yale have picked up the total salary tab for an employee who spent so much of his time doing the work of another organization?

Whatever the facts about Fisher's financial status, it was not the hope of financial reward that motivated him. His swan song, like his debut, was a rhapsody to morality:

> My good wife and I hope to spend the few years left to us in an entirely new type of service to the Church at large, namely *Prayer Evangels.* . . . We have a firm convection [*sic*] that PEACE cannot come, and if it came it could not be maintained until the PRESENCE OF PRAYER returns to the Church, to the Homes, to the Schools, and to the Colleges and Universities. . . .
>
> If the truth must be known—After 28 years of *"Investigations"* I am tired of all these *"Investigations."* At times I have felt that at the rate we are going within a few years we shall be seeking scientific means of "Investigating" the Third and Fourth Generations of the Men of Yale and every other University and Community in America.

For Yale, Fisher had only the deepest respect and affection. He had "known just about all the bad at Yale," but his years there had "increased [his] belief in God[,] . . . strengthened [his] faith in Man, and enlarged and deepened [his] admiration for Yale. . . . Yale had been a GOOD person to SERVE."[31]

Yale was concerned about Fisher's financial difficulties. On December 22, 1952, the Audit Division of the Connecticut Internal Revenue Service inquired as to the type of work performed by Fisher when he was employed by the university in 1951, in order to "ascertain whether or not Mr. Fisher was subject to self employment tax." Carl Lohmann replied:

> During the year 1951 Mr. Fisher's services were engaged by Yale University for the purpose of centralizing the inquiries made by Government agencies in their investigations of graduates of the University, members of its Faculty and students. . . . The investigators from Government agencies were assisted by Mr. Fisher in making their inquiries with a minimum of disruption of the regular work of University officers and the University depended on him to protect its records form unauthorized search.
>
> Mr. Fisher was also helpful in assisting students who got into trouble with the police, frequently settling their problems out of court.
>
> Mr. Fisher's professional services, backed by years of experience in investigative work, were considered by the University in the same category as those rendered by legal counsel or accounting firms.

Yale granted his request for paid leave. On January 7, 1953, he wrote from Gulfport, Florida, to express his gratitude:

> I just cannot . . . say to you good people at Yale what I would like to say for those checks that have been filling in my leave you so graciously granted me.
>   . . . Yale has been wonderful to work with.[32]

The shift of the Yale Deans' Committee on Social Research from enforcement of a moral code to political intelligence-gathering has some interesting parallels with other investigations of moral belief and political belief.

Such investigations during World War I involved a vast cooperative undertaking by both government and private agencies. Politics was morality by other means; moral surveillance guarded the corporate body from the sins that corrupted it. The appeal of the program was not confined to the religious fundamentalists; it was sanctioned by science and the new professions of public administration, public health, and public welfare. Charles W. Eliot and Newton D. Baker were not Torquemadas, but at times they showed a distinct resemblance to Anthony Comstock.[33]

In this effort, the American Protective League, formed in 1917 as a "private" organization, played a leading role, becoming, for all practical purposes, an agency of the Bureau of Investigation of the Department of Justice. By 1918, thousands of APL agents were working as quasi-government administrators, every federal attorney had an APL chapter at his beck and call, and the APL directors met daily at the Department of Justice with A. Bruce Bielaski and John Lord O'Brian, special assistant to the attorney general. The APL enforced vice and liquor regulations in the vicinity of army camps, in effect becoming a federal vice squad. Its members hunted draft-evaders and investigated alleged subversion among professors, labor unions, and foreign-language and left-wing political groups. It engaged in breaking and entering and wiretapping, influenced the withholding of passports, and gained entrance into private premises by agents masquerading as repairmen, insurance agents, and the like. Moral and political surveillance supplemented each other:

> Like the harassment of aliens and dissenters . . . the APL's control over the sex and drinking customs of Americans was hardly questioned.
>
> Federal sanction of these investigations allowed the APL to probe deep into the lives of American citizens. The last step, one that brought the APL into the life of almost every citizen, was its assignment to collect domestic intelligence for the War Department.

The similarity between Yale's investigations and other investigations of morality and politics may be accounted for by the climate of opinion, but Fisher's zeal may have been more directly inspired. The APL was especially active in the Methodist Church, of which he was a minister and his brother a bishop. The official in charge of military training camp activities, concerned with the suppression of vice, was Raymond B. Fosdick, an associate of U.S. Attorney Emory Buckner, for whom Fisher worked, and almost certainly known to Fisher in Fisher's capacity as metropolitan secretary of the New York Civic League. Finally, the director of the Bureau of Investigation and special patron of the APL was A. Bruce Bielaski, who, as a private attorney in New York during the 1920s, was an undercover agent for Buckner, as Fisher was.[34]

For the founders of classical economics, private vice was transformed by the hidden hand into public welfare. But for many of the founders of republican political theory, as well as for disciples of the modern moral majority, the republic of virtue requires a foundation of private morality. Public virtue, the willingness of the people to surrender everything, even their lives, for the good of the state, was primarily the product of each person's private virtues. Samuel Adams's words to John Scollay in 1780—that the city on the hill would be the "Christian Sparta"—suggest that morality may have its totalitarian side. Since the consequence of private vice was, at the very least, some form of political disorder, its eradication was a matter of public health. The founders of republican political theory dissected the historical corpses of dead states as corpses of the dead are autopsied, to discover the causes of the disorder of which the patients died. David Ramsay wrote his history of "the predisposing causes of the revolution" in what he called "the medical stile." By the end of the eighteenth century, some republican theorists were fearful of basing public virtue on such a constricted view of private morality. Freedom would be destroyed "by the establishment of the opinion that the state has a *perpetual* right to the services of all its members," Jefferson wrote to Monroe.[35]

By the end of the nineteenth century, many of those interested in public morality and social health were not content to explain them as the outward expression of an essentially inner discipline. The preventive society came into being, armed with police powers—such as the power of arrest and the power to use secret agents—to enforce compliance with a moral code that was also an expression of a broad set of social values. Labor unrest was a symptom of degeneration and corruption, as much in need of elimination as prostitution and other forms of vice. Abram Hewitt warned that in order to control "our lower nature" and protect Americans "against the evil impulse and the examples of depravity . . . we must counteract such arrant plotters and imposters as [Terence V.] Powderly [head of the Knights of Labor] and [leading economic and social reformer Henry] George." A vote for Henry George and organized labor was "a vote to undo what has been done for law and order." In moving from moral to political surveillance and in its co-optation into the law enforcement system of the state, the preventive society of 1900 established a precedent—in philosophy and in policy—for the sanitization of politics in the 1950s.[36]

Treatment of the political Typhoid Marys focused on isolation or expulsion. To be properly disposed of, however, they had first to be identified—and that required both "private" organizations and government to join forces to ferret out the beliefs and behavior that to some are nobody's business, to others, everybody's business.[37]

In 1914 the Ford Motor Company established a Sociological Department—the title smacks of Yale's Committee on Social Research—to pass on the qualities of "thrift" and "character" required of employees to qualify for its $5-a-day wage. In 1915 the Sociological Department was under the direction of the Rev. Samuel S. Marquis, dean of the Episcopal Cathedral of Detroit. By 1919 Marquis directed 150 employees in investigations of the marital status, religion, nationality, citizenship, economic status, hygienic standards, drinking habits, sexual practices, budgeting practices, church attendance, recreations, and social relations of Ford employees. All information, including gossip and suspicions retailed by informers, was recorded. By 1921 the Sociological Department no longer existed. It had a brief revival in 1937 under the notorious Harry Bennett, but by then the "welfare" functions of Bennett's Service Department—supervising relief payments to unemployed

Ford workers, setting up vegetable gardens, and the like—were over-shadowed by its main function: preventing unionization of the Ford Motor Company by espionage and intimidation.

Other parallels with the Yale Committee on Social Research are striking. Just as the committee had close relations with the FBI, so, too, did the Ford Motor Company. In 1944 John S. Bugas, SAC Detroit, who had been an intimate of Harry Bennett for a number of years, was appointed an assistant to Bennett. Eventually he replaced him and became vice-president for labor relations.[38]

Not that Fisher was a Bugas, nor Yale a Ford Motor Company, nor that the Ford Service Department provided the model for the Deans' Committee on Social Research. Rather, both situations exemplify the adaptation of existing organizational structures to their leaders' perceptions of new circumstances and the conflicting pressures from the elements of which those organizations are made up. Labor unions came to be on Ford's agenda—and the company responded. Relations with the government came to be on Yale's agenda—and the university responded, in such a way, moreover, as to bring it into conflict with some of the traditional values of universities, like academic freedom. The erosion of autonomy was the price paid to retain the good will and cooperation of the government. Did the Yale authorities know that that would be the price of acceding to the wishes of government authorities? Probably not; their behavior is less that of traitors to the principles they professed than that of poor little sheep who had gone astray. Who has not gone astray in the face of temptation or coercion? And in an institution devoted to the most radical examination of certainties, who can be sure of the principles that only yesterday seemed to be those that at all costs had to be defended? It is likely that H. B. Fisher and the FBI had a clearer view of their principles than the university authorities had of theirs.

The pressures on Yale—and other universities—of temptation and coercion still exist. Are they being responded to as the Deans' Committee on Social Research responded?[39] Central to that response was secrecy. It was not to the interest of the government to reveal its secrets. To have done that would have exposed government agencies to the specific targets of their investigations and revealed to others that they were potential targets. And it would have revealed the general secret that government agencies had established a network of surveillance that penetrated everywhere and created the possibility that nothing—and nobody—was what it seemed to be.[40] Within Yale itself, knowledge of the existence of the committee was confined to a handful of persons, mainly administrators. Some social arrangements cannot survive in the presence of light. Who was to say no to the small group of administrators who established the policy and carried it out? Who was even to bring them the news that perhaps it was not working as intended, that it violated important principles of the university, that there were alternatives?

What did the government gain from the secrecy? What did Yale gain? Both were in the business of collecting intelligence; like all intelligence agencies they had to weigh the value of the information obtained against the risks of obtaining it. Those risks were minimized by the policy of secrecy. For the government, that meant greater aggressiveness in the collection of information. For Yale, it meant immunity from the embarrassment that might result from public awareness that it had departed from the norms of academic autonomy. The cost of winning government approval would not be borne by the institution, but by those who were the present and future targets of investigation. Under the arrangement that emerged, the beliefs and behavior of individuals were not protected by privacy. The behavior of institutions, including government, was protected by privacy—called secrecy. The increase in institutional and government secrecy was marked by an increase in institutional and governmental intrusiveness and power. The decline in personal privacy was marked by a decline in personal freedom and professional autonomy.[41] The persistent and secret invasion of privacy, legitimized as a hunt for heretics, for the immoral, for the mentally ill, or for traitors, freezes the self-confidence people need to express their beliefs and breaks the social connections necessary to translate beliefs into behavior. Natural history has its ice ages; so does political history.

9. Lux et Veritas

Communist infiltration was always at the center of the FBI's interest. SAC New Haven, therefore, devoted considerable attention to his reply to the great investigation of universities ordered by Hoover in the spring of 1953. On April 24, 1953, the New Haven FBI office submitted its first report; additions were submitted sporadically, but their information was so similar to that of the first lengthy report that it may be taken as paradigmatic of them all. In that first report, seventeen persons—including faculty, students, and staff—were included; fourteen were on the Security Index, slated for arrest in event of a national emergency. They came from a variety of departments and divisions of the university—botany, the Institute of Human Relations, the Law School, physiology, zoology, mathematics, medicine, the library, linguistics, chemistry, among others. In addition, SAC New Haven listed six persons from the University of Connecticut at Storrs, one from Wesleyan, and one from New Haven State Teachers College; of these, six were on the Security Index. A few had been identified by informants as being members of the Communist party or one of its affiliates, like the Labor Youth League; one, a distinguished member of the law school faculty, was said by Louis F. Budenz, a former Communist official who had become a professional witness for congressional committees, to have been called a Communist by a third person and by Jay Lovestone. But most had attracted the attention of the FBI because of participation in the Connecticut People's Party—the Henry A. Wallace campaign—the National Lawyers Guild, the Civil Rights Congress, the North American Committee to Aid Spanish Democracy, the Rosenberg case, the "Save Willie McGee Committee," the

National Council of the Arts, Sciences, and Professions, the American Jewish Congress, and anything connected with world peace.

The FBI sent me three copies of the New Haven report of April 24, 1953; variations in the way they have been edited provide interesting information. Sometimes the censor slips, and material that is deleted from two copies may not be deleted from the third.

In two copies of the FBI report, for example, the names of informants have been deleted. In the third copy, however, the following appears: "Mrs. Walter D. Lee, 55 Park St. (whose identity is to be protected)" reported that she had seen literature from the People's party in the apartment of one of the suspected Communists. In another case, the name of the informant has been deleted from two copies, but the phrase "whose identity should be protected" has been allowed to stand. In the third copy, the name of the informant has not been deleted; he was William M. Acker, Jr., a Law School student, who reported to army intelligence concerning the activities of the Yale chapter of the Lawyers Guild. Acker's report, which was forwarded to the FBI, states that although one of the persons about whom he was informing "has made no assertion that he is a member of the Communist Party, he has frequently expressed his favoritism for the communistic form of government. . . . Acker added that he is willing to contribute further information to authorized persons concerning the activities of [name deleted by S.D.] and other individuals of dubious political sympathies with whom he is acquainted at the Yale University Law School."

Only recently the name of Acker surfaced. Now Federal Judge William Acker, Jr., of the Northern District of Alabama, he was sharply reprimanded by the Circuit Court of Appeals for his rulings in a civil rights case.[1]

Notwithstanding FBI and Yale denials of the use of "liaison men," both continued to use H. B. Fisher. On September 17, 1951, SAC New Haven forwarded to the director a letter and its envelope sent to the Student Council of the Yale Medical School from the Czechoslovak Student Council in Prague. The letter was an invitation to join the "XX International Students Summer Games and the III Festival. . . . [We] would welcome the opportunity to meet your students and discuss with them mutual views and experiences. The III Festival . . . will be a glorious meeting of all progressive students. . . . With the best wishes for PEACE and the most sincere greetings." SAC New Haven wrote: "Mr. H. B. Fisher, Liaison Officer, Yale University, made this letter available to the Bureau."

Persistent deceptiveness by the FBI in denying the *Harvard Crimson* allegations about "liaison agents" makes it clear that it was not the *Crimson* that, in Hoover's words, was "distorted, inaccurate and untrue" in its reporting about the FBI and Yale; the FBI was untruthful in reporting its own activities. One final example of Hoover's deceptiveness:

Yale Law School professor Ralph S. Brown, Jr., who was doing research
on loyalty tests for employment, wrote to Hoover asking to what extent
the bureau's files were made available to state and local administrators
or to their special investigators, adding, inaccurately but in consonance
with what the FBI stated its policy to be, "I am aware of the Bureau's
policy of not making such files available to private employers." Hoover
replied that information in the files of the FBI was strictly confidential,
available for official use only, and provided only to those federal government agencies entitled by law to receive it.[2]

The FBI, in its pursuit of subversion on the Yale campus, tacked
between the most significant and the most trivial of interests. Had it
been dependent entirely upon its own personnel, the effort might have
been too great for its resources, but it had the cooperation, informal and
formal, of Yale personnel. During the course of a "routine contact in an
applicant investigation," for example, John S. Nicholas, Sterling Professor of Biology and director of the Osborn Zoological Laboratory, notified a special agent of the FBI that an International Congress of Cell
Biology would be held at Yale September 4–8, 1950, at which four or
five representatives from behind the Iron Curtain would be present. Nicholas told the FBI agent that he had written the State Department to
request that "in the event these representatives from said countries are
admitted to the United States . . . they be placed under surveillance
while in this country." He did not know the identity of these persons or
the countries from which they will come; "however, should he receive
this information he advised that he will furnish same to the New Haven
Office of the FBI." Hoover forwarded the information given by Nicholas
to Jack D. Neal, associate chief of the State Department Division of
Security, with the request that all information about the scientific meeting, especially the identity of the Iron Curtain delegates and the status
of their visa applications, be sent to the FBI. Professor Nicholas kept his
promise to the FBI; he provided the New Haven office with the names
of all foreign delegates. Four pages of the document have been entirely
withheld. All the names on the list provided by Nicholas were checked
against FBI files.[3]

The FBI cultivated its Yale connections. Professor R. Barry Farrell,
convinced that an article that was to appear in the *Yale Daily News* about
FBI investigations was incorrect, informed the FBI that he had advised
its author to "go to the New Haven Office of the FBI and secure the
correct information concerning FBI investigations on the Yale campus."
The student reporter was interviewed by agents of the FBI, including
SAC New Haven. Notwithstanding its denials, the FBI collected information about applicants and made its own information available to the
Yale authorities over a long period of time. Some of its informants were
highly placed in the Yale administration. Prospective appointments in
the physics, philosophy, and history departments, for example, were dis-

cussed by Provost Furniss with informants who then notified the FBI that Furniss "doubts that [the] appointments will go through": "The position of Yale University is apparently swinging around to the point which [two-thirds of a line deleted] that it is much better to look men over and know exactly what they are before they are appointed, and that it is much easier to get rid of them by not appointing them than after they have been once appointed."[4] One informant reported on a conversation he had had with Furniss regarding a prospective appointee:

> [Three lines deleted] the University was quite taken aback by the glib manner in which Mr. [name deleted by S.D.] had spread the news that he was to receive a three-year appointment at Yale and more specifically were they, the officers of the University, taken aback by Mr. [name deleted by S.D.]'s associates and companions in the pink field and darker shade of Communist hue.[5]

Alumni connections were used, sometimes as much through the solicitation of the alumni as through the FBI, which was always eager to tap potential sources of information. It was worth the time and trouble of Assistant Director Nichols to notify Clyde Tolson that Assistant SAC Belmont in New York had had lunch with several executives of the Empire Trust Company, all alumni of Yale, who were concerned "about Communist tactics and the advances they have made at Yale. . . . They talked of the possibility of securing the Director's assistance in combating infiltration of Communism," perhaps in the form of a meeting between Hoover and the presidents of the Ivy League colleges. Student contacts were used to obtain information about the activities of the John Dewey Forum and, as we see repeatedly, about articles in the *Yale Daily News* concerning FBI investigations on the campus. In these matters, H. B. Fisher was often involved, as when, for example, he denied a statement by a student who claimed to have been warned not to seek university approval for a group interested in race relations because it would be investigated by the FBI.[6]

What the FBI considered grave enough to warrant its attention raises issues of sufficient importance to warrant our attention. Few would disagree that the designation of a new university president is likely to be of interest to the FBI, though not all would agree that the matter is a proper concern of the agency or requires any action on its part. When A. Whitney Griswold was elected in 1950 to succeed Charles Seymour as Yale president, his name was checked in the FBI files. Assistant Director Nichols was notified about Griswold's publications. He was also told that FBI documents "reflect that Dr. Griswold wrote his Congressman during October 1933" recommending that the Justice Department "use propaganda in the form of anti-crime posters pointing out the cost of crime to the tax payers. We had no correspondence with Dr. Griswold about this matter." Nichols was told that Griswold was a contributor in 1937 to a new magazine, *Events,* "devoted to international affairs, American foreign policy, etc." We may suppose that it was of greater interest to the FBI that Griswold was vice-chairman of the New Haven branch of Russian War Relief in 1944 and had signed a letter to the *New York Times* in 1945 with a number of other Yale professors, writing "in the cause of world peace and [declaring] that relations between the United States and Russia must be improved" and that academic exchanges should be extended.

Fewer would feel that it was a proper concern of the FBI to check on the publications sent by American university libraries to deposit libraries in various European countries, in pursuance of agreements for the international exchange of scholarly publications. Yet that is what the FBI did in 1951 in connection with literature sent, under law and with the approval of the State Department, to the Czech National and University Library in Prague. Despite the fact that the exchanges were authorized under an international agreement of 1886, the boxes were seized in Germany.[7]

And surely only a handful would find that reviewing an undergraduate musical farce was a proper function of the FBI, or even, save under conditions reflecting an extraordinary degree of paranoia, understandable. On May 21, 1951, having been alerted by New Haven newspaper articles that the Yale "F" Society was producing *A French Affair* on behalf of the Yale–New Haven DP Sponsorship Committee—to help finance displaced persons in New Haven until they could become self-supporting—SAC New Haven sent a lengthy report to Hoover about the play. On April 24 the *New Haven Register* had announced that "the plot deals with what might occur when a group of case-hardened FBI men take over an exclusive Southern school of girls on the Potomac in an effort to apprehend a beautiful French spy posing as an exchange student from Paris." Exchange students, colleges, spies, the FBI—all the elements for mischief-making or for enlightenment were present. Special Agent Charles H. Fisher, Jr., was assigned to attend the opening night performance. He reported to SAC New Haven, who then reported to Hoover:

> The story briefly concerns a mythical government agency named the Federal Bureau of Espionage or F.B.E. Agent Fisher has stated that there are no direct references to the FBI, and nothing defamatory was noted. . . . The opening of the play consisted of a recording of the so-called FBI March, which was taken from the Lava Soap program. . . . Several of the characters were dressed in trench coats and snap brim hats and worked for the F.B.E., but . . . there was nothing caustic or vitriolic in the entire production. However, it is noted that when SAM SLADE . . . called his workers into his office . . . he summoned them by firing his gun into the air. . . . SLADE and his assistants drink

whisky in order to get up enough courage to participate in this danger-ous assignment.

The FBI must have been relieved. The *Yale Daily News* critic found a "good deal of corn in the script and most of the lyrics are only ade-quate," but there was "humor . . . and enthusiasm." The FBI was re-assured.[8]

The Yale documents allow us to see clearly how Yale's assessment of the political climate made cooperation with the FBI and congres-sional investigating committees seem logical—logical, if kept secret.

Yale was no more insulated from the political hot and cold of the time than any other university, and ample precedent existed for taking political considerations into account in the making of appointments and promotions. The most widely known of these earlier episodes had to do with the refusal to grant tenure to the sociologist Jerome Davis of the Divinity School because of his alleged pro-Soviet views, but other inci-dents, less well known or known only to their participants, show the pressures on university administrators and the political finesse they thought they had to show to keep the loyalty of alumni whose goodwill was nec-essary for the flow of funds.

On June 12, 1933, Professor Ray B. Westerfield of the Yale Econom-ics Department wrote to Dean Furniss, chairman of the Department of the Social Sciences, to protest Yale's recent invitation to the distin-guished Italian antifascist historian Gaetano Salvemini, on behalf of a number of prominent Italians who wanted to know whether "it would not be possible for Yale to engage for a year (or half year) some Italian economist or political scientist who could and would present more fairly and adequately the Fascist development, system and philosophy." Westerfield was himself perturbed by the Salvemini invitation; in 1927–28, when he lectured in Italy, he had heard Salvemini: "I must say from what I heard Salvemini say and what I heard he had said to his classes and elsewhere, he did present a most distorted, if not grotesque, picture of Fascism. Fascism is prominently before the world, not only in Italy, but elsewhere, and it seems a shame to have it so falsely presented at Yale." Westerfield then submitted to Furniss the names of three econ-omists, all of whom "are Fascists and have a good command of En-glish."[9]

George T. Adee, an active Yale alumnus and stockbroker, was a fre-quent and determined, but friendly, critic of the Yale administration in the 1930s. His concern was that "not any one of us who love the Insti-tution"—Yale—could afford to make "statements that might be inter-preted as perhaps extreme liberal beliefs, or as encouraging extreme lib-eralism." Such statements encouraged a lack of confidence among students "in our institutions and unconsciously" made them "more ready to accept any new order, even communism." There was, in fact, a "direct Subversive campaign underway to undermine the fundamental Christian philosophy of our national political thought." The campaign involved many organizations appealing to the "unthinking" through slogans in favor of "pacifism, internationalism, social security, production for use and not for profit, etc." Adee told president Angell that if his classmates confirmed his suspicions about what was happening at Yale he would ask for discussions at the highest administrative level:

> I feel sure . . . you will realize my one and only reason for taking so much trouble about this subject is my abiding affection and devotion to Yale, and my desire to do my utmost to preserve intact her traditional conservatism, which has made her what she is. . . . I want . . . to give you my views and fears in regard to the danger of the spread of socialistic and communistic propaganda and particularly as it applies to dear old Yale.

He enclosed a copy of a letter he had written to Dean Charles H. Warren, identical to the letters he had written to other Yale faculty members and alumni. He was particularly concerned about the invitation to the English Communist John Strachey; the talks at Yale by Heywood Broun and Joseph P. Lash; and the questionable lectures by such faculty members as Dean Charles E. Clark of the Law School and Professors Doob, Brooks, and Bakke. Mainly, though, he wanted to know about student organizations—the Social Problems Club, the Graduate Forum, the National Student League, the Radical Party of the Yale Political Union: when were they started; by whom; who were their student and faculty members? Angell gave a soft answer: "I am sure that of all the institutions of comparable character, the student body at Yale is more fundamentally conservative than any other." Yale's few disturbing episodes were largely the result of the teaching of a few radical professors at the Law and Divinity Schools; "no one appreciates more fully than I the deep and devoted loyalty which you have always manifested for Yale." [10]

U.S. Senator Robert A. Taft, a member of the Yale Corporation, opposed the granting of an honorary degree to Soviet Foreign Minister Maxim Litvinoff in 1942; he stated his political objections, but before he got around to mentioning them he wrote: "Mr. Litvinoff, whose name was Wallach, was born and brought up in the City of Bialystok." Political views of a different kind did not meet with Taft's disapproval. In 1938 he wrote to Yale Secretary Carl A. Lohmann, recommending the appointment of Samuel B. Pettingill, a Democratic representative from Indiana, as professor of law: "He does not intend to run for reelection. He is a distinguished lawyer. . . . I know he is a man to whom serious consideration ought to be given if he is available." To this suggestion,

Law School Dean Clark did not give a soft reply. He wrote Lohmann, who had forwarded Taft's letter, that the same suggestion, made by many others, was troubling because it was so clearly inappropriate. Pettingill had been graduated in 1911 with a good record, primarily as a debater. His record in Congress was nothing if not conservative; in fact, "he had been one of the most bitter opponents of new developments and has served as counsel for Mr. Frank Gannett's Constitutional League." His retirement from Congress was voluntary in form, but "quite with the approval of his constituents." It would be too much of a task "to try to work him over into a professor fully in touch with modern developments in legal education." [11]

During the decade 1945–55, the Yale authorities felt under considerable pressure to take action concerning several appointees whose political views had been questioned. As we have already seen, the FBI was aware of a number of these situations and may even have been involved in the making of the decisions. The New Haven FBI office knew during the last years of the Seymour regime of the Yale policy of inquiry into the political activities of prospective faculty members prior to their appointment, on the ground that it was easier to prevent an appointment than to remove a faculty member who had already been appointed. On September 26, 1945, Law School Dean Pyle Gulliver gave Seymour the names of fourteen persons to be considered for appointment. Three were recommended as full professors with tenure: "Thomas I. Emerson, Abe Fortas, and Harold Laswell. All three encountered stiff opposition from alumni. The recommendation of Fortas, who had taught at the Law School in the 1930s, was withdrawn, probably because it was opposed within the Yale Corporation itself. Dean Gulliver knew that his faculty's recommendation would incur the disapproval of "the more conservative elements of the legal profession [who] will probably consider the appointment a mistake." He told Seymour that, on questioning several of those who objected to Fortas, he had received no answers that made any impression upon him; and he reminded Seymour that Supreme Court Justice William O. Douglas, while a teacher at Yale, had chosen Fortas as his associate and recommended him as first choice to be his successor. Laswell, while not a lawyer, would assist in the integration of law and the social sciences and in the development of new courses.

The opponents of the three flooded the Yale administration with letters, let loose by a broadcast made by conservative news commentator Fulton Lewis, Jr., based apparently on a leak to him by someone at Yale.[12] A. W. Mace, a Law School graduate and official of the Allegheny Ludlum Steel Corporation, followed a telegram with a letter to President Seymour protesting the appointment of all three, two of whom had "no place to go," while the third—almost certainly Emerson—though he had a brilliant mind, was "distinctly not in step with those philosophical and political concepts that brought this country its blessings *and its strength* [emphasis in original], and, being brilliant, is the more [*sic*] dangerous of the three. Why should Yale take on what even Harvard doesn't want more of?" His solution was simple: many of the alumni felt that Yale's problems would diminish if its "educational plans would continue as presently constituted—based on Christian concepts. Why should not a Christian university openly counter the totalitarian propaganda that a university, to be a university, must be basically irreligious?" He quoted a friend who asked, "If Yale teaching is based on Christian concepts . . . why don't they say so?" He wanted his boys to be taught the ideals and ambitions that had guided "their Mother and their Grandmother," but he didn't know whether "Yale is the place to send them."

The senior partner of a Puerto Rican law firm was outraged by the proposal that Fortas and Emerson be appointed; their "peculiar views and philosophy . . . were regarded by the majority of Yale parents and graduates as inimical to our government and its institutions." George T. Adee was still on the prowl; all three candidates were "extreme left wing radicals" whose views were "contrary to the American way of life." If they were added to a faculty that already contained so many "extreme liberals," radical ideologies would control the school. He volunteered his services "to aid in preventing the nomination in the future of extreme radicals" and wrote letters to Law School alumni soliciting their support.

Within a short time, the three candidates had become two. On January 10, 1946, President Seymour wrote the new Law School dean, Wesley A. Sturges, that he was withdrawing his commitment to support all three nominations:

> It appears that the Corporation will be divided if all three professorial appointments are acted upon. For the welfare of the University and the Law School itself it is vital that this division should not occur.
>
> Accordingly I am prepared, in order to avoid such a contingency, to withdraw my support from one or another of the candidates if so requested by the Corporation. It seemed to me that you should have this warning of my withdrawal from the commitment I gave you.
>
> Please regard this information as confidential, except as you may desire to discuss it with members of the faculty, who will also regard it as confidential.

How the nominee to be sacrificed was chosen is not known. It was Abe Fortas. Given the possibility of embarrassment, the matter was handled with consummate discretion: Fortas told the authorities that he was unable "to join the Law School Faculty at this time." Dean Sturges so informed Seymour in a letter requesting him to withdraw the name of Fortas for appointment. Fortas's "situation, which he has heretofore dis-

cussed with me at length," made it necessary for him "with real reluctance" to withdraw. The faculty hoped that Fortas would be able to reconsider at some future date. Sturges requested that the withdrawal of
his recommendation be without prejudice to its possible later renewal.

One alumnus, active in the affairs of the Law School, threatened to
take no further interest in the school if the appointment should be made:
"I used to be able to put up a pretty good argument for men like Clark,
Douglas and [Thurman] Arnold, but I cannot think of any excuse whatever for the Rodells, the Hamiltons, and the Emersons." The issue could
not be clearer: "Is Yale to have a school dominated and controlled by
men who do not believe in our form of government or in our system of
economic freedom, men who will use their positions as teachers to spread
the doctrine of collectivism and even Communism?" It was a sentiment
often expressed to the president, even at the level of the corporation
itself. John W. Hanes, a prominent business executive and member of
the Yale Corporation, wired President Seymour that he wanted the record to show that he opposed all the nominees:

> I have worked with Fortas in the Securities and Exchange Commission
> and I do not believe his philosophy is one that we want at Yale. The
> record of Emerson is so blatantly Communistic that his selection seems
> to be nothing short of tragic. The third member I do not know much
> about but feeling that the other two are so dreadful I must vote against
> him also. I sincerely hope you will convey my strong conviction to the
> other members of the Corporation and assure them that this is too se-
> rious a matter to let pass without the fullest investigation.[13]

Through the final years of Seymour's administration and into the
early years of his successor's, Emerson continued to raise the hackles of
conservative Law School alumni and to frighten university administrators concerned about the possible cutting off of funds. His participation
in the Henry Wallace campaign in 1948—the "Wallace-Communist
ticket" as one letter-writer called it—seemed to jeopardize the Law
School's $10,000,000 Scholarship Endowment Fund. Officials in the
central administration checked the backgrounds of the letter-writers; when
they were felt to be important enough, Seymour replied to them. He
generally made quite clear his opposition to Emerson's political views,
but he denied that he was a Communist and stated his disapproval of
Emerson's active political campaigning. On the copy he sent to Dean
Sturges of his reply to one alumnus, he wrote: "The Cole letter ex-
presses what has come to me in more violent terms from other quarters.
The vital point is, Can we permit a professor supposedly on full time to
engage in a political campaign? The Corporation will ask, Is Yale through
Emerson's salary financing a Wallace movement? Emerson may have
asked your permission. He never asked me." For other alumni, it was

Emerson's activity in the National Lawyers Guild that led to threats to cut off funds.

Like Seymour, Griswold had to support Emerson's civil liberties while disapproving of his politics. Griswold wrote one of his critics that Emerson "has something of a martyr complex and is a born champion of unpopular causes. No matter what the extenuating circumstances I may cite, he is the single most time-consuming member of the faculty as far as my alumni mail is concerned. I earnestly wish he would concentrate on his teaching and I am trying by patience and example to persuade him of this course."

If pressure from alumni led Yale presidents to state their feelings about faculty members so openly, one wonders what they said in reply to attacks from members of the Yale Corporation. Seymour was quite right when he said that the corporation would cast a cold eye on the political activities of faculty members. Writing to Seymour about Professor Fowler Harper, another Law School faculty member frequently attacked by alumni and newspaper columnists, Prescott S. Bush, a member of the corporation and former U.S. senator, expressed his own dismay and that of other Yale alumni at Harper's activities. He made clear that the politics of faculty appointees was a concern of the corporation: "I remember raising some questions about Harper at the time his confirmation was asked because I did not like the looks of his record." But, after "calming assurances" by the provost, approval was granted:

> Then, within a few weeks, I read in the paper that he had gone to the American Hardware plant at New Britain and addressed the members of the Electrical Workers Union of the CIO which is listed as a communist-led union and has not complied with the law by signing the Anti-Communist pledge. This is very disturbing to me indeed, not only because I don't like it myself but because of the effect I am sure it has on our graduates and on the public at large.

He wanted Seymour to know that "continued indulgence of this left-wing element will hurt Yale and I think in connection with further recommendations for appointments and professorships you should be in a position to assure the Corporation that no such difficulties or embarrassments are to be expected."[14]

Emerson and Harper had tenure at Yale and were protected by it; Vern Countryman of the Law School did not, and was denied the promotion that would have granted tenure. Nearly all instances of the denial of tenure are complex, and not all accusations that academic freedom has been invaded are warranted, but there is no doubt that in this situation political pressures were brought to bear and the ultimate decision was made by Griswold in defiance of the overwhelming support of Countryman by the Law School faculty. There is some indication that intramural Law School politics played a part.

Fred Rodell believed so, and he later accused Dean Harry Shulman of duplicity in first having supported the unanimous vote for the promotion, then opposing it to curry favor with the Yale administration. Why should Griswold have been so strongly opposed to Countryman as to go before the Law School faculty in an effort to change its judgment and then to veto it? Perhaps the pressures on Griswold were already so strong—they were to become stronger—as to lead him to knuckle under. What these pressures were are suggested by the correspondence with one Yale alumnus, Charles F. Clise of Seattle, who had earlier complained about Fowler Harper.

On December 1, 1953, he had written to his friend Reuben A. Holden, secretary of the university, about Countryman:

> He is strictly "no good." I don't know this of my own knowledge . . . but my information comes from people out here of the highest authority and in whose judgment I have complete confidence. Vern Countryman may not be Communist, but if not, it is simply because he thinks it is safer and more effective to work without taking on the risks and responsibility that are involved if he joins up with the Party. He goes with the wrong people and has always done so. . . . It is impossible to determine whether he is a member of the Communist Party or not (my guess is that he is not), but he is just as dangerous if he is out of the Party, and possibly more so. . . .

He wrote also to Frederick H. Wiggin, chief counsel to the university, who passed his letter on to Griswold. He was still not in a position to give "fully conclusive" information about Countryman, but his investigation had turned up some interesting facts from people at the University of Washington, "on a conservative basis." His main sources of information were Dick Everest, who had been acting president and was an "unusually sound thinker in all respects," and Tracy E. Griffin, who had been in charge of the legal work involved in "trying to clear up the communistic and radical difficulties" that beset the university. The information available to these men and "their own conservativeness" led him to have complete faith in their judgment. The facts were that

> Vern Countryman comes from a home in Oregon where the record is an unfortunate one. . . . His father suffered repeated reverses during his life, which he blamed on the economy of the nation, with the result that Vern Countryman had a really revolutionary philosophy bred into his thinking. His record out here is very clear to read but . . . he is currently doing an extraordinary [sic] good job in "covering his tracks."

Clise's letter to Wiggin was in response to Wiggin's invitation to provide more information on Countryman's life before he came to Yale and on those activities that provided "serious reasons why we should be very alert in respect to him." He wanted "definite specifications of disloyalty or sinister activities."

Clise was also in touch with Griswold; they were on "Dear Whit— Dear Charlie" terms. He was particularly involved in raising endowment funds from West Coast corporations for the Yale Forestry School and had found that the fund drive was jeopardized by fear of "radical or socialistic trends" at Yale, especially at the Law School. His own investigation disclosed that the dean of the Law School was not forceful enough in handling the "radicals and troublemakers. . . . The men I don't like are Harper, Emerson, and one or two more of their type but I have no great concern in their being kept there temporarily even though I do feel that it would be desirable if they recognized that their pay checks come from Yale" and would curtail their embarrassing activities. But Vern Countryman, about whom Griswold was unlikely to have much information, was even more dangerous. What must have been of concern to Griswold and Wiggin was the information that Clise had been in touch with the noted New York attorney Arthur Palmer, who agreed that the Law School situation was interfering with the financial drive. Griswold was grateful for the advice, and told "Dear Charlie" that he would be seeing Palmer within a week to discuss the matter.

Clise admitted that he had been unable to produce evidence of Countryman's Communist affiliation. It was unnecessary to do so; Countryman's activities in the National Lawyers Guild and in defense of John P. Peters, a distinguished member of the Medical School faculty who was under continuous attack from government agencies, and his having been law clerk to Justice William O. Douglas were enough to cast suspicion on him.

Douglas himself wrote to Griswold on Countryman's behalf:

> A law school certainly should not be a "conservative" school, a "radical" school, a "New Deal" school, or a school slanted to any one school of economic or political thought. That is the liberal tradition—the tradition that tolerates men of all schools because it knows that none has a monopoly on truth.
>
> The many Yale alumni who have come to see me or called me about Countryman fear that this tradition will be violated if he is not kept on. He is by all odds the best classroom teacher in the Law School—according to the students. He has a keen-edged mind, one of the best I have known. He has, I understand, been active in certain loyalty cases. But that too is in the tradition of the law, at least from the time of Erskine who defended Tom Paine in court.
>
> I write with feeling partly because of my attachment to Countryman, partly because Yale has always been for me a beloved place where the measure of disagreement with a man's ideas is no measure of the man nor of his contribution.

Griswold's reply was polite, but adamant. He denied the assumption that politics had anything to do with the decision on Countryman. In fact, he did not know very much about Countryman's views. His decision was made because "I did not think he was yet qualified for a full professorship in what purports to be one of the country's leading law schools." In time Countryman might demonstrate the necessary "qualifications by more substantial accomplishments." For now, Griswold had recommended renewal of his associate professorship for three years. Countryman had rejected the offer.

Douglas offered to come to New Haven to discuss the matter. Griswold was too busy. He sympathized with Douglas's feelings, but his own experience as a teacher taught him that "youthful promise is not always fulfilled in mature accomplishment—at all events . . . in so short a time as five or six years." The decision stood.

Countryman left Yale, and some of his supporters, like Fred Rodell—who was in any case a gadfly to the administration—paid a price for their support. Griswold, writing to Rodell after speaking to the Yale Law faculty and noting how "distressed" he was by Rodell's letter to the Law School dean, said: "I have since re-read this letter, and find it so offensive in both tone and substance that it is very difficult for me, in the light of it, to believe the assurances you have given me either as to your friendship, your confidence in me, or your devotion to Yale or the Law School." [15]

Given the correspondence between Griswold and Clise, it is difficult to credit the assurance Griswold gave to Justice Douglas that he knew virtually nothing about Countryman's political views. It is easier to see in his letter to Rodell that he was approaching the position that opposition to the policy of the president was *lèse majesté*.

Griswold's activities, especially in connection with the famous statement of the Association of American Universities on whether Communists had the right to be teachers, support that conclusion.

Even before Griswold's active participation in the writing of the AAU statement, he had been concerned with alleged subversion by Communists in the universities. Like other academic administrators, he had to walk a narrow line—appearing to defend academic freedom without thereby at the same time seeming to defy those groups, especially congressional investigating committees, which were attacking it. It was an uncomfortable position to be in, and there were times when Griswold showed his discomfort—though not publicly.

Louis M. Rabinowitz, a wealthy New York businessman who was also a strong supporter of civil liberties and for many years a major benefactor of the Yale library, art museums, and various academic programs, offered to finance a study at Yale of academic freedom. On July

11, 1950, after a lengthy period of apparent indecision, Yale rejected the offer. Provost Furniss notified Rabinowitz of the rejection after consultation with Griswold, who, though claiming to recognize the importance of the project and appreciating Rabinowitz's offer, "decided that it would be unwise for Yale to undertake the project." During the next ten months Yale would be deeply involved in a retrenchment program, the burden of which would fall on the very people who were best qualified to handle the academic freedom project; it would be "unwise to distract our key people from this other urgent job."

Moreover, the country was faced "by the threat of war. We don't know how far the conflict will spread or what it will mean for the University. But we must lay plans to adjust all our operations to the needs of the country; and if by any wild chance we have to go on a war footing again the academic freedom convocation would have to be given up anyway." He assured Rabinowitz that President Griswold and the entire Yale administration were committed, "of course," to the principle of academic freedom, and that any "appropriate opportunity presented by our forthcoming anniversary celebration will be utilized for a declaration of policy on this matter." Rabinowitz was a generous contributor to the university, and prudence suggested that the president also write to him. Griswold did.

His first reaction, he said, was to favor Rabinowitz's proposal, for both general and personal reasons. He had studied and spoken about academic freedom in British universities, at academic seminars, and at the Harvard commencement. Although he did not know Rabinowitz personally, he had known of him for a long time and had "the greatest possible personal desire to accede to your wishes." But "practical considerations" dictated otherwise: straitened financial circumstances and "the very real possibility of another world war and the ebbing away of faculty manpower to Washington and the armed services." If, however, the 250th anniversary of Yale could be celebrated despite present portents, the theme of academic freedom would certainly be stressed: "I believe in the cause as passionately as you do and I should like then, as always, to justify your faith in Yale." [16]

Griswold felt at least a big uneasy that the rejection of Rabinowitz's offer might have unfortunate effects on his generosity toward Yale. He notified professor of religion Erwin R. Goodenough, whose department had been among the beneficiaries of Rabinowitz's philanthropy, of his decision and received Goodenough's approval:

> I think you have handled the matter exactly right. We all know what academic freedom is; it has been investigated and defined many times. The chief thing is to practice it in spirit and truth. This requires adjustment to each immediate problem which no general statement can ever

anticipate. For such adjustment I feel that we have always been in good hands here at Yale, but now are in excellent hands.

As one of your many subordinates, Whit, I ain't worrying.[17]

When Yale rejected Rabinowitz's offer, his foundation proposed a study of academic freedom to Columbia University, which accepted it. Griswold became a member of the advisory committee and remained so until he resigned on December 12, 1952. His resignation almost certainly resulted from the fact that Professor Robert M. MacIver, in charge of the Columbia project, had sent him for his comments the draft of a book on the rights of teachers and students that was decidedly different from the statement Griswold was quietly writing for the AAU.

The conclusions of the MacIver Committee on Academic Freedom were:

1. Though the Party communist is bound by a discipline which is destructive of academic freedom, "no competent educator should be dismissed or disciplined [because] the majority disapproves of his opinions."

2. No college or university educator should be dismissed or disciplined on the ground that he is an ex-communist, a theoretical Marxist (without Party connection), a socialist or "radical" or political nonconformist.

2a. The principle of academic freedom is violated when a faculty nomination to a position on the staff is vetoed by administrative or other authority on any of the grounds referred to under conclusion (2).

3. In view of the charges to which the Communist Party is open, a communist, whether he carries a Party card or not, may properly be dismissed or disciplined if he injects Communist propaganda with his teaching or into his relationships with students.

4. When questions arise concerning the presence of a communist on the faculty, the proper body to undertake an investigation of whatever charges are made is the faculty itself. . . . While the final authority is the governing board, that body should pay high respect to faculty judgment in the matter.

5. Any general investigation designed to uncover possible communists on the faculty is wholly undesirable.

6. The imposition of special loyalty oaths on faculty members, that is, oaths requiring a denial of communist affiliation, is a derogatory, injudicious, and futile expedient.

7. If an organization of college or university students invites a communist to address them they should be permitted to hear what he has to say.

8. No student should be debarred or dismissed from any institution of learning because he professes communist ideas.

Griswold turned over the draft chapters to former dean Clarence W. Mendell for his comments, together with a batch of other materials dealing with the Academic Freedom Project—minutes of past meetings of the Advisory Panel and the Executive Committee, agendas for future meetings, papers prepared for conferences. On December 12 he wrote to MacIver that owing to the press of business he had been unable to complete his reading of the materials sent to him; indeed, he had neglected his duties as a member of the Advisory Panel: "I read fitfully through the material you send me, and form critical opinions thereof, but find no time to set them on paper or even to express them." The situation was "frustrating and disturbing to [his] conscience." He had no choice but to resign from the committee. He assured MacIver that the only reason for his resignation was the press of business and said he would be glad to suggest a substitute from the Yale faculty should he be asked to do so.

On the same day he sent a copy of his letter, together with all the material he had received from MacIver, to Rabinowitz: "I can no longer endure the sight of material lying unread on my desk month after month and the perpetually nagging thought that I am shirking my duties." He also sent a copy of the letter to Frederick B. Adams of the Morgan Library, indicating that his decision had been at least a month in the making: "Here at last are the fateful notes I discussed with you a month ago. I hope you will use your good offices with Louis Rabinowitz if you can find it in your heart to do so."

There were aspects of the situation that Griswold was reluctant to write about. Rabinowitz answered Griswold's letter:

> In your postscript to me you say "I can say things to you about this pressure that I do not care to say publicly." This intrigues me a great deal.
>
> Is this pressure in general, or pressure in connection with the Academic Freedom Project? If it is the latter I sure would be greatfull [*sic*] to hear about it.
>
> Could you spare a few minutes for a short chat in the near future.

The copy of Griswold's letter in his files does not contain the postscript to which Rabinowitz refers. Two lines are drawn in the margin of Rabinowitz's reply at the place where he requests an appointment, and at the top of that letter Griswold has written: "Ansd. by phone." We do not know what Griswold said.[18]

We cannot be sure what Griswold said, but it is not hard to know what he was thinking. By the time Griswold sent his letter of resignation to MacIver and Rabinowitz, he was already knee-deep in activities at considerable variance with the MacIver recommendations—and so was the Yale administration. Griswold's own critical role in writing the statement of the Association of American Universities restricting the rights of Communists as teachers; his behind-the-scenes activities in connection with the protests over the teaching at the Law School of Harper, Emerson, and Countryman; the participation by Yale in the affairs of the inter-university Listening Post, which showed involvement by universities in efforts to purge faculties; the evidence of cooperation with the McCarran, Reece, and other committees—these suggest that Griswold and other members of the Yale administration, whatever reservations they might have had about the uncouth tactics of government investigations, were not about to oppose them. Accommodation, not opposition, was the strategy. The defense of academic freedom was confined, as Griswold and Furniss implied to Rabinowitz, to general statements before alumni groups and ceremonial occasions like Harvard commencements and Yale anniversary celebrations. Even a sketchy review of some of these situations shows the pressures to which Griswold and others felt they had to respond—had to or wanted to, for there is no evidence that accommodation was a tactic they were reluctant to adopt.

In 1950 the Association of American Universities, consisting of the presidents of thirty-seven leading universities, decided to draft a statement setting forth a policy on "the privileges and responsibilities inherent in academic freedom and tenure" in response to the political pressures of the Cold War. After a number of false starts, some the result of abortive efforts to consult with the AAUP (American Association of University Professors), and some the result of personnel changes on the drafting committee, a new committee chaired by Griswold was appointed.

When the AAU met in New York in February 1953 to discuss Griswold's draft, it had the impending hearings on education of the House Un-American Activities Committee very much in mind. It felt that the statement should deal with the problem of Communist teachers—which was the crux of the statement MacIver had sent to Griswold—and, at the suggestion of President Henry M. Wriston of Brown, with the general "Communist issue" and the specific Fifth Amendment issue. Griswold and Wriston were assigned to polish and publish it as quickly as possible. When the official statement was released on March 24, all thirty-seven presidents signed it. It proclaimed the main threat to academic freedom to be "world Communism"; accordingly, teachers who were associated with that movement, dependent on thought control and deceit, disqualified themselves from the teaching profession. Universities and faculties owed cooperation to official inquiries, not defiance. Sounding like the Sutherland-Chafee letter, the AAU found that certain public acts and utterances, even though not illegal, might be ill advised because they did harm to the profession, the university, education, and the general welfare. Such acts and utterances jeopardized the reputation of the universities; even more, they were a denial of the "complete candor and perfect integrity" that teachers owed the university and the public. The use of the Fifth Amendment, though legal, "places upon a professor a heavy burden of proof of his fitness to hold a teaching position and lays upon his university an obligation to re-examine his qualifications for membership in its society."

Harold Dodds, president of Princeton and of the AAU, wrote a self-congratulatory letter to his members; he had seen hundreds of newspaper clippings, but the only editorial attacking the statement, aside from two or three small papers on the extreme right, was in the *Daily Worker.*[19] Dodds showed his colleagues less than the "complete candor and perfect integrity" he urged on professors—and so did Griswold. Four years after the AAU issued its statement, the American Civil Liberties Union finally got around to considering it. The University of Michigan had fired two professors and had justified its action in part on the AAU statement deploring the use of the Fifth Amendment, even though legal. The Academic Freedom Committee of the ACLU sent a copy of its report on the matter to Griswold. Griswold must have been sensitive to the criticism, late as it was in coming, for he telephoned and wrote to Roger Baldwin of the ACLU about the letter he had received from Ernest Angell, chairman of the Board of Directors of the ACLU, and sent a copy of his letter to Angell to at least one other university president, C. W. deKiewiet of the University of Rochester. Both Baldwin and deKiewiet assured him of their support. deKiewiet gave the ACLU the back of his hand and told Griswold that his reply was "altogether an admirable statement"; Baldwin, though an officer of the ACLU, told Griswold he would not have dignified the ACLU statement "by such meticulous analysis."

Griswold's defense of the AAU statement was curious: in only one case, that of the University of Michigan in 1956–57, had it been cited to justify the firing of faculty members; moreover, the statement had never been intended to be, as the dean at Michigan had said, authoritative and binding on AAU members. In a second letter to Angell, Griswold argued that the real point of the AAU statement was to take a "united stand" against "the McCarthyite attack against the universities." He had himself been attacked—by William F. Buckley, Jr., by Fulton Lewis, and in a daily flood of mail pressing him to fire specific faculty members. He had spent endless hours discussing the matter with members of the Yale Corporation, alumni, and presidents of nearby universities at emergency meetings in New York "with all the gravity inspired by a sense of impending disaster." The AAU statement, given the urgency of the situation and the pressures of time, could not have been submitted for approval to the governing boards and faculties of all thirty-seven member universities: "It was a hard enough job as it was to get all the Presidents to agree to a text that was not smothered in ambiguity." He rejected Angell's suggestion that a meeting of university administrators, faculties, governing board members, and civil libertarians be held to discuss the matter. He was afraid that such a discussion would lead to consideration of the Michigan case, and he did not want to get involved in that.[20]

Griswold's statement was less than an example of perfect candor. His correspondence shows that at the time the AAU statement was sent out to the university presidents, there was opposition, some of which was "smothered in ambiguity," some of which—at points where the statement was especially vulnerable—was simply ignored or steam-rollered. President Grayson Kirk of Columbia University wrote that he objected to certain parts of the statement but would sign it because he did not want to be accused of holding it up by "quibbling." No effort was made to find out what his objections were. President E. B. Fred of the University of Wisconsin was quite explicit in his objections and asked Dodds to take his suggested revisions into account if the statement were to be printed. Those revisions, on which he had had the advice of Deans Mark H. Ingraham and O. S. Ruedell, concerned three points in particular. The first was the obligation of a professor for "complete candor" to both his colleagues and the public. The reasoning of the AAU statement led "from an impossible premise to a doubtful conclusion." Fred argued that the "obligation of the professor to say what he thinks does not include the obligation to say everything he thinks." His sense of fitness had to be relied on to determine "what of his thoughts he shall retain as his alone," and he was on sound legal and moral grounds in refusing to tell all he knows or thinks "on the ground that it is his legal privilege to do so." The AAU statement was seriously flawed when it imputed unfitness to one who exercised the privilege, "one of the great protections of the bill of rights." The protection had always been annoying to prosecutors and police, "but it hardly seems consistent with our traditional notions of academic freedom for academic authorities to say to the teacher: You answer when asked, or else!"

President Fred found the position of the AAU that it was the duty of universities to cooperate with investigating committees far too vague. How can one say definitely that there is a duty to cooperate "until we know more about who is investigating what and whom"? "Unless the paragraph can be made more specific, it should be omitted." The "definite threats of dismissal of faculty members who follow the communist line" posed a danger to every member of a university faculty. To make the threat effective "a surveillance would be required which is highly inconsistent with the kind of academic freedom we have enjoyed and under which we have thrived." The risk of Communist infiltration had to be great indeed to warrant the "imposition upon our faculties of the circumspection in thought and word that would be required. It is doubtful that the danger warrants this treatment of them."

Dodds wrote Griswold that he had squeezed a reluctant affirmative vote from Fred with the promise that his proposals would be considered "should the demand for printed copies justify this form of publication." The promise seems not to have been kept. Several thousand copies of the AAU report were printed with financial assistance from the Rockefeller Foundation, but no account was taken of Fred's suggestions.[21]

Griswold told the ACLU that the purpose of the AAU statement was to make possible a "united stand" by the presidents against the onslaughts of the McCarthys. His notes and correspondence, as well as the minutes of the AAU meetings, raise serious questions as to the meaning of the phrase "united stand" and how it was to be achieved—by opposing McCarthy or by joining him.

The early draft of the statement Griswold submitted to the AAU had the benefit of consultations with colleagues at Yale and elsewhere. Law professor Arthur L. Corbin, for example, recommended that consideration be given to distinguishing between "various theoretical forms of communism" (like Brook Farm and the Shakers) which "may not advocate either violence or lying" and adherence to "the Russian form and practice." He suggested the following sentence for inclusion in the draft, and it was accepted in substance if not in form: "Such purposes and methods are squarely in conflict with those of every American University; and no person adhering to them is worthy of a place on any faculty for either teaching or research, even though he commits no legal offense."

When his draft statement was submitted to the AAU on February 15, 1953, Griswold made clear what it was and was not intended to be. It was not "a new philosophy of academic freedom"; rather, it was "a tactical and political document." The document should not "excite those members of society who had been in opposition on numerous national issues during the last twenty years." Moreover, it should show patience with those people in whom "the national crisis had produced a feeling of anxiety."

The statement produced considerable discussion. President Dodds was sure that there would be congressional investigations by the Velde and Jenner committees. This made the issuance of a statement all the more urgent. Griswold concurred, though he felt that there would be substantial differences in approach between the two committees: Jenner's Senate committee would concentrate "on the alleged existence of Communist cells in universities and would follow the lead of the FBI"; Velde's "would probably concentrate on individuals." He predicted that the Senate committee would be the more thoughtful and statesmanlike. President Henry Wriston of Brown, a member of the drafting committee, had objections to the statement as submitted: the final document should place more emphasis on "the institutional responsibility of the universities" and should give more "saliency and emphasis to the Communist issue. . . . A clear, compact and quotable statement on the Communist issue would add greatly to the significance of the document." Others felt that the use of the Fifth Amendment required more discussion. The consensus seemed to be that, while "it would be unwise to lay down any hard and fast rules for cases arising from the refusal of members of universities to testify," the fact was that "actual or supposed abuse of this right had done damage to the universities." President deKiewiet of Rochester believed that the document made the serious mistake of presenting the university essentially as the originator of new ideas "at variance with trends in its own society" and "devoted specially and preponderantly to the expression of differences." Any document that did not emphasize that "university education was a major factor in imparting shape and stability to the nation" would be expressing "an imperfect educational philosophy and be seriously vulnerable to attack." The association concluded that the draft needed revision, especially the section dealing with the Fifth Amendment. Griswold and Wriston were named to do the job.

For the final draft, too, Griswold consulted with his colleagues. From the notes of some of his conversations it appears that James B. Conant was of special importance to him. Conant's comments and implied advice are consonant with what we have seen:

> Conant: Line betw[een] investig[ation] of indivs. & invest. of institutions and what they are teaching. Congr. hasn't crossed line yet. May not do so. At pres[ent] in[vestigation] of indivs. "Ac. freedom" not a shield. Indiv. has to defend himself.

Marked with an asterisk is the following: "Harvard counsel advises mem[bership]. in Com P [Communist Party] under Smith Act = gross misconduct & dismissal. (also Brown)."

And back to Conant:

> Doesn't like Wriston's metaphor of "shield." Doesn't think there is a shield. Initiative by education. Three disinterested grp [group] to ensure continuing independence of institution. "Lay committee"—to observe tactical line, *not* to defend indiv. martyrs, screwballs etc. but proced[ures] with [?] def.[ense] of institutions—to defend basic procedures of univs.
>   1) Weakness of apptment procedures—
>   2) Most negligent on questions of tenure
> N.B.:
>   Disregard Chafee in Harvard Law Review.
> N.B.:
>   Very bad advice. Way out of perspective.
>   Better fight perjury or contempt charges than refuse to answer.[22]

But the dubiousness of Griswold's assurances to the ACLU that the purpose of the AAU statement was to make possible a "united stand" of the university presidents against congressional and other attacks need hardly be inferred from the notes and drafts he prepared for the AAU statement. That a "united stand" meant cooperation rather than conflict can be seen in the record of Griswold's activities—and those of other Yale authorities—relating to committee investigations. To begin with, Yale made every effort—in close collaboration with Harvard and, somewhat less, with MIT—to keep itself thoroughly informed of the activities of the committees, even to the point of hiring special counsel in Washington to keep track of the committees' agenda, probable witnesses, advising on university strategy, and the like.

The Yale legal representative in Washington was Sturgis Warner, who had been designated by Yale's chief counsel, Frederick H. Wiggin. Warner performed the same services for Harvard by arrangement with Oscar M. Shaw, of the Boston law firm of Ropes, Gray, Best, Coolidge, and Rugg. As Wiggin wrote to Shaw, "I told him [Warner] that you had authorized me to say to him that he might represent Harvard as well as Yale, that he was not in any sense to represent any member of either faculty but that he was to serve as the eyes and ears of the two universities with no authority to state any official position by either of them. I told him of your preference that he do not take on any others than these two and that I agreed with that." That stricture was eased shortly afterward when Wiggin notified counsel for MIT that Yale would "be glad to make common cause with MIT as far as our interests may coincide." For Wiggin, "common cause" involved the development of a common strategy in the face of impending legislative investigations. So far there had been "no positive indications" that Yale was to become a target, but in view of the fact that some Yale professors had been mentioned in *Counterattack*, which was edited by ex–FBI agents, it had to be assumed that "information in the hands of the present F.B.I. organization is available not only" to *Counterattack* "but also to the investigators for the Congressional committees."[23]

Being the "eyes and ears" of Yale—and Harvard—in Washington meant, first of all, that Warner and his staff kept close watch on the activities of the investigating committees, even acting on occasion as if they were liaison officers between the committees and the universities, and on the activities of executive agencies of the government. They maintained connections with important Yale alumni who were in a position to influence government policies and reported on the activities of Yale faculty members when they spoke in Washington. He wrote to Wiggin, for example, about a television debate between law professor Fowler Harper and a University of Southern California student, in which

Harper "took the negative on the question 'Is Communism a Real Danger in Our Colleges.'"

Reuben Holden, assistant to the secretary of Yale University, drafted a letter to the House Un-American Activities Committee to introduce Warner to Frank S. Tavenner, committee counsel. Griswold objected to the draft until it was modified by Yale counsel Frederick Wiggin. The main difference between the rejected draft and the accepted letter was that the draft specifically mentioned the fact that an investigator of the committee who had visited New Haven "was given the information he requested in connection with the work of [the] committee." The letter, in the form acceptable to Griswold, granted Warner authority "to talk to Mr. Tavenner at any time and to say to him that you are informed that Mr. [Donald T.] Appell has been making inquiries at Yale and that Yale has retained you to represent its interests for the purpose of obtaining direct first-hand information as to investigations by Congress in the field of education." In fact, as we shall see, the rejected draft came closer to complete candor; Yale had provided information to Appell and to others. For example, Holden sent Wiggin a memorandum, "Information Given to D. T. Appell," about a former graduate student who had received his Ph.D. in English and was now teaching at another university, and about a former staff member of a research project.

Warner also forwarded to Yale pertinent extracts from testimony before the committees, statements by the committees commending positions taken by the university, such as the Un-American Activities Committee's praise for the statement by the AAU, and testimony that might possibly have important implications for university policy regarding the employment of suspected subversives. He notified Yale, for example, that Richard E. Combs, counsel to the California Senate Committee on Un-American Activities, had given the Jenner committee "answers which are of more than routine interest." The California committee had an "agreement of cooperation with about a dozen colleges for the prevention of Communist infiltration under which 100 teachers had been dismissed and more than 100 have been prevented from gaining tenure— i.e., have not been hired in the first place—through their combined and cooperative effort." Appropriate university officials and the committee would come "into some sort of agreement as to the finding on any particular professor and whether he should be dismissed, and it further appears that men who are being considered for teaching positions are screened by the Committee for any comment that may be found on them in the Committee's extensive files." The California colleges were cooperating voluntarily. All parties to the understanding agreed that "prior screening" was preferable to the "rooting out of Communists after some damage had been done." State investigating committees, moreover, could provide services colleges could not provide for themselves, like administering oaths and providing documentation accumulated over the years. Small wonder, then, that California colleges were hiring "loyalty and security experts—men of former police and FBI training or naval intelligence experience. There was emphasis on the need for expertise in the selection of security specialists."

The testimony of witnesses from government and from other universities that mentioned Yale professors or organizations at Yale was collected and forwarded to New Haven. So, too, was information that had no direct relation to Yale but seemed to have some bearing on the interests of the investigating committees and, therefore, on what Yale might expect if its turn came. The usual suspects, like Thomas Emerson, were mentioned, but there were also others, less prominent, like Professor Ralph Turner of the history department. Both of these faculty members, and others, were discussed privately by Warner and Congressman John Vorys of the House Un-American Activities Committee, who was especially concerned about the Yale Law School and the fact that Yale, like Harvard, had not publicly announced that "refuge in the Fifth Amendment" would result in automatic suspension. Warner's memorandum on his conference with Vorys was the subject of discussion between Wiggin and Griswold. When Warner reported that a former Yale undergraduate, now a journalist, spoke about the John Reed Club and mentioned the names of members, Wiggin recommended that Griswold "should at once set someone to work to obtain all the information available about that institution and its members or former members."

Information was provided to the Un-American Activities Committee by Yale at the request of Committee Investigator Donald T. Appell, who had already been in touch with the chairman of the Yale Physics Department, W. W. Watson, about three persons who had been scientists on an Office of Naval Research project some time before. Watson reported that "he had made every effort to be courteous and helpful to Mr. Appell who realized that Yale was not responsible in any way."

Neither was the navy responsible for the choice of these men. Watson "was anxious that we not involve the Navy unless we felt so obliged. The Navy has been generous in its research grants and since it did not pick or clear the personnel, it should not be held responsible." But if neither Yale nor the navy was responsible, who was? The three men had been brought to Yale by a former University of Wisconsin physicist with whom they had been doing research. Watson gave the same information to the chairman of the Physics Department at Ohio State, where one of the three was now employed, but at the request of the professor who had brought the three men to Yale, he had "deleted all references" to him in his letter to Ohio State.

Warner was also expected, when authorized, to issue press releases in the name of the university, though, to make sure there were no slipups, these were drafted in New Haven, not Washington. One such

press release, to be issued only on instructions from Wiggin, Carl Lohmann, or Holden, is of special importance as an indication of the nature
of Griswold's "opposition" to the attacks of the McCarthys. Signed by
Griswold himself, the proposed press release stated:

> Yale has not been blind to the existence of an international communist
> conspiracy that seeks to destroy our universities as well as our country.
> We are determined to safeguard both against this conspiracy.

He reaffirmed the position taken earlier that Yale knew of no present
member of its faculty who was "trying to undermine our society," but
that, since membership in the Communist Party was incompatible with
the intellectual and moral standards of the teaching profession, "Yale
does not knowingly appoint members of the Communist Party to its faculty." Moreover, "action incompatible with the stated principles of the
University . . . will receive appropriate attention from the University
administration."

Warner reported to his Yale superiors about his investigation of relations with the Office of Naval Intelligence arising over whether particular projects involved classified or unclassified research and whether,
therefore, particular suspected subversives might be employed. From
Yale's point of view, the danger was that such persons might be called
before a committee: "As I said over the telephone," he later wrote Wiggin, "it is a very long shot as to whether you can ever dam such a story,
but it might give you a lead as to a possible future witness. The relationship between the Office of Naval Intelligence and the FBI is probably a
rather close one on matters such as these."

The FBI documents and Yale's own make clear that Yale cooperated
closely with the FBI in investigations of faculty and students and with
congressional investigating committees, to the point of providing information to them. How high in the Yale chain of command did knowledge
of such activities and participation in them exist? The answer is, up to
President Griswold himself. Griswold, of course, delegated authority,
especially to Yale counsel Wiggin, but he was the ultimate destination
of the information provided by Warner in Washington and made decisions that called for cooperation with the investigating committees.

On June 11, 1953, Warner sent Wiggin a memorandum on the recent hearings before the Jenner committee in Chicago. One of the witnesses was Donald Horton, who had "rejoined" the Communist Party
(he had originally joined as an undergraduate at the University of Pennsylvania) while a graduate student at Yale sometime after 1939. He refused to give the names of other Party members—faculty and student—
at Penn and Yale. In 1943 he was appointed research assistant at the
Yale Institute of Human Relations and became a consultant to the Morale Services Division, Research Branch, of the War Department. Shortly

thereafter, he left Yale and, according to his testimony, the Communist Party as well. When Wiggin forwarded Warner's letter and memorandum to Griswold, he wrote that it "might be useful if you should have someone send me a memorandum of the records on Donald Horton. I hope the committees will not get around to Yale just as you leave the dock for a nice sail out at Martha's Vineyard on your new yacht." In the margin of the letter, Griswold wrote: "Ben [Reuben A. Holden]: Will you do this please? AWG." It was done; and on June 18, Holden sent Wiggin—at the request of "Whit"—"the information we have on Donald Horton."

The Un-American Activities Committee was interested in Byron T. Darling, a physicist formerly at Yale and later at Ohio State. On March 16, 1953, Wiggin wrote Holden asking him to call to the attention of Griswold a packet of materials, which included, among other documents:

1. A press release concerning Darling, "to be used if necessary"
2. "Information given [Donald] Appell [Un-American Activities Committee investigator] from the Alumni Records office"
3. Memorandum on Holden's conference with Appell
4. Memorandum on Holden's conversation with Professor Watson of the Yale physics department
5. Memorandum prepared in the office of Sturgis Warner on Darling's testimony to the House Committee in which Yale was mentioned

Griswold, in short, had complete information about the matter and approved how it was handled by his subordinates, including the providing of information to Appell. Some of the documents that Wiggin told Holden to send on to Griswold are noteworthy, especially Holden's memorandum on his conference with Appell:

> Mr. Appell had some names of former students at Yale whose present activities he wanted to verify. I took him to the Alumni records and had a few of the sheets which gave this information pulled out and he took a few notes. (See special sheet for names.) [On the "special sheet" attached to Holden's memorandum are biographical data on seven former Yale students.]

Appell later went to Professor Watson to discuss the navy research project on which three persons the committee was interested in were employed. When Appell returned to Holden's office, "he said that Professor Watson had expected investigators to make a check on the work of some of these people and had already had a visit from a representative of the F.B.I."[24]

Appell told Holden that a member of the Yale faculty would be subpoenaed for an executive session of the committee on March 19. If the faculty member failed to notify the Yale administration of his subpoena, "Appell himself would give us his name if we phoned him in Washington. . . . When Mr. Appell later returned, he said that he had not had any luck in finding the person concerned and asked if I would see if it were possible to locate Professor Ralph Turner of the History Department." Holden learned from the History Department that Turner was in Paris editing a series of books on world history for UNESCO. He had Yale prepare a memorandum on Turner based on information in its files.[25]

In President Griswold's file, attached to Holden's memorandum, is a single page of handwritten notes on a meeting with Appell. The notes were probably made by Holden. They are important as an indication of the attitudes and interests of the Un-American Activities Committee about which Griswold was clearly informed. They also refer to matters about which Holden's formal memorandum is silent, though he must have discussed them:

> Appell—pumpkin—4 children—Catholic
> UAC [Un-American Activities Committee] don't get info. from other investigating comms. but make their findings open. Approves idea of FBI keeping all info quiet.
> "If I were pres. would tell profs. to tell whole truth—not necessarily fire Communists but would take some action if required on return of same [?] informing us."
> Benj. Wright vs. Prof [Robert Gorham] Davis [of Smith College]
> [Wendell] Furry [of Harvard] was stupid and *did* incriminate self.
> UAC will protect individual and university—hope educators will understand.
> Turner—led students into groups which were questionable influence
> Comm. *has* to *get back* info. to build up picture and get evidence on others

It would be difficult to find a more succinct statement than that final sentence of the importance to the congressional committees—and to the FBI—of obtaining information from universities and elsewhere. No one can now say—except the universities in their official statements—that the universities did not comply with requests for information or were unaware of the uses to which it was put.

———

Warner was the eyes and ears of Yale in Washington, not its tongue. For that, it had its own powerful alumni, some of whom were members of the Yale Corporation while serving in the U.S. Senate. On March 25, 1953, Lloyd Cutler, an influential Washington attorney, sent to Wiggin at the suggestion of Warner a report on the recent meeting of the Yale Law School Association at Washington, at which five Law School alumni, members of the House of Representatives, spoke. One of them, Republican Representative Albert W. Cretella of Connecticut, was distinctly hostile; the Law School harbored Communists who, he hoped, "would be exposed and driven off the faculty as soon as possible." Cutler, Washington representative on the Executive Committee of the National Yale Law School Association, took the responsibility of explaining Yale's position, as it had been presented by Griswold, on the pending congressional investigations. He especially emphasized

> Mr. Griswold's statements that the University had no intention of issuing public statements attacking the Congressional inquiries, that Yale respected the right of the Congress to inquire as it saw fit, that Yale would urge any faculty member receiving a subpoena to testify, that it would recommend that any such faculty member retain a conservative lawyer, and that if the faculty member required financial assistance to hire such a lawyer, the University would find a way to assist him.

Since Cretella adamantly opposed university financial support for legal assistance to subpoenaed professors, Cutler suggested another way to get "competent and conservative counsel"—Griswold should ask Law School alumni to undertake the task as a service to Yale. He and Gerhard A. Gesell, with whom he had discussed the matter, were sure that many Law School alumni would respond to such a request without compensation.

On April 13, 1953, Cutler sent Warner a report on addresses made by U.S. Senators Bush and Taft—both members of the Yale Corporation—to the Yale Committee of Washington. Bush took what by now had become the official position—defense of the congressional committees and of Yale, which really was above suspicion. He defended the right of congressional committees to inquire into whether teachers were now or had ever been Communists, and objected to the use of the Fifth Amendment. Present Communist faculty members should be discharged; according to Cutler, "he did not distinguish between present Party members and non-party members who profess Communist ideals." He "had taken the trouble to investigate the matter" since arriving in Washington, and he was convinced there were no Communists at Yale, which "had little to worry about in the present investigations." President Griswold and his administration deserved the highest praise, and Yale alumni could feel as confident as he that Yale was "as good a place to send their sons as when he was in school, some thirty years ago."

Senator Taft on the whole agreed with Bush. He saw "no basis whatever for questioning the right of a Congressional committee to investigate" faculties, and he felt that faculty members should testify because the use of the Fifth Amendment was tantamount to an admission of guilt. Present members of the Communist Party should be discharged because Party discipline was incompatible with the search for truth, but the holding of Communist ideas, if they were not taught in class, was not sufficient grounds for dismissal. He did not believe that Yale had any Communist Party members on its faculty, though he was "strongly opposed to engaging some of the Yale professors" whose views were now being attacked. In language almost identical with that of the Yale administration and some of the investigating committees, he said "that the time to consider a professor's ideas is when he is first engaged by the university, or first placed on permanent tenure. . . . It was the duty of the Corporation to exercise its judgment at the time of the appointment, and not to hire anyone merely because the faculty of a particular school in the University recommended him." That was, as we now know, the position taken by the Yale administration more than once in connection with Law School appointments, although we do not know whether the vetoes exercised by the presidents were on their own behalf or on behalf of the Yale Corporation. We know, too, that the policy Taft advocated of inquiring into "a professor's ideas" at the time of appointment or promotion was the basis for the screening of professors, with information provided by state investigating committees and the FBI, throughout the state of California and elsewhere. The best statement Taft had seen on the subject was that of the AAU, which was largely the work of Griswold. So long as he was in charge, the university was in safe hands. He ended on a note of ambiguity: "As he looks back now he is in far more doubt about the wisdom of the votes he has cast as a member of the Yale Corporation than his votes as a United States Senator."

It seems hard to reconcile Taft's and Bush's statements, the Yale record in providing congressional investigating committees with information about students and faculty members, and Griswold's own contemporaneous notes, with Griswold's assurance to the ACLU that the AAU statement must be seen as opposition to intrusive committee investigations. The statement was more one of concealment than of candor, to cover up the fact of accommodation. Yale had reason to feel pleased that it seemed to be achieving its purpose, and that it could count on the cooperation of its alumni in the Senate: "I should say that our Yale Senators are doing stalwart service," Wiggin wrote proudly to Griswold.[26]

Other matters in Washington required the attention of Yale and Griswold; here, too, in addition to the services of Sturgis Warner, they could count on the cooperation of powerful alumni—among them, Dean Acheson.

Sturgis Warner's law firm was to follow the "progress of the Reece Resolution in the House Rules Committee." The resolution was important to Yale and Harvard because it—and a companion resolution in the Senate, the McCarran Amendment—would deprive universities and foundations of tax exemption if they had subversives on their staffs or made contributions or grants to subversive organizations and individuals. Warner's reports made Wiggin nervous. What might be done to slow down the Reece committee? He suggested that Griswold pay particular attention to developments in California, where there had been a policy, "particularly in the larger institutions, of employing full time people who had had practical experience in the field of counter-Communist activities, ex-F.B.I. agents, and ex-Navy and military intelligence men. This practice of employing spies on the campus seems to have met with the approval of the Committee." At the time, Yale had had on its staff for twenty-five years the undercover agent H. B. Fisher. Requests from the Reece committee for information concerning how the foundations dealt grants to the universities and how the universities managed them set off a flurry of activity in presidential offices. Should the universities voluntarily comply, or should they wait for their records to be subpoenaed? How would the foundations respond? Should they, as the Reece committee urged, make suggestions, or should they simply provide short answers? What should they do to prevent looking defensive?

Yale took no official public position before the Reece committee, though one member of the faculty—Professor David Rowe, a Far Eastern specialist in the Department of Political Science—testified that some foundations (he specifically mentioned the Carnegie Corporation) were clamping down on independent "scholarly enterprise" by supporting "monopolies in research projects" in certain universities. In addition, they showed political bias in the making of grants. He was commended by the committee, whose general counsel sent Griswold a letter congratulating him for having such a person on the Yale faculty. Wiggin was dubious: "When the Professor said that . . . the Marxist infection has spread among us, he was saying exactly what Reece and Company wanted him to say."

The McCarran Amendment to the Internal Revenue bill seemed to present a more serious problem. A number of universities—Yale included—worked hard to kill it in committee. Legal counsel and other representatives of the Yale and Harvard administrations cooperated to knock out the provision that would deprive charitable organizations of tax exemption if they made a grant to a Communist. The McCarran Amendment was opposed less on constitutional and legal grounds than on political. Charles S. Gage, Yale treasurer, wired the committee that Yale was unalterably opposed to communism: "Therefore as far as Yale is concerned there is no necessity for including in H.R. 8300 the provision of the amendment embodied in Section 505. . . . A single act of bad judgment by some minor official or employee would penalize hundreds of innocent beneficiaries of Yale's charitable work." The McCarran Amendment was thrown out by the conference committee, not because it was obnoxious to its members, who were "strongly opposed" to donations "to subversive organizations or individuals," but because the committee did not feel that it had sufficient information to cope with the problem justly. It solicited advice from foundations and universities. The ball was now in the universities' court. How would they respond to the request for suggestions?

The staff of the Joint Committee on Internal Revenue Taxation requested a meeting with university representatives on November 5, 1954, to discuss among others the following questions:

1. How are faculty members and employees of representative colleges selected with particular regard to their loyalty? . . .
2. How are recipients . . . of grants from representative colleges selected, with particular regard to their loyalty to the United States? . . .
6. Should . . . an organization that makes grants to an individual known to a trustee to be an official of an organization on the Attorney General's list be tax exempt on the ground that it is operated exclusively for the promotion of social welfare?

Yale submitted a lengthy brief to the joint committee, but it declined—on advice from Acheson—to participate in the meeting with its staff. It was Yale's position that the two systems of higher education in the United States, one public and supported by taxation, the other private and not taxed, were equally necessary: "There are, for example, certain guarantees of free thought and free speech in the endowed universities. That this does not imply freedom to overthrow the government by force is admirably shown in the bulletin issued by the Association of American Universities under date of March 24, 1953." Did the Yale brief imply that in the tax-supported colleges there were no guarantees—or fewer—of free thought and free speech? In any case, the AAU statement, pointed to by Griswold as evidence of opposition to snooping committee investigators, was in fact being cited as evidence of university cooperativeness.

University reasonableness could be seen, furthermore, in the answers given to the first two questions asked by the joint committee staff. Faculty appointments involved searching inquiry into "education, intellectual qualifications and moral character. The last of these involves the question of loyalty." In the past, loyalty could be taken for granted, but "today the subject is more carefully considered." A further guarantee against the employment of the disloyal lay in the quasi-probationary status of faculty members before being appointed to tenure: "Thus, their early work comes under the constant scrutiny of department heads and other responsible professional observers." The inquiry into the fitness of a teacher to obtain tenure involved consideration of "moral character," including "the question of loyalty." As to students, every precaution was taken to assure the selection of those of "proper character, ability and promise of future development." There was the added precaution that "scholarships are granted for a year at a time only." Students came under a prolonged period of observation.

Yale sent no official representative to the meeting with the staff of the joint committee—Pennsylvania, Michigan, DePauw, Chicago, Columbia, Stanford, and Harvard (represented by Dean McGeorge Bundy) did—but Sturgis Warner was there as note-taker. His notes, already referred to in our discussion of Harvard University, make clear that the defense used by the universities was not to challenge the actions of the committees on constitutional and legal grounds but to demonstrate that university cooperativeness made new legislation unnecessary. In the selection of faculty members, "widespread investigation" was routine, not only into professional competence but also into "the relationship of the prospective faculty member to his entire community." A congressional enactment requiring a non-Communist oath would not be helpful, nor would bringing the FBI and the Department of Justice into the situation as a result of an apparent violation of such an oath. The reason was chilling: "The university representatives pointed out that the Department of Justice and the FBI are not today following up and prosecuting cases which the universities have already handed over to them under existing law." Warner felt that "the entire atmosphere of the meeting was one of cordiality and cooperation."

Griswold himself was in touch with fellow presidents and others regarding the strategy to be followed in the meeting with the committee staff. He approved of the advice from Dean Acheson—lie low and stay out now. His notes on his conversations are illuminating:

> Stam [Chief of Staff of the Joint Committee] and assocs. entirely friendly—no preconceived idea of what they wanted—took idea seriously.
> 1) Mand[ate] from Milliken [chairman of the Committee] to come up with [?] to McC. Comm.
> 2) Red problem, not with major founds. or univs. but with small founds. truly subv., e.g., Blair Found. for World Government. . . . Dollard and Wood advocate full reporting etc. . . .
> Tactics: Colls. and Univs. would do well to have someone able to speak for them, to talk with Stam—doesn't seem at present stage Pres. of Yale shd. be in there pitching—hasn't reached that stage—might be later. What's needed now painstaking spade work on the staff level.
> A. Convince Stam prob. not as serious as they think.
> B. Better remedies. . . .
> At moment, nothing to shoot at. We'd be maneuvered into suggesting remedies. Not proper for us. *Later* when something to shoot at. . . .
> Might be dangerous. Stay out now. Let lawyers rep[resent] us now. . . .
> Dodds [president of Princeton] agrees with me. . . .
> Harold also felt mistake to go *now*. Drag feet at this stage of game.[27]

It could not have been easy always to lie low. Griswold and the other presidents must have felt under constant pressure, some of which can be explained by the charged atmosphere of the period. What else accounts for the nervous letter that Warner wrote to Wiggin, who then passed it along with a letter of his own, to Harvard counsel Shaw and to Griswold, about the suicide of a CIA official in Washington who had been a Yale undergraduate and a Harvard M.A.? Though the initial reports spoke of "overwork" as the cause of the suicide, Warner and Wiggin were alert to the possibility that "allegations of disloyalty" might be made. The *Washington Times-Herald*, in reporting the event, had mentioned the suicides of Lawrence Duggan, Laird Goldsborough, and F. O. Matthiessen. Might they not all have been involved "in some way in subversive activities"? Helpfully, Warner advised Shaw: "In view of the fact that [name deleted by S.D.] appears to have been on the Harvard faculty at one time, it might be worth while to make a check into the matter at your end." When the solicitor of the Post Office Department informed Griswold that the Yale Divinity School Library was receiving material from Russia and elsewhere containing propaganda, which universities could receive legally if "they undertake to study such propaganda" without disseminating it, Griswold informed him that Yale "has no use for such publications and does not desire to receive them." Wallace Sterling, president of Stanford, must have added to Griswold's nervousness when he complained that a number of Stanford faculty members "endorsed in a paid advertisement the statement on behalf of [Adlai] Stevenson that emanated from Columbia. . . . This endorsement was clumsily done." [28]

But what must have been of most concern was the effect of the political atmosphere on fund-raising. Would funds dry up because the universities were thought to be refuges for Reds? Might it not be possible to convince Congress that because universities were continuing to receive corporate gifts they could not possibly be such sanctuaries? When Sturgis Warner sent Wiggin a copy of an MIT professor's testimony before the House Un-American Activities Committee, he enclosed the text of a press release and a recent speech by the president of the National Association of Manufacturers "with regard to the need for obtaining moral and financial support for colleges from industrial groups. I suppose that Yale is thoroughly up-to-date on the speech and on the program which [NAM] President Sligh mentioned, but it occurs to me that participation in such a program would be an affirmative step in building up the case for the university."

On October 5, 1950, J. M. Kaplan, president of the Welch Grape Juice Company and of the Kaplan Foundation (later identified as a conduit for the distribution of CIA funds), wrote Griswold requesting "guidance" in solving a personal problem—how to combat the "deep sense of frustration" he felt because, after a "lifetime devoted to competitive business and the accumulation of wealth," he was now convinced that

"materialism alone" was "devoid of enduring personal satisfaction."
Shortly after he wrote Griswold, he wrote to his friend, former attorney-
general Francis Biddle (with a copy to Griswold), national chairman of
Americans for Democratic Action, suggesting more specifically what might
be done to reconcile humane values and wealth: "I want to propose to
ADA's leaders a program of action on India, designed to help save it
from Soviet and Communist-China imperialism. . . . It is vital, too, for
all other Far and Middle Eastern countries not yet under Communist
control."

That provided the political context for Kaplan's interest, but at the
time he wrote to Griswold his interest was more philosophical; at least
it was expressed in more philosophical terms: "It is clear that a fair
share of the world's material goods and a secure and decent standard of
living are necessary to human dignity and enjoyment of the fullness of
life," yet materialism alone cannot perpetuate "the essential human values and the impulses of the human spirit which have through the ages
motivated the greatest and most wholesome creative efforts of civilized
man." Could Griswold and other university presidents help? "I assume
that the search for moral as well as intellectual direction is [the] proper
responsibility" of universities. "But what institutions are best qualified
to pursue this course, and how can my funds be made of greatest help
to them?"

Griswold knew what had to be done. The physical and social sciences had friends galore; the humanities, "the source 'of those essential
human values and the impulses of the human spirit' " of which Kaplan
had written needed support. Griswold proposed "something like . . .
the Rhodes Scholarships . . . for graduate work in the humanities." He
expressed the desire to carry on the discussion with Kaplan.

At the same time, Griswold received a letter from David Potter, professor of history:

> By the way, I wonder if you have had any correspondence with a man
> named Kaplan or Caplan who wants to give a million dollars to the
> right university as soon as he finds out what the right one is. I was
> talking not long ago to a man who knows him and who thinks he knows
> the origin of the whole idea. If he is on your list, let me know, and I
> will tell you what I have heard about him.

Griswold asked Potter to let him know what he had found out about
Kaplan; at the same time, Kaplan thanked Griswold for his interest in
the matter and promised to visit him on "completion of this season's
[grape] harvest."

Potter had no philosophical burdens to bear and came quickly to the
point:

About Mr. Kaplan, I really do not know much, but where a million dollars are concerned, even the trivia are hardly trivial. Eliot Janeway, who writes for *Newsweek* and who is some kind of business consultant, apparently is an adviser of Mr. Kaplan's and had a hand in Mr. K's letter. Janeway tells me that Mr. Kaplan has a deep sense of his own unworthiness (perhaps resulting from a realistic appraisal of his own business practices), and that he wants, thinks he wants to make a gift that will foster spiritual values. Spiritual in this sense does not mean religious, but rather non-materialistic. . . .

Mr. Janeway thinks that Mr. Kaplan yearns to yield to a higher authority, and that he is less likely to bestow his gifts on those who roll out the red carpet than on those who remind him, almost sternly, of their role as custodians of the truth. But clearly, this is where I drop out and the seasoned strategists of many fiscal campaigns come in.

As "a seasoned strategist of . . . fiscal campaigns," Griswold sought to demonstrate his own—and Yale's—political orthodoxy.

That is in part conjectural, though hardly implausible. What is not conjectural is Griswold's response, not so much to windfall contributions from little-known philanthropists but to contributors tormented by doubt whether they should continue to contribute to an alma mater that coddled Communists. Griswold's files are studded with letters from doubting alumni and with encouraging responses from him and other administrative officials.

Bern Dibner, president of the Burndy Engineering Company, a well-known collector of rare books and manuscripts in the history of science, denounced the university for harboring Communists in the Law School: "This reality spells *[sic]* little credit on the management of your university." To Griswold's reply that the charges against Yale made by the editors of *Counterattack* were false, he warned that, nevertheless, "an inordinate number of professors who should know better were *active* [emphasis in original] in Communist front organizations (as determined by our national authorities)." Then came the threat: "You may be interested in my conviction that if I had a son preparing to study law, I would not encourage him to do it at Yale under its present faculty."

Samuel G. Colt, of Pittsfield, Massachusetts, class agent for the Alumni Fund, asked what "steps are being taken to get rid of the PINKS or the FELLOW TRAVELERS." He endorsed a similar letter from one of his classmates, Col. Sanford H. Wadhams, 1894. During the past few years Wadhams had reduced his contributions because of "pinks and fellow travelers" at the Divinity School and the Law School: "I dislike the idea of contributing to their support and there are others who share the same view." Someone in the Yale administration wrote at the bottom of the letter that Wadhams's contributions ranged from $500 to 1951 to $100 in 1953. Griswold replied to Colt, reaffirming the policy set forth by Seymour "that Yale would appoint no Communists to its faculty" and denying that there were any. Yale was "a great constructive and patriotic force in our society and fully deserving of the best you and I can do to support it."

When Carlos F. Stoddard, Jr., of the Yale Development Office sent Griswold the draft of a reply he had written to a similar complainant, he identified him to Griswold: "Robert H. Ives Goddard, to whom my letter is addressed, is Ben Sturges' uncle, and beyond doubt the most important Yale alumnus in Rhode Island (both in dollars and influence)." Stoddard's defense of Yale included a denial that Thomas Emerson was a Communist and a statement that the AAU resolution on "The Rights and Responsibilities of Universities and Their Faculties" had been written—"every word of it"—by Griswold himself. No one was in a better position to speak for America than Griswold, who "as a scholar understands more fully the origins and development of his country, or who as a man with the traditions of over 300 years of New England Griswolds behind him, is more a part of our heritage." He included a collection of addresses by Griswold and a nine-page, single-spaced letter by Eugene V. Rostow, professor of law, denying that Yale was a haven for Communists. There were "no Communists or Communist apologists on the faculty." If there were, they would be fired, in accordance with the statement of the AAU, for which Griswold was largely responsible. Rostow was grateful to alumni for pressing the issue:

> In view of the threat of communism to our national security, and the significant activities of the communist fifth-column in many parts of our national life . . . [it] is a real act of loyalty to Yale to inquire about such charges.

In truth, however, Rostow said, the persons mentioned in Goddard's letter of complaint were not Communists. Thomas Emerson was never even a member of any organization on the attorney general's list. Fowler Harper had resigned from organizations in danger of becoming Communist fronts. Dr. John Peters, though he had been "an enthusiastic joiner in his time, had withdrawn as sponsor of the Scientific and Cultural Conference for World Peace." The distinguished historian George Vernadsky had "close friends" among White Russians and was "decidedly to the right of Kerensky."

Yale received so many letters of complaint from alumni contributors based on the *Counterattack* article accusing it of providing a haven for Communists that it prepared a standard letter of reply, the final draft of which was accepted on January 6, 1953. Earlier versions of that letter were edited by Griswold himself; he even composed a complete draft of his own. We have no need, therefore, to wonder whether Griswold accepted all that was written over his name; we have his notes and, through them, direct knowledge of his views. Among the sentences written by Griswold himself were:

> I am just as much opposed to Communism and the subversive influences connected with it as you are, and if I saw the facts as you see them I should feel very much as you do. . . . Nor can we find evidence of such [radical] teaching among our students or graduates. On the contrary, the conservative complexion of both is well known. In their poll last fall, our students gave the Republicans a two to one majority (in my 27 years of life and work at Yale I have never known a student poll to go otherwise). . . . Yale abhors Communism as a mortal enemy. Our Corporation, Faculty and students recognize it as the destroyer of the very foundations upon which Yale rests. . . . This attitude is vigorously represented in Yale's official policy and daily life.[29]

Some years later, a quite different letter was sent to Griswold. Griswold had written an article in the *Sunday Magazine* of the *New York Times*, "Loyalty: An Issue of Academic Freedom," opposing a provision for loyalty oaths in the National Defense Education Act. The letter-writer congratulated Griswold for "its literate style" but confessed that had the article been written "with more parochial references," he might have "dismissed [it] with a comment on the limited courage of a man taking a stand on an issue of importance only to himself and his own private interests." But Griswold's article contained many historical references showing the much broader implications of loyalty oaths and investigations, "some of which have touched Yale University, in the case of Vern Countryman." Therefore the article could not so easily be dismissed. The historical events referred to by Griswold had occurred years before the "phenomena subsumed under the heading of 'McCarthyism' " and could, therefore, have been used as "a guide to courageous action of more general and generous scope than that of standing up to the implications of the National Defense Act." But Griswold had never spoken out against "those practices until they began to wash over into his special field":

> Nor, so far as I know, have you added the weight of your office and of your knowledge to the fight on behalf of individuals (not institutions) who were being punished under the tyrranical [sic] laws and usurpations.

He asked:

> What is the purpose of a liberal education? Learning has no value unless it culminates in action; and the liberal arts are merely snobbery if not used to inform and direct action, especially for socially and morally good ends and against the socially and morally bad. To the extent that

learning is treated as a personal decoration or for armchair philoso-
phizing educators are open to the charge of eggheads and educational
institutions to that of ivory towers.

Is your open stand on the issue of the loyalty oath . . . the opening
gun in a continuing fight for a liberal, democratic ideal throughout all
aspects of our public policies; or is it to be merely a parochial protest?
I should be pleased to know.

The letter was written by hand and the signature was barely legible,
but someone in Griswold's office took the trouble to decipher it: Bertram
Cole, 63 Curtis Drive, New Haven 15. Cole never learned the answer to
his question. Griswold, so painstaking in his replies to letters threatening the cutting off of funds, did not bother to answer Cole, nor did
anyone from the Development Office.[30]

10. The FBI Dissemination Program

How DID THE FBI get its list of subversives to be investigated in its inquest of 1953? What it knew and what it did with what it knew required the use of informers and the co-optation of private persons like university presidents and other educational officials. The FBI, the educational administrators, and the political leaders who were often their go-betweens never made public what they were doing. Secrecy made deceit possible.

So far as the university administrators were concerned, the deceit characteristically took the form of denying that they made inquiries into the political beliefs and activities of teachers when, in fact, they bartered what they knew to the FBI in exchange for what the FBI knew. So far as the political go-betweens were concerned, it took the form of silence, scrupulously protecting the educators and the FBI. So far as the FBI was concerned, secrecy allowed it to make available the information in its files while proclaiming that that information was not provided to private persons and organizations. The parties to the arrangement, concealing their activities, conducted a political purge and established a blacklist that many of them hoped would guarantee that the effects of the purge would be permanent. The deceit that made it possible to conduct the purge and establish the blacklist was not, for the most part, idiosyncratic; it was institutional. The relationship between the partners did not depend on who they were; it depended on the positions they occupied.

But how exactly was the purge conducted and the blacklist established? Hoover's directive of March 26, 1953, to all twenty-three FBI field offices ordering an immediate investigation of "Communist sub-version" in fifty-five colleges and universities provides a number of clues. The names of the subversives to be investigated were to be obtained from the Security Index, pending security files, and "any confidential informants and established sources which might be expected to have information concerning persons connected with these institutions." FBI deception was partially revealed in Hoover's letter of instructions. The SACs were instructed to investigate "all suspected Communist subver-sives without inquiring into the extent of Communist infiltration." But how was it possible to do the first without doing the second? Moreover, the SACs were "specifically instructed not to make any contacts which might give the impression that the Bureau is conducting any such inves-tigation of institutions of higher learning." The bureau wanted to sug-gest that neither education nor particular institutions were being inves-tigated; only people were.

Though the returns from the fifty-five universities investigated are skimpy in certain respects and have been heavily censored by the FBI, enough remains to show that Hoover's caution not to give the impres-sion that institutions were being investigated was more for the record than for the instruction of the SACs. Institutions as well as individuals were investigated. Even more useful are clues showing how the files were leaked so that a suspect's dossier was made available to employers unless the suspect "cleared" himself. What was the price of clearance, and how was it obtained? The returns from Hoover's great political Domesday inquest contain many references to the "Dissemination Pol-icy" and "Responsibility Program." What were they, and what was their bearing on the purges and blacklist?

On April 7, 1947, all SACs received printed instructions to adhere to the "long-established policy that no information is to be furnished from our files to other than approved representatives of the executive agencies of the Federal Government, such as Army and Navy Intelligence, etc., except to advise cooperating law enforcement agencies of data which are matters of public record. This policy is to be adhered to rigidly."[1] Whether this statement can be taken as an accurate description of FBI policy at any time is to be doubted; if it ever was, it was not so for long. On July 22, 1954, Hoover, in a memorandum to Attorney General Brownell, re-minded him of "our Responsibilities Program," which had been in ex-istence since early 1951. The policy had been worked out by Hoover and Governor Frank Lausche of Ohio, with a committee of other gov-ernors representing the National Governors' Conference, to meet the need that "responsible officials of state governments should have knowl-edge of dangerous Communists and other subversives employed in state and municipally operated institutions" such as public utilities and school systems. Information in the FBI files was "volunteered orally" to the state governor "or, if circumstances require, to some other high level state official." Hoover indignantly rejected a proposal that no information should be "disseminated regarding dangerous Communists who are employed in the public school systems of the various states. In my opinion, Communist infiltration of the public school systems would present a most serious threat to the internal security of this Nation."

That policy had been reaffirmed more than once by the Executives' Conference of the FBI. Indeed, the list of those considered suspects about whom information could be given to the governors had been broadened. So had the list of those to whom the information could be given. The latter now included "a large number of state and local officials" in addition to the governors, even those governors who had indiscreetly blabbed that they had been given information by the FBI, a number of judges (including former Chief Justice Fred Vinson and Justice Tom Clark), and local police departments. The former now included, in addition to employees of utilities and teachers, persons on whom name checks were requested by governors, members of Congress, and the Red Cross. Investigations were made of "sex deviates" among "present and past employees of any branch of the United States Government" and of applicants to the bar of the various states and those involved in disbarment proceedings. Information regarding these categories of persons—and others—had, by July 22, 1954, been given to various Senate and House committees, including the McCarthy committee, the Un-American Activities Committee, the Subcommittee on Labor-Management Relations of the Senate Committee on Labor, and, under "a continuing program of cooperation which was established by the Attorney-General personally on March 15, 1951," to the Senate Internal Security Committee and the Select Committee to Investigate Foundations.

Despite the censorship of the returns, it is easy to see how the FBI conducted its investigations of teachers and leaked its files. The FBI information was given to the state governors or their designated representatives, with the understanding that nothing would be revealed about the source; the governors transmitted the information to high-ranking state school officials; they in turn sent it on to local school systems and college and university officials. The successful operation of the system depended on the discretion of all the parties—FBI, politicians, school officials. Discretion meant concealing the fact that the FBI was the source of the information. If the FBI refused to play ball, the information would cease to flow; if the information flowed, politicians and school officials could claim credit for holding back the tides of subversion.

What is most telling about the policy is the evidence it provides of the breadth of support for the underlying assumption of the FBI: surveillance, investigation, and blacklisting were necessary for national security. But there were other aspects of the policy that must have especially delighted Hoover. It had been worked out during the Democratic years, not the Republican years. "I particularly related to him [Brownell]," Hoover later told his FBI executives, "the concern of then Governor Adlai Stevenson of Illinois that state legislators were starting to move toward investigation of state educational institutions as to subversives in such institutions and that he, the Governor, felt that this would tend to create a certain amount of witch-hunting whereas if Governors could be furnished, on a strictly confidential basis, information from the FBI, they could protect themselves from ill-considered and often-time unwarranted inquiries by well-meaning legislators and patriotic groups." By the time the Governors' Conference decided at its meeting of January 26, 1951, to send a committee to meet with the president to discuss "the policy of the federal government in the field of sabotage and internal security generally," the FBI had already briefed Department of Justice officials about its "cooperative arrangements with state and local police" in the investigation of subversives. But every precaution had to be taken to make believable the "firm position . . . that the files of this Bureau are confidential and that information cannot be released outside the Executive Branch of the Federal Government." On February 12, 1951, Hoover met with the committee of state governors—Frank Lausche, Gordon Browning, Elbert Carvel, Frederick Payne, and Sherman Adams—with Walter Kohler and Adlai Stevenson in attendance, to discuss the subversion problem and the FBI's Security Index. He suggested that the governors get in touch with the SACs when they "have a problem" concerning Communists in colleges.[2]

And check with each other about their problems the FBI, the governors, and university officials certainly did.[3] Even in the disemboweled form in which they have been provided, the FBI documents give profuse illustrations of the operation of the blacklist, only a few of which are cited here. "Les preuves fatiguerent la vérité"—proofs weaken the truth—Georges Braque wrote. These cases have been chosen because the documentation is relatively full and because they highlight a number of important aspects of the blacklisting policy: secrecy, collaborative lying by the FBI and the universities, and the manufacture of pseudo-history.

We shall begin with one of the clearest cases of FBI–university cooperation.

The University of Washington in Seattle was the setting of perhaps the earliest major academic freedom controversy of our period. It has been the subject of considerable investigation and has been presented as paradigmatic in a number of respects—for example, in the fact that the affair was deeply embedded in a context of both national and state politics, in the way in which organizations of teachers and their allies tried to identify the attack on them with broader attacks on civil liberties, and in the effect that the defeat of the teachers in Seattle had on controversies elsewhere.

Certain aspects of the affair, however, which seem now to have been decisive both for the way in which it originated and for its conclusion, have been neglected. The role of the FBI has not been noted; because of that the degree of involvement on the part of the University of Washington officials with the FBI has not been fully recognized. This limitation is testimony to the success of those who, aside from the teachers themselves, were the main participants—high administrators of the university, the FBI, and leading members of the Canwell committee, the Washington State Un-American Activities Committee. The administrative officers of the university had their reasons for wanting the cooperation of the FBI; the FBI had its reasons for wanting the cooperation of the university. The reasons were not the same and not as important to the participants as the hoped-for consequences of cooperation. Those could be attained only by secrecy. If that secrecy continues to cloak the historical record, as it did contemporary events, those consequences of cooperation will persist.

On March 3, 1947, the Washington state legislature established the Joint Legislative Fact-Finding Committee on Un-American Activities under the chairmanship of Representative Albert F. Canwell, former deputy sheriff in charge of the Spokane County Identification Bureau. From the start it was clear that educational institutions would be investigated, and University of Washington President Raymond B. Allen met with the Washington chapter of the AAUP and with committees of the faculty to discuss the situation. The Canwell investigation was supported by a majority of the university regents; the faculty was divided, though most seemed to be in opposition. President Allen presented himself as taking a middle course. He recognized the legitimacy of the investigation, but would try to mitigate it by working with Republican U.S. Senator Harry P. Cain, whose reputation as a fierce opponent of communism gave him credibility with the Canwell committee and others on the far right, and by asserting his support of hearings and other procedural safeguards for faculty members accused of Communist infiltration. He would support due process, but would not defend individuals "engaged in secret activities of a dubious character." Canwell gave Allen the names of the faculty members who would be subpoenaed. After a number of meetings of a special faculty committee appointed by Allen and of the Senate Committee on Tenure and Academic Freedom, charges were brought against six faculty members. In January 1949 the regents dismissed three of the six professors; the other three were put on probation.[4]

President Allen was diligent in trying to unite his own faculty—and the academic profession in general—in support of a policy he presented as solicitous both of the concern of the political authorities that Communist subversion be investigated and of the faculty that academic freedom should not be infringed. In October 1948 he issued an "Open Letter to Friends of the University of Washington" entitled "Communism and Education," in which he nicely balanced his two concerns:

> Academic freedom has not been abridged. . . . The Legislative Com-
> mittee's investigation has sought to establish the pertinent facts: first,
> that membership in the Communist Party is incompatible with service
> to a public-supported institution of higher learning; and, second, that
> certain members of the University of Washington faculty are or have
> been members of the Communist Party. . . . Taking cognizance of these
> issues does not abridge academic freedom.

The "usefulness and legality" of such investigations "can scarcely be questioned. . . . A university, and surely a state-supported one, has no special immunity from such investigations." Allen wanted to clear up certain "misconceptions," particularly that the "University has acted in collusion with the Legislative Committee . . . [and] that the President of the University is the 'prisoner' of some mysterious 'understanding' between the Board of Regents and the Committee." His personal conviction was that Communist affiliation was a bar to teaching not because of the ideas of communism, but because of its deceptiveness: "The subversion we fear is subversion of ideas that are hidden or falsely painted in colors not their own." Teachers "must be free, of course, but they must also be willing to stand up and profess what they believe so that all may learn."[5]

Allen carried his campaign outside the University of Washington. In the summer of 1948, he went east to visit Dwight Eisenhower at Columbia and the general secretary of the AAUP, Ralph Himstead. Allen was a member of the Hoover Commission studying national security organizations and of the Armed Forces Medical Advisory Committee, and his visit with the new president of Columbia was "designed to elicit his advice on a number of topics." They discussed the Canwell committee hearings, which Allen was sure would be "extremely healthy for the University and the State as well as for the individuals concerned." Allen spoke also to Henry Luce and Whittaker Chambers.[6] He was in touch with the FBI—and had been for some time and would continue to be. On September 2, 1948, Assistant FBI Director Nichols wrote Clyde Tolson:

> For record purposes, Dr. Raymond S. [sic] Allen of the University of
> Washington called on August 25. He was in town for one day only in
> connection with the Hoover Commission's study of the organization of
> military establishments. I had talked with him earlier about some Com-
> munists on the faculty out there, and he requested the following infor-
> mation, which I sent over to him by special messenger:
>   Copy of the Constitution of the USSR
>   Copy of the Constitution of the Communist Party, USA

Typed copy of a membership card of the Communist Party
List of required reading material of the Communist Party membership
Attorney General's list of subversive organizations

Allen's path to the FBI had been smoothed by U.S. Senator Harry P. Cain, whose administrative assistant called Hoover's office on May 3, 1948, to arrange an appointment for Allen to see a "top assistant" that day. He saw Nichols that very morning. His mission on that first occasion was not general education about the Communist Party, but the forging of links with the FBI and the Canwell committee.

Nichols reported that Allen told him that Canwell had come to him early "in the investigation . . . and outlined to him what the Committee wanted to do; namely, to ferret out Communists in the University of Washington. Dr. Allen stated he was very favorably impressed and the college offered its full cooperation." Allen told Nichols that one of Canwell's investigators, Everett Pomeroy, "who he believes to be a former Special Agent of this Bureau, conducted numerous interviews, excited very little suspicion and succeeded in securing the cooperation of the faculty." Allen also reported that he had "made an agreement with Canwell whereby after the investigation Canwell would turn over to him the names of any faculty members prior to any public hearings and permit Dr. Allen to have a representative to his staff go over the file of the Investigating Committee; further that Canwell had promised to advise Allen of the information of a derogatory nature which would enable Allen to go to the faculty committee and go through the process of a hearing."

Canwell and Allen apparently had some disagreement over the timing of the release of the names of the faculty members under investigation. At a meeting between Canwell and the regents, Canwell agreed to give the names to Allen three or four days in advance of their general release. But now two or three additional investigators had been working on the campus, and they "have openly said that not only would they publicize individuals found wrong but anybody who had anything to do with them."

Nichols then came to the point of Allen's visit:

Dr. Allen said he had heard that at UCLA an arrangement had been worked out whereby a Bureau representative cooperates with University officials and he was hoping that some arrangements could be perfected with our Seattle Office whereby he could take matters up with the SAC and the SAC could contact him. He likewise expressed the hope that if we secured any information on any of his faculty members we could at least put him on his guard and conceivably if he wanted to hire new faculty members he could check their names with us.

Acknowledgment of the arrangement that Allen had heard about—
by which the FBI and a university exchanged information on a regular
basis—would have embarrassed the FBI; and Nichols was quick to deny
it:

> I told Dr. Allen as far as I knew we had no such arrangements with
> UCLA; that undoubtedly in connection with the Atomic Energy Act
> and the like we did a lot of work on the college campus and accordingly
> we endeavored to have one Agent make the various contacts and cover
> the various leads. I told him that of course he should know Mr. Wilcox,
> the SAC of our Seattle Office; that conceivably at some time he might
> be able to be of assistance. He then said he had three or four college
> professors under inquiry and wondered if we could furnish him any
> information on them. I told him if he would furnish us with the names
> we would see what we have and conceivably we might furnish him with
> some leads where he might secure information himself.

On May 4, the day after his meeting with Nichols, Allen, in a telegram from Princeton, gave him the names of the four Canwell committee investigators and cited a Seattle newspaper as authority that Canwell
would not give the names of faculty members to the university before
public hearings. Allen's wire ended: "Please talk to Canwell about this.
Thank you." The press of other business had kept Nichols from pursuing the matter. Now that he was ready to follow up, he noted "that on
May 6th the Director [Hoover] saw Canwell and it would appear to be
rather awkward to answer Allen's wire now." The Canwell investigators
were apparently not former FBI agents. Perhaps the best that could now
be done was to notify SAC Wilcox of Allen's visit, tell him to call on
Allen sometime in the future, and "warn him of being caught in a cross-
fire between Allen and Canwell." He then summarized the information
in the FBI files on the faculty members whose names had been given by
Allen. Tolson okayed the recommendation for Wilcox, and Hoover endorsed it: "Yes at once. H." [7]
On May 19, 1948, Nichols told Tolson he had checked with SAC
Los Angeles about the UCLA arrangement and had been assured that
while "they do have an Agent who endeavors to cover all the leads at
UCLA, . . . they do not furnish information." He had notified the Seattle office of Allen's visit and cautioned Seattle that "any information"
forwarded to Allen should be limited to matters of "public record." [8]
Nichols learned from Seattle that Canwell had been at the FBI office
only the day before to make arrangements for more regular meetings
with his chief investigator. He told Seattle to notify Allen he had been
misinformed about the nature of the relationship between the FBI and
UCLA, but added there would be no objection if SAC Wilcox took with
him on his visit to Allen "the Agent who covers the leads at the University of Washington."

SAC Seattle reported to the director on May 25, 1948. He had interviewed Allen on May 24. Allen had again been in touch with Canwell and the speaker of the lower house of the Washington legislature; both had assured him that "the University would be given advance notice of any information alleging Communist Party membership or activities on the part of the faculty members . . . thereby affording the University the opportunity of holding faculty hearings and taking administrative action against those members." Allen remained interested in the FBI–UCLA relationship: "He was still under the impression that an agent of this Bureau was stationed at the University and in cases of some import at the University would furnish information to them." He was, "of course," told that such was not the case; "the impression may have been gained by virtue of the fact that one agent in that office was assigned exclusively to make all of the office contacts on the campus." The same arrangement existed at the University of Washington:

> Dr. Allen stated that he could readily understand how the false impression might be gained from that arrangement. He added, however, that he would like to meet the Agent in Seattle who makes all of the University contacts, and he was assured that this would be done immediately.

Allen wanted to know if "it would be possible in certain cases for the Bureau to furnish the University information concerning members of the faculty or *applicants for faculty positions* [emphasis added]. He was particularly concerned with information on their association with the Communist Party or their involvement in front organizations or Communist Party activities." Upon being told that this would be impossible under Department of Justice orders, Allen said "he had gained the impression from his discussion with Assistant Director Nichols . . . that in certain selected cases the Bureau would tell him, Dr. Allen, where such information could be secured." Would the Seattle office give Allen the information he wanted? "In view of the impression he gained from his discussion with Assistant Director Nichols no further action or commitment" would be "taken by this office without specific Bureau authorization."

Hoover answered SAC Seattle on June 2, 1948. Nichols had told Allen that it would not be possible to provide the information as a routine matter, but that "if any special situation arose and Dr. Allen would communicate with the Bureau, we might possibly be of assistance in furnishing leads. What the Bureau had in mind was that we could check our indexes and if any matters of public record were found which could be referred to Dr. Allen, we could then consider this course of action." The general Dissemination Policy of the FBI and the apparent restriction of the material to "public records" served less to limit the information the FBI released than to limit its liability for having released it.

On June 9, 1948, Allen wired Hoover for an appointment the following day in Washington to discuss the Canwell committee investigation. "He will have to see someone else," the wary Hoover wrote. And he did.

He met on June 11 with Nichols and told him that he had talked at length with Professor Sophus Winthur, "once a member of the Communist Party, and . . . now reformed." Winthur had identified four faculty members "as being at least one time [*sic*] active in the Communist Party and two others who were suspected": Ralph Gundlach, Harold "Ebey" (Eby), "Ethel Garland" (Garland Ethel), "Melvin" (Melville) Jacobs, Joseph Butterworth, and Herbert Phillips. Allen had talked to all six and was convinced that four "are still members of the Party." He had tried to call Canwell because he had learned that the committee had the names of twelve members of the Communist Party on the University of Washington faculty. "The purpose of Allen's visit was to inquire whether we had any record on the other six." Nichols told Allen he doubted whether the FBI would "identify them for him; however, I would talk to our Seattle office and if we could be of any assistance, we would let him know."[9]

By the fall of 1948, Allen was deeply involved in preparing the case against the six faculty members against whom charges had been filed; his involvement included continued contact with the FBI. On October 19 Nichols wrote Tolson that Allen had phoned the FBI with a request for specific information concerning the six professors who were being called "on the carpet to see whether or not they should be retained on the staff." He admitted to having a serious problem, which he proposed to solve in the following way:

> Dr. Allen said the University case is not too strong as a matter of proof. They have a few witnesses who can place these Professors at Party meetings and who can show that they belonged to front organizations but they have very little else. Dr. Allen wondered if it would be possible for the Bureau to render some assistance to them. He stated he fully appreciates the confidential nature of our records but thought possibly if it could be arranged to throw some leads in his way he would be most appreciative of any help that we could render.

Nichols promised he would be in touch before Allen left Washington the next day. What he had in mind, he told Tolson, was to review the files immediately, "and should there by any leads of a public source nature we can furnish them to SAC Wilcox to pass on to Dr. Allen." It turned out that "while the Bureau's files" were "replete with information about the" six, there was nothing "of a public source nature which had not previously been furnished by the Seattle Office in accord with instructions previously given to SAC Wilcox there."[10] SAC Wilcox had told headquarters by phone that the agent covering the university "is in personal contact with Allen on a weekly basis" and had been making all "public source" data available to him. Allen "understands perfectly we have given him everything we can." Still, he would get in touch with Allen again to reassure him that all that could be done was being done.

SAC Wilcox did meet with Allen, and he reported to the director on November 4, 1948:

> Dr. Allen was concerned that one of the professors not presently being afforded a hearing, namely Melvin Rader, might be as closely connected with the Communist Party as some of the others and yet he might still be permitted to remain at the University. Dr. Allen requested that he be informed of any information that the Bureau could furnish him which would indicate Dr. Rader's position. This information will be furnished to Dr. Allen, bearing in mind previous instructions concerning this matter which were issued to me by Assistant Director Nichols.[11]

According to SAC Seattle, President Allen was confident that the six professors would be fired: "For the Bureau's information, Dr. Allen advised me confidentially that he felt quite sure that the committee of faculty members hearing the charges against the six professors . . . would bring in a recommendation that the professors be dismissed from the University. He said that in the event such a recommendation was not made, he felt the Board of Regents would without doubt dismiss the six professors concerned." Arrangements with the FBI were very good, and he hoped they would continue.

Allen continued to be in close touch with the Seattle FBI office. On January 26, 1949, SAC Seattle brought Washington headquarters up to date on the hearings. The FBI report on Allen's "views and actions" was based on "numerous contacts" with him. He had accepted the presidency with the understanding that there was considerable Communist activity at the university. His own position was that those who had "seen the light" and left the Party should not be dismissed provided they were competent and "were no longer engaged in subversive activities." Those who were "presently engaged in subversive activities and were secretive about their position" had to be eliminated. There were, however, "numerous stumbling blocks cast in the way of any successful investigation or prosecution of University professors."

First, there was the difficulty of obtaining adequate proof of membership in the Communist Party. Second, there was the tenure system, which protected from dismissal professors who had reached a certain rank or served a specified number of years, except for incompetence, neglect of duty, physical or mental impairment, dishonesty, or immorality and conviction of a crime involving moral turpitude. The president himself could not dismiss a tenured professor. The Tenure Committee of the faculty, after proper hearings, could make recommendations as to dismissal to the regents, but the regents were not bound to follow its recommendations. Third, the regents themselves might object to the dismissal of certain professors "unless some good and sufficient reason were shown." Finally, "there was public reaction to be considered." The Teachers Union had "objected to most everything the President has done. He [Allen] indicated that he was convinced that there was a subversive element of no small proportion in the Teachers Union."

Allen told SAC Seattle that he had often spoken with Canwell before the hearings began and that, on the whole, Canwell had lived up to his promise to inform him in advance which professors would be called to testify. He had interviewed every such professor, "for the purpose of laying the foundation for dismissal of the professors on the grounds of neglect of duty." When the faculty hearings began in October 1948, Allen was "convinced that the University would be able to rid itself of all six accused professors, or nearly all of them." Defense counsel had made such a good showing, however, that now "he was doubtful that more than two would be dismissed." Allen was particularly concerned that Professors Jacobs and Gundlach might not be recommended for dismissal. He was also anxious for "proof of Communist activities" on the part of professors who denied membership. He knew that "Communists removed from the University would soon be replaced by others, and he expressed a keen desire to hold down any new Party members who were attempting to obtain a foothold on the campus."

The majority of the Tenure Committee on January 7, 1949, recommended that all the professors but Gundlach be retained, because none of the five stated causes for dismissal could be stretched to include past or present membership in the Communist Party. Gundlach's dismissal was recommended by a majority not because of "subversive activities," but for "neglect of duty, in that he was evasive and hostile . . . and generally uncooperative with the administration." Allen recommended the dismissal of Butterworth, Phillips, and Gundlach and probation for the others; the regents concurred. SAC Seattle conveyed Allen's offer to make the entire stenographic record of the hearings—including the transcript of three thousand pages of testimony—available to the FBI. FBI headquarters recommended that Allen's offer be accepted.[12]

On November 22, 1951, Allen resigned as president of the University of Washington. He became chairman of the Psychological Strategy Board, coordinating the information policies of the State Department, the Department of Defense, and the CIA. In December 1951 he became the first chancellor of the University of California at Los Angeles.[13] His departure from Washington did not end the FBI's interests there, nor did it end his own influence.

On April 22 and June 23, 1953, SAC Seattle reported to FBI headquarters in response to Hoover's request for the survey of Communist infiltration. It was based on documents in the files of the FBI, discussions with "Agents having comprehensive experience in the security field in this division," and interviews with "two women who have worked closely with investigative committees, with the American Legion, and possibly with other individuals and organizations in compiling information regarding the Communist Party and persons associated therewith." One of these informants was Mrs. Fred Niendorff, whose husband, a reporter for the *Seattle Post-Intelligencer*, was especially close to the Canwell committee.[14] Reports were submitted on seventeen faculty members and employees of the university. None was then included on the Security Index nor under investigation by the Seattle office, but some were reported to have been members of the Communist Party in the past, and others had participated in American Youth for Democracy, the Pacific Northwest Labor School, the Teachers Union, the Independent Citizens' Committee of the Arts, Sciences, and Professions, and the defense of Professor Frank Oppenheimer at the University of Minnesota.[15]

Allen's influence continued after his departure from Washington. When, in April 1952, the English Department recommended the appointment of literary critic Kenneth Burke as Walker-Ames Lecturer, Donald Anderson, director of university relations, began a "routine" check of Burke's political background. He called Allen, his former chief, to ask Sidney Hook, professor of philosophy at NYU, who had given advice to Allen during the Canwell Committee hearings, about Burke's recent political views. Anderson's notes on Allen's phone call read: "Sidney Hook reports that [Burke] is a mildly confused leftist and fellow travellr [*sic*]—was probably gotten into that line by Malcolm Cowley—is a very poor teacher—very obscure—terribly exaggerated (his ability)—is not a Communist author and has not been active politically recently."[16] The offer to Burke was withdrawn.

To prevent further embarrassments like the Burke affair, the regents, in conformity with practices already established during the Allen regime, decided to formalize the screening procedure for new appointments. In November 1952 President Henry Schmitz appointed a committee to assist him in the formation of policy "relative to the appointment of persons whose political backgrounds raise questions as to the appropriateness of University sponsorship." The university sought assistance from, among others, Richard E. Combs, counsel for the California State Senate Fact-Finding Committee on Un-American Activities (Burns committee). By that time every university in California, including UCLA—where Allen was now chancellor—had an "agreement of cooperation"

with the Burns committee and Combs under which present and prospective faculty members were screened through the committee files by
a "liaison officer" who was usually, if not always, the president of the
university. The University of Washington committee report for the most
part endorsed the practice of screening faculty appointments for political
purposes, the only significant exception being for acting or temporary
appointees, in whom some otherwise disqualifying quality would not be
a major impediment.[17]

Sometimes the Dissemination Policy inhibited the FBI from giving
to university administrators as much information as the administrators
would have liked to get, but it never prevented it from giving as much
information as the FBI wanted to give. That flow of information, which
depended at the start on the personal views of the university presidents
and on their political judgment that cooperation with the FBI might
prevent even more rampant witch-hunting, soon began to overflow the
channels that had been designed to contain it. Regardless of who was
university president, the information passed back and forth—justified by
one party as essential to national security, by the other as essential to
organizational survival as well. To provide information to the FBI became part of the job description of the university president.

To provide information to the universities was always part of the job
description of the director of the FBI.

On December 22, 1953, SAC New York wrote to Washington headquarters that Dr. Buell Gallagher, president of the City College of New
York, had been interviewed in his office at his own request on December
16, 1953. He wanted help from the FBI in rooting out subversive professors, about whom he had been receiving "adverse publicity," especially since the recent hearings before the Jenner committee of the U.S.
Senate. Three CCNY professors had been forced to resign as a result of
their testimony; a fourth did so following an investigation by the Board
of Higher Education. But it was not enough. Gallagher told his FBI
interviewers that "he still believes there are other professors at the College who might be suspect and that he had been approaching every avenue of information in an effort to determine whether or not these people he suspected should be asked to resign." He was up against a deadline.
On January 15, 1954, he had to submit an affidavit to the Board of
Higher Education to the effect that he knew no professor to be a member of or affiliated in any way with the Communist Party:

> He stated that he had cooperated closely with the Jenner, McCarthy,
> and Velde Committees and had secured their cooperation in attempting
> to determine if any of the professors on the staff were in anyway [sic]
> subversive. He stated that he himself had spent considerable time look-
> ing into the background and reading articles, papers, and books by the
> professors he thought were suspect.

To no avail—he had not been able to turn up conclusive evidence of their Communist connections. His purpose in talking to the FBI "was to determine whether that organization would come to his assistance and supply him, possibly on a confidential basis, information concerning suspected professors." He understood the FBI's position—that "by order of the Attorney General" such information "could not be made available"—and explained that he had requested the interview to assure himself that he had pursued every source of information. The interview ended on a cordial note, with Gallagher assuring the FBI that he would have treated any information given him with complete confidentiality and promising that his affidavit would say that he had cooperated with various congressional committees and the FBI.

That ended the interview, but not the relationship or the flow of information. SAC New York called Hoover's attention to a letter of April 25, 1953, listing the names of professors in New York who were, or should be, on the Security Index, including a number at CCNY: "The Bureau may desire, under its responsibilities program, to make this information known to Governor Dewey who may in turn make this information available to Dr. Gallagher or some other administrator of City College of New York."

Hoover responded on January 8, 1954:

> In the event there are professors or other employees of the City College of New York whose names are presently included in the Security Index of your office, you should immediately in each case make a proper request to the Bureau for authority to disseminate information under the Responsibilities Program.

On January 19 SAC New York assured FBI headquarters that "all Security Index subjects who were formerly employed at CCNY are no longer employed there in any capacity." Governor Dewey was informed about the situation at CCNY and elsewhere, and information provided him was passed on to Gallagher and the Board of Higher Education. The arrangement was a continuing one. On September 1, 1954, SAC New York notified Washington headquarters that the head of the Albany office had given information to Dewey under the Responsibilities Program, and that the Board of Higher Education and Gallagher had been given derogatory information about someone who "up to this time has been a tutor at CCNY."[18]

SAC New York wrote Hoover on May 26, 1954, that "liaison continues to be maintained with [name deleted]" of the Board of Higher Education to get the transcripts of the trials of teachers accused of Communist affiliation. The board was of particular interest to the FBI. It received, courtesy of an employee of the board, the transcript of testimony and the documentary evidence presented before the board's Trial

Committee at the hearing of suspected Communist teachers. The information was used to supplement the FBI's own files and was compared with the testimony of the same persons before the Senate Internal Security Committee in the hope that discrepancies would be found to sustain a charge of perjury. The trial transcripts were provided by William F. Hartnett, Jr., assistant counsel of the Board of Higher Education. He called at FBI headquarters to speak with Hoover, was interviewed by FBI Domestic Intelligence Director F. J. Baumgardner, and delivered the 111-page transcript of the trial of three Hunter College professors at the instructions of Michael Casteldi, special counsel, Special Investigating Unit of the Board of Higher Education.[19] We know, too, that FBI contacts with the New York Board of Education provided it with information about teachers in the public schools. On March 27, 1953, Hoover called SAC New York's attention to the recent testimony before the Jenner committee of William Jansen, superintendent of the New York public school system. Hoover instructed SAC New York

> to advise the Bureau whether . . . Jansen has reported to you the identities of the 81 teachers ousted and the identities of the additional 180 teachers who are reported to be under investigation. If you are not in possession of the identities of these teachers, you are instructed to take immediate steps to obtain this information.

Security investigations were to be started on the 261 persons. The FBI wanted information from Jansen, but it was reluctant to give information to him. Instead, information on the Communist affiliation of teachers was given by the FBI to New York Police Commissioner George P. Monaghan under the Responsibilities Program.

SAC New York quickly responded to Hoover's demand for the names of the New York schoolteachers. On April 20, 1953, he notified headquarters that an informant with the Board of Education who had earlier "declined to furnish information concerning the complete investigation of communist infiltration" into the public schools now agreed to do so. He turned over 271 names to the FBI, including those who resigned while being investigated, those "suspended or discharged by the Board for insubordination based on the results of a hearing," those who resigned or retired rather than keep an appointment for a hearing, those who refused to answer questions asked by the Jenner committee, and those currently being investigated by the board.

What was the FBI's justification for leaking from its files information about teachers? As far back as April 29, 1951, the FBI Executives' Conference had decided:

> The educational field is considered a prime target by the Communist Party because it reaches the youth of our nation. A daily contact of teachers with pupils forms a close association and enables the teachers

to effectively control the thinking of the pupils and thus insidiously instill into the minds of children the Communist Party line. . . . The FBI may be considered to have a responsibility to advise responsible local officials of the identities of communists in the schools.

The blacklist was constructed and worked by trading information for exemption or possible exemption from being blacklisted. By the time the University of Washington sought the assistance of the California State Senate Fact-Finding Committee on Un-American Activities to develop procedures for sifting out subversive teachers, the educational authorities of California—with the assistance of the FBI and political leaders—had been doing the job for some time. What they did was done throughout the country, but since the documentation is particularly rich in the case of California and since no state governor was more diligent in using the FBI than Earl Warren, most of our illustrations of the triangular trade in information among political leaders, educational authorities, and the FBI derive from there.

UCLA authorities, under pressure from various groups to prove their diligence in eliminating suspected Communists from the faculty, tried to clear themselves, as did university authorities elsewhere, by stating that they were already checking their faculty against FBI files. On April 13, 1950, SAC Los Angeles notified Hoover that an administrative officer at UCLA had just been interviewed by the FBI about his statement, quoted in the *Los Angeles Times,* "that he checked FBI records in connection with interviews of applicants for faculty positions at UCLA." Public disclosure that information in the FBI files was made available to the universities irritated the nerve endings of the FBI and stimulated major efforts to deny what university officials and local politicians sometimes blunderingly admitted.

UCLA—and other educational institutions in California, including the public schools—became aware of what was in the FBI files regarding "subversive" teachers in the way President Buell Gallagher of CCNY was informed: through the governor, who was himself informed by the FBI. To judge from the FBI files, no state governor received more FBI information than Earl Warren.

For example:

Captioned individual, who is the subject of a Security Index card, is employed as [several words deleted].

The Los Angeles Office has requested authority from the San Francisco Office to furnish information regarding the subject to Governor Earl Warren of California. Information has previously been furnished to Governor Warren under the responsibilities program and he has been proved to be reliable.

It is recommended that the SAC at San Francisco be authorized to

furnish certain information regarding the subject to Governor Warren.[20]

Captioned individual whose name is included on the Security Index
is presently employed by [few words deleted]. . . .

It is recommended that the SAC at San Francisco be authorized to
orally furnish information regarding the subject to Governor Warren.[21]

Sometimes local FBI officers requested permission to pass along information to governors pending the results of interviews with suspected
subversives. On April 28, 1953, SAC San Francisco asked permission to
give Governor Warren information about a subject "in view of his employment" depending on the cooperativeness shown by the subject in a
scheduled interview. The FBI was well aware of the risk it ran if such
subjects were fired, but it was prepared to run the risk if it was persuaded that the governor could be trusted with the information. On May
21, 1953, for example, the director notified SAC San Francisco that information regarding a suspect be given to "the proper local authority"
under the Responsibilities Program:

It is probable that should subject lose his position [several words de-
leted] the Bureau will be accused of such action. [several words de-
leted] who you state is the proper individual to whom information should
be furnished, would undoubtedly be directly involved in any controversy arising as a result of subject's losing his position. The Bureau
feels, therefore, that information regarding subject should be given to
Governor Warren of California in this instance, since Governor Warren
has been the recipient of information under the Responsibilities Program in the past and has proved to be reliable.[22]

For a suspect to demonstrate lack of cooperation in an interview meant
information would be given to the governor. To demonstrate cooperativeness—that is, to become an informant—meant that the information
might not be passed along to the governor. On June 2, 1953, SAC San
Francisco notified Washington headquarters that two subjects in an interview at their residence showed they "did not intend to cooperate with
the Agents." The interview had been ended, but the subjects had not
objected to speaking at a later date. The agents felt that "the subjects
should be reinterviewed because it is believed that if they can be convinced that the Communist Party is controlled by the Soviet Union and
is a threat to the security of this country and also a threat to the working
man rather than a benefactor, they will be cooperative and furnish valuable information regarding [half line deleted]." SAC San Francisco,
therefore, requested permission to reinterview the subjects before "furnishing information to the Governor of California under the Responsibilities Program."

Even in the case of discreet governors like Warren, the FBI was nervous about leaks. On June 12, 1953, SAC San Francisco wrote the director denying that someone whose name has been deleted could "have seen a copy of an FBI report in the office of [name deleted]. Information concerning security matters is furnished to Governor Earl Warren . . . by this office only, and, of course, no copies of reports are supplied to him. . . . Since Governor Warren fully understands that information obtained from this Bureau is given to him confidentially and that he is not to refer to the FBI as his source of information, it appears that [name deleted] statements are based primarily on his own assumption."

SAC Los Angeles notified Washington headquarters on June 3, 1953, that a state official, name deleted, notified the FBI "that he knew that information concerning Communist activities in the California School System was being disseminated from the Office of Governor Warren, and that [line deleted] had been receiving this information from an unnamed source. [Name deleted] further stated that he knew that this information was coming directly from the FBI and that the procedure was strictly confidential."

SAC San Francisco cautioned Warren about the leaks, and Warren discussed with him the procedure he followed for dissemination of FBI information. On July 9, 1953, SAC San Francisco notified Hoover that Warren "described in considerable detail his method of handling information received by him from the Bureau. He pointed out first that only he and his secretary [few words deleted] are aware of the relationship which exists between the Governor's Office and the Bureau, and that both of them use considerable caution in insuring that this relationship will be kept confidential." But the fact that California had a state loyalty oath required the governor to forward the FBI information to the state attorney general as well as to the department in which the suspect was employed. Warren said that in forwarding the information he simply stated that he had received it from "a reliable source," without specifying the FBI. SAC San Francisco assured Hoover that he had seen Warren's letters and "found that they are most discreet." Warren was sure "that the program . . . has prevented people who are or have been members of the Party from obtaining State employment. For this reason, as well as because of the high regard the Governor has for the Director and the Bureau, he is most anxious that nothing occur which would interfere with this relationship." Warren was much favored by the FBI. As A. H. Belmont wrote to Assistant Director Ladd on December 21, 1951, whereas state governors requesting information on present or future employees were provided with what was euphemistically called "public source information," Warren was given information from "reliable sources" of the FBI itself.

———

Notwithstanding Warren's assurances and the precautions he undoubtedly took, the problem of leaks did not disappear. After his appointment as chief justice, it focused on the University of California. On March 30, 1954, Hoover sent a memorandum to four top officials of the FBI: Tolson, Boardman, Belmont, and Nichols. He had just been visited by Assistant Attorney General Warren Olney, who reported that on his recent trip to California he had learned that "over some period of time there would turn up upon the desks of high officials of the University of California blank memoranda containing information about individuals employed at the University. Such memoranda have turned up on the desks of the President and Chancellor of the University" and also in the governor's office when "Warren was Governor of California and had been forwarded to [name and title deleted]:

> Mr. Olney stated that there had been engendered a very bad impression among the people at the University about this procedure as it had been ascertained through an inquiry which had been made that these so-called mysterious anonymous memoranda had come from the FBI.

Hoover wrote his colleagues that he had told Olney that "this did not seem to make sense. . . . as I did not believe we were furnishing any such type of memoranda to the University but I did know that we had over a period of time supplied information to Governor Warren concerning the subversive background of State employees. I stated that when Governor Warren left the Governorship we had then sent such material to [line and a half deleted]."

While Olney was in his office, Hoover telephoned SAC San Francisco to order an immediate inquiry. If the information had been handled as reported, "we should again reevaluate the entire program on the dissemination of information to State officials." The FBI was embarrassed: "Mr. Olney stated that much of the information which had been supplied to the University of California . . . had been found to be unsubstantiated; vague; and had in turn created considerable criticism of the FBI for the so-called smearing of persons employed by the University without giving any substantive facts to support the allegations made."

On the same day, SAC San Francisco teletyped his reply. Five full pages have been deleted, but the general outline of the FBI's procedure can be reconstructed. Under Warren, the information was given orally; that procedure was still being followed, but the information now was being given to someone else. Under Warren and at present, two letters were prepared in the office of the governor. The first was a personal letter, signed by the governor, sent to the agency employing the suspect. "It stated in substance that attached to it is a memorandum concerning the subject containing info received from a reliable confidential source and requesting the employing agency to conduct an investigation of the subject and advise the governor's office of the results." The attachment was a synopsis of the information "orally provided by the FBI." The second letter was a personal letter signed by the governor to the state attorney general, containing the same information and requesting "an investigation of the subject by the State AG's office. Where the employing agency has an investigative staff, the head of that agency ordinarily makes the info available to the investigator without revealing the fact that it came from the Governor's Office and, of course, without revealing the source." The investigative reports by the attorney general and the employing agency, containing information from the Tenney committee (California State Un-American Activities Committee), local law enforcement agencies, "and various semi-public info-gathering services," were sent to the governor. They "usually resulted in [an] interview of the state employee and a final report on actions taken." About the University of California:

> The letter from the Governor's office with the attachment is directed personally to [name deleted], the President of the University. President [name deleted] gives the info in the attachment to [two lines deleted], who conducts additional investigation, contacts all sources available to him and reports back to the President of the University in blind memo form without giving his sources. The President then makes a report to the office of the Governor.

The FBI refuted the charge that its memoranda contained "vague and unsubstantiated information" by insisting that all the information had "been obtained from reliable informants and that all organizations mentioned have been documented. . . . Governor Warren . . . has not been known to have betrayed our confidence." [23]

On April 2, 1954, Boardman notified Hoover that as of the end of March the bureau had authorized dissemination on 875 Security Index subjects, of whom 204 were from California. These figures did not include "name checks which were made at the specific request of Governor Warren, now Chief Justice of the United States Supreme Court. . . . It is interesting to note that a large proportion of the Security Index subjects on whom we have disseminated information under this program were school teachers."

The rumors about the FBI–University of California connection could not be entirely contained. SAC San Francisco notified FBI headquarters that *The Nation*, in an article on January 30, 1954, on the "contact man" system at the university, had reported that the university had a "liaison officer" with investigating agencies, including state and federal legislative committees. The liaison officer on the Berkeley campus was William Wardman, "an FBI–trained man." The president and the chancellor denied the charge, but copies of the article were distributed by Students to Combat McCarthyism, and the affair made headlines in the *Daily Californian*. Humorlessly, the FBI report continued:

The alleged purpose of the [student] group is to oppose "Mc-Carthyism" in all its forms. "McCarthyism," according to a potential security informant of the San Francisco Office, was roughly defined on February 23, 1954, as "a system designed to curb civil liberties, free action of the individual and domestic rights."

True to form, the San Francisco Office of the FBI placed "Students to Combat McCarthyism . . . under investigation . . . as a Communist-front organization since January, 1954."[24]

The leak at the University of California could not be prevented, nor could those at many other universities. On May 11, 1954, A. H. Belmont notified L. V. Boardman that SAC Milwaukee had been confidentially advised by a good friend of the bureau that the FBI and the Responsibilities Program were a matter of secret discussion by about thirty high officials of leading universities meeting in Chicago during the last week of April 1954: "Several officials mentioned that they had received instructions from their state governor to dismiss certain faculty members on the grounds of questioned loyalty. It was generally surmised . . . that the Governors have been receiving information from some such reliable source as the FBI." The university officials directed no "specific criticism" against the FBI, but they did express "considerable resentment" over being held responsible for firing faculty members on the basis of charges made by anonymous sources. Belmont once again pressed for secrecy to prevent embarrassment to the FBI.

Public school authorities, especially in Los Angeles, and universities in Southern California were made privy to information in the FBI files, secretly and deviously. On March 27, 1953, SAC Los Angeles wrote to Hoover:

The following individuals, who have been subpoenaed to appear before the House Committee on Un-American Activities (HCUA) at Los Angeles, California, are in the educational field [three paragraphs deleted].

Appropriate officials in connection with the Responsibilities of the FBI in the Internal Security Field have been advised of the Communist Party membership or activities of all of the above individuals, who are the subjects of Security Index cards, with the exception of [line deleted].

The appropriate authorities under the Responsibilities . . . program have been notified of the Communist Party activities of the following individuals, who formerly were in the educational field in the Los Angeles Division territory. These individuals are no longer in the educational field in the Los Angeles Division territory. [seven paragraphs deleted]

By March 18, 1954, the Los Angeles office could report to the director that it was "unaware of any Communist Party program with any vitality pointed toward the infiltration of Education in this vicinity." Still, wariness was called for—"the Los Angeles Federation of Teachers, also Academic Freedom Committee" and the Teachers Defense Committee needed especially to be watched.

Hoover told Attorney General Brownell that Adlai Stevenson had pressed for access by the governors to information in the FBI files as a matter of general policy. He apparently requested such information himself as well, and made use of it.

On August 3, 1953, SAC Springfield telegraphed Washington head-quarters that the *Chicago Daily Tribune* had that day carried a press release from Dr. George D. Stoddard, who had resigned as president of the University of Illinois, under fire by the university's trustees and Illinois politicians for having been lax in hunting down Communists on the Illinois faculty. Stoddard said that while the politicians "shout them-selves hoarse about communism in the university, those of us in charge have worked quietly through our own security officers, the FBI, the State Department and the military establishments to make sure that no Communists are on the staff." The *Chicago Herald-American* had called the Springfield FBI office to ask "whether or not the statement of Stoddard as regards the FBI was correct." SAC Springfield's reply had been "No comment." Now he was informing Washington:

> It is to be observed the names of the following three professors [names deleted by S. D.] were previously furnished Governor Adlai E. Steven-son in the program entitled FBI Responsibilities in the Internal Security Field, which info was passed on to the University by Governor Steven-son, resulting in Professors [names deleted by S. D.] being dropped from the rolls. The name of Professor [name deleted by S. D.] has recently been given to Governor William G. Stratton in the above mat-ter.

Hoover wrote at the bottom of the telegram: "Stick to 'no comment.' H."[25]

On August 27, 1953, SAC Hosteny of Springfield wired Hoover that he had received an inquiry from an Illinois state representative about Stoddard's claim that he had "worked quietly through the FBI to make sure that no Communists are on the staff." She wanted to know if the FBI had made sure there were no Communists at the University of Illinois: "I think I know you did not, and if you did not, I submit that the false inference from his statement should be corrected." Hosteny sent a suggested reply for Hoover's approval. Back came the evasive answer Hoover insisted should be sent to the representative:

> Although I would like to be of service . . . I must advise that in ac-cordance with a departmental regulation data contained in the files of

this Bureau is maintained as confidential and available for official use only. . . . The FBI is strictly a fact-finding agency and it is not within the limits of its prescribed function to draw conclusions or make evaluations concerning the character or integrity of any organization or individual.

Liberal political and educational leaders like Stevenson and Stoddard felt that to cooperate with Hoover in fighting communism might avert even more rabid witch-hunting. It did not. The FBI accepted their cooperation and used them in firing and blacklisting subversives, but it did not reward them by acknowledging publicly their cooperation. To the contrary: by adhering to its firm denial that it ever released information from its files or "cleared" suspected persons, it allowed Stevenson, Stoddard, and others to continue to bear the brunt of right-wing attacks. To the charge that they were "soft" on communism was now added the charge that they lied in saying they received information about suspected Communists from the FBI. Did not the FBI deny constantly that it ever released information from its files? So far as the FBI was concerned, Stevenson and Stoddard could twist in the wind.

The FBI documents reveal that the FBI created a network of informants through the trading of information for exemption from being fired. On February 5, 1953, SAC Baltimore wrote the director:

Information concerning [name deleted] was furnished to [name deleted] on 12/2/52. Subsequently, [name deleted] Office advised that they are going to attempt to develop [name deleted] as an informant by pointing out to her that if she did not cooperate with them, she would undoubtedly lose her employment [few words deleted]. . . . On February 2, 1953, [name deleted] advised SA [name deleted] orally that his investigators had in fact attempted to develop [name deleted] as an informant, but that she had absolutely refused to talk with them.

The paradigmatic example is presented in the interoffice memorandum between A. H. Belmont and D. M. Ladd, February 13, 1953:

The San Francisco Office on January 2, 1953, requested authority to furnish information concerning the subject to [name and title deleted].
    Since the subject had been interviewed and a second interview with him was contemplated, we advised the San Francisco Office that no action would be taken on its request to furnish information to [name deleted] until the results of the interview were furnished.
    On January 30, 1953, San Francisco advised that the subject stated that he had no additional information to furnish with regard to his past activity and that another interview would serve no purpose. San Francisco recommended that the subject's name be retained in the Security Index. Also . . . to furnish information concerning the subject to [name

deleted] who is believed to be both reliable and discreet in matters of this type.

It is recommended that we authorize the SAC at San Francisco to orally furnish certain information concerning the subject to [name deleted].

When a San Francisco subject was unwilling to "talk to the agents" during his interview, information concerning him was given to an officer of an organization "in view of the fact that the subject may seek employment there."[26]

On June 15, 1951, SAC Louisville notified the director that "an established reliable source," who had been the recipient of information in the past, said that "he would immediately look for an opportunity to terminate" the employment of a Security Index subject about whom he "quickly and correctly deduced that the Bureau's interest . . . was because of some current or former subversive connection." He did not believe that there were "many Communists in [half line deleted] but that there is a group of so-called 'Liberals,' whom he refers to as 'incompetents' and 'educational bums.' " SAC Louisville requested authority to pass on information to the informant, and his request was approved on June 25 by the director.

Louis C. Wyman, attorney general of New Hampshire, was especially zealous in his pursuit of Communists and succeeded in enlisting the assistance of the FBI, with whom he had established close connections as a member of the staff of U.S. Senator Styles Bridges. On July 9, 1953, Nichols wrote Tolson that Wyman had called to solicit the help of the FBI in the investigation of subversive activities:

> He stated that the whole action of the Legislature was directed primarily at school teachers; however, to avoid any kickback from teachers in class, the resolution came out without names of school teachers. But the investigation would concentrate on teachers, of whom there were four to five thousand.

He was checking their names with the various Senate and House committees, but could the FBI help? Nichols informed Tolson that he had advised Wyman to get in touch with the American Legion, various patriotic groups, *Counterattack* magazine, the California State Committee on Un-American Activities, and newspaper files on the organizations on the attorney general's subversives list. The FBI could not check the names of the thousands of New Hampshire teachers, but "if he had a half-dozen cases in which he was particularly interested," the FBI would help. SAC Boston was then instructed, if Wyman provided a list of names, "to search those names through the indices of your office." Whatever information Wyman was given was, of course, to be kept confidential.[27]

With time the relation of the FBI to congressional committees came to be of crucial importance in the tactics of blacklist and purge. It had been a subject of concern to the Executives' Conference of the FBI at least as early as the fall of 1953, probably earlier, when the conference considered whether the FBI should respond to all requests for assistance from congressional committees and in what form it should respond. The decision of the Executives' Conference was probably made in response to an order by Deputy Attorney General (later Secretary of State) William Rogers modifying the Dissemination Policy in certain respects.

The FBI informed the attorney general on October 20, 1953, that it wanted no change in current policy which was, "as a general rule," to notify congressional committees asking the FBI to conduct name checks that such requests had to be made through the attorney general, except in the case of the Senate and House Appropriation Committees, the Senate and House Judiciary Committees, the Joint Committee on Atomic Energy, and—on the basis of an understanding with former attorney general J. Howard McGrath on March 15, 1951—the Subcommittee to Investigate the Administration of the Internal Security Act and Other Internal Security Laws. FBI policy regarding congressional committees antedated the return to power of the Republican Party with the Eisenhower victory of 1952. An agreement with Attorney General Tom Clark on December 3, 1947, endorsed the FBI "practice of passing to Government departments and agencies information coming to our attention in connection with conducting investigations." Attorney General McGrath had approved the special relationship with the McCarran committee in 1951. In a conference with Deputy Attorney General Rogers on March 9, 1953, Assistant FBI Director Nichols said "there had been instances wherein we had ascertained that a Congressional Committee was on the verge of uncovering a valuable informant; that in such a case, we had no choice but to go to the committee, and, if it meant the saving of our informant, furnishing them information on another individual where no harm would be done to the Bureau or the Department and the public interests [*sic*] would be served." [28]

At the March 9 conference between Rogers and Nichols, Rogers expressed his willingness to give no FBI information to any committee. At a dinner with Vice-President Nixon, Senator McCarthy, Don Lourie, and Scott McCleod, he was surprised that McCarthy asked for FBI information concerning an employee of the Voice of America. "He wondered how McCarthy knew this. [Nichols] told him this was very simple; that we had told Roy Cohn . . . in response to his request for Voice of America data, that before forwarding the data, we were calling it to Rogers' attention. . . . Rogers stated this was perfectly okay." Nichols told Rogers about other occasions on which information had been given to the Senate Internal Security Committee:

I told Mr. Rogers the initial agreement with the Internal Security Committee was that we would privately tell them what we had covered so they would not be wasting time going up blind alleys in the IPR [Institute of Pacific Relations] case; that we would furnish them leads and, in a few isolated instances, informally and confidentially furnish them with information which they could use for the purpose of examining witnesses; . . . that the former Attorney General had approved this agreement and established it as a Departmental policy. . . . I did cite certain benefits, such as Morris' [Robert Morris, committee counsel] attitude in holding the possibility of public testimony over the head of a Harvard University professor; that he had been deferring it until he talked to the Bureau.

Perhaps the most bone-chilling example of an FBI leak to an investigating committee involved no complicated razzle-dazzle at all, but a straightforward request from the committee and an equally direct response from the FBI.

On February 11, 1953, Assistant FBI Director Nichols sent a memo to Clyde Tolson:

Robert Morris stated the Senators were very happy over their hearing yesterday with reference to the teachers. Morris would like to have another hearing some time week after next and would like to get hold of a good case at Bennington College, Sarah Lawrence College and Harvard. He wondered if we could give him any leads. I told him we would give some thought to this.

I asked Morris whether he had given any thought to Professor [name deleted] Cornell University. He thought this was an excellent idea and would do so. I further asked him whether he had given any thought to [name deleted] whose maiden name was [name deleted] and who, as I recalled, joined the Party at Sarah Lawrence College. He thought this was an excellent idea and would give it consideration. . . .

I think if we could get a good Communist Party professor at Harvard, Sarah Lawrence and Bennington, this would be a worth-while venture.

At the bottom of the memo, J. Edgar Hoover wrote: "Yes. Help if we can. H."

Instructions were sent to the three concerned field offices to provide the help the Jenner committee wanted.[29] Disappointingly, Bennington College had no professors on the Security Index. Harvard had six, but only two were felt to provide the "good cases" the committee wanted. As to one of those, "investigation has not developed actual proof of his Communist Party membership although it has indicated that he has identified himself and lent his name in support of Communist Party sponsored programs and front organizations such as the Joint Anti-

Fascist Refugee Committee, the Paris Peace Conference, the National Council of American-Soviet Friendship, the Progressive Citizens of America, the Committee of One Thousand, the American Peace Crusade, and the National Council of the Arts, Sciences, and Professions." Investigation had not turned up admissible information on the other subject's Communist Party membership, but he had "expressed sympathetic statements for the Russian Government" and was associated with the Samuel Adams School of Social Science in Boston, "which has been cited by the Attorney General under Executive Order 9835." A few days later, at Morris's request, Nichols provided additional information on still other professors.[30]

The Responsibilities Program preserved the virtual monopoly of the FBI in internal security matters. The Dissemination Policy allowed it to give information to whom it pleased under circumstances of its own choosing. Together they expanded enormously the power of the FBI to act as it wished and to protect itself from critics. To charges that it leaked information from its files, depriving suspects of their constitutional rights, that it went beyond its legal authority, and that its behavior made possible the repressiveness of government and private organizations, the FBI had only to lie and to keep secret what it was lying about.

Hoover had endorsed Nichols's memorandum of February 11, 1953, that information in the FBI files be given to the Jenner committee with the comment: "Yes. Help if we can. H." On April 16, 1954, he sent the following memorandum to Tolson and Nichols:

On April 15, 1954, I saw Mr. Ralph McGill, Editor of the "Atlanta Journal," who was in town attending the annual meeting of the American Society of Newspaper Editors. He called to pay his respects.

During his visit I . . . stressed the fact that the FBI did not evaluate information which it procured and forwarded to other Government agencies, and I also took the occasion to point out to him the confidential character of the FBI files and the fact that access to them was not had by members of Congress or Committees of Congress, notwithstanding some of the public statements which had been made by certain members of Congress.[31]

═══

Hoover could keep secrets—from the public, from the press, from the attorney general.

On October 29, 1954, FBI official Boardman sent Hoover a lengthy memorandum, "Exemptions to Restrictions Limiting Dissemination of FBI Data to Executive Branch of Federal Government." Its purpose was to brief Hoover on what he should tell Brownell that might assist Brownell in the decision he was about to make on the Dissemination Program. He recommended that the attorney general be advised of the instances set forth in the details of this memorandum wherein FBI data is disseminated outside the Executive Branch . . . (such as limited access for selected Congressional committees, name checks when requested by the judiciary, information given to state and local officials under the Responsibility Program) *with the following exceptions* [emphasis supplied]:

    a. That we do not advise him of the fact that . . . on occasions when common sense dictates and it appears in the best interest of the Bureau to do so we furnish limited information on a confidential basis to private organizations and individuals. It is not believed that the Attorney General should be advised regarding the above exception to the general rule that FBI data is not disseminated outside the Executive Branch of the Federal Government inasmuch as such dissemination is not made on a continuing basis to any one person or organization and such dissemination is never made without the expressed *[sic]* authority of a high Bureau official.

    b. That we do not advise the Attorney General of the information disseminated by the Administration Director . . . as such information is disseminated in connection with Budget and Appropriations materials or in the course of business practices normally exchanged on a courtesy basis with other organizations. . . . It is recommended that the Bureau's policy in this regard *not* be brought to the attention of the Attorney General [emphasis supplied].

Boardman's advice to Hoover seems to have been heeded. In all the memoranda that I have seen by Hoover to the attorney general on the Responsibilities Program and Dissemination Policy of the FBI, not a single one mentions the exceptions that Boardman felt should be kept secret even from the attorney general.

Thirty-five years after these events, in the congressional investigation of the diversion of funds from the sale of arms to Iran to the opponents of the government of Nicaragua, the phrase "plausible deniability" was often used. It meant to be able to lie convincingly when denying knowledge that the law was being broken. Crucial to plausible deniability was the absence of any document showing that the superior had given instructions that the policy be carried out or even that he knew there was such a policy. In short, there was no "smoking gun"—the chief had not been caught in the act, nor had he confessed. But does the absence of the smoking gun imply innocence of knowledge of the policy and of complicity in the action? Hoover's memoranda serve more to prove the innocence of those who believed him than to prove his own innocence. When he told Tolson and Nichols he had denied leaking FBI files to any congressional committee, he had already been doing it for years. Tolson and Nichols knew that, for they had been participants in the leaks. They did not need the truth from Hoover. What they got from Hoover was the signal that the lie—the confidentiality of the files of the FBI—would continue. The absence of a smoking gun is less surprising than its presence would have been, for in that case the continuation of a policy based on deception and secrecy would have been jeopardized.

Documents released by the FBI from its Dissemination File between 1947 and 1955 show that the policy was a cause of constant concern to the FBI, confronted with the need to alert its agents to the importance of releasing information while denying they were doing so.[32]

Sometimes the FBI was concerned that the state or local official to whom it was releasing information was not reliable, and headquarters was at pains to notify its agents to check these officials against their own office files to make sure there was no derogatory information against them. Sometimes the need to maintain the anonymity of its "reliable contacts" was its concern. When Maryland adopted the Ober Law, requiring state and local government employees, including schoolteachers, to sign loyalty oaths, the FBI was afraid that the officials to whom it released information would be required to make the information available to the state attorney general in order for the suspects to be prosecuted or dismissed: "Reporting of this information to the State officials might conceivably result in embarrassment to the Bureau in that the subject is a teacher in the public schools and any attempt by our contact to have him removed as a result of the information furnished by us would eventually place our contact in the position that he would have to prove his charges and thereby disclose that his source for the information was the FBI."[33]

Limitations on the range of recipients to whom information was supplied were never inhibiting. The instructions to agents of October 27, 1951, read:

> The Bureau desires to reiterate the long-standing rule that information received from any source which is of interest to another governmental agency must be passed on to that agency. Information received from informants must also be furnished to whatever agency would be interested in receiving it.

In June 1953 the FBI revised Section 5 of its Manual of Rules and Regulations to codify its procedures for the dissemination of information. The manual pointed out exceptions to the apparent limitations in the Dissemination Policy. One of these limitations was the restriction of released information to material obtained as the result of FBI investigations. Headquarters called the attention of its agents to a major exception to this rule—"i.e., information received from reliable sources which reflects membership in any group declared as subversive by the

Attorney-General and public source information." Another limitation was the restriction of released information "only within the Executive Branch of the government," but there was a major exception here as well—"information pertaining to subversive activities" in certain public utilities and "in public and semi-public organizations within a state, should be furnished to a responsible local authority such as a governor, mayor or chief of police." The manual provided even for exceptions to exceptions. The general policy, for example, was that the information released must come from the FBI's own investigations. The exception was that information from "reliable sources" suggesting membership in an organization on the attorney general's list of subversive organizations or indicating that an individual is a security risk could be released. The exceptions to the exception were as follows: (1) the individual need not be a member of a subversive organization, but only on its mailing list; (2) the organization need not be on the attorney general's list, but should be "shown in Bureau files to be dominated or infiltrated by Communists." Given this degree of latitude, it is difficult to see how the FBI was limited in any way it chose not to be. It was, however, concerned that the leaks not be attributed to it: "In those instances where the Bureau's identity must not be revealed as the source," blind memoranda were to be used. These were to be "on plain white bond unwatermarked paper, be dated, and should bear the name of the subject across the top center of the first page"; they were not to use the symbols of FBI informants "or any phraseology which might identify the FBI as the source."[34]

The information the FBI collected—and the information it leaked—went beyond subversion. For the FBI, sexual deviance created security risks: "Wherever information is developed indicating that the subject (if a past or present employee of the government) may be a sex deviate or a security risk by reason of association with sex deviates, reports will be sent to the Civil Service Commission in order that they may keep up to date their central file on such individuals." Information on "sex deviates in the Legislative Branch" was disseminated to "designated individuals in the United States Senate, the House of Representatives," and—curiously—the "General Accounting Office, Government Printing Office, the Library of Congress and the Botanical Gardens. A specified individual was designated to receive information concerning sex deviates among employees of the Judicial Branch of the Government." Were these agencies selected by the FBI to be "safe" repositories of information it would be embarrassing to admit was kept in its own files? Repeated FOIA requests for information on the matter have produced only the statement that no documents can be found dealing with the policy set forth in the FBI memorandum of October 21, 1954.

The dissemination policy of the FBI was nondiscriminatory; anyone could become a victim of FBI violations of the law. Employees of the three branches of government were not exempt from the treatment afforded teachers. Derogatory information, however tenuous its connection with subversion, was leaked when and as it pleased the FBI to do so.[35] If the purpose of the effort was to provide evidence of criminality, it failed. But that was not its purpose—it was to intimidate, and in that it succeeded.

Conclusion

THIRTY YEARS AGO Louis M. Hacker, in an introduction to a new edition of Thorstein Veblen's *The Higher Learning in America*, pointed to some important differences between universities in Veblen's America and in ours. Veblen was right in worrying about the direction the universities were taking, Hacker wrote. In his time the direction was set largely by governing boards and presidents. Today we "would worry about the growing intrusiveness of the federal government, through its financing," which "more and more is directing research and compelling conformity." Hacker went on to say that many of the questions Veblen asked "are still with us today, although in somewhat different form."

The trail we have followed suggests that if fifty years were required for Hacker to bring Veblen up to date, only thirty years are required for us to bring Hacker up to date. Hacker's reference to government intrusiveness as responsible for directing research and compelling conformity is an important half-truth. The other half has to do with the university's side of the relationship. The government has not been an unwelcome guest; it has been an invited guest in campuses and quadrangles, and there is precious little evidence that the universities objected to, or even thought much about, the price that was being exacted for the benefits they sought. In a sense, a great potlatch was being celebrated: the government brought gifts, highly visible ones; the universities also brought gifts, research results in permissible areas. Each successful ceremony established the basis for another; and in time academic potlatching, like Kwakiutl potlatching, changed the character of the relationship between the two parties. Even more dangerous was the fact that, with time, the memory that matters had once been different—and therefore might be different again—was lost. A practice established presumably to support a culture eroded it. So it was with the Northwest native Americans.[1] And so it threatens to be with the universities and the government. The cure has created a disease that is not seen as pathology, but as "the way things are."

Accepting Hacker's critique, Veblen's description of the "academic executive" remains a useful point at which to start our analysis of the particular pathology we are concerned with. There is no code for the guidance of academic executives, Veblen writes, "with the sole exception of that mandatory inter-presidential courtesy that binds all members of the craft to a strict enforcement of the academic black-list—all of which leaves an exceptionally broad field for casuistry." Unlike the situation in the business community, "no standardization has here determined the limits of legitimate prevarication." Nor can such standardization be achieved so long as the academic executive must function as both the employer of the academic staff for whom he is responsible and, at the same time, "their confidential spokesman and their colleague in the corporation of learning." Under the circumstances, the academic executive has been "guided in effect by a meretricious subservience to extra-scholastic conventions, all the while that he must profess an unbiased pursuit" of knowledge and its diffusion. And he concludes: "One who purports to be a scientist . . . can gain popular approval of his scientific capacity, particularly the businessman's approval, only by accepting and confirming current convictions regarding those elements of the accepted scheme of life with which his science is occupied."[2]

Veblen's view that the tendency toward conformity in the university arises from the pressures of business is limited. In our world, the danger comes more from government and the response of academic statesmen to its pressures and blandishments. Nor does Veblen give enough weight to the culture of professionalism in providing a common outlook for both government and universities, and others too, for that matter. The problem is to explain how professionalism provides the cement that binds government and university together. How is a common culture created, Auden asked:

> Malinowski, Rivers,
> Benedict and others
> Show how common culture
>   Shapes the separate lives. . . .
> Who when looking over
> Faces in the subway
> Each with its uniqueness . . .
> Would not like to know what
> Influence occupation
> Has on human vision

Of the human fate:
Do all the clerks for instance
Pigeon-hole creation,
Brokers, see the Ding-an-
sich as Real Estate?[3]

E. M. Forster had an answer to Auden's question:

> We may expect a society that is highly centralised . . .; it shall be very tightly knit; it will be planned; and it will be bureaucratic. Bureaucracy, in a technical age like ours, is inevitable. The advance of science means the growth of bureaucracy and the reign of the expert. And as a result, society and the state will be the same thing. . . . In the future the only effective patron will be the State. The State is in a position to commission pictures, statues, symphonies, novels, epics, films, hot jazz—anything. It has the money, and it commands the available talent.

Like Max Weber, Forster saw the threat as coming from a bureaucracy that advanced like a glacier, a bureaucracy whose members were single-minded in pursuit of their mission—to do their duty and to convince others that they had to do the same. It was relentless and insidious—"Fabio-Fascism," Forster called it, "the dictator-spirit working quietly away behind the facade of constitutional forms, passing a little law (like the Sedition Act) here, endorsing a departmental tyranny there, emphasizing the national need of secrecy elsewhere, and whispering and cooing the so-called 'news' every evening over the wireless, until opposition is tamed and gulled. . . . This Fabio-Fascism," he says, is an old enemy. He quotes Kipling:

> He shall mark our going, question whence we come,
> Set his guards about us, as in Freedom's name.
> He shall peep and mutter, and the night shall bring
> Watchers 'neath our windows, lest we mock the King.[4]

Henry A. Kissinger has become famous for the practice of "shuttle diplomacy," but winging through the skies of the Middle East was not the only shuttle he was on, nor the most important. That was the shuttle among Cambridge, New York, and Washington—the red-eye express between academia and government—on which, no matter what he wore, he was fashionably dressed because he was consummately professional. In 1969 CIA Director Richard Helms, in pursuance of operation CHAOS, which had begun under President Johnson in 1967, to unearth alleged Russian, Chinese, and Cuban support for student and civil rights militancy, sent Kissinger in the Nixon White House a letter accompanying a CIA report on "Restless Youth." The report was based on an illegal investigation; Helms knew it—and so did Kissinger. Helms's letter of February 18, 1969, reads:

> In an effort to round out our discussion of this subject, we have included a section on American students. This is an area not within the charter of this Agency, so I need not emphasize how extremely sensitive this makes the paper. Should anyone learn of its existence, it would prove most embarrassing for all concerned.[5]

"And the night shall bring/ Watchers 'neath our windows"—Kipling and Forster were right. Helms had no reason to doubt Kissinger's prudence; the professor had become a bureaucrat. Or rather, what was the difference, when both accepted the same goal and agreed on the means to attain it?

Writing in the *New York Times* of August 25, 1991, about recent developments in the Soviet Union, Serge Schmemann asks why "the greatest evils were not the overt persecution of dissidents or the silly newspeak of Communist propaganda, nor even the pervasive controls of the political police, but the habits of the average Soviet citizen—the innate caution, the quickness to inform, the lack of initiative, the constant compromises." The power of the regime derived less from muscle than from corruption. In language reminiscent of that used by Forster and Kipling in describing tendencies in their own society, Schmemann describes the source of Soviet corruption—government "control of all benefits, services, pleasures and their distribution according to the loyalty of their citizenry." Many friends and scientific associates of Andrei Sakharov failed to support him "not so much because they feared direct retaliation, but because they stood to lose the comforts and privileges of their office, and especially the trips abroad." It is easier to say yes than to say no.

———

Why is it important to remember the history of the FBI and education, especially when so much of it deals with activities that were obviously grotesque, and when many concede the damage that was done but consign it to the bad old days? It's all so different now, we are told. Even if that were so, it would be no reason for forgetting the past. The memory of what was once done—and the consequences of what was done—alert us to the possibility that we are capable of doing it again. But is it true that it all belongs to an ancient and different past?[6]

Hardly a week goes by without reports of activities engaged in by the FBI and other intelligence agencies that are strikingly similar to the surveillance and harrying we have just examined. These include the harassing of political refugees and those who would give them asylum; the role of intelligence agencies themselves in matters running from illegal trafficking in drugs to end-around plays to circumvent existing laws and policies; the surveillance of hundreds of citizens and groups, beginning at least as early as 1981, opposed to Reagan administration policies in Central America, including the Council of Churches in New York, a number of union locals, the Maryknoll Sisters, and the Southern Christian Leadership Conference in Atlanta; the continuing animus of the FBI against blacks, extending to the treatment of its own agents.

Predictably, the White House denies that anyone there or on the National Security Council has any information about these matters. On those rare occasions when news of official misconduct erupts into the open, the FBI promises an internal investigation to "let the chips fall where they may." The chips never seem to fall; the investigations are interminable. An FBI spokesman, referring to the harassment of more than one hundred organizations in connection with its investigation of CISPES (Committee in Solidarity with the People of El Salvador), said cryptically: "Generically speaking, we're very hard on our own when mistakes are made." One of the most serious accusations made against the FBI was not cryptic at all: its investigation of CISPES was based almost exclusively on the information of an undercover informer, who later admitted that the investigation was simply an excuse for intimidation. The FBI directed its wrath against the admitted and contrite informer. William H. Webster, who was FBI director at the time the investigation began, was later promoted to be CIA director. Is this what the FBI spokesman meant by "we're very hard on our own?"

Following the FBI's admission of illegality in its CISPES investigation, the General Accounting Office attempted to inquire into violations of constitutional rights in connection with other investigations. According to the *New York Times*, it was stymied by FBI refusal to grant full access to its files. A federal judge in Arizona ruled that the FBI could not engage in "unbridled and inappropriate covert activity"—in this case involving undercover FBI informers in churches—that abridge the First Amendment right to freedom of religion. The FBI has recently admitted seizing tapes of tapped telephone calls without a warrant and keeping files on foundations—like the J. Roderick MacArthur Foundation—that have been critical of U.S. foreign policy.[7]

It is possible that some in the White House do lack information about these matters, though not for the reason they imply. The American Library Association, in its report "Less Access to Less Information by and about the U.S. Government," has charged that a "Government policy of secrecy existed" under which "documents were shredded and concealed, documents that should have been deposited in Government archives. . . . The Office of Management and Budget has clearly consolidated its government information control powers." The situation is this: the government engages in questionable, even illegal, activities; the government destroys the record of its activities; no matter—it's not a political problem anyway, but professional and managerial; finally, the White House knows nothing about it.

One such recent activity is the Library Awareness Program to get libraries to report on "suspicious characters" who use them. On September 18, 1987, the *New York Times* reported that staff members at a number of libraries in New York had been spoken to as "part of a national counterintelligence effort. . . . 'We're just going around telling people what to be alert for,' " said James Fox, deputy assistant director of the New York FBI office. "I find it amazing that a librarian could be supposed to recognize someone who is a national of a hostile power. . . . Does anyone with an accent come under suspicion?" the executive director of the American Library Association said. The director of Academic Information Services at Columbia University wrote to the American Library Association that she had been approached by two FBI agents who said the "library awareness program" was designed to alert librarians " 'to the use of their libraries by persons from countries hostile to the United States' and to provide the F.B.I. with information about these activities. I explained that we were not prepared to cooperate with them in any way [and] described our philosophies and policies respecting privacy, confidentiality and academic freedom." FBI Director William S. Sessions issued a report, "The K.G.B. and the Library Target, 1962–Present," claiming that Russian agents had been seeking information from libraries for twenty-six years, though "none of the information sought at the libraries was classified." He said the program would continue. On May 30, 1988, the *New Yorker* referred to the FBI's statement about the program: "It's a misconception that the F.B.I. is swarming around libraries. What we're doing in New York is educating librarians about what's going on. . . . Nobody's *making* them talk to us." The chairman of the American Library Association Committee on Intellectual Freedom, reporting on an FBI visit to the University of Utah library, said: "If Judge Sessions . . . wants us to believe that the program is restricted to New York, he has a map of the United States different from the one I have." Assistant FBI Director James H. Geer presented a frightening picture of the theft of "hundreds of thousands of items of microfiche" from scientific and technical collections. Have such thefts occurred? "I am sure that the widespread loss of hundreds of thousands of microfiche pieces would not have gone unnoticed by the library community," the Columbia University librarian said. Nearly two years after its pledge that "librarians don't have to talk to us," the FBI was identifying its critics: "After a number of librarians criticized the surveillance program . . . the bureau conducted inquiries to determine whether some of the critics had been influenced by a Soviet-backed effort to discredit the program." Within a few days after that disclosure, FBI Director Sessions denied knowing anything about the FBI check on librarians, but said he would have approved the investigation had he been asked: "It is natural for us to check. It is routinely done." Exactly: If it is "routinely done," Sessions did not need to be told. And if it is "natural," *not* to check is what would be surprising.[8]

═══

As for FBI involvement in matters affecting universities even more directly, what reason is there for believing that the sun now shines where once there were darkness and stealth? The hiring of former FBI and intelligence agents as campus security directors is even more common now that it was earlier. Can change for the better be detected in the memorandum of SAC Boston to Hoover, May 20, 1968, to which is attached a *Harvard Crimson* editorial of that same day:

> This article attacks the Director because of his testimony before the House Appropriations Committee relative to Students for a Democratic Society. The Harvard Crimson, of course, has never been favorable toward the Bureau or the Director and the editorial reflects that the Director has obviously incurred the wrath of these "kooks" because he spoke the truth. I do not think any purpose would be served in attempting to discuss this matter with any of the staff of this "rag."

The *Crimson* editorial had said: "It is the responsibility of the next President of the United States to remove him [Hoover] from office, and it is the responsibility of University administrators now to clarify the nature of maligned political organizations." If investigations are "routine" and "natural," must we not assume that the editorial earned the editors an FBI dossier?

More to the point is the question whether the FBI maintained the "arrangement" with Harvard officials that it worked out in the bad old days. On December 4, 1964, SAC Boston notified Washington headquarters that a *Crimson* reporter had called recently in connection with a meeting of *Crimson* representatives with Robert B. Watson, dean of students at Harvard College. The reporter had wanted "to ascertain exactly how confidential records are maintained by the various officers of Harvard University." The *Crimson* was interested in:

1. The nature of SA [name deleted] relationship with Harvard University
2. The kind of information SA [name deleted] asks for
3. What he is told by Harvard University personnel concerning these requests for information. . . .

Immediately thereafter SA [name deleted] called [three full paragraphs deleted].

Boston was advised to answer "No comment."

Two articles from the *Crimson* made clear why its reporter asked these questions. In the first, Dean Watson was accused of trying to depose the president of the Harvard-Radcliffe Socialist Club, who, he said, was ineligible because she was a special student. Another officer of the club reported that he had been called into Watson's office to be told "that a friend of Watson's—who was an FBI agent—wished to talk with him about the Second of May Movement." Watson said he had been contacted by an FBI agent who wanted to interrogate the student and that "he had simply wanted to notify the student that the FBI was investigating him."

In the second article, Robert Tonis, chief of the Harvard University police and a twenty-seven-year veteran of the FBI, admitted he had accompanied two federal customs agents to a meeting of the Socialist Club where they had interrogated a member in connection with an investigation of a Viet Cong movie "smuggled" into the United States. Tonis said it was the policy of the Harvard police to cooperate with the Customs Service, the Justice Department, the FBI, and other law enforcement agencies, but not to make its files accessible to them. Dean Watson also denied making university files available but admitted that his office sometimes arranged for meetings between the FBI and students. On December 9, 1964, SAC Boston, in a heavily expurgated memorandum to headquarters, reported that a Harvard official, very likely Watson, had told the FBI that the *Crimson* articles "represent 'the preconceived notions of one vicious, destructive guy who went into the interview with his mind already made up and who did a very poor job of reporting the true essence of the interview. . . .' Boston feels the articles in the 'Crimson' represent speculation on the part of its reporters as well as irresponsible reporting of the interview of Dean Watson. . . . Contacts of this Office with Harvard University have been consistent with Bureau policy."

These FBI documents of the late 1960s read like the earlier documents. On March 13, 1948, SAC Denver wrote Hoover that the Denver office used no student informants. Really? Well, yes; but then again, no. Denver had no need to use students; information could be obtained through other sources: "In most instances we obtain information from students, directly through third parties who are not students. The students are not aware that information they furnish to these third parties is being made available to the Bureau." Who were the third parties? No doubt there were many, but chief among them were university administrators.

On June 10, 1948, SAC Boston, engaged in an investigation of the American Association of Scientific Workers, requested permission of FBI headquarters, in pompous FBI English, "to go upon the campi of Harvard College and Massachusetts Institute of Technology in order to conduct investigation in these cases. It is noted that currently the Boston Division has informants in both organizations and that the greater bulk of the work will be done by these informants." Sometimes, however, it was necessary "to visit record offices of these schools in order to obtain additional identifying data concerning the members" of the organizations being investigated. Hence the request for permission for FBI agents to enter the campus to search out records. On July 8, 1948, permission was granted, with the usual proviso that "care and discretion" must be used so that "no embarrassment to the Bureau will result."

Shortly thereafter the FBI extended its role on college campuses—with the cooperation of college authorities. On August 24, 1948, SAC Boston asked FBI headquarters for blanket authority "to examine the records maintained by the office of the Registrar of various universities within this Field Division . . . from which records pertinent background data is available for identification purposes in investigative reports, and for possible future investigative leads." In making his request, SAC Boston was acting on well-established precedent:

> It appears that no serious consequence should arise from such blanket authority as Agents of this office are constantly interviewing college Registrars and examining college records, for example, at Harvard University, Boston University, Massachusetts Institute of Technology, and other schools and colleges within this Field Division. . . . In addition, inquiries are generally made of various alumni offices maintained by the colleges.

SAC Boston asked that the search through university documents, with the cooperation of university authorities, be allowed "in connection with Internal Security inquiries" as well as applicant investigations. Extending the scope of FBI activity would create no new danger of exposure. It was already being done. The main advantage would be that the FBI field office would be spared the necessity of requesting permission each time it entered the campus to use official documents. SAC Boston was asking for

> blanket authority to examine the records of the Registrar's office at schools or colleges in connection with Internal Security matters, in the same manner that such records are presently being examined with the volume of Applicant inquiries. . . . The Registrar's office of Harvard University is being contacted daily by Agents in connection with such inquiries and it would appear that no embarrassment could come to the Bureau by extension of such authority in connection with Internal Security matters.

Hoover saw the usefulness of SAC Boston's suggestion. Based on the endorsement by D. M. Ladd of the suggestion by SAC Boston, on October 5, 1948, SAC Letter No. 128, Series 1948, was sent to all FBI field offices. It would no longer be necessary to ask headquarters for authority "to contact the Registrars of any school, college, or other institution of public learning . . . for the purpose of obtaining from the school records pertinent background data and information useful for identification purposes or for the proper development of other investigative leads in security type investigations." There was one cautionary note:

> Of course, you must be assured that the Registrar is reliable and can be depended upon not to divulge the Bureau's interest in any inquiry. The Bureau will hold you personally responsible to see that no embarrassing situations arise from the exercise of this authority.

Even more chilling is the evidence of FBI–MIT cooperation in matters of faculty appointments and promotions well after the FBI was supposed to have reformed itself. On June 20, 1969, SAC Boston wrote to Hoover, "Subject—Cointelpro—New Left," concerning two persons, one a "Key Activist," the other on the Security Index. The first, a former president of SDS and then an organizer for the Boston Draft Resistance Group, was employed as a humanities instructor by MIT. The second, also employed in the Department of Humanities, was an assistant to "[name deleted] Associate Professor of Humanities." The appointments of both were subject to renewal as of July 15, 1969,

> at which time recommendations will be made as to whether or not they will be supported for the coming academic year. Boston currently enjoys an excellent relationship with [line and one-half deleted] is an established source of the Boston Office and is also a member of the [half line deleted]. Boston proposes to furnish [name deleted] with numerous public source data concerning [name deleted] and [name deleted] background, which identifies their connections and associations with SDS and the BDRE. . . .[9]
>
> It is believed that if MIT is in possession of all the public source material concerning [name deleted] and [name deleted] they would not reappoint them to their respective positions with the Humanities Department at MIT. This counterintelligence action would also frustrate [name deleted] who has been attempting to build up the Humanities Department at MIT with radical-type instructors. . . .
>
> The Bureau can be assured that any information furnished to [name deleted] will be kept confidential and that the Bureau's interest in this matter will be fully protected.
>
> The Bureau's thoughts on the above will be appreciated so that this counterintelligence action can be shortly initiated.

Within two weeks, SAC Boston had his answer:

> Provided you can be assured that the information will be used with discretion, you are authorized to contact and furnish [few words deleted] with public source material relating to [names deleted]. . . . On the occasion of your contact with [word deleted] you are to impress

upon [name deleted] the necessity for keeping the Bureau's interest in this matter in the strictest confidence. In addition, you are to make no recommendations to [name deleted] as to how [word deleted] is to use this information.

And it was done. On August 18, 1969, an employee of MIT, who was "an established source of the Boston Office, advised that as a result of the . . . material that was furnished to him confidentially relating to [names deleted] he was able to have their re-appointments to the staff of MIT cancelled. . . . [Name deleted] was very grateful . . . and indicated that all aspects of this operation would be kept confidential. Boston will remain alert for any other potential counter intelligence actions in regard to captioned group [Cointelpro—New Left]."[10]

It should be clear by now why it is no exaggeration to write of the "struggle" to write history and to remember it. "Is it true that a nation cannot cross a desert of organized forgetting?" Milan Kundera asks. If so, it is not for lack of trying. To forget the past or to alter it is the point of some of our most subtle, and ferocious, political battles. "People are always shouting they want to create a better future," he writes:

> It's not true. The future is an apathetic void of no interest to anyone. The past is full of life, eager to irritate us, provoke and insult us, tempt us to destroy or repaint it. The only reason the people want to be masters of the future is to change the past. They are fighting for access to the laboratories where photographs are retouched and biographies and histories rewritten.

To change the past by mastery of the future is an important point, but not, I think, Kundera's most important point: "Since we can no longer assume any single historical event, no matter how recent, to be common knowledge, I must treat events dating back only a few years as if they were a thousand years old." But why bother? Because "the struggle of man against power is the struggle of memory against forgetting."[11]

Since historical memory is one of the weapons against abuse and power, there is no question why those who have power create a "desert of organized forgetting." But why should those who have been the victims sometimes act as if they, too, had forgotten? Speaking of the blacklist in Hollywood, the daughter of one of the victims of the 1950s tells why it has been so difficult to communicate the pain and complexities of the period: it is "partly because people . . . are unwilling to re-experience the bitter emotions of the past by examining them [and] partly because the left itself is still so precious that everyone who fought for it wants to protect it from the ignorance of those who might not understand." In his last book, Primo Levi depoliticizes the point and makes it one of anguish. Both the guards and the prisoners at Auschwitz knew that by the standards outside the walls, what was taking place inside was incredible. Even if someone survived to tell the tale, who would believe it? Levi tells of a recurrent dream of the prisoners during their captivity: "They had returned home and with passion and relief were describing their past sufferings, addressing themselves to a loved one, and were not believed, indeed some not even listened to." If no one is listening, why speak? And yet, and yet . . . there must be a witness. He quotes "The Rime of the Ancient Mariner":

> Since then, at an uncertain hour,
> That agony returns
> And till my ghastly tale is told
> This heart within me burns.[12]

Not all the tales to be told are as ghastly as Levi's, but they are testimony to the struggle against power and abuse. William Lecky, the historian, was once invited as guest of honor to a dinner given by the Duchess of So-and-so. He was seated next to her, but she never addressed a word to him until the savory was being served. "And what is your name?" "Lecky, ma'am." "And what do you do?" "I'm a historian." "What a pity. I've always believed in letting bygones by bygones."

So do I, but history is not the story of bygones. It has been said that history is like another country; they live differently there. As migrants from that history we can no more escape it than those who migrate from country to country ever fully leave the place and time of their birth. History is more than the chronological precursor of the present. Walter Benjamin said that even the dead will not be safe from the enemy if he wins, because the battles of the past might be lost again if they are not fought and refought. Was this what the great Jewish historian Simon Dubnow meant, when in Riga in 1941, he cried out as he was dumped into the truck that took him to his execution?: *"Schreibt und far-schreibt"*—Write and record. Not to do so would be a great betrayal.[13]

Notes

Introduction

1. Reagan had been in touch with the FBI at least as early as September 17, 1941, when his name, along with a number of others, was sent to Hugh Clegg, assistant SAC in Los Angeles, as a possible informer. By 1943 he was meeting with FBI agents at Camp Roach, California. Anne Edwards, *Early Reagan* (New York, 1987), 302–6.

2. The FBI wrote on June 23, 1988, that it was providing a document concerning James B. Carey as a supplement to a release of *August 31, 1983;* it explained that deletions had been made under Exemptions (b)(1) and (b)(7)(D). The document itself is four pages long; every word has been deleted except the file caption, "Comintern Apparatus," and the city and date of origin, San Francisco, August 14, 1945. One wonders why the FBI considers this a "supplemental release." To conserve space, the FBI documents will not be separately cited by their specific serial numbers. They will, however, be identified in the text by date and some other distinguishing characteristic, such as author or recipient.

3. See, among dozens, Francis Dvornik, *Origins of Intelligence Services* (New Brunswick, N.J., 1974); George L. Mosse, ed., *Police Forces in History* (London and Beverly Hills, Cal., 1975); Richard Cobb, *The Police and the People: French Popular Protest, 1789–1820* (Oxford, Eng., 1970), esp. 49–54. On conspiracy theories, see Gordon S. Wood, "Conspiracy and the Paranoid Style: Causality and Dissent in the Eighteenth Century," *William and Mary Quarterly*, 3rd series, 39, no. 3 (July 1982): 407; Bernard Bailyn, ed., *Pamphlets of the American Revolution, 1750–1776* (Cambridge, Mass., 1965), vol. 1, p. 88. Nearly seventy years ago, Richard C. Cabot found the co-optation of "private" citizens into the secret police network as informers already so widespread in the United States as to

"render all civilized life impossible" because it destroys "our ability to trust our fellows." Richard C. Cabot, "Spies," *The Survey* 52, no. 7 (July 1, 1924): 379–81.

4. See the excellent study by Mary O. Furner, *Advocacy and Objectivity: A Crisis in the Professionalization of American Social Science, 1865–1905* (Lexington, Ky., 1975). Compare the conclusion of Dorothy Ross, who argues that after 1900 the professions perfected "the role of the academic expert who carried out the political goals of society rather than" lead "society to reformulate its goals. . . . Whether social scientists wished to retreat from the public arena altogether or only to hide the political implications of their work," basic quantitative or behavioral science and "scientistic euphemisms . . . were appropriate shields." Charles Rosenberg adds that in the half-century before 1920, it became increasingly clear that social intervention could be dangerous both to individuals and "the disciplinary needs of the nascent social sciences." Ross, "The Development of the Social Sciences," in Alexandra Oleson and John Voss, eds., *The Organization of Knowledge in Modern America 1860–1920* (Baltimore, 1979), 123–28; Rosenberg, "Toward an Ecology of Knowledge: On Discipline, Context, and History," in ibid., 443. Is the decline of university autonomy the result of unwelcome intrusiveness by government agencies, even intelligence agencies, or has it been sacrificed by university administrators to gain goodwill and cut costs? The CIA has recently announced that in 1985 it created an "officer in residence" program under which some of its "best and brightest" agents are sent to colleges and universities on one- or two-year teaching sabbaticals. At present, ten CIA agents are posted at universities from Harvard to Jacksonville in Florida. Since the start of the program, twenty-three agents have participated—paid for by the CIA, not the universities. At Boston University, two courses are offered: Intelligence in a Democratic Society for undergraduates and Problems in Strategic Intelligence for graduates. The CIA agent who teaches the courses says he "can't teach students to be spies. But I can teach them the theory of it. Any student studying history, political science or international relations ought to know about intelligence." The CIA–provided and CIA–paid instructor adds: "The only thing I have to avoid is confirming whether or not things are true." "Veritas," "Veritas Vos Liberabit," "Lux et Veritas"—university variations on the theme are endless. But Truth seems expendable when "theory" is free. Do the universities offering such courses seek faculty approval in the way new courses and teachers normally are approved? Are faculty members and students told about the auspices of these courses? *New York Times*, April 14, August 11, 1991.

5. McGeorge Bundy, "The Battlefields of Power and the Searchlights of the Academy," in E. A. J. Johnson, ed., *The Dimensions of Diplomacy* (Baltimore, Md., 1964), 2–3, 12, 14–15.

6. Jane Takeuchi, Fredric Solomon, and W. Walter Menninger, eds., *Behavioral Science and the Secret Service: Towards the Prevention of Assassination* (Washington, D.C., 1981), Report of an Invitational Workshop on Behavioral Research and The Secret Service: Problems in Assessing and Managing Dangerous Behavior, March 8–10, 1981, sponsored by the Institute of Medicine of the National Academy of Sciences, esp. 7–11, 33, 40–41, 53–54, 56–57, 76, 112. See also the fascinating paper by Dr. Joseph T. English, director of psychiatry, St. Vincent's Hospital, New York City, "The Secret Service and the Mental Health Delivery System: Problems and Prospects," in ibid., 155–58.

7. Philip Green, "The Obligations of American Social Scientists," *The Annals of the American Academy of Political and Social Science*, vol. 394 (March 1971), *Social Science and the Federal Government*, 13–16, 26–27; U.S. Congress, Senate, Committee on the Judiciary, Subcommittee on Constitutional Rights, *Army Surveillance of Civilians: A Documentary Analysis* (Government Printing Office: Washington, D.C., 1972), 4, 9, 21, 42, 44, 45, 51, 69, 72, 76, 81, 91; Frank Donner, *The Age of Surveillance* (New York, 1980), 301–4. The Subcommittee on Constitutional Rights of the Committee on the Judiciary pried loose from the Department of the Army considerable material on its investigations of persons and organizations suspected of possible involvement in expected urban uprisings. Information was systematically collected on, among other things, increases "in number of incidents which reflect minority group rebellion against authority," "sharp increases in absentee rate of discontented minority groups," "identity of newspapers, radio, or television stations and prominent persons who are friendly with the leaders of the disturbance," "high unemployment or menial work rate among discontented minority groups," "efforts by minority groups to upset the balance of power and the political system," "collaboration between subversive groups and non-white organizations," "women members" (of suspect groups), "manifestations of support by 'peace' organizations." Among the dozens of agencies receiving copies of the report were the National Security Council, CIA, FBI, Internal Revenue Service, Immigration and Naturalization Service, and the Subversive Activities Control Board. U.S. Congress, Senate, Committee on the Judiciary, Subcommittee on Constitutional Rights, Hearings, *Federal Data Banks, Computers, and the Bill of Rights* (Government Printing Office: Washington, D.C., 1971), 1125–37. The following two examples, which could be multiplied almost indefinitely, show the involvement of universities in these investigations. When Columbia University gave its students the option of closing their academic records to routine inspection by government investigators, the 108th Military Intelligence group in Manhattan persuaded someone in the registrar's office to disclose information from the closed files surreptitiously. President Malcolm Moos of the University of Minnesota testified that military intelligence agents regularly received reports, including surveillance photographs, from the university's office of admissions and records and police department on students and faculty. Ibid., Hearings, *Military Surveillance* (Government Printing Office: Washington, D.C., 1974), 185.

8. Bernard Malamud, *The Fixer* (New York, 1966), 314–15; Marc Bloch, *The Historian's Craft* (New York, 1953), 75–76, 91–92; "To Posterity," *Selected Poems of Bertolt Brecht*, trans. H. R. Hays (New York, 1959), 173.

9. Arthur Kinoy, *Rights on Trial: The Odyssey of a People's Lawyer* (Cambridge, Mass., and London, 1983), 129–35.

10. Harrison Salisbury writes that CIA director Allen Dulles came to the *Times* with the ubiquitous C. Tracy Barnes (of whom, more later) to meet with Orville Dryfoos, John Oakes, "Punch" Sulzberger, and Clifton Daniel about the Bay of Pigs, and he reports the claim made by Carl Bernstein that the Sulzbergers had agreements not to reveal information given the *Times* by the CIA. General Adler and Dulles, who had been classmates at Princeton, were "good friends" all their lives. When Dulles told Adler that he was suspicious of Sidney Gruson's "political reliability" and wished that he did not cover Guatemala, Gruson was removed; Adler passed Dulles's tip on to Sulzberger. Salisbury is pretty sure that

the *Times* went beyond its agreement not to publish material made available by the CIA; it provided cover for "intelligence people" on the *Times* staff and had a "liaison relationship" with Alfred C. Clark, the agency's man in New York. Cord Meyer of the CIA said that the "cooperation between the *Times* and the CIA" rested on "trust between the CIA and *Times* correspondents" that was based on social connections, their conception of the position of the United States in world politics, and their common view of the nature of the Communist danger. The reference to "trust" is noteworthy, since one of the main objectives of intelligence agencies everywhere is to sow distrust. Fear dissolves cohesion; each person stands alone, fearful of being watched and feeling that security lies only in cooperating. Harrison E. Salisbury, *Without Fear or Favor* (New York, 1980), 464–67, 493–99, 505–6, 585–86, 595–97. As to the relationship between the breakdown of trust and secret intelligence gathering and covert action, President Robert D. Cross of Swarthmore College wrote to U.S. Senator Sam Ervin, Jr., on May 3, 1971, asking that on-campus intelligence gathering and covert operations by the FBI be ended: "Even without the documents which report the FBI's intention to further paranoia . . . the upshot has been an extremely unhealthy growth of mutual distrust, in a college . . . where trust is essential to inquiry, debate, disagreement, and controversy." A university "must retain some autonomy if it is to remain a free institution. To the extent that that autonomy is subverted, unilaterally, clandestinely and by misrepresentation . . . the free college is effectively subverted." Subcommittee on Constitutional Rights of the Committee on the Judiciary, Hearings, *Federal Data Banks, Computers and the Bill of Rights*, U.S. Senate, 92nd Cong., 1st sess. (Government Printing Office: Washington, D.C., 1971), 1525.

On the friendship of General Greenbaum, who accompanied Adler to FBI headquarters, with the Sulzbergers and, going back to his Princeton days, with then cold-warrior George F. Kennan, see Salisbury, *Without Fear or Favor*, 114, and Gay Talese, *The Kingdom and the Power* (New York, 1969), 547–49.

11. Months after this introduction was written, Shirley Hazzard reported on U.S. investigative activities in the UN that are astoundingly like some of the major findings of this work. She reports, for example, that U.S. investigating agencies were not unwelcome intruders into the UN. In 1949 Secretary General Trygve Lie made a secret written agreement with the State Department whereby, in violation of basic civil liberties and of the UN charter, U.S. applicants for and incumbents of positions in the secretariat were screened, without their knowledge, by U.S. agents. The chief architect of "that conspiracy," as Hazzard calls it, was Byron Price, head of the U.S. Office of Censorship during World War II and assistant UN secretary general for administration and financial services, who told the McCarran Subcommittee on Internal Security that while in official written documents between the U.S. government and the UN every precaution was taken to make it appear that no laws or regulations were being violated, in practice "American directives for dismissals of U.N. personnel" were presented, in the words of the State Department witnesses before the subcommittee, through "informal, confidential, word-of-mouth channels." Why did the State Department make known to the McCarran committee its secret practices in the UN? To show how far it would go to frustrate UN internationalism. What was the reaction of the McCarranites and McCarthyites? In later chapters we shall see

that cooperation by university administrators and public officials to prove to the FBI the sincerity of their efforts to purge radicals only whetted the appetite of J. Edgar Hoover for more victims. In early 1953, after President Harry Truman ordered the official screening of all U.S. employees of the UN, Trygve Lie approved the setting up of a branch office of the FBI at UN headquarters; surveillance, interrogation, and fingerprinting of U.S. staff members were involved. Neither the press nor any high UN official protested the action. The UN attitude, like that of university administrators who hoped to win FBI approval, was stated by Oscar Schachter, a senior legal officer at the UN and later a professor of law at Columbia University. Nearly fifty years later he expressed bewilderment that "what I could not get across to them [the staff] is that the investigation was concerned only with loyalty and that they had nothing to fear in replying to these personal questions." Schachter still seemed puzzled that though "only" loyalty was involved, some employees insisted on taking the matter seriously. Nor did he seem to understand that there might be some to whom principles like the maintenance of a nonpolitical international civil service and due process were worth defending, even at great personal risk.

One of Hazzard's greatest contributions is her assessment of the long-term social and political costs of the UN's kowtowing to U.S. political power. That contributed to the degeneration of the UN, of course, but it had additional serious consequences. It led, she writes, to a state of arrested moral judgment, marked by the habitual emblems of immaturity: demands for approval, an incapacity for individual or collective self-questioning, no admission of error, no effort at self-recognition.

Similarly, the secret arrangements between the FBI and the universities and labor unions affected those organizations but, in addition, were of considerable importance in prolonging the Vietnam War, producing the climate in which Watergate and Irangate could flourish, and affecting the course of the civil rights movement. Dissenters were purged; centers of potential dissent were destroyed; dissent itself became illegitimate because unpatriotic; and, very quickly, the very conception that there might be alternatives to current policy literally became unthinkable. Hazzard concludes with the words of Edward Gibbon: "The freedom of the mind, the source of every generous and rational sentiment was destroyed by the habits of credulity and submission." Shirley Hazzard, *Countenance of Truth: The United Nations and the Waldheim Case* (New York, 1990), 7, 8, 14–15, 20, 27–29, 75.

A particularly pertinent example of the domestic consequences of foreign policy can be found in the conclusion of Alfred W. McCoy, *The Politics of Heroin in Southeast Asia* (New York, 1972), 362, which shows how U.S. drug involvement was an artifact of Cold War foreign policy: "In the final analysis the American people will have to choose between supporting doggedly anti-Communist governments in Southeast Asia or getting heroin out of their high-schools." But how could U.S. drug involvement be challenged when it was a consequence of a foreign policy that met opposition by equating dissent with treason? In 1972 Cord Meyer, Jr., a high-ranking officer of the CIA, and Laurence R. Huston, CIA general counsel, approached the publisher of the McCoy book in an effort to have it altered. David Wise, *The American Police State: The Government Against the People* (New York, 1970), 198.

Chapter 1

1. *New York Review of Books,* April 28, May 26, July 14, 1977.

2. An FBI document I received after I had written my letter casts light on this. On July 28, 1954, SAC Boston wrote to the director: "From information provided the Boston Division by other individuals having Harvard Corporation appointments, it appears that Dean Bundy is insisting that former Communist Party members who now have Harvard Corporation appointments shall provide the Federal Bureau of Investigation a full and complete account of their activities in the Communist Party and shall at the same time identify all individuals known to them as participants in activities of the Communist Party and its related front organizations."

3. Wise, *American Police State,* 205, 222.

Chapter 2

1. SAC Los Angeles to Director, April 22, 1948; SAC Cincinnati to Director, April 24, 1948.

2. SAC Cincinnati to Director, Feb. 8, 1949.

3. Memorandum for the Director, June 1, 2, 1932.

4. Col. L. R. Forney to Hoover, May 27, 1943, with enclosure; Confidential Memorandum, Army Base, Boston, March 2, 1945.

5. FBI Report, Boston, May 24, Aug. 21, 1943.

6. FBI Report, Boston, March 10, May 16, Dec. 5, 1947, April 30, Nov. 19, 1948; memo, SAC Boston to Director, July 16, 1948; Director to SAC Boston, July 27, 1948; FBI Report, Feb. 1, Aug. 8, 1948, March 7, Nov. 1, 1950. It could only have been a Harvard official who told the FBI that "the John Reed Club had not registered as a student organization for the 1950–51 academic year at Harvard. . . . No formal communication had been received from the John Reed Club to indicate its existence as an organization and particularly in connection with the requirement that all student organizations formally register with the Dean's Office at Harvard University each year for approval prior to their activity on the university campus." SAC Boston to Director, Nov. 7, 1950. The FBI reported, also on the basis of information supplied by an informant, that the John Reed Club chose not to comply with the Harvard requirement to submit membership lists for fear that "the government might at some future date demand these lists in relation to its loyalty investigations of Government employees." FBI Report, Boston, Feb. 28, 1952. By that time, the university had already made the membership lists available to the FBI.

7. Memo, SA [name deleted] to SAC Boston, Dec. 19, 1960; memo, SAC Boston to Director, Jan. 4, 1961.

8. Attached to FBI Serial No. 100-28341-17-13.

9. *Harvard Crimson,* June 9, 1949.

10. *Harvard Crimson,* June 23, 1949. For more on the Ober-Clark episode and Conant's participation in it, see chapter 5.

11. "Rules and Regulations on Conduct of Interviews," Section 87, Security Investigations, paragraph 5A: "Restrictions upon . . . investigations and interviews with individuals connected with institutions of learning."

12. FBI Report, "Donald Howard Menzel," Boston, Aug. 25, Sept. 1, 1949,

New York, Sept. 14, 1949; memo, SAC Albuquerque to Director, March 22, 1950; memo, A. Rosen to A. H. Belmont, May 29, 1950; Director to SAC Chicago, May 10, 1951; SAC Chicago to Director, May 26, 1951. On March 30, 1950, the head of the Washington field office sent Hoover four copies of a letter from the American Committee for Democracy and Intellectual Freedom, cited by the House Committee on Un-American Activities as "subversive," of which Menzel was listed as a National Committee member. Others included Walter Rautenstrauch, Ruth Benedict, Robert S. Lynd, Wesley C. Mitchell, Harlow Shapley, Roland Bainton, Joseph Warren Beach, Walter B. Cannon, Henry Steele Commager, Abraham Flexner, Christian Gauss, Frank P. Graham, Alice Hamilton, Kirtley Mather, Allan Nevins, George Sarton, and James T. Shotwell. On October 25, 1955, Hoover sent a memorandum to the director of the National Security Agency concerning Menzel, now identified as "Consultant, National Security Administration." Attached to the memo is a note: "Donald Howard Menzel, prominent scientist, Harvard University, admitted former membership American Committee for Democratic and Intellectual Freedom which was cited by HCUA as subversive. In 1942 he attended meeting sponsored by Congress of American-Soviet Friendship and made short speech (complimentary to Russia) on his expedition to Russia in 1936 . . . to study effects of eclipse in that country. . . . Reportedly closely associated with Harlow Shapley."

13. Material on Parsons can be found in FBI Main Files #62-60527-16867, #62-60527-16872, #62-60527-28031, all relating to the UNESCO investigation. FBI reports on Parsons are in files #100-390459-1 through 55. It is from these serials that the quotations in the text have been taken. When, in his written interrogatory and in his appearance at his hearing, Parsons claimed that his relations with Harlow Shapley were limited largely to matters relating to the National Science Foundation, he no doubt thought that no one could take exception to his involvement in such a professional, nonpolitical matter. He did not know, as we do, that for J. Edgar Hoover the establishment of the National Science Foundation and Harlow Shapley's interest in it were proof of the Communist conspiracy.

14. FBI Report, San Francisco, Oct. 2, 1950; FBI Report, Washington, D.C., Oct. 10, 1946; memo, SAC Washington Field to Director, Sept. 24, Oct. 2, Nov. 6, 1946, with enclosures.

15. This account is based largely on the following documents (letters, unless otherwise noted) in the DeVoto file: Stanley J. Tracey, assistant director, FBI, to Jay Hughes, *Harper's Magazine*, Oct. 21, 1949; Caskie Stinnett to Hoover, Oct. 3, 1949; Hoover to Stinnett, Oct. 11, 1949; SAC Letter No. 96, Series 1949, Oct. 13, 1949, calling attention to DeVoto's article and Hoover's reply and asking that both be made the subject of a special conference of all FBI agents; Hoover to Frederick Lewis Allen, Oct. 17, 1949; memo, V. P. Keay to H. B. Fletcher, Nov. 2, 1949; Allen to Hoover, Oct. 17, 1949; Hoover to Allen, Oct. 20, 1949; Russell Lynes to Tracey, Oct. 28, 1949; Keay to Fletcher, Oct. 18, 1949; L. B. Nichols to Clyde Tolson, Nov. 23, 1949; Tracey to Russell Lyons [*sic*], Dec. 3, 1949; Charles O. Blaisdell, Pres., Society of Former Special Agents of the FBI, to Editor, *Harper's*, Dec. 19, 1949; between Daniel Mebane, Publisher, *New Republic*, and Hoover, Oct. 20, 1949, et seq.; Keay to A. H. Belmont, March 29, 1950.

16. The navy file on DeVoto was indeed checked. Hoover was notified that

it included (1) an article in the *People's World* of February 27, 1948, listing him as one of the signers of a statement attacking the House Un-American Activities Committee, and (2) "a short sketch of DeVoto's life . . . which reflected that . . . upon enrolling as a Freshman at the University of Utah in 1915 he quickly established himself as an 'intellectual revolutionary.' That particular year four professors on the University of Utah faculty were dismissed for subversive teachings. . . . DeVoto had among his collection of books a copy of 'Das Kapital' which he prized very highly." Memo, D. M. Ladd to Hoover, Oct. 19, 1949. Both the FBI and ONI were concerned that DeVoto's call for noncooperation with the intelligence agencies would tend to dry up intelligence sources. On November 17, 1949, Edward Scheidt, SAC New York, wrote the director about the FBI's having been turned down on a request for information by someone who had cited the DeVoto article as his reason for refusal. The next day the informant called the FBI to agree to be interviewed; he was. Hoover wrote on Scheidt's memorandum: "[Name deleted] after his first crack should not have been interviewed subsequently. He should never be approached in the future. If one wishes to align himself with the DeVoto school of thought as against his country's interest then he is privileged to do so and should be so listed.—H." The ONI report supplemented what the FBI had ferreted out: DeVoto had protested the refusal of the mayor of Boston to issue a license for a public meeting at which Mrs. Gerhart Eisler, the wife of a Communist official, was to speak; he attacked the ban in Boston on the sale of Lillian Smith's *Strange Fruit;* he had urged "utmost care" in the conduct of loyalty investigations. Telegram, SAC Boston to Director, Oct. 4, 1949. He was a member of the advisory council of the Society for the Prevention of World War III, which "includes among its officials individuals who have been associated with pro-Communistic activities," as well as of the Cambridge chapter of Americans for Democratic Action, and had been denounced by William H. Chamberlin in the *New Leader* and by a rural Illinois newspaper, which advised "New York authorities: keep your eye on Bernard DeVoto, this guy is playing 'possum, he is a package of dynamite and when you least suspect or expect it, he'll drive a knife into the heart of New York." Memo, M. A. Jones to L. B. Nichols, Oct. 5, 1949.

17. Jacobson had been in touch with the FBI earlier about anti–FBI statements allegedly made by DeVoto. Memo, Nichols to Tolson, Nov. 23, 1949.

18. A copy of DeVoto's "Easy Chair" article is filed with the Jones-Nichols memorandum. Only with DeVoto's death did the FBI call off its investigative dogs. On November 18, 1955, SAC New York sent the director a clipping from the New York *Journal-American* of November 14, reporting the death of DeVoto: "As the Bureau is well aware, DeVoto wrote a scurrilous attack against the Bureau in *Harpers* in October 1949." Someone in Hoover's office added: "DeVoto removed from 'List of Persons Not to be Contacted—11/28/55.' " It is the last item in his FBI file.

19. Quinlan J. Shea, Director, Office of Privacy and Information Appeals, U.S. Department of Justice, to Sigmund Diamond, March 9, 1981.

20. The quotation from Fisher is from his letter to Hoover, marked "Personal and Confidential," of October 27, 1949.

21. Affidavit of Special Agent David L. Smith, *Sigmund Diamond v. FBI et al.*, Ca 79-C-3770, U.S. District Court, Southern District of New York, pp. 48–50.

22. Memorandum to the Members of the Listening Post, Report of December 8, 1954, Meeting with Staff of Joint Committee on Internal Revenue Taxation, pp. 1–6, Records of the University, Columbia University Files, Low Library, New York, N.Y. I am indebted to the authorities of Columbia University for access to this and other university documents. The same document may be found in the archives of Yale University. Whether it is in the Harvard University archives cannot now be determined, because Harvard has invoked its rule barring access to its corporation records for a period of fifty years.

23. "Admittedly, it is difficult to scrutinize an organization from either the information with which it is willing to part, or from those effects of its activities which by sheer accident become a matter of public knowledge." Otto Kirchheimer, *Political Justice: The Use of Legal Procedure for Political Ends* (Princeton, N.J., 1961), 204 n61.

Chapter 3

1. For a discussion of the effort to persuade President Bok to change the Harvard fifty-year official secrets rule, see Sigmund Diamond, "Keeping Secrets," *Harvard Crimson*, Jan. 11, April 5, 1984. The announcement reaffirming the fifty-year rule was made on the day Harvard officially opened the papers of President A. Lawrence Lowell on the Sacco-Vanzetti case—fifty years after the deposit of the Lowell papers and fifty years after the execution of Sacco and Vanzetti. One might wonder whether President Bok takes seriously the arguments in the much-praised books by his wife, Professor Sissela Bok, *Lying* and *Secrets: On the Ethics of Concealment and Revelation*. But one has no cause to wonder about the consequences of his decision: he provided a defense of executive privilege that not even presidents of the United States used.

2. Robin W. Winks, *Cloak and Gown: Scholars in the Secret War, 1934–1961* (New York, 1987), 41–45, 79–80, 315, 382–83.

3. Bundy, "The Battlefields of Power and the Searchlights of the Academy," in Johnson, *Dimensions of Diplomacy*, 2–3, 15. Five of the six lecturers represented in the volume were from the academy—Bundy, Henry Kissinger, Walt Rostow, James R. Killian, Jr., and A. A. Berle. The publication of the book was made possible by a grant from the J. M. Kaplan Fund, which had earlier provided financial assistance to the Johns Hopkins School of Advanced International Studies. As if in illustration of the main point of Bundy's lecture, the Kaplan Fund was later identified as a CIA conduit.

4. Stephen F. Cohen, *Rethinking the Soviet Experience: Politics and History Since 1917* (New York, 1985), 8–9, 10, 12–13, 16–17. One of the major themes of Cohen's book is the interpenetration of bad history and bad policy. This is a problem that Cohen does not fully resolve. His book, useful in many ways, hardly begins to show the intimacy of university-government cooperation at Harvard and elsewhere, and the cloak of secrecy in which that cooperation was concealed. As a result, it fails to suggest problems that have both a historical dimension and current policy implications—the disappearance of the autonomy of "private" organizations and the historical roots of executive secrecy characteristic of Watergate, Irangate, and similar episodes.

5. Anthony Cave Brown, ed., *Drop Shot: The United States Plan for War with the Soviet Union in 1957* (New York, 1978), 15, 19, 22–23, 25–28; T. H.

Etzold and J. L. Gaddis, eds., *Containment: Documents on American Policy and Strategy, 1945–1956* (New York, 1978); *Foreign Relations of the United States, 1950*, vol. 1 (Washington, 1977), 282–91. Recently more evidence was disclosed on the close connection between political intelligence and military planning during the Cold War when a number of European political leaders, including Prime Minister Giulio Andreotti of Italy, revealed that NATO, under CIA auspices, had organized, armed, and trained clandestine organizations in all Western European countries to carry out military operations against the Soviet Union. It has been charged that the organizations, right-wing politically, stockpiled some of the weapons they were provided with and may still be operating. *New York Times*, Nov. 14, 16, 1990; *Time*, Nov. 26, 1990, p. 44.

6. Winks, *Cloak and Gown*, 382–84; Cohen, *Rethinking the Soviet Experience*, 10.

7. George Fischer, *Soviet Opposition to Stalin: A Case Study in World War II* (Cambridge, Mass., 1952), 114, 144.

8. Memo, SAC Boston to Director, Jan. 27, 1949. On October 27, 1952, SAC Boston notified FBI headquarters that an earlier Boston letter of March 2, 1949, had reported that Dimitri Shimkin, a senior research center staff member, had been told by Baroch that "Baroch could be placed in a position having to do with intelligence work in the Department of State, and that Professor Donald McKay was to spend one day each week from March until June, 1949, in Washington, D.C., attempting to place graduate students of the RRC in the intelligence services of the War, Navy, Air Corps and State Departments." A Boston letter of February 25, 1949, stated that Baroch had reported "that Merle Fainsod of the RRC told him that the RRC would supply intelligence officers to the USAF." I have been informed by Mr. Charles O'Connell of the Sociology Department of UCLA that in these same FBI documents, sent to him *after* having been sent to me, Baroch's name has been deleted.

9. Memos, SAC Boston to Director, Aug. 17, 1951, Oct. 27, 1952. Kluckhohn had been the subject of FBI investigation since 1943, when accusations were made against him in connection with an episode on the Navajo reservation in New Mexico. One official of the Bureau of Indian Affairs, who spoke to the FBI about the matter in July 1954, was concerned that an investigation "made at Harvard College . . . might result in an unfavorable reaction there and the ultimate loss of this individual [Kluckhohn] as a consultant. . . . He advised that they are vitally concerned with the outcome of the investigation no matter which way it turns and are equally interested in seeing it terminated as soon as possible so that they can be governed in their future dealings with this person, whose services they value highly and who they are anxious to use if prosecution is not instituted or the investigation fails to support the original accusation." The Bureau of Indian Affairs official was told that the FBI had no intention to investigate, and that the U.S. attorney had declined to prosecute "because the case could not successfully be presented. . . ." In fact, the FBI had investigated the charges at the request of the U.S. attorney in Santa Fe, who asked in November 1943 that "an investigation be conducted with a view toward prosecution." All this information was then sent by Hoover to James P. McGranery, assistant to the attorney general. We do not know whether Harvard University knew of this FBI investigation. If so, it did not damage his career there. Equally important is whether Kluckhohn knew that the U.S. attorney in Santa Fe had requested an

investigation "with a view toward prosecution." If Kluckhohn did know, he would have had powerful incentive for being cooperative. Memo, SAC Boston to Director, July 5, 1944, with attachment; FBI Report, El Paso, Nov. 4, 1943; FBI Report, Phoenix, January 12, 25, 1944. On December 7, 1943, George J. Gould, director of the Security Division of the Office of the Secretary of Defense, wrote Hoover for the FBI reports of the episode on the Navajo reservation: "In view of the [half line deleted] subject's critical position in the Department of Defense, it is believed the above statements may be vital to a pending interrogation of subject and proper determination of subject's security reliability." Memo, sender's and recipient's names deleted, Aug. 13, 1951; memo, SAC Boston to Director, Sept. 7, 1951; Gould to Hoover, Dec. 7, 1953.

10. Memos, Brenton Gordon to SAC Boston, April 12, 1949; SAC Boston to Director, Feb. 11, 16, 25, 1948; March 2, April 12, May 5, June 11, Aug. 18, 1951; March 12, May 5, 1952.

11. Memos, SAC Boston to Director, Nov. 29, 1947; SA [name deleted] to SAC Boston, April 3, 1948; Jan. 17, 1949; Oct. 3, 1950; May 24, 1951.

12. Cherrington to Hoover, Dec. 7, 1949.

13. Letter, [name deleted] to Hoover, Boston, Oct. 30, 1952; Hoover to [name deleted], Nov. 6, 1952.

14. Memos, SAC Washington Field to Director, March 17, 1954; Director to SAC Boston, April 9, 1954; FBI Report, Boston, April 14, 1954; memo, M. A. Jones to Mr. Wick, Oct. 19, 1966; memo, SAC Chicago to Director, March 29, 1954; FBI Reports, Washington, D.C., July 15, 1954; Boston, May 24, 1954; Washington, D.C., June 24, 1954; memo, Raymond A. Bauer, Fund for the Republic, Sept. 9 (?), 1955. The Erlichman notation may be found in FBI Reports, Atlanta, June 2, 1954, and New York, June 16, 1954. The documents themselves do not reveal exactly why Erlichman was sent copies, but it should be remembered that in the Nixon White House he coordinated political intelligence for the administration. This included wiretapping, hiring John Caulfield and Anthony Ulasewicz for political espionage and surveillance and arranging to pay Ulasewicz's salary, receiving reports from the FBI, supervising—with the assistance of Charles Colson—the work of the White House Plumbers Unit, arranging with high CIA officials, including Director William Colby, to help E. Howard Hunt in his "black box" jobs for the White House, and ordering the Internal Revenue Service to investigate the tax returns of political enemies. About the investigation of the tax return of Lawrence O'Brien, Democratic Party chairman, he said: "I ordered them [the IRS] to turn up something and send him to jail before the election. . . . Unfortunately it didn't materialize." He was convicted for his role in the illegal breaking and entering of the office of Daniel Ellsberg's psychiatrist. Considering the connection of Bauer and William Remington, it is not unlikely that Erlichman, ever on the prowl for conspiracies, was looking for one that might provide political mileage for Nixon. Wise, *American Police State*, 17, 21, 62, 79, 109–10, 156, 228, 251, 253, 336, 338.

Chapter 4

1. I am greatly indebted to Mr. Charles O'Connell of the Sociology Department of the University of California (LA) for suggestions that led to additional research on the Russian Research Center and the Carnegie Corporation.

Mr. O'Connell's work-in-progress goes beyond a discussion of the Russian Research Center; it is, as well, an inquiry into the sociology of knowledge—the relations between intellectual work and the milieu in which that work is created.

2. I gratefully acknowledge the permission of the Carnegie Corporation of New York to examine and quote from their archives (hereafter cited as CC).

3. E. R. Guthrie, Executive Officer, Academic Personnel, University of Washington, to John W. Gardner, June 13, 1947, Harvard University–Russian Research Center file, Carnegie Corporation Archives (hereafter cited as HU-RRC, CC); JG, Office of the President, Record of Interview, Subject: Russian Studies, July 11, 1947, HU-RRC, CC; memorandum, "Russian Studies," July 14, 1947, HU-RRC, CC. Compare Gardner's list of major research projects with those in the May 1953 "Five Year Report and Current Projects" of the Russian Research Center. That inventory includes projects on Soviet bureaucracy, Communist ideology, the relation of the Soviet Communist Party to Communist parties elsewhere, the acceptance or rejection of Communist ideology by older cultures, psychology and social life (based on interviews with former Soviet citizens), attitudes toward authority in the factory and in the polity, religion, public opinion, all themes that had been emphasized by Gardner. The center was under the supervision of an all-Harvard Executive Committee of which Kluckhohn was chairman and Parsons and Inkeles were members. Raymond V. Bowers was not a member of the research center staff, as had been recommended by Gardner; he was, however, director of the Human Resources Research Institute of the U.S. Air Force—about which more later—which granted a large contract to the research center for fieldwork in Germany in connection with the interviewing of Soviet émigrés, the program that so interested Alexander Leighton. Gardner's second suggestion concerning immediate activities at Harvard was echoed by Kluckhohn. Announcing the Carnegie grant, he said that "a 'planning seminar' to survey and collate existing American information on Russia will be started by the center in February." In short, both of Gardner's objectives were adopted. SAC Boston to Director, Dec. 12, 1947, Sept. 10, 1953.

4. Gardner to Kluckhohn, July 29, Sept. 5, 1947; Kluckhohn to Gardner, July 23, 1947; memorandum, "CD and Frederick Osborn," Sept. 30, 1947; memorandum, JG, Oct. 6, 1947; unsigned memoranda but dictated by JG, Oct. 13, 16, 1947; unsigned memorandum, "Proposed Program on Russia, Harvard University," Oct. 15, 1947—all in HU-RRC, CC.

5. Memo, "SHS and Walter Ellis—Russian Program at Harvard," Jan. 5, 1948, HU-RRC, CC.

6. Calendar of "Follow Up Correspondence and Conferences Relative to the Russian Research Center at Harvard University," undated but sometime after June 2, 1948; memoranda, "JG and Irene Hay," "JG and Stuart Hughes, Assistant Director," Feb. 18, 1948—all HU-RRC, CC; Kluckhohn to Gardner, Russian Research Center, Correspondence, 1947–48, A–G, Harvard University. The John Gardner of these documents is not easily assimilated into the picture that developed especially after his service in Lyndon Johnson's cabinet. But some credibility is added to a story told in the recent biography of William F. Buckley, Jr. In July 1968 Richard M. Nixon asked his assistant Pat Buchanan to get Buckley's advice on a vice-presidential running mate. Buckley suggested Gardner, "a renowned liberal." Perhaps Buckley knew something the rest of the world

did not know. John B. Judis, *William F. Buckley, Jr.: Patron Saint of the Conservatives* (New York, 1988), 295.

7. Kluckhohn to Gardner, March 9, 1948, with attached Interim Report—HU-RRC, CC.

8. Memorandum, "JG and Clyde Kluckhohn, Director," March 30, 1948; "Blue Sheet—JG and Kluckhohn," Sept. 7–10, 1948; Dollard to Kluckhohn, Feb. 23, 1949; Kluckhohn to Dollard, Feb. 10, 1949; memorandum, "JG and Clyde Kluckhohn, Director," June 1, 1949—all HU-RRC, CC.

9. Assistant Secretary, Carnegie Corporation, to James Bryant Conant, Jan. 23, 1951, with enclosure; Frederick Osborn to Clark Armstrong, Aug. 1, 1951—both HU-RRC, CC.

10. Record of Interview—CD and James B. Conant—breakfast in Washington, Sept. 7, 1951—J.B. Conant file, CC; Cross Reference Sheet, Blue Sheet—CD and James B. Conant, Sept. 4, 1951; D.D.T., Memorandum for Counsel, Harvard Russian Research Center—HU-RRC, CC. The statement that the Champlain faculty member was not one of those under FBI suspicion raises questions: How did the Carnegie Corporation know which faculty members were suspected by the FBI? How did it know that this one was not?

11. "Notes on Russian Research Center Achievement," HU-RRC, CC.

12. Carnegie Corporation Project, Oral History Research Office, Columbia University: transcripts of interviews with Buck, 3–4, 25, 36, 40, 45, 48; Osborn, 62, 67–68, 83–84; Parsons, 21, 23, 28, 30–31, 32–34; Josephs, 122–23, 125–26, 128; Dollard, I, 146–47, 156; II, 173–79, 193–95, 270–72; Burgess, 40–42; Wriston, 213; Haskins, 236–38, 241–42, 243–46, 249–50; Marvel, 62, 68, 70. Buck's distinction between academic and administrative appointments is almost identical with McGeorge Bundy's. He makes clear that Harvard's continuation of Hughes in his teaching position depended on Carnegie's picking up the tab for the four remaining years of Hughes's five-year appointment. But suppose Carnegie had not done so. Would Harvard have kept Hughes on? If not, as Buck strongly suggests, what remains of the distinction, at least as far as academic freedom is concerned, between academic and administrative appointments? Hughes remembers the episode differently. S. M. Lipset, in *Education and Politics at Harvard,* basing his account on what Hughes had told him, writes that Hughes had said that no one at Harvard put any pressure on him to resign. Years later, Hughes wrote that the prevailing view at Harvard was that the Carnegie Corporation had gone too far and that he "had shown commendable institutional loyalty in resigning." Was it "institutional loyalty" or Provost's Buck's warning that he would do himself great harm by making an issue of the matter? It was a disturbing situation for Hughes: "Certainly the best indication of my divided mind was that I escaped by departing for a long summer in Europe." H. Stuart Hughes, *Gentleman Rebel: The Memoirs of H. Stuart Hughes* (New York, 1990), 207–9.

Florence Anderson, a longtime Carnegie staff member, was stunningly frank in discussing Carnegie-government relations. The corporation had never been concerned with political beliefs before the McCarthy period, she said. And since then? "Yes, we have, since. I think, again, it is a matter of degree. I don't think we have supported scholars whom we knew were way to the left. We certainly haven't supported any whom we knew was an avowed Communist":

INTERVIEWER: But your tendency now, or your practice, is to check a man out before you give him a grant?

ANDERSON: We always check them out.

Florence Anderson's statements sound like a script for a contemporary play. On November 13, 1989, Lynne V. Cheney, chairman of the National Endowment for the Humanities, issued new rules governing how recipients of direct grants from the endowment—including foundations and universities—must handle subgrants. How far has the endowment gone in screening subgrantees? In the case of the National Humanities Center in North Carolina, an observer for the endowment sat in on the discussion of the selection of "the entire list of fellows, most of whom are supported by non–N.E.H. funds." As the director of the center said: "One could imagine that the presence of government observers in a private institution might produce results which none of us can fully foresee." Of course they can be foreseen, because they already have occurred. *New York Times,* Dec. 17, 1989.

Was Carnegie ever offered financial support or asked to do special studies, Anderson was asked. "No"; the CIA did that only with dummy foundations or those without professional staffs. Transcript, Anderson interview, II, 260–69, 278–80, 283; III, 456. The corporation was sensitive to the issue of CIA funding. When, in the late 1960s, it was revealed that the Kaplan Foundation had received CIA funds, Carnegie counsel must have inquired about two grants it received from the Kaplan Foundation to help finance an art directory. The Kaplan Foundation assured Carnegie that the money had not come from the CIA: "Their Board has passed a resolution stating that neither one of those grants came through C.I.A. funds. The C.I.A. funds that they received, they state, went into their Central-American leaders project, I believe." Transcript, Kenneth Holland interview, 24.

13. Briefs Prepared for Congressional Investigations, List of Microfilm Reels—Cox Committee—Working Papers, CC. Reels destroyed were Harvard U.—Russian Research Center, 1947 through 1953.

How Carnegie's general policy considerations manifested themselves in specific cases can be seen in the documents prepared by the staff for use by officers of the corporation and by counsel. The records of the corporation were meticulously combed to find out what connections it had with persons mentioned by the House Committee on Un-American Activities, the Cox committee and other investigating committees, and the FBI and in trials of suspected subversives. Charles Dollard was advised to consider the following questions:

When Louis Adamic made his proposal for a grant in 1938, what did you know about his general background? . . . Had you read his book *Dynamite—a History of Class Violence* published in about 1933? . . . What do you know of Adamic's activities in connection with the American Slav Congress, an organization condemned by the Un-American Activities Committee? . . . What part did the Corporation play in the selection of [Alger] Hiss as president of the [Carnegie] Endowment in 1947? What is your explanation of the cordial welcome given Hiss by the Corporation? This includes providing Hiss with free office space and [Pendleton] Herring and [Devereux] Josephs' nomination of Hiss for the Harvard Club. . . . What is your present belief concerning the truth about Alger Hiss?

Fortunately, the corporation "had little or nothing to do with" some suspects, like Alan Lomax (who had sometimes gone with his father on folk-song collecting trips, which had been supported by Carnegie grants to the Library of Congress), Carey McWilliams, the dancer Pearl Primus, and Frank Lloyd Wright. But there were closer connections with, among others, Mary Van Kleeck of Russell Sage (she was a "lifetime friend of Keppel, but the Corporation did not have many business dealings with her"), Mark Van Doren, Francis Henry Taylor of the Metropolitan Museum of Art, Ernest Simmons of Columbia, Harlow Shapley, Meyer Schapiro, the art historian, Frederick Schuman of Williams College, Ira Reid, Arthur Upham Pope, Gardner Murphy, Lewis Mumford, Robert S. Lynd, Philip Evergood, the painter, Irwin Edman, and Aaron Copland.

Carnegie felt forced to defend its connection with particular organizations and projects as well. Among the former, some hardly seem to require an attitude of defensiveness, like the American Council of Learned Societies and the Social Science Research Council. But some of those associated with the ACLS were troublesome. Dirk Bodde of the University of Pennsylvania, Arthur M. Schlesinger, Sr. (". . . identified with a few front organizations"), and Henry Sigerist, the historian of medicine, had been or were then members of the council; and members of ACLS committees had attended the so-called Waldorf Peace Conference. As to the SSRC, one of its directors in 1946 had attended the Waldorf Peace Conference and had written letters against the deportation of the composer Hanns Eisler, brother of the Communist Gerhart Eisler. Since Lindsley Kimball of the Rockefeller Foundation conceded that it had been a mistake for the foundation to have awarded a fellowship in music to Eisler in 1940—"Knowing what we now know, we would not today award this fellowship"—the nervousness of the Carnegie officials is not surprising. The organization and project that seem to have caused the corporation the most trouble were the Institute of Pacific Relations and the famous Gunnar Myrdal study of race. Of special concern about IPR was its connection with alleged Communists Frederick Vanderbilt Field and Owen Lattimore and with the journal *Amerasia,* and the fact that it had become the chief target of Alfred Kohlberg, leader of the so-called China Lobby, and of Senator Pat McCarran. More surprising was the list of questions prepared for counsel that he might expect about the Myrdal study: "Q. Why did the Corporation select . . . Myrdal . . . ? A. It was felt that the man selected should be a citizen of a country having no colonial or racial problems of its own. . . . Myrdal's name was originally suggested by Beardsley Ruml. . . . Q. Why was Doxey Wilkerson, even then an active Communist, placed in charge of one section of the study? A. . . . The Corporation . . . gave the assurance that Myrdal was to have the final decision to select whomever he pleased to collaborate in the study. Wilkerson was Myrdal's suggestion, and, particularly in the light of the results, this selection was a mistake, as Myrdal himself recognized. . . . The Corporation found [his work] contained too much radical partisanship." Questions were also asked about Myrdal's tolerant, sometimes even friendly, attitude toward the National Negro Congress, the Southern Negro Youth Congress, the Southern Conference on Human Welfare, the Urban League, and the NAACP. The suggested answer was that Myrdal attempted to take into account the activities of all reform organizations, but that, with the help of Ralph Bunche, he knew which organizations were under Communist influence: "Perhaps the best endorsement of the study is the Communist attack upon it." Answers to

Basic Questions . . . on the Role of Foundations, Their Policies, etc.; "Memorandum for Counsel on Basic Principles . . .," May 15, 1952; memorandum to Mr. Dollard from Mr. Good, June 6, 1952; "Memorandum for Counsel—Miscellaneous Individuals," F. A., June 30, 1952; Memorandum to Mr. Dollard, J.[ohn] P. G.[ood], Nov. 17, 1952; memorandum, "Questions Submitted by Counsel," April 29, 1952; "Memorandum for Counsel—Proposed Revision of Questions and Answers on Support of IPR," May 29, 1952; *ibid.:* "Questions and Answers on Support of IPR," June 10, 1952; "Questions and Answers on Support of IPR," May 6, 1952; "List of Names in John Good's IPR Brief of 1/25/52"; "Notes on Lattimore's Grants," June 30, 1952; "Memorandum for Counsel—Questions and Answers re *The Negro in America,*" undated but 1951. All in Cox Committee—Working Papers, CC.

On cooperation with the Rockefeller Foundation, see Elling Aannestad to Lindsley Kimball, Counsel, Rockefeller Foundation, with copy to Charles Dollard, July 7, 1952; Memorandum for Counsel from E. A., June 9, 1952, responding to Dean Rusk's request for information on "governmental efforts to establish and encourage . . . cultural interchange with Russia"; memorandum, Dollard to Staff, Dec. 11, 1951.

Two recent books by Ellen Condliffe Lagemann, *Private Power for the Public Good: A History of the Carnegie Foundation for the Advancement of Teaching* (Middletown, Conn., 1983) and *The Politics of Knowledge: The Carnegie Corporation, Philanthropy, and Public Policy* (Middletown, Conn., 1989), exemplify "official stories"—what an organization would like others to believe of it. She does not raise the possibility that intelligence considerations may have had something to do with the support Carnegie gave to the Russian Research Center, and she is virtually silent on the Cox and Reece investigations. But why? The documents are in the Carnegie archives, to which she had access and must have seen. We know the panicky response of Carnegie to the Cox committee investigation. Yet Professor Lagemann's discussion of that reaction is limited to a statement that Carnegie redesigned its annual reports and increased their circulation to improve its public image.

14. Raymond A. Bauer, Alex Inkeles, and Clyde Kluckhohn, *How the Soviet System Works: Cultural, Psychological, and Social Themes* (Cambridge, Mass., 1964), v–vii, chapter 1. The project, under Air Force contract No. 33(038)-12909, ran from June 1950 until September 1954. The unpublished reports of the project were submitted to the client agency—Air Research and Development Command, Human Resources Research Institute, Maxwell Air Force Base, Alabama—and from there to various other intelligence agencies. Technical Research Report No. 23, "Structure and Functioning of the Lower Party Organizations in the Soviet Union," for example, was approved for release by the acting director of research and commander of HRRI, sent on to the Counter Intelligence Division, director of Special Investigations of the Air Force, and by it to J. Edgar Hoover of the FBI. F. L. Welch to Hoover, Sept. 7, 1954, FBI Files.

15. Raymond V. Bowers, "The Military Establishment," in Paul F. Lazarsfeld, William H. Sewell, and Harold L. Wilenski, eds., *The Uses of Sociology* (New York, 1967), 234–74. For a time, Charles Dollard of Carnegie was chairman of the academic panel on human relations and morale. Bowers was executive director of the Committee on Human Resources from 1947 to 1949 and did staff work for a number of panels. The postwar connections in social science

research among Harvard, the military, and the Carnegie Corporation capitalized on relations established earlier. Professor Samuel A. Stouffer directed studies for the Research Branch of the army's Information and Education Division. That branch had its origins in the Joint Army and Navy Committee on Welfare and Recreation, set up in 1941 through a grant from the Carnegie Corporation to assist the military services by enlisting support from private community groups. At the same time, the army's Intelligence Division was planning a survey of army morale under Stouffer. The work was facilitated by Major General Frederick H. Osborn, director of the Information and Education Division, who had his own connections with the Social Science Research Council and the Carnegie Corporation. Within a few years of the end of the war, the military had established an intricate series of connections with the Defense Research and Development Board, the Operations Research Office of the Johns Hopkins University, the Rand Corporation, HumRRO at George Washington University, the Human Resources Research Center, the Human Resources Research Laboratory, the Human Resources Research Institute at Maxwell Air Base—whose largest beneficiary was the Harvard Russian Research Center—and many others. Gene M. Lyons, *The Uneasy Partnership: Social Science and the Federal Government in the Twentieth Century* (New York, 1969), 103–9, 138, 141–45, 172–73.

16. FBI Report, Washington, D.C., March 17, 1954. Bauer informed Kluckhohn about his security problems and the FBI interest in him. The "biggest security problem is my relationship with William Remington. . . . As I have already informed you, I agreed to meet Remington on the evening of the day I testified to the counsel of the House Committee." He had been persuaded by a "security-minded friend" to meet in a private apartment. Since he was "more worried about newspaper publicity than being shadowed by any Federal agent," he did so. "If I had thought for a moment" that either was being shadowed— "as I now suspect—I would have insisted on meeting him in the hotel lobby." Bauer to Kluckhohn, undated, Russian Research Center, Refugee Interview Program, Correspondence A–Bi, Harvard University Archives.

17. Memorandum, Director to SAC Washington Field Office, Nov. 19, 1953. On the military side, the investigation was carried out by special agents of the 116th CIC Detachment, and the results were forwarded to John Sullivan of the FBI. All names of suspected employees are censored, but they are numbered. Some of the information is especially interesting:

> 5. [Name deleted] was once an official of the Jewish Anti-Defamation League of Chicago, an organization suspected of having some Communist affiliations. . . .
> 74. [Name deleted] was engaged in Communist activities to such an extent that his landlady was under the impression that he was studying to be a Communist at Harvard University.
> 131. [Name deleted] has been described as a strong believer in Civil Rights, so much so, that his reasoning is dominated by his emotions.
> 152. [Name deleted] is married to [name deleted] who is the former wife of [name deleted] in whose apartment subversive literature was found.

T. E. Smullin, Chief, Special Operations Branch, G2, to John Sullivan, FBI Liaison, Oct. 8, 1953, FBI Documents, HumRRO.

18. Memorandum, SAC Washington Field to Director, July 22, 1954, with attachments.

19. Microfiche copy of Davis Progress Report on the World Urban Resources Index, March 1, 1952, in BASR Collection, Lehman Library, Columbia University.

20. Bowers, in Lazarsfeld et al., *Uses of Sociology*, 241–42; Judith S. Barton, ed., *Guide to the Bureau of Applied Social Research* (New York and Toronto, 1984). Compare the results of the Iklé studies on the limited effects of atomic bombing with the conclusion of M. S. Sherry, *Preparing for the Next War: American Plans for Postwar Defense, 1941–1945* (New Haven, Conn., and London, 1977), 212–13: the Joint Intelligence Committee of the Joint Chiefs of Staff, after suggesting twenty Soviet cities as suitable for atomic bombing, added that such bombing was relatively ineffective against conventional military forces and transportation systems. Was this a left-handed admission that atomic bombing was useful only for the mass destruction of urban targets? See microfiche copies of BASR Reports, BASR Collection, Lehman Library, Columbia University; Siegfried Kracauer and Paul L. Behrman, *Satellite Peoples: Political Attitudes and Propaganda Susceptibilities of Non-Communists in Hungary, Poland, and Czechoslovakia* (New York, 1956). The vice-president of International Public Opinion Research Corp., one of the subcontractors for HumRRO, which provided émigré interviews to the Bureau of Applied Social Research, was Richard C. Sheldon, who had been a student fellow at the Harvard Russian Research Center and a graduate in anthropology there. On May 29, 1950, Inkeles wrote Kingsley Davis about the proposal to interview Soviet DPs on the effects of Voice of America radio programs. Could the Bureau of Applied Social Research do the job? "The Air Forces are very interested in problems of psychological warfare, and some of the results of a study . . . would have both direct and indirect importance and implications for Air Forces activities in this area." If the bureau should go ahead, the research center could offer space in Cambridge and Germany, provided Columbia paid the bill. Inkeles to Kingsley Davis, May 29, 1950, Refugee Interview Project, Correspondence, Bo–C, Harvard Archives.

21. Russian Research Center, Harvard University, "Five Year Report and Current Projects" (Cambridge, Mass., May 1953), attached to memorandum, SAC Boston to Director, Sept. 10, 1953.

22. The letters are in the Merle Fainsod Papers, Correspondence Relating to Russian Research Center, N–Re, Pusey Library, Harvard University. At the end of his letter of June 30, 1948, to Kluckhohn, Parsons wrote: "By the way, it might be worthwhile for you to have these letters typed and I'd like a copy. I am keeping only very fragmentary notes—putting all the connected story into the letters. You can see that some of this stuff is of a character best not carried around with one but I am told U.S. mail is perfectly safe from here." On July 7 Kluckhohn answered: "I am having your letters typed in sequence." He asked Parsons if he had any objection to showing them to Professors Fainsod and McKay. On July 15 Parsons wrote Kluckhohn: "By all means show all my stuff to Merle and Don and Ed Mason if he's interested. Beyond that probably it wouldn't be wise to go with the more confidential things, but use your judgment." Some of the originals of Parsons's letters to Kluckhohn are in the folder "Parsons, Talcott—Letters from Europe," in RRC—Corresp. 1948–49, O–Si,

Pusey Library. These letters were first called to my attention by Charles O'Connell, to whom I am grateful. I have examined them in the archives myself.

Edward S. Mason, professor of economics and member of the Executive Committee of the Russian Research Center, at the time of the congressional committee hearings involving Harvard faculty members, was a member of the Faculty Advisory Committee, appointed by the Harvard administration. According to corporation member William Marbury, it was Mason who suggested the formula under which Professor Wendell Furry was put on probation. Ellen Schrecker, *No Ivory Tower: McCarthyism and the Universities* (New York, 1986), 398 n14. Jeremy Bernstein, in his review of physicist Victor Weisskopf's autobiography, says that the Harvard position put Furry at risk of imprisonment for contempt, by insisting that he testify about himself but need not name names. One must ask why Mason, appointed to assist Harvard faculty members, recommended a course of action that would lead to a contempt citation. Jeremy Bernstein, "The Charms of a Physicist," *New York Review of Books* 38, no. 7 (April 11, 1991): 48.

On August 3 Kluckhohn wrote Parsons to see one of the Russian experts in Germany, Dr. Ivan Nyman, whom Parsons had already cautiously referred to as Mr. N. RRC-RIP, Corresp. 1947–48, File M–Po. Kluckhohn wrote to Fainsod in Germany on August 18 about Nyman. His possible appointment to the Russian Research Center had been discussed by the Executive Committee and "presents real difficulties. Talcott took this up with PHB [Paul Herman Buck, the Provost] also, who said 'Harvard could not take any responsibility for getting him to the USA.'" If, however, Nyman were able to get to the United States, Buck would have no objection to paying him by voucher "as a consultant, but a corporation appointment is out of the question." He asked Fainsod to inform Nyman and Colonel Hoffman directly about the matter. Nyman was bitter about the Harvard turndown. The United States was admitting as immigrants its "direct former enemies whose hands are very often covered with the American blood," while rejecting those who considered Stalin as Enemy #1 and Hitler as Enemy #2. He was grateful for what Fainsod and others were doing to get him a job with the government, and felt he had to provide "more precise personal data than I released to you and, especially, to Prof. Parsons whom I gave a not quite adequate version of my past." He insisted that he had never been a member of the Communist Party or the Vlasov movement. He wrote Fainsod again requesting reconsideration of his apparent rejection by Harvard. His usefulness to the research center was not an issue; the only question was "the suspicion of political unreliability," that is, how deep were his anti-Soviet feelings? Colonel Hoffman and the CIC were the only ones to know his real story; he had concealed the full truth from Parsons and others to protect his parents. "I appeal to you and to Professor Kluckhohn to assist me in my difficult struggle for justice and to live as a free man." Nyman to Fainsod, Nov. 17, Oct. 31, 1949. Fainsod Papers, Corresp. Relating to RRC, File N–Re.

23. Poppe worked hard on his Harvard connections. On February 24, 1949, he wrote Eliseev about some of his work in the Caucasus and in Berlin; once again he claimed credit for saving "Mountain Jews" who were not "genuine" Jews. Kluckhohn wrote Professor Richard Frye of Harvard for a recommendation. On April 8, 1948, Frye wrote Kluckhohn that he knew of Poppe's connec-

tion with General Vlasov. He made the point that the State Department wanted him: "John Davies . . . is interested in him and would like to see him in some academic position in this country, especially if he could be available as a consultant to the State Department." On April 20 Kluckhohn informed Provost Buck that the Executive Committee of the Russian Research Center had authorized an appointment for Poppe for one year at $4,500 as research associate: "It seems to all of us that in Mr. Poppe we would be obtaining both a first class scholar and an invaluable informant on conditions in Russia, especially the workings of certain aspects of the government." Both the State Department and the army so much wanted to bring Poppe to the United States that they "would transport Mr. Poppe and his family without charge." Buck was prepared to approve the proposed appointment, on condition (1) that both the army and the State Department cleared Poppe and (2) that statements from Davies of the State Department and from Professor Carl Friedrich be obtained: "I need not remind you that you are working in a delicate field and it would be well in all such appointments to be protected in advance by documentary evidence." He also felt strongly that Poppe should be told that the appointment was for one year only. Buck to Kluckhohn, April 22, 1948. During the negotiations about the Harvard appointment, Poppe was aware that his work in Germany might create difficulties. On April 26 he wrote Kluckhohn that he had a clean record as to crimes, despite having been in Germany during the war:

> People who escaped from Russia or who were deported by the Germans to Germany and still remain there are suspected of having committed the most disgusting crimes in their native country. From this point of view I am perfectly all right and I have been cleared politically by the authorities. You can get complete information from the CIC in Frankfurt. . . . I was visited by Dr. Frye [of Harvard] and an American intelligence officer. The latter know everything about me. Do you know there was in Germany an institute called The Wannsee-Institut? [It was there that the Final Solution of the Jewish question was worked out.] That Institute possessed a very valuable library on Russia (80,000 volumes). If your new center has no library you must get the remainder of that library."

He added: "If the difficulty will be that the USA cannot openly take a former Russian subject because the Soviet authorities will protest, I can change my name if this is necessary." Since the Soviets were continuing to search for him, mail from Kluckhohn to him should be sent to Frankfurt, to the home of the father of his friend, Karl Heinrich Menges.

Not surprisingly, Poppe seems to have been less than completely candid in discussing his own activities. After the capture by the Wehrmacht of the city of Mikoyan-Shakhar, where he was teaching at the Pedagogical Institute, he defected to the Nazis and reported on Soviet targets, concentrations of Jewish populations, and the like. He worked for both British and U.S. intelligence after the war. The director of CIC Intelligence wrote: "The British feel that Mr. Poppe is valuable as an intelligence source and have asked me if it is possible for U.S. intelligence authorities to take him off their hands and see that he is sent to the U.S. where he can be 'lost.' " It certainly was possible. He was given the name of Joseph Alexandros and brought to the United States in 1949 under the protection of George Kennan and John Paton Davies. He was flown to Washington, where he worked with Carmel Offie, who, under State Department cover, was an official of the Office for Policy Coordination of the CIA, under covert operations chief Frank Wisner. Christopher Simpson, *Blowback: America's Recruitment of Nazis and Its Effects on the Cold War* (New York, 1988), 108–23.

Eliseev seems to have jumped the gun when he assured Poppe that the Harvard appointment would be made. Helen Parsons, Talcott Parsons's wife and administrative director of the research center, wrote Kluckhohn that she was "stunned" by Eliseev's guarantee to Poppe, in the light of a "hitch on State Department clearance." She also wrote to Poppe, in care of Menges's father in Frankfurt, that he should not count on an appointment by the fall of 1948 because "in your case various complications have arisen." The letters may be found in RRC—Corresp., 1947–48, Files A–G and M–Po. Poppe reports that Gustav Hilger, with whom he worked in Washington, had been brought to the United States "in order to help with plans for a future German government. . . . I became good friends with the Hilgers and visited them several times in Bonn after their return to Germany." Nicholas Poppe, *Reminiscences*, Henry G. Schwarz, ed. (Western Washington, 1983), passim, 200. George Fischer, who interviewed Hilger for his book on Vlasov, says that during the war Hilger worked in the German Foreign Office Committee on Russian Affairs and was quite close to Vlasov. Fischer, *Soviet Opposition*, 26, 32, 82, 137, 222. Hilger's guardian angel was George Kennan, who secretly obtained visas for him, together with new identification papers and top security clearance, and arranged for U.S. military transportation to bring him out of Europe. By the time of the Nazi invasion of Russia, he had been at the German embassy in Moscow for many years. He worked for Ribbentrop and became the chief political officer for Eastern Front questions in the foreign ministry. As liaison representative to the SS on German occupation of the Soviet Union, he was involved in the processing of the reports of the special killing detachments, the Einsatzgruppen. After he came to the United States in 1945, he shuttled for several years between Washington and Germany, protected by Kennan and Robert Murphy, the U.S. political adviser in Germany. Alfred G. Meyer, an associate of the Harvard Russian Research Center who collaborated on Hilger's book, *The Incompatible Allies: A Memoir-History of German Soviet Relations, 1918–1941* (New York, 1953), reports that Hilger got a generous gift from the Carnegie Corporation and did much of his work in the United States at the Russian Research Center and at the Johns Hopkins University, which served as a cover for his consulting assignment for the CIA's Office of National Estimates. Kennan very likely had Hilger in mind when he wrote to U.S. Ambassador John G. Winant: "If others wish . . . to pursue the illumination of those sinister recesses in which the brutalities of this war find their record, they may do so. [But] the degree of relative guilt which such inquiries may bring to light is something of which I, as an American, prefer to remain ignorant." That being so, he opposed the de-Nazification policy in Germany; rather than remove "the present ruling class of Germany," he would rather "hold it strictly to its task and teach it the lessons we wish it to learn." Simpson, *Blowback*, 6, 82, 88–89, 118; George P. Kennan, *Memoirs, 1925–1950* (Boston and Toronto, 1967), 179. Hilger's role helps provide the political context for the research center.

Poppe's friendship with Menges probably began in the late 1920s, when Menges was studying languages in Russia, where he was especially interested in the linguistic-cultural problems of Soviet nationalities. Karl A. Wittfogel, *China und die Osteuräische Kavallerie-Revolution* (Wiesbaden, 1978), 6–11. Wittfogel had known Menges since their association in Frankfurt at the Institute of Social Research in the early 1920s. They were in Russia together in 1928 and in Berlin in 1929, and they met again in New York when the institute became affiliated with Columbia University. In his autobiography, Poppe insinuates that the failure of the Harvard appointment to come through may have been due to Owen Lattimore, who had already raised "some objections . . . to my having stayed in war-time Germany as a refugee from the Soviet Union and worked for the German government."

Whether or not Lattimore had raised objections to Poppe, Poppe raised objections to Lattimore. Toward the end of 1951, Poppe writes, Professor George E. Taylor introduced him in Seattle to "a Mr. Benjamin Mandel," not otherwise identified, who asked him questions about Mongolia. The next day, the two met in Poppe's apartment; Mandel inquired further about Mongolia and the Institute of Pacific Relations. It is difficult to believe that Poppe did not know—or was not told by Taylor—who Mandel was. He had been a Communist; in fact, he was involved in the recruitment of Whittaker Chambers into the Communist Party. He became an investigator for the Dies Committee on Un-American Activities and chief investigator of the later House Un-American Activities Committee. He then moved on to the Senate Internal Security Subcommittee. At the time he interviewed Poppe, he was preparing a perjury case against Lattimore. Whittaker Chambers, *Witness* (New York, 1952), 207. In early 1952 Poppe was asked to testify before the McCarran committee about China, Mongolia, and the IPR: "Finally [February 12, 1952] the Committee got around to the main subject; they asked me whether I knew Owen Lattimore. . . . Soon more embarrassing questions were asked: Why is Lattimore giving a false picture of Mongolia? Is he not a secret Communist? Does he not want to mislead public opinion?" Poppe would say only, "I don't know." He claims he got a letter from Lattimore thanking him for not accusing him of being a secret Communist, but objecting to calling his work superficial. Poppe feels that what he said about Lattimore "under the circumstances prevailing at those hearings . . . was the least harmful thing I could have said. Therefore I regard it as unkind [of Lattimore] to call me an SS officer in one of his later books." In *Nomads and Commissars* (New York, 1962), 125, Lattimore called Poppe "a Soviet defector to the Nazis during the war and an officer in the Nazi S.S. [who] is even more anti-Soviet than anti-Mongol." Poppe's refutation was: "The Wannsee Institute in Berlin where I was assigned to work in 1943 was a branch of the Stiftung für Landerkunde [Geography Foundation] which, in turn, was an SS organization. However, I was not a member of the SS and, as a foreigner, could not have easily become one." Poppe, *Reminiscences*, 208–15, 303 n9; Kenneth O'Reilly, *Hoover and the Un-Americans* (Philadelphia, 1983), 186–87.

24. Record of Interview, "CD, JWG and Talcott Parsons," signed C. D., Sept. 17, 1948, HU-RRC, CC.

25. Record of Interview, "WM's Visit to Russian Research Center, Harvard University," signed W. M., Sept. 24, 1952, in HU-RRC, CC.

26. Bernard M. Malloy, Chief, Psychiatric Staff, Office of Medical Services, CIA, to Parsons, July 29, 1974, confirming an appointment he had with Parsons and another CIA officer, Dr. Bradt, in William James Hall on August 7, 1974, Talcott Parsons Papers, Harvard University Library. Parsons's political activities—especially his views on Berlin and his acting as psychiatric consultant to

the CIA—could only have contributed, had she known them fully, to the distress of his daughter, who died tragically in 1964. She had been overwhelmed, to the point of panic, by the Berlin crisis of 1961 and was dismissed from the Boston Psychoanalytic Institute, where she was a postdoctoral student, ostensibly because she was not treatable by psychoanalysis. She felt betrayed by her doctor. In the last of the letters she wrote to her father in Moscow in 1964, she said: "This is what an . . . important part of my conflict with Dr. A. [the analyst] . . . was about, since when I was in such a panic about nuclear war and the possibility of American fascism, he simply could not or did not see that people can have strong emotions about anything but their immediate personal relationships or whatever it is that happens before one is six years old." More than once she commented on her father's conservatism. She wrote Dr. Jerome Frank of the Johns Hopkins University in 1963 that she had been reading about the U.S. military-industrial complex. Whatever she knew of her father's political views and activities she could not have found sympathetic. See Winifred Breines, "Alone in the 1950's: Ann Parsons and the Feminine Mystique," *Theory and Society* 15, no. 6 (1986): 805–44.

27. Here, too, I acknowledge the kind assistance of Mr. Charles O'Connell of UCLA. His tracking down of many of the dramatis personae is an example of intelligent questioning and dogged determination. We emphasize somewhat different points; O'Connell is interested mainly in the sociological problem of the relationship between "scientific" knowledge and the social context in which it is produced; I, in how the specific details of Research Center activities throw light on intelligence agency–university relations.

Case's statement is in the *Washington Post*, Jan. 24, 1971.

28. Memos, Fred Wyle to Raymond A. Bauer, Nov. 12, 15, 1950, RRC-RIP, Corresp., A–Bi, Pusey Library. For examples of letters written to DP newspapers and others, attempting to answer rumors about the research center, see Alex Inkeles to E. R. Romanov, Verlag "Posev," June 21, 1950, RRC-RIP, Corresp., Pr–R; L. K. Andreev, editor, *Nabat*, to Bauer, Jan. 17, 1951, and Bauer to Andreev, Jan. 23, 1951, RRC-RIP, Corresp., M–Po; Inkeles to V. V. Pozdniakov, June 26, 1950, RRC-RIP, Corresp. M–Po.

29. #46, Memorandum on Conversations with Russian Members of the Faculty of the Regensburg School, July 5, 1949, Merle Fainsod Papers, Correspondence Relating Chiefly to RRC, Folder G–M; Fainsod to Dallin, Sept. 15, 1952, Barghoorn to Fainsod, Aug. 28, 1952, Merle Fainsod Papers, Corresp., 1930's–1970, Subject File—Faer–Ge folder, General Correspondence. Kunta wrote a report for the Harvard Project on the Soviet Social System. RRC—Project Reports of the Harvard Project on the Soviet Social System, 1950–54, Box 1.

30. Kluckhohn to Lt. Col. T. E. Hoffman, June 5, Aug. 10, 1950, RRC-RIP, Corresp. G–Human Resources; Inkeles to Hoffman, June 20, 1950, RRC-RIP, Corresp. G–Human Resources; Parsons to Hoffman, undated but 1948, RRC—Corresp., 1948–49, O–Si; Kluckhohn to Parsons, July 7, 1948, RRC—Corresp., 1947–48, P–Z; Hoffman to Conant, undated but 1948, RRC—Corresp., H–N.

31. Fischer to Fainsod, July 20, 1950, with attached Report, Merle Fainsod Papers, Correspondence, Miscellaneous.

32. Yakovlev and Kunta to Inkeles, Aug. 2, 1950, RRC-RIP, Corresp. Pr–R.

33. Bauer to Kluckhohn, Nov. 29, 1950, RRC-RIP, Corresp. A–Bi. Bauer

was optimistic, at least philosophical, about the political problem. Nothing could be done to prevent the attacks of the right-wing refugees: "My prediction . . . is that the decision of the State Department to work with the new emigration and more liberal political groups will eventuate in a rivalry and dissident policy, similar to what one found under the Nazis. I would not be too surprised if a strong cleavage developed." To help the institute obtain the legal status it needed, Bauer called on the assistance of Harvard Law School professor Robert Bowie, who was General Lucius Clay's legal adviser. Bauer did not want "our relations with it [the Institute] destroyed [because] it is essential for our continued operations." Bauer to Inkeles, Sept. 28, 1950, RRC-RIP, Corresp. A–Bi.

34. Kluckhohn to Yakovlev, June 29, Aug. 10, Oct. 9, 1950, RRC-RIP, Corresp. Pa–R. Some of the DPs used the submission of essays to seek admission to the United States and employment at the Russian Research Center. See, for example, Kulishev to "Deeply Respected Professor" [probably Kluckhohn], Dec. 30, 1951, RRC-RIP, Corresp., Human Resources–L: "If I might trouble you also with a question—is it possible for the Institute to provide for me real work of permanent collaboration at Harvard University. . . . With your cooperation I would willingly move to the USA." He claimed to have been a professor at Kiev, which he left in 1943 for Germany.

35. Memorandum on Defector Interview Project Agreement with Russian Library, Alex Inkeles, June 28, 1950, RRC-RIP, Corresp., Pr–R; William F. Diefenbach to Bauer and Inkeles, Feb. 6, 1951, RRC-RIP, Corresp., Pr–R.

36. Fischer to Kluckhohn, Aug. 17 (?), 1950, RRC-RIP, Corresp., D–F; Fischer to Kluckhohn, Inkeles, and Bauer, July 15, 1950, RRC-RIP, Corresp., D–F; Inkeles to Brig. Gen. M. Lewis, July 28, 1950, RRC-RIP, Corresp., Human Resources–L; Kluckhohn to Lewis, July 17, 1950, RRC-RIP, Corresp., Human Resources–L; Fischer to F. B. Stevens, Dec. 2, 1950, RRC-RIP, Corresp., D–F.

37. London to Belosselsky, June 15, 1951, RRC-RIP, 1950–1953, Paper on N.Y. Operation and Germany, Box No. 1–NY Operation; Belosselsky to London, Feb. 1, 1951, *ibid.*; Dallin to Inkeles, June 21, 1950, RRC-RIP, Corresp., D–F.

38. Minutes of Planning Meeting of July 18, 1950, RRC-RIP, Planning Memoranda and Minutes; memo, Inkeles to Bauer, Aug. 22, 1951, RRC-RIP, Corresp., A–Bi; Garland to Bowers, with copy to Kluckhohn, Nov. 15, 1951, RRC-RIP, Corresp., Bo–C: "Requirements of Estimates Division for Social Science Information," undated but almost certainly 1950; Evaluation Division, Special D/1 Requirements for Social Science Information; TAB "A," Air Targets Division Requirements for Social Science Information, APOIT-TP/Lt. Col. Sleeper . . . 26 May, 1950; summaries of correspondence, probably sent to Bauer; Inkeles to Wyle, Aug. 12, 1950; all in RRC-RIP, Corresp., A–Bi.

39. PPS 22/1, Policy Planning Staff, "Utilization of Refugees from the Soviet Union in U.S. National Interest," Department of State, March 4, 1948, "Secret," Copy No. 11, National Archives, Washington, D.C.; Simpson, *Blowback*, xiv–xv, 32–34, 102–3, 292–93; Clarence G. Lasby, *Project Paperclip: German Scientists and the Cold War* (New York, 1971), 5, 9, 58–59, 78–79, 90–98, 102–3, 134–35, 148, 174–77, 181, 195–98, 234, 265, 273–76. Paley's association with intelligence agencies was long-standing. In 1976 Sig Mickelson, former CBS News president, disclosed that Paley had had a relationship with the CIA at least since the 1950s; CBS had given press credentials to a CIA undercover

agent, the William S. Paley Foundation was a CIA financial conduit, and CBS had given the CIA outtakes from its programs and allowed the CIA to use its control booth at the UN to read the lips of Soviet delegates when Khruschev spoke. Frank Stanton and Edward R. Murrow kept J. Edgar Hoover informed of CBS programs and requested his comments. Louis J. Paper, *Empire: William S. Paley and the Making of CBS* (New York, 1987), 303–4, 162–63, 183–84.

The conclusion of the 1944 National Academy of Sciences report that German professors were "an island of nonconformity in the Nazified body politic" and withdrew into "the traditional ivory tower which offered the only possibility of security" hardly commanded universal assent then, nor does it now. Ten years earlier Professor I. L. Kandel, discussing the Nazi view of German universities in *The Making of Nazis* (New York, 1935), had written: "As centers of culture and education universities must cooperate in political and national tasks. . . . In place of the humanistic university there must be created the national political university. . . . institutions of higher learning . . . must give up their traditional aloofness and preoccupation with the quibblings of so-called research" (121–22). Did the universities provide a haven for the neutral, the disaffected, those in opposition? A half-century after Kandel another scholar concluded that by "1943 . . . the universities had shown that they had no stomach for conflict. Even Hitler recognized that, and while he expressed frustration at not being able to get the cooperation he desired from the churches, he often said that there was no such problem with the universities." Alice Gallin, *Midwives to Nazism: University Professors in Weimar Germany, 1925–1933* (Macon, Ga., 1986), 105, 86, 97.

One must wonder, therefore, why in 1988 McGeorge Bundy resurrected the 1944 argument of the National Academy of Sciences, indeed embellished it. Why did not German scientists produce an atomic bomb, he asked? Why, in fact, had they opposed making one? Bundy says that German scientists, led by Werner Heisenberg, never pressed their government to make a nuclear weapon during 1941 and 1942. They saw that weapons could not be produced in time to affect the war and were content to work to give Germany a leading role in "future peaceful uses of atomic energy." Their reluctance to push for a bomb, says Bundy, was overwhelmingly the result of Hitler's "personality"; his views of physics were "hopelessly confused" by anti-Semitism; "Jewish physics, he called it." From 1939 on, "the dominant motive" of most German physicists was to protect their science and themselves from Hitler's war. With Albert Speer's knowing help they succeeded. "There is a certain decency in what they did and did not do." He concludes with an appeal to remember that the Germans never entered the race for the bomb and that "the best of the German physicists never really tried." Bundy, *New York Times Magazine*, Nov. 13, 1988, pp. 45, 60, 64.

Bundy's conclusions are marred by an error especially unfortunate among historians: the notion that the outcome of an event is the result of the intention of those who precipitated it, as if the wills of other people, opportunity, resources, and the like play no part. If German physicists did not produce an atomic bomb, Bundy says, it is because they did not want to—and we should honor them for that. The argument has been rejected by a number of scholars. One major study of the physicists of the Third Reich concludes that an important reason for their lack of resistance to the Nazis was that they based their actions on "predictable consequences." Leo Szilard was convinced as early as

1931 that Hitler would take power, not because of his irresistibility but because there would be no resistance. Every possible action was evaluated by a single criterion: what would be its predictable consequence? Since it could not be logically demonstrated that any single act of opposition would upset the Nazi juggernaut, nothing, or far too little, was done. But in political life, since the consequences of an action are not wholly predictable, the basis for an act cannot be its presumed logical consequences alone but must include some consideration of moral and social responsibility. But, specifically, what about the physicists and their alleged aversion to the construction of an atom bomb? Was this aversion, if it existed, based on their character, their training, their professional code—or perhaps something else? A recent student, Alan D. Beyerchen, says the Germans did not produce a bomb because of (1) Nazi economic policy, including the decision to concentrate on short-term rather than long-range projects, (2) the inability of the theoretical physicists to organize the huge projects necessary for the production of an atomic bomb, and (3) the lack of a real sense of urgency—since German science could not produce a bomb in short order, how could American or British science? These reasons may not be entirely adequate, of course, but in no case do they suggest that the German physicists are entitled to the accolade of "a certain decency." Some, yes; the profession, no. Jonothan Logan argues that German physicists, even by the end of the war, failed to appreciate the implications of plutonium breeding or to determine the critical mass; therefore, they had not done the experimental work necessary for the production of the bomb. To cover up their slim accomplishments, they themselves invented the explanation that they had chosen not to develop atomic weapons—a tale now being transformed from a German "official story" to an international story. Jonothan L. Logan, Letter, *Physics Today* 44, no. 5 (1991). In his recent review of Victor Weisskopf, *The Joy of Insight: Passions of a Physicist,* Jeremy Bernstein argues persuasively that Heisenberg's failure to develop the bomb had to do with technical incompetence, not moral reservations. He quotes Hans Bethe as having told him that Heisenberg had never said anything to him or others about the morality of making a nuclear bomb. Bernstein concludes that the surviving documents show that German scientists were as eager as the Allies to make the bomb. They failed because of scientific errors. Bernstein, "The Charms of a Physicist," *New York Review of Books* 38, no. 7 (April 11, 1991): 47–50. Robert H. Marsh, professor of physics at the University of Wisconsin, writes that the notion that German scientists never seriously intended to present Hitler with a nuclear bomb, but instead were engaged in a subterfuge designed to preserve German physics, protect young scientists from conscription, and provide a source of energy for Germany's postwar reconstruction, is a "myth" that originated in Heisenberg's *Physics and Beyond.* The "myth" may correctly represent "Heisenberg's thinking after 1943, when the war was clearly lost and his project in the doldrums [but] it is clear that prior to this time he tried very hard (with limited success) to interest the Nazi regime in a vigorous nuclear weapons program." Letter to the Editor, *New York Review of Books,* June 27, 1991, p. 62.

But there are other difficulties with Bundy's analysis as well. Was Hitler's role decisive? "His view of nuclear physics, in particular, was hopelessly confused by his pathological anti-Semitism; Jewish physics, he called it." But the term "Jewish physics"—and its correlatives "German" or "Aryan" physics—were not of Hitler's coinage. The terms were developed and publicized not by Hitler nor even Alfred Rosenberg, but by two distinguished German physicists, both Nobel laureates, Philipp Lenard and Johannes Stark. The first volume of Lenard's treatise on physics, *Deutsche Physik*, is dedicated to Nazi official Wilhelm Frick. " 'German Physics?' one asks," and Lenard answers:

> I might rather have said Aryan Physics or Physics of the Nordic Species of Man, the Physics of the very founders of science. . . . There has developed a peculiar and wide-spread Jewish Physics. . . . Jewish Physics is only a delusive picture and a manifestation of the debasement of fundamental Aryan Physics. (Quoted in L. G. Montefiore, *The Spirit of the German Universities* [London, n.d.], 12, 13, 15)

Lenard and Stark never succeeded in winning the degree of support from their colleagues that they lusted for, but the fact remains that the concept of "Jewish physics" was of academic origin. One of the reasons for its failure to sweep the field lay in the opposition it encountered for political reasons from parts of the Nazi bureaucracy. Himmler, for example, did not back it, and Stark and Lenard had the bad judgment to seek the approval of Himmler's opponent, Wilhelm Frick. Werner Heisenberg, the hero of Bundy's account, sought—and won—the support of Himmler, an old family friend, in his fight against Stark and Lenard. Perhaps "there is a certain decency in what" Himmler did. When Heisenberg was interviewed by Samuel Goudsmit at the end of the war, Goudsmit wondered how much truth and falsehood would be blended to "give the impression of an 'inner exile,' despite the evidence." Malcolm C. MacPherson, *Time Bomb: Fermi, Heisenberg, and the Race for the Atomic Bomb* (New York, 1986), 165, 283, 290. Hitler's profound mistrust of "academic people" seems more often to have been contempt, based on a view of the professoriate that is not irrelevant to the response of the physicists to the Nazi program and to wartime science. Speaking of the professional civil service—of which the professoriate was part—Hitler said:

> Do you think perhaps that . . . we would not inherit the brains in droves? Do you believe that . . . this flower of the intelligentsia would refuse to serve us and place their minds at our disposal? This German middle class would take its stand on the famed ground of the accomplished fact. (Quoted in Beyerchen, *Scientists Under Hitler*, 10)

Finally, concerning the statement of the National Academy of Sciences that the professors withdrew into "the traditional ivory tower which offered the only possibility of security," the distinguished linguist Max Weinreich, examining the role of the German universities at the very time the NAS was issuing its report, concluded:

> As time progressed, the bulk of university scholars, of scholarly periodicals, of publishing houses were entirely Nazified. . . . With the political and military leaders, they proposed, instituted, and blessed the program of villification, disfranchisement, dispossession, expatriation, imprisonment, deportation, enslavement, torture, and murder. (Max Weinreich, *Hitler's Professors: The Part of Scholarship in Germany's Crimes Against the Jewish People* [New York, 1946], 241–42)

Gerald Reitlinger, *The SS: Alibi of a Nation, 1922–1945* (London, Melbourne, Toronto, 1956), 42, 477; Charles Wighton, *Heydrich: Hitler's Most Evil Henchman* (Philadelphia and New York, 1962), 210. See also the essays by Fritz K. Ringer (German universities), Telford Taylor (the legal profession), Gert H. Brieger (the medical profession), Alan Beyerchen (the physical sciences), and Thomas Hughes (technology), in Henry Friedlander and Sybil Milton, eds., *Holocaust: Ideology, Bureaucracy, and Genocide* (Milwood, N.Y., 1980); Alan D. Beyerchen, *Scientists under Hitler: Politics and the Physics Community in the Third Reich* (New Haven and London, 1977), x, 9, 197–98, 202, 206–7, 209. Beyerchen's general conclusion is of special relevance to one of the motifs of our own inquiry, the relation of academic professionalism to political behavior: "To what extent did adherence to professional values constitute opposition to National Socialism? The answer must be that it was not opposition at all. The maintenance of professional values amounted only to the denial of active support, not denial of support per se. . . . Professional opposition to Nazi theory was not the same as political opposition to the Nazi regime" (206–7). Particularly pertinent to the statement by the NAS that the "critical" attitude characteristic of scientific thinking would be especially useful for the democratization of postwar Germany is the conclusion of another scholar: "Did [the professors] express anger at the shameful interference of the State in the affairs of the university? . . . The year 1933 was crucial, and it slipped through the fingers of those very persons who were famous throughout the world for their careful research and their critical thinking. There was apparently no transfer of these values to the political scene." Gallin, *Midwives to Nazism*, 97.

This is a dangerous aspect of professionalism that seems to exist in quite different social and political contexts. In his foreword to Grigori Medvedev, *The Truth about Chernobyl* (New York, 1991), Andrei Sakharov wrote just a few months before he died: "These issues are so crucial that they cannot be left to technical experts and still less to bureaucrats, whose approach is too narrowly technical, too tendentious and sometimes prejudiced, as it is paralyzed by a network of mutual solidarity." See also Abraham Pais, *Niels Bohr's Times* (Oxford, 1991).

40. McKay to Young, Jan. 15, 1948, RRC, Corresp., 1947–48, H–O; Gardner to Kluckhohn, Dec. 23, 1947, RRC, Corresp., 1947–48, A–G; Kluckhohn to Davies, July 21, 1948, RRC, Corresp., 1947–48, A–G; Davies to Kluckhohn, July 27, 1948, RRC, Corresp., 1947–48, A–G; Kluckhohn to Kirkpatrick, July 9, 1948, RRC, Corresp., 1947–48, H–O; Kirkpatrick to Kluckhohn, May 10, 21, Aug. 3, 1948, RRC, Corresp., 1947–48, H–O. The Poppe episode is a salutary reminder that the political groups involved in the heating up of the Cold War did not all come from what has been called the Radical Right or the Paranoid Fringe, and to recall that Davies was under severe pressure from the China Lobby, McCarran, and McCarthy. He was fired by Secretary of State John Foster Dulles for "lack of judgment" in his political advice concerning Chiang Kaishek. That seems not to have caused him to change the views he expressed in his discussions with the research center. John Paton Davies, Jr., *Foreign and Other Affairs* (New York, 1966), 11.

41. Memorandum, McKay to Kluckhohn, March 8, Nov. 18, 1947, RRC, Corresp., 1947–48, H–O; Reynolds to McKay, March 5, 1948, RRC, Corresp., 1947–48, H–O; Shimkin to Kluckhohn, Aug. 3, 1948, RRC, Corresp., 1947–48, P–Z; Kluckhohn to Buck, June 13, 1949, RRC, Corresp., 1948–49, A–B. Like

university officials, foundation executives became nervous when CIA contacts threatened to become public; they protested that CIA use of foundation-supported field researchers endangered the CIA–foundation relations. Ford Foundation Director of Research Cleon Swayzee was sent to CIA headquarters to show that a different approach would be more productive: "If the cover blows on any one of these things, everything we're doing will be jeopardized. . . . It was much more in the national interest that we train a bunch of people who at a later time might want to go into the CIA . . . than it was for them to have one guy they could call their source of information." It was publicly disclosed in 1967 that the CIA had provided "the largest proportion" of the more than $1,000,000 spent by the African-American Institute in the 1950s. Well before, McGeorge Bundy, then President Kennedy's special assistant for national security affairs, gave assurances that any loss of CIA funds to the institute would be replaced by funds from the Agency for International Development. Edward H. Berman, *The Influence of the Carnegie, Ford, and Rockefeller Foundations on American Foreign Policy: The Ideology of Philanthropy* (Albany, N.Y., 1983), 61, 132. When the Congress for Cultural Freedom experienced serious financial difficulties in 1966 and 1967 after the exposé of its secret funding by the CIA, the Ford Foundation under Bundy agreed to provide it with a grant for five years of $4,650,000. Michael Josselson, executive director of the CCF, stated that the Ford Foundation had replaced the CIA as the CCF's main financial supporter. When Shepard Stone, who had been director of the Ford Foundation's International Affairs Program for the preceding fourteen years, was made Josselson's successor, George Kennan congratulated him: "The flap about CIA money was quite unwarranted. . . . I never felt the slightest pangs of conscience about it. . . . This country has no ministry of culture, and the CIA was obliged to do what it could to fill the gap. It should be praised for having done so, not criticized." This was neither the first nor the last time that Kennan referred to the use by others of "conscience" as a criterion for policy. In the politics of the Cold War, he was not himself bothered by the concept of "conscience." (See, for example, p.305 n.23). Peter Coleman, *The Liberal Conspiracy: The Congress for Cultural Freedom and the Struggle for the Mind of Postwar Europe* (New York, 1989), 220, 226–34.

Chapter 5

1. Director to SACs, March 27, 1953, FBI James B. Conant File.

2. FBI Special Inquiry on James Bryant Conant, Boston, April 3, 1953. David's comments about Conant should be taken seriously. They had been assistant professors at Harvard, and Conant accounted it "a great triumph . . . when I persuaded him to return to Harvard as a dean. . . . He was one of my oldest friends and certainly my most loyal and helpful one." James B. Conant, *My Several Lives: Memoirs of a Social Inventor* (New York, 1970), 440.

3. FBI Special Inquiry on James Bryant Conant, New York, April 3, 1953, Newark, April 6, 1953, Cleveland, April 7, 1953.

4. Ruth N. Wright (Clark's private secretary) to Sigmund Diamond, July 17, 1986; Clark's children, "with their inside knowledge of the Arboretum controversy made the happy decision that GC's papers" go to Dartmouth. Gerald T. Dunne, *Grenville Clark: Public Citizen* (New York, 1986), 170.

5. Conant, *Several Lives*, 213; the letters quoted here are appended to Conant to Clark, Nov. 14, 1937, Clark Papers, Dartmouth. I am indebted to the
Dartmouth College Library and to Clark's heirs for permission to quote from
his letters. Conant's attitude toward refugee Jewish professors has a history about
which *My Several Lives* is also silent. On June 2, 1922, during the debate on
President Lowell's proposal to adopt restrictive quotas on the admission of Jews
to Harvard College, the faculty voted down a motion by Professor Lawrence J.
Henderson to maintain the existing proportion of Jews until a special committee
on the matter submitted a report. Among those appointed by Lowell to the special committee was Henderson himself, on this matter perhaps Lowell's strongest supporter on the faculty. Conant voted in support of Henderson's motion.
Conant was being disingenuous when in his letter to Grenville Clark he implied
that he had little knowledge of Judge Mack. Judge Mack was a leader of the
opposition to Lowell, and Conant would certainly have known of him. Mack,
Professor Paul Sachs, and Walter Lippmann met with Henderson to get him to
change his mind about anti-Jewish quotas, but Henderson was adamant: Russian and Polish Jews were "very objectionable and morally inferior." A recent
student of the subject says that restrictive admissions continued throughout
Lowell's presidency and into Conant's. Marcia Graham Synnott, *The Half-Opened
Door: Discrimination and Admissions at Harvard, Yale, and Princeton, 1900–1970*
(Westport, Conn., and London, 1979), 63–71, 252 n33, 106–10, 117. The con-
frontation of early-Conant and late-Conant suggests that on other matters as
well, such as Harvard practice in the McCarthy period, discrepant accounts by
the two Conants might reveal the limitations of the "official" stories.

6. Conant, *My Several Lives*, 446, 452, 454–59.

7. Ober to Conant, April 26, 1949; Conant to Clark, May 9, 1949; Conant
to Ober, May 11, 1949, Clark Papers.

8. Chafee to Clark, May 11, 1949; Clark to Conant, May 17, 24, 1949,
Clark Papers.

9. Chafee to Robert M. Williams, May 10, June 22, 1949; Chafee to Clark,
June 14, 1949, with copy of Williams to Chafee, June 9, 1949; Conant to Chafee, June 18, 1949; Chafee to Clark, June 29, 1949—all in Chafee Papers, Harvard Law School Library.

10. Clark to Ober, May 27, 1949, Clark Papers.

11. Chafee to Clark, June 14, 1949, Clark Papers; Clark to Chafee, June
17, 1949, Chafee Papers. One wonders whether Clark and Chafee would have
been so agreeable to falling in with Conant's plans if they had known how limited were his views on academic freedom and on civil liberties in general. In his
Godkin Lectures at Harvard in 1958, delivered on his return from Germany as
high commissioner, he said:

> The government [of West Germany] is given authority to act against a po-
> litical party or group which aims to abolish the libertarian democratic order
> or to jeopardize the existence of the Federal Republic. This is a powerful
> innovation. . . . Many of us took the revolutionary lines of the Declaration
> of Independence literally as basic American doctrine. This was before the
> rise of Mussolini, Stalin, and Hitler. Most, if not all of us, have long since
> modified our views.

James Bryant Conant, *Germany and Freedom* (Cambridge, Mass., 1958), 39.

The publication of the Clark-Ober correspondence and its distribution as a pamphlet, on Conant's orders, gave rise to a flood of letters, most of them favorable to Clark. David W. Bailey, secretary of the Harvard Corporation, again on Conant's orders, sent each member of the corporation a tally of gifts and letters received at the president's office following publication of the letters. Within a month, favorable letters exceeded unfavorable ones, 70 to 15. Memorandum to Members of the Corporation from D.W.B., July 25, 1949, Clark Papers. Conant must have been especially pleased to see that he was being given credit for the position that we know was far more Clark's than his. See, among scores of such letters, Rabbi Joseph S. Shubow to Conant:

> I cannot help but inform you, as a Harvard alumnus of the Class of 1920, how thrilled and delighted I was to . . . see the wonderful letter which you sent to Mr. Frank Ober and the superb statement made by Grenville Clark in connection with Harvard's classic tradition of liberalism. It was . . . among the most exhilarating and stirring statements I have ever seen. . . . Here, as a mere clergyman, a local rabbi in Boston, who owes to Harvard more than he can ever repay, I am sending my check, which is that of a poor man, of $100, and which is much more than I give annually to the Harvard Fund, as a symbol of my faith in you, in your great administration and in our enduring Truth which our University represents. (Shubow to Conant, June 20, 1949, copy in Clark Papers)

The distinguished historian and editor Lyman H. Butterfield made the same identification of Conant and Clark: "I cannot help feeling that Harvard, thanks to you and Mr. Conant, has given a proper direction to national sentiment on this difficult topic. That makes me proud of Harvard, and I have not invariably been so." Butterfield to Clark, Sept. 6, 1949, Clark Papers. When former U.S. senator Edward R. Burke, who had been one of the leaders of the opposition to President Roosevelt's "court-packing plan," made a contribution of $250 to the Harvard Law School Fund, he wrote Dean Erwin Griswold that he was doing so out of admiration for Clark's letter to Ober: "By its prompt and vigorous action in refusing to submit to this challenge to academic freedom, Harvard has demonstrated again its devotion to a great cause. . . . The statement of Harvard's position prepared by Mr. Grenville Clark will for all time make the name of Harvard synonymous with liberty of thought and expression." Burke to Griswold, July 20, 1949, copy in Clark Papers.

12. Burke to Clark, June 18, July 5, 1949; Clark to Burke, June 9, July 30, 1949; Chafee to Clark, June 22, 1949, Clark Papers; Clark to Chafee, June 13, 1949; Conant to Chafee, June 20, 1949, Chafee Papers; Smith, *Chafee*, 256–57.

13. Smith, *Chafee*, passim; Chafee to Taft, June 21, 1949; Chafee to Brewster, April 10, 1950; Schlesinger to Chafee, June 10, 1949; Rauh to Chafee, June 13, 1949; Baldwin to Chafee, June 13, 1949; Chafee to Schlesinger, June 17, 1949; Chafee to Rauh, June 17, 1949; Chafee to Baldwin, June 17, 1949, Chafee Papers. Among the other members of the National Committee to Defeat the Mundt Bill were Thurman Arnold, Stringfellow Barr, Alexander Meiklejohn, Louis Untermeyer, Mark Van Doren, and Harlow Shapley. "I am proud to be associated with such men," Chafee wrote to Doris Cammett. Smith, *Chafee*, 336 n31.

14. Schrecker, *No Ivory Tower*, 183. I have not seen Marbury's letter of De-

cember 8 to Conant; ibid., 184, 394 n49. Marbury wrote to Chafee acknowledging receipt of a letter of January 3 from Chafee. He says: "I shall look forward with greatest interest to the statement which is to appear in the *Crimson.*" Marbury to Chafee, Jan. 12, 1953, Chafee Papers. Sidney Hook writes that Marbury withdrew as Alger Hiss's attorney because he was "convinced that even if Hiss was not guilty of all the charges Chambers made against him, he was withholding important relevant truths." Did Marbury tell this to Hook? Sidney Hook, *Out of Order: An Unquiet Life in the 20th Century* (New York, 1987), 291.

15. *Harvard Crimson*, Jan. 8, 1953; Chafee to Marbury, Jan. 14, 1953; Chafee to Sutherland, Jan. 14, 1953, Chafee Papers. For letters expressing interest in the Sutherland-Chafee statement and suggesting that it would be a "valuable guide," see, among a great many, Charles B. Nutting, Vice Chancellor, University of Pittsburgh, Nov. 23, 1954; Curt N. Taylor, the College of Wooster, March 31, 1954; Grayson Kirk, Columbia University, Jan. 17, 1954, all to Chafee, Chafee Papers; and Sarah Gibson Blanding, Vassar College, March 2, 1953; Warren E. Burger, Assistant Attorney General, March 20, 1953; and John M. Gaus, Harvard, on behalf of other members of the Board of Trustees of Bennington College, all to Sutherland, Sutherland Papers, Harvard Law School Library. Assistant Attorney General Burger was very much interested in loyalty-security problems. J. Edgar Hoover told Clyde Tolson and Louis Nichols that Burger had sounded him out on March 30, 1955, on an idea that he wanted to take up with Attorney General Brownell. Burger confessed his earlier ignorance about the Employee Security Program and said that his ignorance had been dispelled by the need to prepare government cases for the Supreme Court. The public in general needed to be informed about that program and about matters on which "there seems to be a vast amount of misinformation such as the use of informants and the use of wire taps." Burger told Hoover that in off-the-record meetings he had had with the press "he was amazed at their lack of understanding and comprehension of exactly what was being done and why." He suggested that a meeting between Hoover and David Lawrence, publisher of *U.S. News and World Report*, would be helpful. Modestly, Hoover declined, though he thought the idea of an interview with Brownell was a good one. Burger promised to see Brownell as soon as possible. Obviously he did. On April 25, 1955, Hoover congratulated Brownell on his interview in the current issue of *U.S. News:* "I think this is one of the most constructive contributions that has been made with reference to the perplexing problem of the informant system in the handling of security cases and other matters." He added: "While on the subject, I want to call to your attention the very effective work which Mr. Warren Burger has been doing and the contributions he has made. This has been a real source of encouragement to me." Memo, Hoover to Tolson and Nichols, March 31, 1955; memo, Hoover to Brownell, April 25, 1955. These serials are part of the FBI Main File, Confidential Security Informant Program, #66-2542-3.

16. Chafee to Charles B. Nutting, Nov. 16, 1954, Chafee Papers.

17. Chafee to Curt N. Taylor, April 7, 1954, with enclosure, Chafee Papers. The enclosure, an excerpt from pp. 27–28 of Chafee's *Thirty-Five Years with Freedom of Speech*, contains the following: "The law, of course, gives no privilege against betraying one's friends, and yet no decent American would request such a betrayal, so long as no heinous crime is involved." It ends with a story of an encounter on the street between a justice of the peace and a litigant against

whom he had recently decided a case. The litigant began to upbraid the JP, who threatened to sentence him for contempt. "You're not in your court. What I say on the street isn't contempt. You can't punish me." "Yes, I can. A Justice of the Peace is always an object of contempt." Chafee hoped the story would be taken to heart by congressional committees that fling threats of contempt charges against reluctant witnesses. In early January, Alexander Meiklejohn, Chafee's old professor at Brown, attacked the Sutherland-Chafee position in the *Harvard Crimson*. Chafee replied on January 14, 1954. His point was that he had been concerned "to do what little I can to prevent my university, and possibly others, from adopting the rigid position that a professor who goes outside his legal rights at a legislative hearing should be automatically discharged." He favored a position between "this abhorrent extreme and the opposite extreme of ignoring the whole matter." The Sutherland-Chafee position in the vast majority of cases became the legitimization of what Chafee called "this abhorrent extreme" of automatic dismissal. Chafee to Meiklejohn, Jan. 14, 1954, Chafee Papers.

18. Smith, *Chafee*, 40–41, 216, 271.

19. FBI memorandum, A. H. Belmont to L. V. Boardman, Nov. 4, 1955.

20. Jakobson to Sutherland, April 23, May 25, 27, 1953; John H. Pratt to Sutherland, May 1, 8, 1953; Sutherland to Pratt, May 4, 1953; Sutherland to Buck, May 27, 1953, Sutherland Papers.

21. Schrecker, *No Ivory Tower*, 157.

22. Stein to Sutherland, March 1, 1954. Westin, whom we have already encountered in the FBI documents as a spokesman for the Harvard Young Progressives, was a student of Sutherland. In June 1953, in an article entitled "Do Silent Witnesses Defend Civil Liberties?" in *Commentary*, he argued on both philosophical and legal grounds that "complete responsiveness" was the only permissible position for a witness; personal codes of honor must give way to national security. Schrecker, *No Ivory Tower*, 192. Sutherland wrote in support of Westin's application for a commission in the judge advocate general's corps of the U.S. Air Force, emphasizing his high integrity and "unquestionable loyalty." Sutherland to Judge Advocate General, U.S. Air Force, Feb. 15, 1955, Sutherland Papers.

23. Stein to Sutherland, March 11, 1954, with Memorandum from the American Committee for Cultural Freedom to the Committee on the Communist Record of the Fund for the Republic. The ACCF offered detailed criticism of the framework of the study proposed by Sutherland's committee and submitted proposals for the three aspects of the study for which it wanted complete responsibility: (1) Communist infiltration in U.S. cultural and educational institutions; (2) communism in the labor movement; (3) "The Party Line"—including "The Vulnerability of Audiences," for example, the "social worker mentality," "the civil libertarians," the "view of the Communist Party as a legitimate political party (rather than as a conspiracy)," "the unexamined cliché—imperialism, capitalism, etc."

The American Committee for Cultural Freedom had another problem that played an important role in its determination to find a place in the Fund for the Republic study—money. According to Sidney Hook, Diana Trilling, a leader of the committee, reported that Sol Stein had said the committee would have to close up shop unless it raised a considerable sum of money at once. Norman Thomas said he would call "Allen"—referring to CIA Director Allen Dulles, who was an old friend—for a contribution to tide the committee over the crisis. Trilling assumed the money came from CIA funds. Hook "questioned Norman Thomas about this incident." Thomas said he and Dulles were longtime friends and Princeton graduates; both had been protégés of Woodrow Wilson. Hook feels certain that Thomas would have denied the Trilling account had it been written before his death. He says, however, that the committee got the money from the Farfield Foundation, which was later shown to be a CIA conduit: "In my own mind I had no doubt that the CIA was making some contribution to the funding. . . , but I was never privy to the amount or to the mechanism of its operation. If anyone had deep moral scruples about it, he should have dropped out. If he did not, he did not want to know." His conclusion is that the committee was influenced not by CIA funding, but by its political convictions. Hook, *Out of Order*, 425–26, 451.

Hook's autobiography provides some interesting clues to the linkages between the world of the FBI and the world of the academy. The clues are suggested by both what he reveals and does not reveal. His memory on such matters as the advice he gave to Lionel Trilling on anti-Semitism at Columbia University, on his meeting with Trilling and Whittaker Chambers, on his near-vaudeville encounter with Harlow Shapley (whom he hated almost as much as J. Edgar Hoover did) at the Waldorf Peace Conference of 1949, and on innumerable other events is prodigious, but on some matters it is nonexistent. We know that he was an unofficial adviser on communism to President Raymond Allen at the University of Washington, giving advice on who was or was not a Communist or Communist sympathizer, but on that his autobiography is silent.

He devotes an entire chapter to Albert Einstein, especially to Einstein's participation in a celebration held in his honor in 1954 by the Emergency Committee for Civil Liberties; but he is silent on the attempt by the Committee for Cultural Freedom to get J. Robert Oppenheimer to persuade Einstein not to participate. The episode is informative. In 1953, the ACCF had attacked Einstein for advising intellectuals not to testify before congressional investigating committees on their political beliefs; now, in honor of Einstein's seventy-fifth birthday, the ECLC was organizing a conference on academic freedom. Oppenheimer, under suspension as chairman of the General Advisory Committee of the Atomic Energy Commission, offered his services to the ACCF, in which his membership was then pending. Oppenheimer got in touch with Einstein, who told him that he did not go to birthday celebrations but that he had agreed to answer questions in writing from the ECLC and would keep his promise. Oppenheimer then got in touch with the ACCF to tell them the bad news: Einstein would not withdraw. Oppenheimer informed the committee of Einstein's decision: "I do not know what we can do unless we can get someone to choke them [the ECLC] off and stop it." Stein urged Oppenheimer again to talk to Einstein; he told Oppenheimer that American Jewish leaders were afraid that Einstein's presence at the ECLC would link Zionism and communism and help spread the commonly-held notion that physical scientists were babes-in-the-wood on political matters. Was Stein suggesting a line of defense to Oppenheimer—that he use the argument of innocence in his own reply to the charges then being leveled against him? He wrote to Einstein repeating the arguments he had used with Oppenheimer, and so did Norman Thomas. Einstein wrote Thomas: "I see with a great deal of disquiet the far-reaching analogy between Germany of 1932 and the U.S.A. of 1954." He loathed the arbitrary rule of the regime in Russia but felt it was the problem "of the Russian people to make changes there." As to a Communist conspiracy in the United States: "In my eyes, [it] is principally a slogan used in order to put those who have no judgment and who are cowards into a condition which makes them entirely defenseless. Again, I must think back to Germany of 1932." Stein got Whittaker Chambers to join the ACCF, despite Chambers's objection to Oppenheimer, by showing Oppenheimer's devotion to anticommunism in the ECLC–Einstein situation. Mary Sperling McAuliffe, *Crisis on the Left: Cold War Politics and American Liberals, 1947–1957* (Amherst, Mass., 1978), 118–20, 126.

As to the Fund for the Republic's study of communism, Hook is silent about a meeting that, fortunately, Paul Jacobs describes rather fully. Jacobs had worked on the fund's report on blacklisting and had become a consultant to the fund. In the fall of 1955, the fund's president, Robert M. Hutchins, was under increasingly sharp attack from newscaster Fulton Lewis and other right-wing commentators and politicians and from Hook and Irving Kristol of the committee. The committee felt that the fund's bibliography was "soft" on communism and implied that the fund did not agree that communism was "the greatest threat to cultural freedom today." Stein told the *New York Times* that the fund had rejected at least three anti-Communist projects submitted by the committee; earlier, under Clifford Case, it had declined three others. Thomas C. Reeves feels that the committee's animus was related to its financial crisis and the fund's rejection of its proposals. Stein wrote to Hook that the committee would have to become more anti-McCarthy to get contributions from the academic world. Winning their approval would be "unpleasant but . . . necessary if we are to get a more sympathetic following in the academic community." McAuliffe, *Crisis on the Left*, 124–25. At a meeting at the Columbia University Faculty Club on December 1, 1955, Hutchins and Jacobs represented the fund; Hook, Diana Trilling, Paul Hays, Norman Thomas, Daniel Bell, and William Gomberg represented the committee. Hook spoke for the committee. The fund was wrong in (1) refusing to concede that some guilt could rightly be attributed to association, (2) being willing to allow subversives to be employed in government, and (3) suggesting that universities and foundations might hire Communists, if they were professionally competent. When two more committee proposals were rejected (on advice of committees of the Board of Directors and of Professor Clinton Rossiter of the staff of the study on communism), Hook reopened the attack, opposing tax exemption for the fund. None of this is mentioned in Hook's autobiography. Paul Jacobs, *Is Curly Jewish? A Political Self-Portrait* (New York, 1965), 223–24; Thomas C. Reeves, *Freedom and the Foundation: The Fund for the Republic in the Era of McCarthyism* (New York, 1969), 180–81; Hook, *Out of Order*, 501.

In 1952 Professor Robert M. MacIver, director of the American Academic Freedom Project at Columbia University, resigned from the American Committee for Cultural Freedom after a sharp exchange with Irving Kristol over what MacIver felt to be the committee's lame defense of academic freedom and ambiguous response to the attacks of Senator McCarthy. In the papers of the Academic Freedom Project are the minutes of the Planning Conference of the Committee for Cultural Freedom of March 1, 1952, which throws light on the policy of the committee in general—against which MacIver was objecting—and

the views of Sidney Hook in particular. James T. Farrell and Dwight Mac-
Donald wanted the committee to declare, as Farrell felt, that "the main job *in
this country* is fighting McCarthyism . . . but we are seeing the development of
a group of McCarthyite intellectuals." MacDonald agreed: "The major danger
now in the U.S. is a 'witch-hunt.'" Most of the members of the committee
disagreed. Hook felt that "there is less hysteria now than has existed at other
times in recent history, and professors have shown more courage and resistance
to infringements of academic freedom than they have ever before shown." Minutes, Planning Conference, American Committee for Cultural Freedom, March
1, 1952. See also MacIver to Kristol, April 16, Nov. 3, 10, 1952; Kristol to MacIver,
March 28, Nov. 4, 1952, American Academic Freedom Project, Box 21, Folder,
American Committee for Cultural Freedom, Inc., Columbia University Library.
On this, too, Hook's autobiography is silent.

24. Sutherland to Case, March 25, 1954, Sutherland Papers.

25. Stouffer to Bundy, Dec. 17, 1953, March 3, 1954; Sutherland to Case,
Dec. 29, 1953; "Matter of Professor Samuel Stouffer. Conference held in office
of A. E. Sutherland, Jan. 27, 1954. Present Professors Maguire, Kaplan, Stouffer, and Sutherland"; also, "Matter of Stouffer—notes on conference among
Maguire, Kaplan, Sutherland, and Dean Griswold, Jan. 29, 1954"; Eastern Industrial Personnel Security Board, Matter of Samuel Andrew Stouffer, Brief in
Summation of the Testimony and Affidavits Presented on Behalf of Samuel Andrew Stouffer before the Appeals Division, March 1, 1954, Arthur E. Sutherland, Counsel; Sutherland to Robert C. Sullivan, Executive Secretary, Eastern
Industrial Personnel Security Board, May 10, 1954; Bundy to Sutherland, March
3, 1954, Sutherland Papers.

The contrast between Sutherland and Chafee is strikingly illustrated in the
letters they wrote. A sixteen-year-old high school student from New York wanted
to know whether arrests under the Smith Act were constitutional and what Chafee thought of congressional investigations of teachers aimed at forcing the resignation of Communists: "I personally believe that those questions should be
answered negatively," he wrote, "but your answer could definitely have an effect
on my thinking." Chafee replied as seriously as the student. He deplored the
Smith Act's reliance on conspiracy: "If one man talks nonsense, the wise policy
of Thomas Jefferson would leave him alone. If several people get together to
talk nonsense, I do not see that the situation is really different." On investigations of teachers: "The American tradition is to leave a man alone until definite
proceedings are brought against him based on definite charges of wrong-doing.
. . . I believe that it is a serious interference with [the] work" of teachers "when
they are subjected to roving investigations, which question people who have not
been charged with any wrong-doing. The hope is to make some men condemn
themselves out of their own mouths." He concluded: "So much for my own
ideas, but you must remember that there are a considerable number of thoughtful people whose views are more or less opposite to mine. Don't swallow what I
say but read all around these issues." Compare the content and tone of Chafee's
letter with the memorandum of Sutherland to Dean Griswold, suggesting what
Griswold should say in his forthcoming Keniston Lecture. The status of a teacher,
he argued, was incompatible with commitment to causes "which require him to
be clandestine, which require him to hide his ideas, to refuse to tell them when
questioned, or otherwise to transcend his own independence of mind and impair

his acceptance in the minds of the public as a genuinely free being. . . . It probably would have been better for the American academic community if no professor had ever attempted to use the Fifth Amendment. As soon as a man begins to concentrate on what he can avoid saying[,] . . . on his immunities . . . instead of his responsibility and duty to spread the word, then he loses his proper function." Daniel Davis to Chafee, Sept. 27, 1952; Chafee to Davis, Sept. 30, 1952, Chafee Papers; memorandum, Sutherland to Griswold, Feb. 28, 1957, Sutherland Papers.

26. Lipset and Riesman, *Education and Politics,* 256; memorandum, SAC Boston to Director, June 19, 1950.

27. Howe to Conant, Jan. 7, 1953; Arthur N. Holcombe to Howe, May 27, 1954; Chairman's Statement, AAUP Testimonial, with citations for Buck, Coolidge, Pusey, Charles Wyzanski, and Griswold; Brewster to Howe, undated; Howe to Archibald MacLeish, May 12, 1954; Coolidge to Helen Deane Markham, copy in Howe Papers, Aug. 11, 1953, Howe Papers, Harvard Law School Library.

What Howe thought of Pusey may be seen in two pieces of testimony, one documentary, the other undocumented. He wrote to Yale President Kingman Brewster: "You must be mildly watchful of the suspicion that Bill Buckley now calls the tune at Yale. Luckily we don't have to worry about that danger up here; the Power behind our throne has the best credentials and when Nate speaks it's not his own—or Buckley's voice—that we hear. It's Bigger—it's Better—it's His": a reference, of course, to Pusey's increasing concern with Christian piety. Howe to Brewster, Feb. 16, 1964, Howe Papers.

As to the undocumented testimony: the AAUP testimonial was held at Sanders Theatre on May 26, 1954. On the morning of that day, I had an appointment with Howe to discuss my own situation at Harvard; I had met with him on a few earlier occasions at the suggestion of some Harvard faculty members. At one point in the discussion, Howe looked at his watch and said our meeting would have to be cut short that day because he had to go to a ceremony honoring President Pusey. "I may puke," he said. I need not say that despite the differences with Professor Howe that I have expressed, I had—and retain—the deepest respect and affection for him. He was a courageous and compassionate man, who did what he could, and I and many others owe much to him. President A. Whitney Griswold of Yale had a slightly jaundiced attitude toward the Harvard AAUP ceremony. When he received, courtesy of Brewster, who at the time was still at the Harvard Law School and who was to become his successor as Yale president, a copy of the press release issued by Harvard, he attached to it the following note:

Memorandum from AWG
to AWG
Isn't Harvard, with all this kind of business and LLD's for its own faculty and Admin. officers faintly Narcissist? (Griswold Papers, Box 41, Yale University)

Chapter 6

1. Henry A. Kissinger, *White House Years* (Boston and Toronto, 1979), 252.
2. *Time,* Oct. 8, 1979, p. 34.

3. 18 U.S. Code, Sec. 1702.

4. The statements of Hyland and Kissinger are from the *Harvard Crimson*, Nov. 16, 1979.

5. Wise, *American Police State*, 80–86. Kissinger has changed stories on more than one occasion. He said in interviews that he had added at most a paragraph and one or two footnotes to his account of Cambodia in his book, *White House Years*, to take into consideration the criticism in William Shawcross's *Sideshow: Kissinger, Nixon, and the Destruction of Cambodia* (New York, 1979). In fact, a comparison of Kissinger's book with the corrected galley proofs shows wholesale changes, for which an explanation was offered by William Hyland, who performed the same service in connection with the letter-opening incident: *New York Times*, Oct. 31, 1979. Kissinger claimed in *White House Years* that his use of classified documents had been "worked out with the office of the National Security Adviser, Dr. Zbigniew Brzezinski," implying that his manuscript had been submitted for review and approved. Replying to a question from Robert L. Bernstein, president of Random House, as to how the clearance was actually performed, a representative of the National Security Council said that only limited quotations had ever been submitted for NSC review and that the "book's foreward vastly overstates, at least by implication, the degree of classification review to which the book was subjected." When Theodore Draper asked the State Department about the method used to review Kissinger's use of classified documents, he was told that only the sentences quoted by Kissinger had been cleared; everything else in the documents continued to be classified and off-limits to other scholars, with the result that no one could check on the validity of Kissinger's inferences from them. He was in the position of determining what others could possibly know of his activities. Further, he argued in federal court that notes made by his secretaries when he was secretary of state, which he deposited in the Library of Congress, were not subject to disclosure under the Freedom of Information Act because they were not documents in the possession of the government. They were not in the possession of the government because, in his final months as Secretary of State, he had removed them. *New York Times*, June 9, 1980; Nov. 1, 1979.

6. *Harvard Crimson*, Nov. 16, 1979.

7. David Landau, *Kissinger: The Uses of Power* (Boston, 1972), 42–43; Stephen Graubard, *Kissinger: Portrait of a Mind* (New York, 1973), 58–59.

8. FBI Report, Washington, D.C., Dec. 7, 1949.

9. Chafee to Elliott, March 9, 1948, Chafee Papers.

10. Hoover wrote at the bottom of a press release concerning the committee: "It might be alright if the 'Ford Fund for the Republic' or something like it didn't put their tentacles into it.—H." The FBI memorandum of February 19, 1957, summarized the investigation. The Richardson Foundation was established by H. Smith Richardson and family, who controlled the Vicks Chemical Company. Richardson had contributed large sums of money to the America First Committee. Former FBI assistant director Tracy worked on a study at George Washington University with funds made available by the foundation. Richardson was interested in making funds available to educate the public against communism: "Mr. Tracy has advised the Bureau that Richardson hates the fund for the Republic."

11. Memorandums, Sullivan to Cartha De Loach, Jan. 19, 1966; Sullivan to

Belmont, May 12, 1961; S. B. Donahoe to Belmont, May 16, 1961; G. H. Scatterday to Belmont, Aug. 22, 1960, with attached newspaper clippings. The first report by Nixon's advisory committee was to deal with "communism as a social philosophy," James R. Shepley, on loan from *Time Magazine* as Nixon's "policy and issues adviser," said. Nixon was "on the prowl for original ideas." Shepley, who had been *Time*'s connection with the Republican center-right in the 1950s, was especially close to Nixon in the early stages of the 1960 campaign and helped prepare Nixon for his first debate with Kennedy. David Halberstam, *The Powers That Be* (New York, 1979), 664–65. Harvard law professor W. Barton Leach was "delighted that [Elliott was] close to Dick Nixon" and suggested that Elliott provide certain material that "ought to be put in Nixon's hands." Leach to Elliott, April 12, 1960, W. Barton Leach Collection, MS Division, Harvard Law School Library.

12. Donner, *Surveillance*, 130, 142–43, 215–16, 187–89, 12, 249.

13. *Orbis* (Summer 1958): 223, 225, 226, 227–28, 231, in FBI file on Elliott.

14. Quotations are from the following FBI memoranda: R. R. Roach to Belmont, March 3, 1959; Belmont to Director, Feb. 20, 27, 1959; Sullivan to Belmont, March 13, 30, June 10, 1959.

15. Landau, *Kissinger*, 43; Graubard, *Kissinger: Portrait*, 58; *Harvard Crimson*, Nov. 16, 1979.

16. Seymour M. Hersh, *The Price of Power: Kissinger in the White House* (New York, 1983), 84. It is one of the minor ironies of history that William C. Sullivan, who was the genius behind many FBI black-bag operations, installed illegal wiretaps, and tried so hard to get Elliott to write a "liberal" article in support of wiretapping and the use of informants, was almost certainly the FBI official who in February 1973 leaked to *Time* the story of Kissinger's seventeen wiretaps on government officials and journalists. Donner, *Surveillance*, 248.

Chapter 7

1. William F. Buckley, Jr., *God and Man at Yale: The Superstitions of "Academic Freedom"* (Chicago, 1951), xix.

2. It was an article by William Beecher, at that time a reporter for the *New York Times*, that led Henry Kissinger to suspect a leak by members of his own staff and resulted in the famous wiretapping episode. In September 1971 Secretary of State William P. Rogers admitted at a press conference that the FBI was investigating leaks involving two *New York Times* stories, one written by Beecher on U.S. strategy at the SALT talks. He hinted that the Espionage Act had been violated. David Wise, *The Politics of Lying* (New York, 1973), 285–86.

3. Memo, Nichols to Tolson, Oct. 8, 1949.

4. Memo, Nichols to Tolson, Oct. 13, 1949.

5. Buckley to Harper, Oct. 14, 1949, blind copy in FBI file on Yale University.

6. Routing slip, Nichols to Hoover, undated.

7. Hoover to Baldwin, Oct. 28, 1949.

8. See also Harrison E. Salisbury, "The Strange Correspondence of Morris Ernst and John Edgar Hoover 1939–1964," *The Nation*, Dec. 1, 1984, pp. 575–89.

9. Memo, SA Thomas M. Murphy to SAC J. J. Gleason, Oct. 24, 1949.

10. Memo, Director to SAC New Haven, Nov. 8, 1949. There are some discrepancies between the story of this affair as it can be pieced together from the documents and interviews with some participants and the story as Buckley tells it. Professor Robert Cohen has stated that he was visited by Buckley at his home in connection with the *Crimson* articles. He felt he had convinced Buckley that the articles were quite correct and that he had been fingered by an FBI man. In the 1980s, when Buckley was talking about the matter to John Judis, his biographer, he could not remember visiting Cohen. He had told Cohen that he had decided not to run an article on the *Crimson*'s charges in the *Yale Daily News* because the story was no longer newsworthy; but he told the FBI and the Yale administration that he had killed the story because the *Crimson*'s allegations were false. He told Judis he was surprised to learn that the FBI had a liaison man at Yale. But on October 27, 1949, H. B. Fisher, FBI liaison man at Yale, wrote Hoover that Buckley, after spending the summer considering how to answer the *Crimson*, went to the FBI office for "frank interviews" with SAC Gleason, to the "administrative heads" of Yale, and to a "long extended luncheon interview" with Fisher himself, "in which I gave him the entire background of the Yale program in relation not only to the Bureau but to some one hundred twenty-six different investigative bodies who have and are using Yale records and files and faculty for background and information concerning Yale men." How could Buckley have been surprised to learn later about FBI liaison men at Yale? John B. Judis, *William F. Buckley, Jr.: Patron Saint of the Conservatives* (New York, 1988), 72–74.

11. W. F. Buckley, Jr., to Regnery, July 18, 1952, Buckley Papers, Box 4. Judis argues that Catawba, which he calls the senior Buckley's "consulting firm," bought the "rights to *God and Man at Yale* from Bill for $16,000" in order "to gain publicity"; Buckley gave $10,000 to Regnery to publicize the book and kept $6,000 to finance his own publicity tour. The argument is not exactly clear. Why was it necessary for Catawba to buy the rights in order to "publicize the book"? Why did not Catawba make a gift or a loan to Regnery? Above all, why the secrecy; and why the insistence that Buckley continue to present himself as the "author and owner" of the book when in fact he sold his rights to Catawba? At the time the SEC was investigating Buckley's Starr Broadcasting Co. in 1978, it was also investigating Catawba. Six of the companies controlled by Catawba ousted Catawba's representatives, including brother John Buckley, from management positions. Judis, *Buckley*, 88–89, 406.

12. Box 4, Buckley Papers.

13. July 28, 1952, Box 4, Buckley Papers. At his death Casey was director of the CIA. He drew up the incorporation papers for the *National Review* and remained its counsel until he resigned in a dispute with Buckley over the purchase of an Omaha radio station. Judis, *Buckley*, 118, 152.

On January 18, 1981, the CBS-TV program "Sixty Minutes" presented an interview with Buckley and chummy scenes from the twenty-fifth anniversary party of the *National Review*. Casey and Henry Kissinger were interviewed by Morley Safer:

SAFER: Mr. Casey became somewhat upset by the suggestion of a good Bill Buckley and then there's the bad Bill Buckley, who will, whenever he gets the opportunity, skewer an opponent.

CASEY: I've never heard about the bad Bill Buckley. Tell me more about him. . . . Where in the hell does this bad Bill Buckley come from? . . . I want you to tell me about the bad Bill Buckley. . . .

KISSINGER: In my experience, there have been occasions when he's disagreed with me, which proves that even Bill Buckley can—

CASEY: Does that make him bad, Henry? . . . That's an awful word for you to throw into this context. . . .

KISSINGER: But he's disagreed with me, which proves that he can't be right a hundred percent of the time. But when he has— . . . He hasn't skewered me. . . . I really think that he's a noble human being.

CASEY: He's a fine person. Now, why the hell do we have him called the bad Bill Buckley? . . .

SAFER: I'm sorry, Mr. Casey. I said that was—there's the . . .

CASEY: What about—what about—what about—what about the bad Dan Rather? And what about, who's that guy, Mike Wallace? Bad Bill Buckley!

Casey also attended the thirtieth anniversary dinner of the *National Review*, at which the main speaker was President Ronald Reagan. Transcript, "60 Minutes," vol. 13, no. 18, Jan. 18, 1981, produced by CBS News, pp. 13–14. *New York Times*, Dec. 6, 1985. Reagan was also supposed to attend the twenty-fifth anniversary of the *National Review*, but claims to have lost track of the date. Judis tells a slightly different story. Buckley fully expected Reagan, to whom he had extended an invitation—Christopher Buckley says three invitations—to attend the celebration, but he was notified by Roy Cohn that Reagan would not attend. Buckley phoned Nancy Reagan and the president, who claimed he had not received the invitation and had to be in California. Buckley's son was convinced the invitation was deliberately lost by Michael Deaver, who was one of Reagan's administrative triumvirate. Judis, *Buckley*, 424–25.

There is a kind of historical appropriateness in the presence of Henry Kissinger at the *National Review* anniversary celebrations. John Judis feels that the relationship with Kissinger was the "most important" Buckley had with the Nixon White House. They had known each other since 1954, when Kissinger rejected an article on McCarthy that Kissinger had commissioned for his journal, *Confluence*. To atone, he invited Buckley to give annual lectures at his international relations seminar at Harvard. In 1956, at Kissinger's invitation, they had lunch at the Yale Club in New York and formed a continuing relationship. Kissinger tried to soften Buckley's opposition to Nelson Rockefeller, Kissinger's patron. He continued to favor Rockefeller even after Nixon's nomination for the presidency, but by August 1968 he was writing Buckley to tell him that he had a "few ideas" about foreign policy that he thought would interest Nixon. Buckley volunteered to put Kissinger in touch with Nixon; Kissinger met with Nixon and informed him of developments in the Vietnam War negotiations. During Kissinger's years in the White House, he invited Buckley to the White House at least twenty times, on occasion sending the White House jet for him, complete with Colonel Alexander Haig. Kissinger used Buckley as his contact with conservatives and ally in his campaign to oust Secretary of State William Rogers. Kissinger also used Buckley to carry messages to Ronald Reagan during the Republican primaries of 1976. For his part, Buckley tried to reconcile the Republican far right to Kissinger. He gave a great deal of editorial assistance to Kissinger in the writing of *White House Years* but refused Kissinger's printed acknowledgment. He felt that *White House Years* was "a modern classic," ranking with Whittaker Chambers's *Witness.* Judis, *Buckley,* 300–302, 303–5, 331–32, 388–89, 417–18.

14. Aug. 4, 1952, Box 4, Buckley Papers.

15. Box 4, Buckley Papers.

16. Regnery to Buckley, Jr., Sept. 2, 1952; Regnery to Buckley, Sr., June 3, 1953, Box 4, Buckley Papers.

17. Kohlberg was one of the leaders of the China Lobby. Matthews was for years research director of the Dies Committee. Hart, chairman of the New York State Economic Council, was a founder of the American Union for Nationalist Spain and the America First Committee. Kamp, a leading official of the Constitutional Educational League, was the author of the pamphlet "Join the CIO and Help Build a Soviet America." Rumely, convicted during World War I as a German agent, was an officer of the Committee for Constitutional Government.

18. Regnery to Buckley, Sept. 29, 1951; Strauss to Buckley, Oct. 19, 1951; Castle to Buckley, Feb. 20, 1952; Tucker to Buckley, Feb. 15, 1952; McCormick to Buckley, Dec. 18, 1951, Box 4, Buckley Papers.

19. Box 4, Buckley Papers. Thomas I. Emerson, David Haber, and Fowler Harper, three professors at the Yale Law School, were often attacked for their political views. Philip Morrison was a distinguished physicist at Cornell. John S. Service was dismissed from the U.S. State Department after the break-in at the office of *Amerasia,* but was later ordered reinstated. Phillip Jessup, a judge of the World Court, was under frequent right-wing attack.

20. Frank C. Hanighen to Higgins, Nov. 28, 1952; Higgins to Hanighen, Nov. 14, 1952; Chodorov to J. H. Gipson, undated but November 1951, Box 4, Buckley Papers.

21. John B. Judis, "William F. Buckley, Jr.: The Consummate Conservative," *Progressive,* Sept. 1981, pp. 25, 27. Buckley was recruited for the CIA by Willmoore Kendall, one of his professors at Yale, who had himself been in the CIA. Kendall introduced him to James Burnham, who later became an associate of Buckley's on the *National Review;* it was in Burnham's Washington apartment that he met Hunt. At the time, Burnham was consultant to the Office of Policy Coordination, the CIA's covert action division, and Hunt was preparing to go to Mexico City as CIA station chief. Hunt, who became a close friend of Buckley, remained in the CIA until April 1970; he played an important part in the overthrow of the Arbenz government in Guatemala in 1954 and in the Bay of Pigs invasion of Cuba. When he appeared on Buckley's "Firing Line" program on January 18, 1973, Buckley sought to establish the fact that the Watergate operation was conducted in the CIA spirit: "Life-long experience . . . with the CIA teaches a person to forget about the legal impediments that lie between him and the accomplishment of a mission that he seeks to achieve." Quoted in Tad Szulc, *Compulsive Spy: The Strange Case of E. Howard Hunt* (New York,

1974), 163. Buckley's colleague, Frank Meyer, reflecting on the fact that Buckley, his sister Priscilla, and his associates Willmoore Kendall and James Burnham all had CIA experience, sometimes thought that the *National Review* was run by Burnham as a CIA operation. Garry Wills, *Confessions of a Conservative* (New York, 1979), 46. Murray Rothbard, once a frequent contributor to the magazine, has no doubt about it: "I'm convinced that the whole *National Review* is a CIA operation." Judis, *Buckley*, 77–78, 89–92, 148.

22. July 11, 1951, Box 4, Buckley Papers.

23. *International Herald-Tribune*, March 3, 1987. In the spring of 1977, at an early stage in the investigation of the murder of Chilean Orlando Letelier and Ronni Moffitt in Washington, Buckley was irritated that it was the assassination that was being investigated, not Letelier's politics. Taylor Branch and Eugene M. Propper, *Labyrinth* (New York, 1982), 228.

24. Judis, *Buckley*, passim; Priscilla L. Buckley and William F. Buckley, Jr., eds., *William F. Buckley—An Appreciation* (New York, 1959).

25. Buckley to Fall, Nov. 4, 1920, Fall Papers, Reel 1, Univ. of New Mexico.

26. Buckley to Bainbridge Colby, May 22, 1922, Buckley Papers, Reel 8, Univ. of Texas.

27. The material in this section is based on documents in Reels 1, 2, 3, 5, 6, 7, and 8, Buckley Papers; Reels 30 and 36, Fall Papers; *Investigation of Mexican Affairs*, Hearings before a Subcommittee of the Committee on Foreign Relations of the United States Senate, 66th Cong., 1st sess. (Washington, D.C., 1919), 85–93, 767–68, 838–39; contemporary newspapers, including the *New York Times*, *New York Commercial*, *New York Herald*, *New York Sun*, *New York American*, *San Antonio Light*, and others found in the Buckley scrapbooks; and Lorenzo Meyer, *Mexico and the United States in the Oil Controversy, 1917–1942* (Austin and London, 1977); Robert Freeman Smith, *The United States and Revolutionary Nationalism in Mexico, 1916–1932* (Chicago and London, 1972); David C. Bailey, *Viva Christo Rey! The Cristero Rebellion and the Church-State Conflict in Mexico* (Austin and London, 1974).

28. The material on Bielaski is based on documents in the Buckley Papers and on Bielaski's FBI dossier. See also the references to Bielaski in Chapter 8.

29. Smith, *The U.S. and Revolutionary Nationalism*, 143, 233.

30. Ron Rosenbaum, "An Elegy for Mumbo Jumbo," *Esquire* 88, no. 3 (Sept. 1977): 85. What the *New Yorker* recently published as an amusing article might be other than amusing. It reflects the continuing odd association of Yale, specifically of Skull and Bones, and Mexico. The Wednesday Group of El Paso, Texas, has resurrected the rumor that the sepulchre of Skull and Bones contains the skull of Pancho Villa, which was separated from the rest of the skeleton in 1926. It has also been said that Skull and Bones has the skull of the Apache chief Geronimo, removed from the grave in 1918 by a raiding party that included Prescott Bush. In 1986 Endicott Peabody Davison, spokesman for the Russell Trust Association, the governing body of Bones, and Jonathan Bush, President Bush's younger brother and son of Prescott Bush, denied having the skull but offered the San Carlos Apache tribe another skull in its place. Mark Singer, "La Cabeza de Villa," *New Yorker*, Nov. 27, 1989, pp. 108–20.

31. How overt intelligence work easily becomes covert and conspiratorial was succinctly stated by James Jesus Angleton, whose father had served with the Pershing expeditionary force in Mexico in 1917 and who himself became head

of CIA counterintelligence. A graduate of Yale and Harvard Law School, he served with OSS during World War II. He testified to the Church committee investigating the intelligence activities of the U.S. government: "It is inconceivable that a secret intelligence arm of the government has to comply with all the overt orders of the government." Quoted in Wise, *American Police State*, 206–9. When President Bush was asked whether the Yale experience was "useful training" for the clandestine trade and politics, he answered that he had tried to "obscure his Yale past," but no longer. Why not? In a word, baseball. His "fondest memories" were "the lasting friendships formed at Yale. Loved watching football in the Bowl. Playing baseball on that great diamond." Had his Yale ties helped or harmed his career? "My Yale education has helped, I'm sure. Running for public office in Texas is not necessarily enhanced by Yale education, however. I come back to 'friends.' If by 'ties' you mean friendships, yes, they have helped me in politics. Loyal friends can move mountains." But were President Bush's answers to the questions asked of him by the editor of the *Yale Daily News* completely candid? Of the eight or nine questions submitted by the editor, two were not answered at all; others were altered. The president's director of press relations argued: "We don't have any commitment" to answer all the student's questions. "It's completely up to us which questions we decide to answer." She was "mystified" that the editor did not appreciate his good fortune in "having the President agree to give a student newspaper his personally typewritten replies." But they were not his personally typewritten replies. She had edited the student-editor's questions and retyped Bush's original draft "to correct some of the misspellings." *New York Times*, May 28, 1989.

Chapter 8

1. Report, H. B. Fisher to Deans' Committee on Social Research, 1949–50, marked "Confidential," Carl Lohmann Papers, Yale University Library. I am indebted to the authorities of Yale University for permission to examine and quote from these papers.

2. On Bishop Fisher, see Marshall Olds, *Analysis of the Interchurch World Movement Report on the Steel Strike* (New York and London, 1922), 396; *New York Times*, Jan. 21, June 19, 1924; March 15, 16, 17, 1926. On Buckner, see Martin Mayer, *Emory Buckner* (New York, Evanston, and London, 1968).

3. *Reform Bulletin*, New York Civic League, vol. 16, no. 29 (Sept. 1925), vol. 17, no. 10 (March 5, 1926); *New York Times*, Oct. 16, Dec. 22, 1925, Sept. 11, Nov. 18, 1926, Jan. 18, April 11, July 5, 1927, Jan. 8, Nov. 25, 1928.

4. Burton J. Bledstein, *The Culture of Professionalism* (New York, 1976), 228–30, 232; George Wilson Pierson, *Yale: The University College, 1921–1937* (New Haven, 1955), 72–73, 88 et seq., 94–99, 221, 259–60, 517–18; Raymond B. Fosdick, *Chronicle of a Generation: An Autobiography* (New York, 1958), 219; Seymour Gelber, *The Role of Campus Security in the College Setting*, U.S. Department of Justice, Law Enforcement Assistance Administration (Washington, 1972), 16. How the medical metaphor linked moral reform and public health and justified the use of coercive measures can be seen in Fosdick's statement: "Prostitution is only incidentally a police problem. It is a disease which cannot be successfully treated symptomatically. . . . Only direct surgical processes in-

volving violent actions, can really hope to remedy it." Fosdick, "Prostitution and the Police," *Social Hygiene* 2 (1915–16): 11.

5. Taft to Angell, Dec. 7, 1927, Angell Papers, Box 78, Yale University Library.

6. Reports of H. B. Fisher, 1929, Angell Papers, Box 78.

7. Fisher to Angell, Nov. 13, 1929, Angell Papers, Box 78; see also Fisher to Angell, March 26, Oct. 14, Nov. 24, 1930, Feb. 5, 1931. The letterhead on his personal stationery read only: "Beaver Knoll in the Hills of Woodbridge, Conn." or "Beaver Knoll, Box 104A, Seymour Road, Woodbridge, Conn."

8. Bernice L. Corbin to Angell, April 16, 1930; Fisher to Angell, March 26, 1930, Angell Papers, Box 78.

9. Fisher to Angell, March 26, Oct. 14, Nov. 24, 1930; Angell to Corbin, April 17, 21, 1930; Angell's secretary to Fisher, Oct. 14, 1930; Corbin to Angell, May 27, 1930, Angell Papers, Box 78.

10. Furniss to Angell, Jan. 29, 1931, Angell Papers, Box 78.

11. Angell to Fisher, Jan. 29, 1931; Fisher to Angell, Feb. 4, 1931, Angell Papers, Box 78.

12. In Cleveland, Mayor Newton D. Baker established a program for policewomen remarkably like the one envisioned for Yale; Sabina Marshall, "Development of the Policewoman's Movement in Cleveland, Ohio," *Social Hygiene* 11 (1925): 193–209. For other discussions of the early history of this emerging profession, see A. W. Towne, "A Community Program for Protective Work with Girls," ibid. 6 (1920): 57–71; Chloe Owings, "Women Police," ibid. 11 (1925): 38–45; Henrietta Additon, "The Functions of Policewomen," ibid. 10 (1924): 323–38. In 1924 the New York School of Social Work established a special program for training the directors of policewomen units; ibid. 10 (1924): 178–84.

13. Mendell to Angell, Feb. 5, 1931; Angell to Mendell, Feb. 6, 1931, Angell Papers, Box 78.

14. Angell to Fisher, Feb. 6, 14, 1931; Fisher to Angell, Feb. 16, 1931. See also Angell to Fisher, Feb. 18, 1931, Angell Papers, Box 78.

15. Fisher to Angell, March 26, 1931; Angell to Fisher, March 27, 1931; Angell to Furniss, March 27, 1931. Angell dropped the matter, but Fisher never gave up. He found that Yale was the only "first rank" educational institution with an enrollment of four to five hundred women that had no "provision for the services of a woman Dean." Memo, Fisher to Angell, "Re—Dean of Women," April 24, 1931, Angell Papers, Box 78.

16. Fisher to Dean Mendell and the Deans' Committee, Report for 1932–33, with covering letter from Mendell to Angell, Oct. 4, 1933, Angell Papers, Box 187. See also the correspondence dealing with Angell's efforts to pursue some of Fisher's proposals: T. W. Farnham, Treasurer, to Mendell (copy in Angell Papers), Oct. 5, 1933, Box 78; Angell to Mendell, Oct. 6, 1933, Box 187; Angell to Gentlemen of the Yale Corporation, Oct. 24, 1933, Angell Papers, Box 187.

17. Fisher to Mendell and the Deans' Committee, Social Research Report, Oct. 14, 1936, Angell Papers, Box 78; id. to id., Annual Report, 1934; Mendell to Angell, Jan. 29, 31, 1935, Angell Papers, Box 78.

18. New England Watch and Ward Society, *Annual Report*, 1897–98 (1898),

40; ibid., 1914–15 (1915), 5–6; Paul S. Boyer, *Purity in Print* (New York, 1968), 26, 46–52, 66; New York Vice Society, *Annual Report* (1918), 5.

19. Fisher to the Deans' Committee, Social Research Report, July 1, 1941, Seymour Papers, Box F; Warren to Farnham, Sept. 11, 1941, with handwritten notation, "Noted and turned over to C.S.—T.W.F.," Seymour Papers, Box F.

20. The form and covering letter, dated Nov. 9, 1942, may be found in the Carl Lohmann Papers.

21. Fisher to Warren, Report of the Deans' Committee on Social Research, 1942, with covering memorandum, Warren to Seymour, undated but stamped "Received Aug. 31, 1942," Seymour Papers, Box F. Warren's endorsement raises an important problem. Assuming that Fisher was "of the FBI" implies more than the usual "liaison" relationship: that in some sense he was an employee of the FBI, perhaps part of his salary and his instructions coming from the FBI. Both possibilities are compatible with the evidence. One may ask whether the FBI had similar arrangements with other universities, or with other types of "private" organizations. What authority permitted such sharing of private and public functions?

We have already met A. Bruce Bielaski, chief of the Bureau of Investigation, in connection with the Buckleys. Bielaski encouraged the use of the American Protective League, a private organization operating under the cloak of government authority, for "espionage" and "subversion" investigations during and after World War I. In February 1919 he entered the private practice of law. Bielaski was the "victim" of a suspicious kidnapping in Mexico during a time of strained relations with the United States. On May 13, 1925, he was secretly appointed by William J. Donovan, of the office of the attorney general, as special assistant to the attorney general "to act in matters arising under the enforcement of the so-called prohibition laws, with compensation . . . payable from the appropriation, 'Pay of Special Assistant-Attorney U.S. Courts.' " He was given a drawing account of $1,000 per month. The appointment was terminated on March 15, 1926. Emory Buckner, the U.S. attorney under whose direction Fisher worked before 1927, was Bielaski's superior. On April 9, 1926, Buckner wired the attorney general that he was notifying the police commissioner of New York City that "our formal approval Bielaski's activities along line discussed by us is withdrawn and . . . any activities of this nature now in operation should be stopped immediately." His activities were terminated because of concern he was himself acting illegally. In 1925–26, as "chief undercover man" in New York for Brigadier General Lincoln G. Andrews, in charge of federal enforcement of the Prohibition laws, he used federal funds to operate the Bridge Whist Club as a decoy speakeasy to trap violators of the law. Bielaski's role as an undercover agent came as a surprise to members of the House Appropriations Committee and Treasury officials. Andrews had intended that Bielaski's appointment "should be an office secret" and his salary paid from the lump-sum $50,000 appropriation by Congress for "information" needed for Prohibition law enforcement. Congressman Fiorello LaGuardia wanted to know by what authority Bielaski had been appointed. He demanded the indictment of Chester P. Mills, New York Prohibition administrator, and of Bielaski and Ralph Bickle, another undercover man, for having secured evidence of crime by entrapment and for having engaged in wiretapping. He also threatened impeachment of Buckner. Government agents, he said, may not "violate the law in order to detect violations of law." He also accused Bielaski and other undercover agents of using information gained through wiretaps for blackmail purposes. Treasury Secretary Andrew Mellon admitted that the money for the club's lease came from government funds. Bielaski's undercover operations had resulted in more than a hundred indictments but fewer than six convictions.

Echoes of the 1920s reverberated later. During World War II, Donovan was head of the OSS. The Bielaskis were as much a political organization as a family. For many years Bielaski's sister, Ruth Shipley, was head of the passport office of the State Department; her refusal to grant passports to many alleged subversives led to a number of notable lawsuits. Bielaski's brother, Frank B. Bielaski, tapped the telephones of prominent Philadelphia Democrats in 1938 on behalf of Joseph N. Pew, Jr., the Republican industrialist. As OSS director of investigation in New York City, he broke into the *Amerasia* office on Sunday, March 11, 1945, "without the knowledge or approval of the Department of Justice." He removed more than twenty documents and "then replaced all the other documents so that there would be no evidence of their illegal search and seizure." He became head of the Research and Security Corporation of New York, which for a fee checked the records of persons and rated their loyalty. He was especially active in the entertainment field during the blacklist period. In 1950, during the first trial for perjury of William Remington, he was hired by Joseph L. Rauh, Remington's attorney, as an investigator. One potential witness for Remington was vulnerable because he had denied under oath that he had ever been a Communist; he was, therefore, subject to a charge of perjury himself. Rauh interviewed the prospective witness, who promptly told the FBI. Rauh notified Bielaski that the witness had been threatened with a perjury indictment and asked Bielaski to try once again to interview him. Bielaski asked two former FBI agents on his staff to do the job. They refused to conduct "an investigation which is on its face in direct opposition to the work of the Federal Bureau of Investigation." They did, though, send a copy of Rauh's memorandum to Bielaski to the FBI; J. Edgar Hoover sent them a letter of gratitude and forwarded Rauh's memorandum to the Remington prosecution. Joan M. Jensen, *The Price of Vigilance* (Chicago and New York, 1946), passim; FBI Papers, Main File, A. Bruce Bielaski: Attorney General to Bielaski, Feb. 7, 1925; Memorandum for the Appointment Clerk, Chief Clerk and Administrative Assistant, Department of Justice, May 13, 1925; Donovan to Bielaski, May 13, 1925; Memorandum for the files, Office of Attorney General John G. Sargent, Feb. 19, 1926; Sargent to Bielaski, March 15, 1926; L. C. Andrews, Assistant Secretary of the Treasury, to the Attorney General, May 22, 1926; Buckner to Attorney General, April 19, 1926; Bielaski to John A. DeGroot, U.S. Attorney, Eastern District of New York, May 4, 1926; DeGroot to Bielaski, May 5, 1926; LaGuardia to Sargent, Aug. 16, 1926; *New York Times*, June 13, 1940; Feb. 20, 1964; Jan. 6, 9, 10, 14, 15, 20, 21, 22, Feb. 25, 1927; *New York World*, July 22, 1926; John S. Service, *The Amerasia Papers: Some Problems in the History of US–China Relations* (Berkeley, 1971), 36; Victor S. Navasky, *Naming Names* (New York, 1980), 92–94; *New York Times*, May 5, 1950; O'Reilly, *Hoover*, 162–63.

22. Fisher to Warren, Report of the Deans' Committee on Social Research, 1942, Seymour Papers, Box F.

23. N. P. Elliott to Furniss, July 16, 1943, Furniss Papers, Box 1. I have been informed by Professor Roger Daniels of the University of Cincinnati that

the Japanese American Student Relocation Council did not add Yale or any other college to the list of those barred to the Japanese. The government did the barring, sometimes in high-handed and mysterious ways. Dean Robert Redfield, distinguished anthropologist at the University of Chicago, could not understand why Japanese-American students were not allowed to go to the University of Chicago but were allowed at other colleges in that city. The barring was the work of General Leslie Groves, head of the Manhattan Project. As late as June 1943, there were no Japanese-American students at Yale or any other Connecticut college, but at the time there were thirty-four at fourteen Massachusetts institutions. Roger Daniels to Sigmund Diamond, March 20, 1985.

24. Memorandum, Fisher to Lohmann, Oct. 28, 1943, Lohmann Papers.

25. Fisher to Lohmann, Dec. 14, 1943; CV of Kenneth Kenkichi Kurihara; summary of telephone conversation, Dec. 17, 1943, Seymour Papers, Box F; Bloch to Lohmann, Oct. 19, 1945, Lohmann Papers.

26. Fisher, Special Report to the Deans' Committee on Social Research, Jan. 1, 1943, Lohmann Papers.

27. Memoranda, Feb. 12, 1944, March 16, 1945, Lohmann Papers.

28. Fisher, Special Report to the Deans' Committee on Social Research, Jan. 1, 1943; Annual Reports, 1943–44, 1944–45. See also Fisher's Reports for 1946–47, 1947–48, 1949–50, Lohmann Papers.

29. Fisher to SAC New Haven, May 1, 8, 1951, Lohmann Papers. The letter of May 8 is so literate in comparison with the other letters by Fisher that I suspect it was written by someone else, probably Carl Lohmann, and signed by Fisher. On May 17, 1951, Fisher transmitted to Lohmann a series of "Quotes Pertinent to Loyalty Checks by Outside Agencies" taken from a memorandum he had received from SAC New Haven, Galen N. Willis. See also FBI memorandum, ATTN: Mr. H. B. Fisher, June 1, 1951, Lohmann Papers.

30. Assistant to the President to Lohmann, June 21, 1951; undated Lohmann memorandum summarizing discussion with Fisher, probably July 1951; memorandum, Secretary's Office to Deans and Masters, July 12, 1951, Lohmann Papers.

31. Report, Fisher to Deans' Committee on Social Research, Jan. 1, 1952, Lohmann Reports. For Fisher's annual budgets, see his reports to the Deans' Committee in the Lohmann, Angell, and Seymour Papers.

32. James T. Healy, Assistant Head, Audit Division, Connecticut Internal Revenue Service, to Yale University, Dec. 27, 1952; Lohmann to Healy, Jan. 6, 1953; Fisher to Edward C. Roberts, Assistant Comptroller, Yale University, Jan. 7, 1953, Lohmann Papers.

33. Paul Boyer presents some examples of the connection between coercive moral reform movements and increased reliance upon close personal surveillance to force compliance; *Urban Masses and Moral Order in America, 1820–1920* (Cambridge, Mass., and London, 1978), 217.

34. Jensen, *Vigilance*, 148, 151–53, 178–79, 185; *Supplementary Reports on Intelligence Activities*, Book 6. Final Report of the Select Committee to Study Governmental Operations with Respect to Intelligence Activities. U.S. Senate, 94th Cong., 2nd sess., Senate Report 94–755 (Washington, D.C., 1976), 102–7; Harold M. Hyman, *To Try Men's Souls: Loyalty Tests in American History* (Berkeley and Los Angeles, 1959), 273–74, 275–81. The APL's influence lived on. When the Ku Klux Klan was revived in the 1920s, it emphasized patriotism far more

than did the old Klan. Its leader, William J. Simmons, who had been with the American Protective League, conceived of the new Klan as a vast secret service agency, coercing conformity to both a moral and a political code. John Higham, *Strangers in the Land* (New York, 1962), 211–12, 286–89, 294.

35. Quoted in Gordon S. Wood, *The Creation of the American Republic, 1776–1782* (New York, 1969), 69, 118, 52 n12, 612.

36. It could easily have been H. B. Fisher who wrote in 1941 a denunciation of motels as "a new home of disease, bribery, corruption, crookedness, rape, white slavery, thievery, and murder," which, among other things, provided innocent married couples with mattresses previously used in "illicit relations." But it was J. Edgar Hoover. Quoted in Donner, *Surveillance*, 121. Policemen become moral leaders, and moral leaders, policemen.

37. Timothy Gilfoyle, "The Moral Origins of Political Surveillance: The Preventive Society in New York City, 1867–1918," *American Quarterly* 38, no. 4 (Fall 1986): 637–52.

38. Keith Sward, *The Legend of Henry Ford* (New York and Toronto, 1948), 59–60, 79, 297–98, 372–429, 447; Samuel S. Marquis, *Henry Ford: An Interpretation* (Boston, 1923), 147; Allan Nevins, *Ford: The Times, the Man, the Company* (New York, 1954), 551–54, 560, 564. Ernest Liebold, Henry Ford's private secretary, kept the medical personnel at the Ford Hospital under constant surveillance. William Greenleaf, *From These Beginnings: The Early Philanthropies of Henry and Edsel Ford, 1911–1936* (Detroit, 1964), 23, 201 n52, 125.

39. A recent study notes that the FBI has had close relations with university administrations at least since the early days of the loyalty program: "Few college officials question the purpose of FBI inquiry"; they share the same political views, and besides, many campus police officials are former FBI agents. At Yale, John W. Powell, a seventeen-year veteran of the FBI, kept files on the "subversive activities" of students and used student informers; William W. Turner, *Hoover's FBI: The Man and the Myth* (Los Angeles, 1970), 207–8. C. Tracy Barnes, who had been a secret operations officer for the OSS during World War II and then a high-ranking official with the CIA, resigned from the CIA in 1968 to become special assistant to Yale President Kingman Brewster, with special duties in the field of "community relations." After duty in Frankfurt and London, he became chief of the CIA Domestic Operations Division. In late 1953 he organized a special team to plan for the overthrow of the Arbenz government in Guatemala. Barnes selected as political chief of the action E. Howard Hunt, whose connections with Buckley and Watergate we have seen. Barnes used Hunt in the Bay of Pigs operation. Hunt claims that Barnes invited him to meet with Arthur M. Schlesinger, Jr., to prepare the White Paper on the Bay of Pigs that was being written for President Kennedy. At the time of the Bay of Pigs operation, Barnes was designated to brief Adlai Stevenson at the United Nations to the effect that the invasion was strictly a Cuban operation, with American involvement limited to training and financing. Barnes's account was rather ambiguous, but Stevenson seems to have been alarmed. He was interviewed in October 1963 in connection with the Bay of Pigs incident and his knowledge of it. His "distress over his role was evident. . . . He confirmed he had been briefed by Tracy Barnes; he said Barnes seemed to be trying to persuade him either that the United States was not involved in the forthcoming invasion of Cuba or that the CIA's role was marginal." Stevenson was convinced that the United States was deeply involved,

but he had "his mission to perform"—and he did it, to the point of denying
United States involvement. On April 10 Arthur Schlesinger, Jr., sent a memorandum to President Kennedy praising the "skill and care" that had gone into
"Cubanizing the operation and doing nothing which would be inconsistent with
a spontaneous Cuban effort." If Castro sent CIA–trained Cubans to the UN to
show CIA involvement, "we will have to be prepared to show that the alleged
CIA personnel were errant idealists or soldiers of fortune working on their own."
Care had to be taken to protect "one of our greatest national resources," the
character and reputation of the president: "When lies must be told, they should
be told by subordinate officials. At no point should the President be asked to
lend himself to the cover operation. For this reason, there seems to be merit in
Secretary Rusk's suggestion that someone other than the President make the
final decision and do so in his absence—someone whose head can later be placed
on the block if things go terribly wrong." Schlesinger quotes this passage from
his memorandum to Kennedy in his book on the Kennedy presidency. Christopher Hitchens wrote to the *Times Literary Supplement* quoting Schlesinger's view
that when "lies must be told, they should be told by subordinate officials." He
concluded: "Clear enough? Schlesinger has been a servant of power and an
inventive courtier," and we have all "learned from his mistakes. But he really
must stop confusing this role with that of the historian." *Times Literary Supplement*, March 31–April 6, 1989, p. 339. John Ranelagh, a historian of the CIA,
calls Barnes one of "the glamor boys" of the agency. Barnes had been one of
the glamor boys at Yale—hockey, rugby, handball, manager of the Glee Club.
After a brief legal practice with Carter, Ledyard, and Milburn, he worked with
Allen Dulles and the OSS in Switzerland. Robin Winks, the chronicler of Yale
men in the OSS, writes that he "knew Barnes when, after his resignation from
the CIA, he became assistant to the president of Yale University. However, Barnes
proves unusually elusive." Was his elusiveness the result of his training, a requirement for his job at Yale, or both? Reference to his special responsibilities
in the area of community relations recalls the early H. B. Fisher, but the similarity stops there. Barnes was an Ivy League "spook"; in comparison, Fisher was
just a cut above Little League. With his experience in overthrowing governments, one cannot see Barnes reporting on student dances. One can, however,
see him handling relations between Yale and military and intelligence agencies
in Washington. Harris Smith, *OSS: The Secret History of America's First Central
Intelligence Agency* (Berkeley, Cal., 1972), 230; Szulc, *Compulsive Spy*, 69–71;
John Ranelagh, *The Agency: The Rise and Decline of the CIA* (London, 1986),
36–61; Peter Wyden, *Bay of Pigs: The Untold Story* (New York, 1979), 20, 31–
32, 39, 156–58, 160–61; E. Howard Hunt, *Give Us This Day* (New York, 1973),
22–23, 38–40, 145–47, 172–74, 219; Winks, *Cloak and Gown*, 554–55, n3;
Wise, *Lying*, 37–38; id., *Police State*, 205–6.

40. Opposition to the Freedom of Information Act and other forms of "sun-
shine laws" is often based on confusion of the two different types of secrets—
the specific and the general. Revelation of the "general" secret that government
is engaged in widespread surveillance does not necessarily disclose the specific
targets of that surveillance. Opponents of these laws do not wish it to be known
that government engages in these acts at all.

41. James B. Rule, after studying a number of surveillance-bureaucracies,
concluded: "The interactions between systems like those studied here and their

social contexts press such systems steadily towards . . . total surveillance. . . . As the new, larger social units come to make more and more demands on the behavior of those who participate in them, the mechanisms which enforce these demands must increase commensurately in strength and effectivenss. . . . The frequent efforts of the elites who control such systems to conceal their activities and to obfuscate the issues involved conduce to the same sort of effect." *Private Lives and Public Surveillance* (London, 1973), 327–29, 358.

Chapter 9

1. After considering whether to mention the names of these informants, I finally decided to do so. Often the FBI does not delete the names of those alleged to be "subversive" faculty members or students; I am not sure that the identity of the informants should be protected, while that of their victims is revealed. The case of Acker reveals another reason for mentioning their names. Could their experience as informants have been important to their careers? Perhaps Acker felt himself under pressure to prove his own patriotism. He sent to G2 a copy of a pamphlet entitled "A Message to American Lawyers," issued by the National Lawyers Guild, which he said was being distributed by the person about whom he was informing. Written on the first page of the pamphlet is a sentence that has been crossed out but is still readable: "Acker is a dirty pinkie." Was Acker afraid that he might be considered a Communist because he had received the pamphlet, and was this the way he sought to clear himself? Colonel Ernest A. Barlow, Chief, Security and Training Group, Intelligence Division, CGUSA, to Director, FBI, Feb. 9, 1950, with attached report, Jan. 30, 1950, from G2, Military District of Washington. On July 29, 1988, the *New York Times* reported that District Judge Acker had instructed federal attorneys to appear before him to consider an "unprecedented" question: should he recuse himself from all cases in which the federal government was a party? Smarting from reversal by the Court of Appeals of the Eleventh Circuit of several of his rulings in a four-year-old criminal case involving the Ku Klux Klan, a reversal in which the court ordered the rehearing of the case by another judge, Acker felt his impartiality had been cast into doubt. He was upset because the circuit court ruled that he had acted improperly in dismissing the indictment against one Klansman, suppressing key evidence against others, and ordering the acquittal of one who had been found guilty by the jury. The Department of Justice had refused to prosecute the Klan after a violent clash in Decatur, Alabama, in 1979, but in 1982 the case was reopened when attorneys for the Southern Poverty Law Center presented new evidence based on depositions made by the Klansmen in a civil suit. A federal grand jury returned nine indictments in 1984. Acker ruled that the depositions were inadmissable because they were involuntary. He also called the Southern Poverty Law Center a "counter-vigilante group" that was trampling on the rights of the KKK. The main difference between the Klan and the Law Center was that the Klansmen "were and are unsophisticated, impecunious and ignorant of legal procedures, while the lawyers and investigators of the center are quite sophisticated, socially acceptable and well financed." Acker heard the case again after the reversal; he again ordered that the evidence be suppressed. On appeal he was again reversed, charged with committing many errors reflecting "that he is no longer able to review these cases impartially. We

direct these cases be reassigned." One of the three-judge panel of the Court of Appeals of the Eleventh Circuit that voted to overrule Acker was Judge Robert S. Vance. On December 16, 1989, Judge Vance was killed in the explosion of a bomb mailed to him. *New York Times,* Dec. 20, 21, 1989.

2. Brown to Hoover, Sept. 17, 1954; Hoover to Brown, Sept. 22, 1954. See also Brown to Hoover, date illegible, and Hoover to Brown, Oct. 6, 1954. By the time Brown wrote his second letter to Hoover, he had himself been checked: "Bufiles contain no derogatory information identifiable with correspondent."

3. Memorandums, SAC New Haven to Director, June 21, 1950; Hoover to Neal, July 14, 1950; Hoover to Donald L. Nicholson, Sept. 5, 1950; SAC New Haven to Director, Sept. 15, 1950.

4. Memorandum, M. A. Jones to Nichols, Nov. 1, 1955; memorandum, SAC New Haven to Director, June 6, 1949.

5. Memorandums, SAC New Haven to Director, April 15, June 6, 1949.

6. Memorandum, Nichols to Tolson, Jan. 2, 1947; SAC New Haven to Director, Dec. 7, 1954; memorandum, SAC New Haven to Director, April 23, 1951, with attachment from *Yale Daily News,* April 23, 1951. The name of the student who made the statement was checked in the FBI records.

7. Memorandum, Jones to Nichols, Feb. 20, 1950; Hoover to Assistant Chief of Staff, G2, Feb. 12, March 7, 1951; FBI Report, Washington, D.C., Feb. 27, 1951; teletype, Washington Field Office, FBI, to Director and SACs Baltimore, New York, and New Haven, Feb. 16, 1951.

8. Memorandum, SAC New Haven to Director, May 21, 1951, with attached newspaper clippings.

9. Copy, Westerfield to Furniss, June 12, 1933, Angell Papers, Box 174.

10. Adee to Angell, May 10, 1935, with enclosure; Adee to Warren, May 2, 1935; Angell to Adee, May 27, 1935, Angell Papers, Box 1. See also the letters that George Parmly Day, Yale treasurer, forwarded to Angell and to Dean Luther Weigle of the Divinity School from a Divinity School alumnus who advocated firing four Divinity School professors. Unidentified correspondent to Day, Feb. 17, 1936; Day to correspondent, Feb. 21, 1936; Day to Angell, Feb. 24, 1936; correspondent to Day, Feb. 26, 1936; Day to correspondent, Feb. 28, 1936, Angell Papers, Box 60.

11. Taft to Seymour, April 9, 1942, Seymour Papers, Box 134. Taft's letter about Pettingill is quoted in the memo from Lohmann to Clark, May 16, 1938; Clark to Lohmann, May 17, 1938, Seymour Papers, Box 80.

12. The tenured members of the Law School faculty on January 4, 1946, with two dissenting votes, adopted a resolution condemning Lewis's broadcast as intended "to block these appointments, not by demonstrating unfitness, but by inflaming prejudice." The resolution added that Lewis's detailed knowledge of the situation showed that he had been given information that should have been held in strictest confidence by the faculty and the corporation. The faculty called on Seymour to conduct an inquiry to discover who was responsible for compromising the integrity of the appointment process through leaks and to deny "the guilty person or persons . . . all future participation in faculty appointments and policy determinations" at Yale. Seymour agreed with the faculty's sentiments about confidentiality but declined to investigate the matter of responsibility. Wesley A. Sturges to Seymour, with attachment, Jan. 7, 1946; Seymour to Sturges, Jan. 9, 1946, Seymour Papers, Box 80.

13. One active Law School alumnus made the emphasis on the Christian character of Yale a bit more specific. In a long letter to Seymour, he explained his objections to all three men: "The reputation of Abe Fortas is perhaps not as vicious as that of Emerson and certainly he has not incurred to the same extent the enmity of conservatives and liberals, who believe in the American form of government." On the same day, he wrote "Dear Charles" another letter, stating a second objection to Fortas, "which I did not mention in my formal letter as perhaps it should not be a matter of record, although I am perfectly willing to have you mention it to the Corporation, if you wish":

> I do not wish to be considered anti-Jewish or prejudiced against the Jews as a race. In fact, I have some very good Jewish friends for whom I have the highest regard. I feel that a Jew of the type of Mr. Shulman [of the Law School faculty], who is a scholar, a gentleman and an excellent teacher, is a desirable member of any faculty. Nevertheless, I believe that there are too many Jews on the Yale Law School Faculty, and especially that there are too many of the wrong kind. From the last law school catalogue, which I have, of 21 professors I believe 6 are Jewish. I may be wrong about one or two but in any event they are out of proportion. Mr. Fortas would add one more of the wrong kind.

In a postscript to his reply, Seymour wrote: "This is a matter which, as you can understand, I can discuss with you orally much more reasonably that I can put all aspects of the situation on paper." John B. Dempsey to Seymour, two letters, Jan. 10, 1946; Seymour to Dempsey, Jan. 15, 1946, Seymour Papers, Box 80; Peyl Gilbert to Seymour, Sept. 26, 1945; telegram, A. W. Mace to Seymour, Dec. 19, 1945, and letter, Dec. 27, 1945; Seymour to Mace, Dec. 29, 1945; Henri Brown to Seymour, Jan. 4, 1946; Adee to Seymour, Jan. 9, 23, 1946; Livingston Platt to Seymour, Jan. 9, 1946; Seymour to Sturges, Jan. 10, 1946; Sturges to Seymour, Jan. 11, 1946; Hanes to Seymour, Jan. 10, 1946; Albert D. Farwell to Seymour, Jan. 18, 1946; telegram, id. to id., Jan. 10, 1946; Seymour to Farwell, Jan. 15, 1946. Not all of Seymour's correspondents agreed. Richard Hooker sent Seymour a copy of a letter he had written to George Adee in which he made the point that, however much he disagreed with Fortas, Rodell, and Arnold, in particular, it was important to have some radicals on the faculty. Hooker to Seymour, with attachment, Jan. 11, 1946; Seymour to Hooker, Jan. 15, 1946, informs him that the nomination of Fortas was withdrawn; Seymour Papers, Box 80.

14. R. H. Cole to Seymour, Aug. 3, 1948, with attached memo; Seymour to Cole, Aug. 11, 1948, Seymour Papers, Box 80. Griswold to Gilbert H. Scribner, Jr., Sept. 12, 1951, Lohmann Papers, File "E." Bush to Seymour, June 29, 1948, Seymour Papers, Box 80. How far Yale officials would go in expressing disapproval of faculty members who incurred the wrath of powerful alumni may be seen in a letter by Carlos F. Stoddard, Jr., of the Yale Development Office. He had read in a newspaper article that Fowler Harper had answered "Why not?" to the question whether Communists should be permitted to teach at a university. Stoddard interviewed Harper about the matter and listened to a tape of the TV program. He pointed out that Harper did have the grace to say that President Griswold disagreed with him about the matter, but felt he was "seri-

ously remiss in not laying adequate emphasis on President Griswold's 'disagreement.' . . . Mr. Harper has, by this failure, even more than by his expression of an unpopular and highly controversial opinion, brought harm to the cause of Yale." As a senior officer in two flourishing businesses for many years before coming to Yale, he would not have acted as Yale acted: "I am perfectly aware of what I would have done with an employee who repeatedly damaged our reputation and interfered with our prosperity. In about two minutes, after second offense. . . . If you want to get Harper a job felling trees in Canada, I'll buy you a drink, and have a special medal struck off 'For Service.' " Stoddard to Charles F. Clise, June 19, 1953, Griswold Papers, Box 1. When Representative John Taber of the House Appropriations Committee threatened to cut off his contributions to Yale as a result of Emerson's activities, Griswold sought to distance himself from Emerson: "Sitting here in this office I sometimes feel pretty discouraged and frustrated when individual members of our faculty sound off with propositions with which I violently disagree." Griswold to Taber, June 18, 1953, Griswold Papers, Box 1.

15. Rodell to Shulman, Jan. 3, 1955; Clise to Holden, Dec. 1, 1953; Wiggin to Clise, Dec. 21, 31, 1953; Wiggin to Griswold, Dec. 31, 1953; Clise to Wiggin, Dec. 28, 1953; Clise to Griswold, Nov. 27, 1953; Griswold to Clise, Dec. 3, 1953; Douglas to Griswold, Jan. 26, Feb. 18, 1955; Griswold to Douglas, Jan. 31, Feb. 23, 1955; Griswold to Rodell, Jan. 10, 1955, Griswold Papers, Box 1. On Countryman's connection with the Peters case, see Peters to Griswold, Dec. 31, 1954; Griswold to Peters, Jan. 3, 1955, Griswold Papers, Box 1. The Executive Committee of the Yale chapter of the American Association of University Professors requested a meeting with Griswold to discuss questions that "arise out of the resignation of Professor Countryman." Among them was whether the administration should "undertake to pass on the qualifications of candidates for full professorship" and whether "unconventional behavior retard[s] advancement." Roland H. Bainton to Griswold, April 4, 1955, Griswold Papers, Box 7.

16. Furniss to Rabinowitz, July 11, 1950; Griswold to Rabinowitz, July 18, 1950, Griswold Papers, Box 20.

17. A copy of Griswold's letter to Rabinowitz was sent to Goodenough on July 21, 1950. Goodenough to Griswold, July 26, 1950, Griswold Papers, Box 20.

18. Report, Academic Freedom Study, Columbia University, March 14, 1951, Griswold Papers, Box 20. Griswold to MacIver, Griswold to Rabinowitz, Griswold to Adams, all Dec. 19, 1952; Rabinowitz to Griswold, Dec. 19, 1952, Griswold Papers, Box 20. Relations between university officials and donors are illuminated by the correspondence relating to Rabinowitz. Provost Furniss wrote Yale Treasurer Charles S. Gage on March 7, 1955, that Rabinowitz "can easily be persuaded to endow a chair bearing his name. . . . During the past fifteen years Yale has been the focus of his life's interest." The establishment of a professorship bearing his name "would be for him the surpassing consummation of his entire career. If this objective caused him to reduce his gifts which only add to our running costs, such as rare books and manuscripts (don't tell Jim Babb) [librarian of Yale] I would regard it as a net gain." Gage was warned to keep the matter confidential: "If our friends in the Library and Gallery [also a major beneficiary of Rabinowitz's gifts] get wind of this development they might take alarm and torpedo the whole proposition." Exactly one year later, Babb wrote

to Furniss about a testimonial dinner honoring Rabinowitz, at which he had represented Yale: "After a day in New York—the night before attending a completely Hebrew dinner in honor of Louis at which we listened to (it seemed to me) ten speeches, all entirely in Hebrew. My wife certainly works hard for Yale University!" And then, handwritten in the margin: "Kosher food."

In his letter soliciting contributions to the Louis M. Rabinowitz Memorial Fund, however, Babb paid tribute to Rabinowitz's "constant and generous" contributions to the library, "which owes some of its greatest scholarly resources to him," especially in Judaica, incunabula, and English literature. His "recognition of beauty and historical importance in any form" secured for Yale outstanding books and manuscripts of many kinds.

After Rabinowitz died on April 27, 1957, the amount of money that Yale might expect from his estate was a subject of considerable interest to Provost Furniss. Furniss to Gage, March 7, 1955; Babb to Furniss, March 6, 1956, June 11, 1957; Furniss to Victor Rabinowitz, Sept. 27, 1957; Victor Rabinowitz to Furniss, Sept. 16, 1957; Note, Conference with Mr. Victor Rabinowitz, signed E.S.F., May 22, 1957, Furniss Papers, Boxes 12, 56.

19. Schrecker, *No Ivory Tower*, 187–90, 395, notes 55–59.

20. Louis Joughin, Assistant Director, ACLU, to Griswold, Sept. 13, 1957; deKiewiet to Griswold, Sept. 30, 1957; Griswold to Baldwin, Oct. 7, 1957; Baldwin to Griswold, Oct. 4, 24, 1957; Angell to Griswold, Oct. 9, 1957; Griswold to Angell, Oct. 16, 1957, Griswold Papers, Box 7. Not all of Griswold's mail was as threatening as he implied. His friend and powerful alumnus, Charles Clise, who pressed for the dismissal of Vern Countryman, congratulated him on the AAU statement: "I understand you had a lot to do with its writing. . . . I am anxious that we be unusually vigilant. 'Tenure' is one of the channels through which the subversive groups have been attempting to gain improper authority for license and therefore needs careful watching. . . . Your competent coverage . . . of the general problem is splendid and I want you to know of my great appreciation." When the same document could be seen by "Dear Whit" as an expression of the defense of university and faculty rights against McCarthyism and by "Dear Charlie" as a long needed curtailment of those rights, it must have been "smothered in [the] ambiguity" Griswold seems to have elsewhere deplored. Clise to Griswold, April 20, 1953, Griswold Papers, Box 11-A.

21. Fred to Dodds, March 24, 1953, with enclosure, Griswold Papers, Box 11-A; Schrecker, *No Ivory Tower*, 189.

22. Corbin to Griswold, Dec. 2, 1952; AAU, Minutes of Meeting, Feb. 15, 1953; undated notes of Griswold, but 1953, Griswold Papers, Box 11-A.

23. Wiggin to Shaw, Feb. 11, 1953; Wiggin to Phillips Ketchum, Feb. 25, 1953, Griswold Papers, Box 1.

24. Draft letter, Secretary of Yale University to Tavenner, March 20, 1953; Wiggin to Griswold, March 26, 1953; Wiggin to Warner, March 2, 26, 1953; memorandum, "Information Given to D. T. Appell," undated but March 1953; Wiggin to Mrs. John Q. Tilson, Jr., Executive Assistant to the President, Yale University, Feb. 12, 1953; Warner to Wiggin, March 3, 20, 23, June 4, 1953; Wiggin to Holden, March 23, 1953; Warner to Shaw, March 20, 1953, with attached memorandum, March 19, 1953; Wiggin to Griswold, with memorandum, "Yale Law School," of telephone conversation with Warner, March 16, 1953; Wiggin to Griswold, with attached memorandum, "Re: Jenner and Velde

Committee Hearings," April 23, 1953; Appell to Holden, March 20, 1953, Griswold Papers, Box 1. For references to Warner's reports on testimony from faculty members at MIT, Harvard, Cornell, Brooklyn, and elsewhere, see Wiggin to Griswold, April 24, 29, May 29, 1953, with memorandum of May 26, Feb. 25, 1953; Wiggin to Warner, Feb. 11, 1953; "Bill" (W. W. Watson) to "Ben" (Reuben A. Holden), March 17, 1953, with attached letter, Watson to Dudley Williams, March 17, 1953; biographical data on seven former Yale students, undated but March 1953; undated memorandum (but March 1953), "A Memorandum Re: Conversation with Professor Watson," almost certainly by Holden, Griswold Papers, Box 1.

25. Warner to Wiggin, June 11, 1953, with attached memorandum; Wiggin to Griswold, June 12, 1953; Holden to Wiggin, June 18, 1953; Wiggin to Holden, March 16, 1953, with attachments, including handwritten notes, memoranda on Professor Turner and students, etc., Griswold Papers, Box 1.

26. Wiggin to Griswold, March 27, April 16, 1953; Cutler to Wiggin, March 25, 1953; Wiggin to Cutler, March 27, 1953; Cutler to Warner, April 13, 1953; Warner to Wiggin, April 15, 1953, Griswold Papers, Box 1.

27. Wiggin to Griswold, July 7, 1953; memorandum, Warner, Re: Functions to be Performed . . . in Connection with Congressional hearings, July 1, 1953; Wiggin to Griswold, Aug. 10, Nov. 27, 1953, with attachment; Karl Ettinger to Griswold, Jan. 14, 1954; handwritten note, Holden to Griswold, undated but January 1954; Warner to Wiggin, June 7, 1954; Griswold to René A. Wormser, June 8, 1954; Wormser to Griswold, June 7, 1954; Wiggin to Mrs. John Q. Tilson, Jr., June 8, 1954; Wiggin to Warner, July 9, 1954; Wiggin to Mrs. Tilson, July 9, 1954; Gage to Eugene D. Millikan, July 12, 23, 1954; Millikan to Gage, July 23, 1954; Warner to Wiggin, Oct. 7, 1954; Colin F. Stam to Paul F. Myers, Oct. 21, 1954; Griswold to Acheson, Dec. 1, 1954; Wiggin to Shaw, Dec. 1, 1954, with attachment; Wiggin to Acheson, Dec. 1, 1954; Warner to Wiggin, Dec. 16, 1954, with attached Memorandum to the Members of the Listening Post; undated handwritten notes by Griswold, but December 1954, Griswold Papers, Box 1.

28. Wiggin to Griswold, April 6, 1953; Warner to Wiggin, April 2, 1953; Warner to Shaw, April 2, 1953; Abe McGregor Goff to Griswold, Jan. 7, 1955; Catherine J. Tilson to Goff, Jan. 18, 1955; Sterling to Griswold, Dec. 1, 1953, Griswold Papers, Box 1.

29. Warner to Wiggin, April 25, 1953; Kaplan to Griswold, Oct. 5, Nov. 17, 1950, Feb. 28, 1951, with copy of Kaplan to Biddle, Feb. 27, 1951; Potter to Griswold, Nov. 10, Dec. 12, 1950; Griswold to Kaplan, Nov. 1, 1950; Griswold to Potter, Nov. 17, 1950; Dibner to Griswold, Jan. 2, 16, 1953; Colt to Griswold, April 9, 1953, with copy of Wadhams to Colt, March 24, 1953; Griswold to Colt, April 13, 1953; form letter, Griswold to (recipient), final draft, June 1, 1953; draft of letter edited by Griswold, undated but before June 1953; handwritten draft by Griswold of form letter, before June 1953, Griswold Papers, Box 1.

30. Cole to Griswold, Dec. 21, 1959, Griswold Papers, Box 1.

Chapter 10

1. SAC Letter No. 40, Series 1947, April 7, 1947. The policy was reaffirmed in June 1948. It was emphasized that under no circumstances should

information be given to "private organizations and individuals." SAC Letter No. 97, Series 1948, June 22, 1948.

2. On February 8, 1951, Louis Nichols received a memorandum from M. A. Jones giving information available in the FBI files on Adams, Browning, Carvel, Lausche, and Payne, the members of the committee. On Lausche, the FBI wrote: "Of hundreds of references in Bufiles to Governor Lausche, the majority are in connection with reports on Communist Party and Communist key figure activities in Ohio. Most of these security references cover the 1944 period. None of them show that Governor Lausche was a Communist Party member or that he had Communist beliefs. It is indicated that he used the Communist Party in Ohio for political purposes, and perhaps the Communists used him also. . . . Lausche has drawn a great deal of political strength from Slavic and other foreign nationality groups." Under the caption "Criminal References," the FBI reported: "The SAC at Cleveland, on 2-23-43, referred to Mayor Lausche as being of Slovenian extraction, currying the favor of nationality groups in the Democratic Party. For this reason, the Mayor appointed his friend, Frank D. Celebrezzi, as Safety Director of Cleveland to appease persons of Italian extraction."

3. For one example, see SAC Albany to Director, Feb. 9, 1951, in which Governor Dewey states that he has appointed R. Burdell Bixby, his executive assistant, to receive FBI information and "laughingly pointed out that Bixby had served as Roosevelt's bodyguard while in the Army." For other meetings with governors, see SAC Philadelphia to Director, Feb. 8, 1951, which reports that the FBI told Governor Fine "that we had contact with plant management in connection with our investigative jurisdiction and problems. . . ."; SAC Boston to Director, Feb. 17, 1951, in which the Boston field office reports on certain FBI investigations in New Hampshire that are too sensitive to involve the State Police—"contacts at Dartmouth College . . . investigation at newspapers . . . inquiries involving member of Greek Orthodox Church."

4. Jane Sanders, *Cold War on the Campus: Academic Freedom at the University of Washington, 1946–64* (Seattle and London, 1979), 3–99.

5. "Communism and Education: An Open Letter to Friends of the University of Washington From President Raymond B. Allen," Seattle, Oct. 7, 1948. The copy of this pamphlet that I have used is in the Main File of the University of Washington at FBI headquarters; it is #100-364439-13.

6. Sanders, *Cold War on the Campus*, 43, 46.

7. Nichols to Tolson, May 17, 1948.

8. "Public source information" does not mean what it would seem to mean— information available to the general public. It includes all materials not acquired as a result of the FBI's own investigations, including those seized in raids by local police. The term protects the FBI from the charge that it has conducted surveillance against subjects or that it has breached the confidentiality of its own files should its role in disseminating the information become known. Donner, *Surveillance*, 129.

9. Nichols to Tolson, June 21, 1948.

10. Nichols to Tolson, Nov. 2, 1948.

11. Rader had been called a Communist at the Canwell hearings by George Hewitt, a former Communist from New York. Rader denied the charge, at the time and later in his book, *False Witness* (Seattle, 1969). Ed Guthman, a re-

porter on the *Seattle Times*, won a Pulitzer Prize for a series of articles that appeared on Oct. 21, 22, 29, 1949, proving that the Canwell committee investigators had tampered with a key piece of evidence—a hotel register—which disproved the testimony of Hewitt. Allen, after examining Guthman's evidence, issued a statement declaring himself convinced that the charges against Rader were false. Before that, however, he acted as if he believed otherwise. He intimated to Rader that he believed the charges against him were false, but he wrote to Provost Albert C. Jacobs of Columbia University, breaking off an exchange teaching agreement between Rader and Columbia philosophy professor Herbert Schneider: "Our friend here [Rader] is going to be in trouble before long, trouble of his own making." Sanders, *Cold War on the Campus* 39, 86, 206 n33.

12. Memorandum, H. B. Fletcher to D. M. Ladd, March 3, 1949; Director to SAC Seattle, March 4, 1949.

13. Sanders, *Cold War on the Campus*, 94–95.

14. Ed Stone, former managing editor of the *Post-Intelligencer*, called Niendorff a major figure in the Canwell investigation. Sanders, *Cold War on the Campus*, 39, 73, 75, 194 n32.

15. For additional evidence of FBI interest in the University of Washington, see the telegrams of SAC Seattle to Director, Feb. 18, 1955, dealing with the withdrawal by President Henry Schmitz of the invitation to J. Robert Oppenheimer to lecture at the University, and Feb. 24, 1949, dealing with President Allen's "confidential" advice to the FBI that a possible decision by the Atomic Energy Commission to make the university a major research and experimental center would "entail considerable investigation and thorough screening of numerous persons attached to the university"; and the documents dealing with whether the FBI should send a covert or overt agent to attend the university's institute on "World Communism and American Policy"—SAC Seattle to Director, March 22, June 8, 1955; Director to SAC Seattle, March 23, June 14, 1955; Memorandum, W. C. Sullivan to A. H. Belmont, June 14, 1955. Professor George Taylor, director of the institute, promised to send the transcript of all talks to the FBI; SAC Seattle to Director, Aug. 24, 1955.

16. Sanders, *Cold War on the Campus*, 105–11.

17. Sanders, *Cold War on the Campus*, 119–22; Sigmund Diamond, "McCarthyism on Campus," *The Nation* 233, no. 8 (Sept. 19, 1981): 238–41.

18. The practice of asking the FBI for information was common. A high official of the University of Rhode Island spoke to the Providence FBI office to ask "if there was some way that he could obtain information concerning applications for positions at the University of Rhode Island which he or some other member of his administrative staff suspected might have Communist leanings. He said the situation might never arise, but the possibility existed." Memo, SAC Boston to Director, Aug. 17, 1951. The number of such documents suggests that university presidents and other officials perhaps developed a common strategy, informally or at meetings of their own associations.

19. Memo, Belmont to Boardman, Oct. 6, 1954.

20. Memo, Belmont to Ladd, April 30, 1953.

21. Memo, Belmont to Ladd, May 7, 1953.

22. See memo, SAC San Francisco to Director, April 30, 1953, in which a request to pass along information to Warren concludes: "No derogatory infor-

mation concerning Governor Warren is contained in the files of the San Francisco Office. Governor Warren is believed to be both reliable and discreet in the handling of matters of this type." Recently released FBI documents show that Warren and Hoover had a particularly close and cooperative relationship that began when Warren was a "law and order" district attorney in Alameda County, California, and continued until shortly after the publication of the Warren Commission report on the assassination of President Kennedy, when Warren was removed from Hoover's "special correspondents list," made up of persons felt to be especially friendly to the FBI. Requests made by Warren for information from the FBI show his concern about Communist subversion, a concern that led Hoover to establish a program entitled "Cooperation with Governor Earl Warren." "Whatever the Governor requests I want prompt attention accorded it," Hoover wrote in 1951. The FBI gave Warren the use of a car and driver on several occasions. *New York Times,* November 29, 1985.

23. Memo, Belmont to Ladd, July 9, 1953; memo, Boardman to Director, March 31, 1954. See also the memorandum from Hoover to Tolson, Boardman, and Nichols, March 30, 1954, in which Hoover reports on his telephone call to SAC San Francisco: "I told Mr. Whelan I wanted to find out right away what information we have been furnishing in such a surreptitious manner to the officials at this University."

24. Memo, Belmont to Boardman, May 12, 1954.

25. Stevenson received information about still other university staff members; SAC Springfield to Director, Feb. 20, 1952. On May 6, 1953, SAC Springfield reported to headquarters on the results of the survey ordered by Hoover. He listed twenty-one subversives at the University of Illinois. One of them, about whom it was said that "investigation at the University of Illinois reflects no information indicating that" he "is active on behalf of the Communist Party or its affiliates or a follower of the Communist Party line," was nevertheless listed in the Springfield FBI files; he was later awarded a Nobel Prize.

26. SAC San Francisco to Director, May 22, 1952.

27. Memo, Director to SAC Boston, July 16, 1953.

28. Memorandum, Executives' Conference to Director, Oct. 28, 1953; Hoover to the Attorney General, Jan. 26, 1952; memorandum, Nichols to Tolson, March 9, 1953. On March 23, 1953, Deputy Attorney General Rogers sent a memorandum to all division heads of the Department of Justice setting forth the policy on release of information to congressional committees. All reports and memoranda were to be removed from the FBI files before the files were made available to the committee. If the committee insisted that the FBI reports and memoranda were essential, a summary would be prepared which would not disclose investigative techniques, the identity of confidential informants, or other matters that might jeopardize FBI procedures. Even so, the FBI would be asked to approve examination of the summary, which would not be made available to the committee unless approved.

29. Communications Section, FBI, to Albany, etc., Feb. 18, 1953.

30. Memorandum, Baumgardner to Belmont, March 3, 1953; Nichols to Tolson, March 4, 1953. Nichols had exceptionally close relations with committee counsel Robert Morris. On March 7, 1953, a month after Morris's request for FBI information on Bennington, Harvard, and Sarah Lawrence, Nichols wrote Tolson about a luncheon meeting on February 27 called by Vice-President Nixon,

at which Congressmen Velde, Kearney, and Dan Jackson, Senator Jenner, Robert Morris, General Persons, Eisenhower's assistant, and Jerry Morgan, Persons's aide, were present. Persons and Nixon "urged that the House Committee on Un-American Activities and the Internal Security Committee of the Senate work as a joint committee in investigation of Communist infiltration into education." The proposal foundered when the Senate Judiciary Committee disapproved it, on the ground that the Senate would be weakened "in its current controversy with the House over the Chairmanship of the Joint Committee on Atomic Energy." Morris "confidentially informed" Nichols that General Persons had told the luncheon guests that the White House was under strong pressure to get the president to issue a statement against congressional investigations into education, but that "so far Persons has been able to avoid this."

31. It seems likely that McGill was the more ready to accept Hoover's assurances because of his own political views. When Henry Wallace went to the South to speak in the winter of 1947, he insisted that his audiences not be segregated. McGill, often regarded as a southern moderate, wrote in the *Atlanta Constitution:*

> In Atlanta, one of the cities where Mr. Wallace will speak, his sponsors, the Communist infiltrated Southern Conference for Human Welfare (with its officials apparently getting most of the "welfare") will be grievously disappointed if someone does not create a disorder so as to give them the publicity they seek. Since there is a great deal of similarity between the mental mechanism of the Ku Kluxers and the officers of the SCHW, we are likely to see a Klan picket line or some other form of protest. Indeed, if there is one I trust someone will look under the robes to see if they be the hired pickets of the SCHW or the real McCoy of the Klaverns.

Threatened with a libel suit, McGill two months later denied that he was impugning the politics or the honesty of the Conference officials. James Aronson, *The Press and the Cold War* (Indianapolis and New York, 1970), 40–41.

The FBI denied it was breaking the confidentiality of its records at the very time it was. Robert McCaughey, administrative assistant to Senator Karl Mundt from 1945 to Mundt's death in 1974, admitted that when an FBI agent would deliver a file to him and discuss it, he would also bring along a letter from Hoover denying access to it. The purpose of the letter, of course, was to alert the recipient of the file as to what to say if questioned. Mundt blundered into an embarrassing error. In November 1953, speaking in Bonneville, Utah, he admitted that the FBI leaked to congressional committees, especially in cases in which there was not enough evidence to produce an indictment. *The Salt Lake Tribune* carried the story; the FBI, Attorney General Brownell, and Senator McCarthy denied it; O'Reilly, *Hoover*, 128–29.

On January 21, 1953, A. H. Belmont wrote D. M. Ladd referring to a memo from Nichols to Tolson stating that "on a personal and confidential basis Senator [John] Bricker of Ohio is advised annually regarding the identity of any Communists on the faculty of Ohio State University. Senator Bricker requested on January 19, 1953, that another check be made." Belmont instructed SAC Cincinnati to give Bricker the names of any Communists at Ohio State. Nichols's memo states the purpose of the Bricker–FBI arrangement: "The Senator has very effectively cleaned them [the Communists] out and he merely takes the position as a member of the Board of Trustees, that those who have a record of Communist Party affiliations not be retained. The manner in which the Senator has handled this has been most refreshing." Bricker had "no suspicions or information" that any Communists had "crept into the faculty" since he had last requested information; he merely wanted to "see to it that Ohio State is clean" in view of the pending House committee investigation. Nichols felt that the FBI "should continue this procedure as we have in the past." "I agree," Hoover wrote.

32. See, for example, SAC Letter No. 40, Series 1947, April 7, 1947; SAC Letter No. 56, Series 1948, April 9, 1948; SAC Letter No. 97, Series 1948, June 22, 1948; Memorandum to Director on Proceedings of the FBI Executives' Conference of Sept. 27, 1949, Oct. 3, 1949.

33. SAC Baltimore to Director, April 20, 1951.

34. V. P. Keay to A. H. Belmont, Jan. 23, 1953.

35. Memorandum, Executives' Conference to Director, Oct. 14, 1953; memorandum, Callan to A. Rosen, Nov. 25, 1953; memorandum, Belmont to Rosen, Oct. 21, 1954. The FBI did not restrict its interest in sexual behavior to government employees. On the explicit instructions of Hoover, it "confidentially made available to George Washington University information concerning sex deviates or Communists employed as teachers there." It did the same at New York University, where it "confidentially advised a contact at the University as to the sex deviate practices of an instructor." Memorandum, [name deleted] to Mr. Rosen, Oct. 22, 1954.

Conclusion

1. Helen Codere, *Fighting with Property: A Study of Kwakiutl Potlatching and Warfare, 1792–1930* (Seattle, 1950).

2. Thorstein Veblen, *The Higher Learning in America*, introduction by Louis M. Hacker (New York, 1957), viii–ix, 191–92, 132–33.

3. "Heavy Date," *The Collected Poetry of W. H. Auden* (New York, 1945), 106–7.

4. E. M. Forster, "The Duty of Society to the Artist" (1942), in G. B. Parker, ed., *E. M. Forster: Selected Writings* (London, 1968), 45–46; "Liberty in England" (1935), in ibid., 29.

5. *Final Report of the Select Committee to Study Governmental Operations with Respect to Intelligence Activities*. U.S. Senate, 94th Cong., 2nd sess., Rpt. No. 94–755 (Washington, D.C., 1976), Book 3, 101. Prefiguring the CIA-to-Kissinger report by Director Helms on "restless youth" was a CIA-to-Bundy report of April 27, 1965, by Director John McCone alleging that the Chinese and North Vietnamese believed that the continuation of antiwar feeling in the United States would lead to U.S. withdrawal from Vietnam. Bundy asked J. Edgar Hoover for a report on Communist activity in the antiwar movement. Hoover obliged. On April 28, 1965, after President Johnson expressed gratitude, Hoover sent Bundy a memorandum on Communist participation in the civil rights campaign and student movement. Theoharis, *Political Surveillance*, 176–77.

No one expressed the danger of governmental secrecy better than Spinoza:

"Those who have it in their power to transact the business of the state in secret, have the state in their power. They lie in their ambuscade constantly striking against the citizens. . . . It is the old story of those who seek after absolute rule. . . . Under the larva of the patriot the oppressor is concealed." Baruch Spinoza, *Tractatus Politicus*, in Geza Engelmann, *Political Philosophy from Plato to Jeremy Bentham* (New York and London, 1927), 192. Others have expressed the danger more succinctly. Commenting on the disclosure of the release of poisonous phenol into the drinking water supply of much of South Korea, a senior official of the Doosan Electro-Materials Co., the chief polluter, said that under Korean tradition, the company cannot really defend itself while it is the focus of public controversy: "If we explain everything, it will only inflame people." *New York Times*, April 16, 1991. H. Jack Geiger, professor of community medicine at the City University of New York Medical School, writing about the recent disclosure that for forty years the government knew about radioactive leaks from the Hanford, Washington, nuclear arms plant and allowed people to receive excessive amounts of radiation, says: "The Government knowingly risked the health of thousands of innocent civilians and then lied to them until forced by Freedom of Information Act lawsuits to disclose some of the facts. . . . Secrecy is the ultimate crime. . . . It denies the right of free people to control their government." *New York Times*, Aug. 5, 1990. But it permits government to control "free people." Fred F. Fielding, legal counselor to President Reagan and a deputy to John Dean, Nixon's legal adviser at the time of Watergate, revealed the "secret" of surviving in a White House staff split by rivalries: " 'I have their FBI files,' he said, breaking into a comfortable laugh." *New York Times*, October 23, 1985.

6. If the constitutional and political dangers arising from "counterespionage" exist over a long period of time, then they are of greater significance than if they had only a short span of life. Similarly, if those dangers exist in more than one place, accounting for them is of greater significance than if they were limited to one place. See the review of Nicholas Hiley, research fellow in the Department of War Studies, King's College, London, of Bernard Porter, *Plots and Paranoia: A History of Political Espionage in Britain 1790–1988* (London, 1989), in which Porter emphasizes the role of secrecy and the domination of the government's covert countersubversion campaign by rightist bureaucrats who " 'never made the mistake of confusing patriotism with loyalty to elected governments.' " Theirs was " 'a higher allegiance than to their constitutionally elected masters.' " *Times Literary Supplement* (London), Dec. 22–28, 1989, p. 1408.

7. *New York Times*, Oct. 19, 1990, Dec. 12, 1990, Nov. 16, 1990, Nov. 28, Dec. 6, 16, 1990.

8. *New York Times*, Jan. 28, 30, May 12, June 14, 21, 26, July 5, 1988; Nov. 7, 8, 1989; on the Library Awareness Program, see ibid., Sept. 18, 1987; May 19, 1988; *New Yorker*, May 30, 1988, 23–24. The FBI has not admitted, for obvious reasons, and the press seems not to have discovered, that the FBI's interest in libraries is no recent development; it goes back at least half a century. On September 25, 1941, SAC Newark wrote Hoover about a suggestion made by an employee of the Newark Public Library to inform on "suspicious persons" who use libraries to get information "valuable to a person bent on subversive activities. . . . She feels that some of these people are not gathering this information to further their education because they do not appear to be the intellec-

tual type. . . . She felt that the Bureau should be informed of these requests, which information should at least be a matter of record with the Bureau." She gave the Newark FBI office a list of all business libraries in the United States. E. E. Conroy, SAC Newark, felt that headquarters should instruct the FBI field offices to make "some arrangements with the libraries whereby they would maintain a register of persons" requesting such information: "These registers may prove valuable to the Bureau in investigations of espionage and sabotage."

9. As has been explained earlier, "public source data" is FBI jargon; it does not mean data available to the public, but data gathered by other agencies, which could be cited as the source, leaving the FBI out of the picture.

10. In addition to the FBI documents identified in the text, see also Memorandum, SAC Boston to Director, July 7, Aug. 21, 1969. In one set of FBI documents I have, the names of both MIT faculty members have been deleted. In the other, only one name has been deleted; but I have decided to delete both.

11. Milan Kundera, *The Book of Laughter and Forgetting* (New York, 1981), 159, 22, 7–8, 3.

12. Larry Ceplair and Steven Englund, *The Inquisition in Hollywood: Politics in the Film Community, 1930–1960* (Berkeley, Los Angeles, London, 1983), 429; Primo Levi, *The Drowned and the Saved* (New York, 1988), 12.

13. Walter Benjamin, *Understanding Brecht*, Anna Bostock, ed. (London, 1973), x; Martin Gilbert, *The Holocaust* (New York, 1985), 229–30.

Index